Transparency and Reflection

Transparency and Reflection

A Study of Self-Knowledge and the Nature of Mind

MATTHEW BOYLE

OXFORD
UNIVERSITY PRESS

Oxford University Press is a department of the University of Oxford. It furthers
the University's objective of excellence in research, scholarship, and education
by publishing worldwide. Oxford is a registered trade mark of Oxford University
Press in the UK and certain other countries.

Published in the United States of America by Oxford University Press
198 Madison Avenue, New York, NY 10016, United States of America.

© Oxford University Press 2024

All rights reserved. No part of this publication may be reproduced, stored in
a retrieval system, or transmitted, in any form or by any means, without the
prior permission in writing of Oxford University Press, or as expressly permitted
by law, by license, or under terms agreed with the appropriate reproduction
rights organization. Inquiries concerning reproduction outside the scope of the
above should be sent to the Rights Department, Oxford University Press, at the
address above.

You must not circulate this work in any other form
and you must impose this same condition on any acquirer.

Library of Congress Cataloging-in-Publication Data
Names: Boyle, Matthew, 1972– author.
Title: Transparency and reflection : a study of self-knowledge and the
nature of mind / Matthew Boyle.
Description: New York, NY : Oxford University Press, [2024] |
Includes bibliographical references and index.
Identifiers: LCCN 2023049374 (print) | LCCN 2023049375 (ebook) |
ISBN 9780199926299 (hardback) | ISBN 9780197765869 (epub)
Subjects: LCSH: Self-knowledge, Theory of.
Classification: LCC BD438.5 .B69 2024 (print) | LCC BD438.5 (ebook) |
DDC 126—dc23/eng/20231204
LC record available at https://lccn.loc.gov/2023049374
LC ebook record available at https://lccn.loc.gov/2023049375

DOI: 10.1093/oso/9780199926299.001.0001

Printed by Integrated Books International, United States of America

Contents

Preface   ix

  Introduction   1
    I.1. Why Study Self-Knowledge?   1
    I.2. Self-Knowledge and the First-Person Perspective   5
    I.3. The Stakes in These Debates   9
    I.4. Epistemic versus Metaphysical Approaches to Self-Knowledge   13
    I.5. Kantian versus Sartrean Conceptions of Self-Consciousness   15
    I.6. Plan of the Chapters   22

PART I: SELF-KNOWLEDGE AND TRANSPARENCY

1. Transparency and Other Problems   27
    1.1. Introduction   27
    1.2. Standard Formulations   29
    1.3. Three Observations about Self-Knowledge   34
    1.4. Generalizing the Problem of Transparency   39
    1.5. Conclusion and Prospect   44

2. Contemporary Approaches   45
    2.1. Introduction   45
    2.2. Transparency versus Alienation: Moran   46
    2.3. Transparency as Inference from World to Mind: Byrne   50
    2.4. Transparency as Inference from Judgment to Belief: Peacocke   56
    2.5. Transparency and Expression: Finkelstein and Bar-On   59
    2.6. Conclusion   62

3. The Reflectivist Approach   64
    3.1. Reflectivism and Its Problems   64
    3.2. Sartre and Reflectivism   66
    3.3. Nonpositional Consciousness and Transparency   68
    3.4. The Structure of the Sartrean Account   74
    3.5. Conclusion   77

PART II: SELF-CONSCIOUSNESS AND THE FIRST-PERSON PERSPECTIVE

4. Consciousness-as-Subject 81
   4.1. Introduction 81
   4.2. Imagining-as-Subject 84
   4.3. Representing-as-Subject in General 85
   4.4. Subjective versus Objective Attitudes: Some Contrasts 89
   4.5. Consciousness-as-Subject and Self-Knowledge 93
   4.6. Consciousness-as-Subject and Nonpositional Consciousness 97

5. Self-Consciousness 101
   5.1. Introduction 101
   5.2. The Anti-Egoist Challenge 105
   5.3. Egocentric Thought: Monadic versus Relational 110
   5.4. Consciousness-as-Subject versus Self-Consciousness 114
   5.5. Introducing the First Person 118
   5.6. The Reflectivist Approach to the First Person 125
   5.7. The First Person and Others 131
   5.8. Implications 134
       5.8.1. Referentialism versus Anti-Referentialism 134
       5.8.2. Essentialism versus Inessentialism 138
       5.8.3. Egoism versus Anti-Egoism 142

6. Bodily Awareness 144
   6.1. Introduction 144
   6.2. The Subject-Object Problem 145
   6.3. Sartre's Enigmatic Intervention 147
   6.4. Positional versus Nonpositional Consciousness Again 149
   6.5. Nonpositional Bodily Awareness 151
   6.6. The Primacy of Nonpositional Bodily Awareness 156
   6.7. Conclusion 160

PART III: REFLECTION AND SELF-UNDERSTANDING

7. Reflection and Rationality 165
   7.1. Introduction 165
   7.2. A Budget of Difficulties 166
   7.3. Rationality and the Taking Condition 171
   7.4. Taking and Reflection 178
   7.5. Self-Reflection 184
   7.6. Responses to Difficulties 186
   7.7. Rational versus Nonrational Minds 191

8. Armchair Psychology 196
   8.1. Introduction 196
   8.2. Two Kinds of Armchair Psychology 198
   8.3. First Illustration: Intentional Action 200
   8.4. Second Illustration: Perception 206
   8.5. Modes of Presentation and Implicit Understanding 209
   8.6. The Nature of Reflection 212
        8.6.1. The Mode-to-Content Shift 212
        8.6.2. Aristotle's Principle 214
        8.6.3. Systematicity 217
   8.7. Implications 222

9. Self-Understanding 227
   9.1. Introduction 227
   9.2. Skepticism about Self-Understanding 229
   9.3. Processualism about Self-Understanding 233
   9.4. Processualism and Skepticism 237
   9.5. Transparency and Self-Understanding 241
   9.6. Conclusion: Intelligibility and Intelligence 246

10. The Examined Life 248
    10.1. Introduction 248
    10.2. Refining the Claim 251
    10.3. Reflection in Good and Bad Faith 255
    10.4. The Point of Self-Reflection 261
    10.5. Socratic and Cartesian Self-Knowledge 269
    10.6. Human Beings as "Beings for Themselves" 273

Bibliography 279
Index 287

Preface

The substance of this book has been written in the years since I moved to the University of Chicago in 2016, but the groundwork for it was laid during the ten years I spent teaching at Harvard (2005–2015), and the interests that guide it were formed even earlier, while I was a graduate student at the University of Pittsburgh (1998–2005). Yet these descriptions make the writing process sound more linear than it was in fact. It would be more accurate to say that this book arose out of the collapse of another book I hoped to write, or anyway fantasized about writing, during that long period. That other book, which grew out of my doctoral dissertation, would have been a defense of what I called "the Kantian thesis": Kant's famous claim that "it must be possible for the *I think* to accompany all of my representations," on pain of their being "nothing to me." I thought of this thesis as encapsulating a crucial idea about the importance of self-consciousness to a rational mind. For a long time I claimed to be writing a book elaborating on this idea, but I wrote only a little of it, as I found myself struggling with various objections that I could not put to rest.

In the end, I came to think that the objections I had been seeking to overcome were in fact the keys to a sound understanding of the topic, and I realized that I needed to begin again. An encounter with Sartre played a crucial role in this transition, and my debts to his peculiar and sometimes frustrating philosophical work will be evident in the pages that follow. Once I began to think in a more Sartrean way about the nature of self-awareness, the book finally began to move forward, and I found that many of the themes I had hoped to approach via a discussion of Kant could find their place in the new book, albeit having suffered a sea change. I thank Peter Ohlin, my editor at Oxford University Press, for his patience through this long process of reformulation, and for his wise guidance and support along the way. It strikes me as I write this that I am also grateful to my parents, James and Ivy Boyle, for exhibiting these same qualities, although in a different capacity, of course.

Having worked on this project for so long leaves me with more debts than I can easily recollect, but I will mention those I can recall, beginning with the most obvious ones. In the first place, I owe a great debt to John McDowell, my long-ago dissertation director: his humane sense of what matters in philosophy, his insistence that it is possible to save the philosophical appearances rather than regimenting or reducing them away, and his striking example of how one might think in conversation with figures in the history of philosophy have been constant sources of inspiration to me. I owe a different but equally significant debt to Sebastian Rödl, who invited me to discuss the manuscript of his book *Self-Consciousness* while I was still a graduate student, an experience that had a transformative effect on my sense of what was at stake in the topic of self-awareness and what was the proper method by which to approach it. And I owe a third debt, not easy to calculate, to Doug Lavin, whom I got to know in this same period, and who was, for the dozen years we spent together, first at Pittsburgh and then at Harvard, my constant philosophical interlocutor, as well as my closest friend. These three people shaped my sense of what sort of philosopher I wanted to become, and although I am all too conscious of how imperfectly this book expresses the depth of my debt to them, I hope they will recognize their several influences on the issues I consider and the form my argument takes.

I owe a more immediate but equally profound debt to Dick Moran, whom I first discovered through reading his papers on self-knowledge, but who then became my colleague at Harvard, my mentor, and my friend. The importance of his work to my thinking will be obvious to any reader of this book, but he also contributed by guiding me through various crises and moments of despair, and by reading and commenting on each chapter as it came to be, always with a view to the whole to which these might one day contribute. Without his help and encouragement, this book would not exist.

Several other friends read all or most of the manuscript, and their comments have improved the book in countless ways. For this kind of help, I offer my heartfelt thanks to Anton Ford, Matthias Haase, Ben Laurence, Beri Marušić, John Schwenkler, Kieran Setiya, and Daniel Sutherland, and all the participants in a graduate seminar I taught on the manuscript in the Fall of 2020. I am also greatly indebted to Andrea Kern for organizing a workshop on the manuscript at the University of Leipzig, and to all of the participants in that workshop for their comments, which led to numerous changes and improvements in the final draft. And I am indebted to Nataliya Palatnik for organizing a reading group on the manuscript at the University of Wisconsin-Milwaukee, and to all the participants in that group for their feedback, which led to significant revisions. Finally, my Chicago colleagues Jim Conant and Jonathan Lear have both contributed crucially to the development of this project through various invitations to present material at workshops and co-teach seminars, and I am most grateful to both of them for their support and for the stimulus of their conversation.

Many other people have responded to bits of this material in ways that made me see the issues and my own contribution to them more clearly. It is here that I feel most liable to lapses of memory, but the people whose responses I do remember include Dorit Bar-On, Ian Blecher, James Bondarchuk, Alex Byrne, John Campbell, Lucy Campbell, Quassim Cassam, Pirachula Chulanon, Sandy Diehl, Stephen Engstrom, David Finkelstein, Jeremy Fix, André Gallois, Melina

Garibovic, Andrea Gianatti, Hannah Ginsborg, Wolfram Gobsch, Adrian Haddock, Pamela Hieronymi, David Hunter, Andrea Kern, Irad Kimhi, Chris Korsgaard, Aryeh Kosman, Thomas Land, Amy Levine, Béatrice Longuenesse, Eric Marcus, Mohan Matten, Alan Millar, Dan Morgan, Evgenia Mylonaki, Ram Neta, Sasha Newton, Lucy O'Brien, David Owens, Eylem Özaltun, Costas Pagondiotis, Sarah Paul, Christopher Peacocke, Thomas Pendlebury, Michael Powell, Ursula Renz, Johannes Roessler, Amélie Rorty, Susanna Siegel, Alison Simmons, Michael Thompson, Anubav Vasudevan, Jennifer Whiting, and Crispin Wright.

Long though this list of debts has become, it would not be complete without mention of two other people whose conversation sustained me during the years it took to produce this book: my brother Latham Boyle and my wife Rachel Cohen. Neither of these is a philosopher by training, but I have felt as well understood by them as by anyone, and their sense of what I am up to and why it matters has kept me going at times when my own sense of this has lapsed. My wife Rachel, who is the author of many books, once drew me a picture of a shelf with my own prospective book on it, and she believed in me and encouraged me during a long period when it looked like this might never amount to more than a picture. I don't suppose that producing the pictured book is any way to repay what she has meant to me, but at least, to borrow a line from Quine, it makes an honest representation out of her drawing.

I dedicate this book to my family, Rachel, Sylvia, and Tobias, with love.

* * *

Some material in this book has been adapted from the following papers: "Sartre on Bodily Transparency," *Manuscrito* 41 (2018); "Transparency and Reflection," *Canadian Journal of Philosophy* 49 (2019); "Longuenesse on Self and Body," *Philosophy and Phenomenological Research* 98 (2019); and "Skepticism about Self-Understanding," in *Mental Action and the Conscious Mind*, ed. Michael Brent and Lisa Miracchi Titus, Routledge, 2022, reproduced courtesy of Taylor and Francis Group, LLC, a division of Informa plc. I thank the publishers for permission to use this material.

Work on this book was supported by fellowships at the Radcliffe Institute for Advanced Study at Harvard University and the Franke Institute for the Humanities at the University of Chicago. I am very grateful to those two institutions for their support.

Introduction

> [F]or human reality, to exist is always to *assume* its being; that is, to be responsible for it instead of receiving it from outside, as a pebble does. . . . This 'assumption' of itself which characterizes human reality implies an understanding of human reality by itself, however obscure this understanding may be. . . . For this understanding is not a quality that comes to human reality from without, but its own mode of existence.
> —Jean-Paul Sartre, *Sketch for a Theory of Emotions* (1994), 9

I.1. Why Study Self-Knowledge?

The topic of self-knowledge has been central to philosophy since antiquity, and even in our highly specialized and professionalized era, it continues to give rise to a steady stream of discussion.[1] It certainly has the prestige of history on its side: the Temple of Apollo at Delphi famously bore the inscription "Know thyself," and this injunction became a touchstone of Greek philosophy, and thereby of the Western philosophical tradition as a whole.[2] But divine injunctions aside, what entitles self-knowledge to its central place on the philosophical agenda? If it deserves to be not simply a goal that each of us ought privately to pursue, but a topic that philosophers should investigate in general terms, on what basis does it claim our attention?

---

[1] Recent book-length studies in English include Gallois 1996, Moran 2001, Finkelstein 2003, Nichols and Stich 2003, Bar-On 2004, Bilgrami 2006, O'Brien 2007, Rödl 2007, Carruthers 2011, Gertler 2011, Fernandez 2013, Cassam 2014, Coliva 2016, and Byrne 2018. Important anthologies of articles include Cassam 1996, Wright, Smith, and MacDonald 1998, Hatzimoysis 2011, and Smithies and Stoljar 2012. These lists are highly incomplete: I merely list the works best known to me, and I do not attempt to list works on closely related topics such as: the nature of self-consciousness, the analysis of *de se* thought, the basis of bodily awareness, the limits of self-knowledge, etc. A full list of such works would be unmanageably large.

[2] The Delphic maxim seems originally to have been meant as an injunction to human beings never to forget the difference between their own mortal standpoint and the standpoint of the gods. Interpreted in this sense, the maxim does not call us to any general project of knowing ourselves. The maxim is, however, repeatedly invoked by Plato's Socrates, and via his influence, it came to be understood in a broader sense.

Answers to this question have varied over the centuries, but a point of longstanding agreement has been that the capacity for self-knowledge is in some way deeply characteristic of human beings. This thought has been developed differently in different eras, but broadly speaking, Western philosophers have tended to hold that human beings differ in some crucial way from other animals—often, this difference is said to consist in our "rationality"—and this distinctiveness, in turn, is held to entail a capacity for and a need to attain self-knowledge. In Plato and Aristotle, this idea took the form of the claim that, since human beings are rational animals, human virtue requires a measure of self-understanding—not so much knowledge of our private thoughts and feelings as a general understanding of our own nature, which is held to be necessary for living well.[3] Medieval thinkers like Augustine and Aquinas placed greater emphasis on the idea that the capacity for knowledge of our own thinking is an essential trait of our minds, so that, as Augustine puts it, the human mind "cannot be altogether ignorant of itself" since it is necessarily "present to itself."[4] And modern philosophers, following Descartes, came to regard self-awareness in thinking, not merely as an essential trait of our minds, but as their defining principle, the basis on which we may characterize the distinctive mode of existence of the human mind itself.

These conspicuous differences of doctrine should not, however, blind us to a broader commonality of theme: the shared topic of these diverse theories is something distinctive of human mindedness, some essential openness to self-awareness, which informs our capacities for knowledge and action and thereby sets our lives apart from those of animals that lack this fundamental capacity for self-reflection. Thus, for thinkers in this tradition, the topic of self-knowledge earns its place on the philosophical agenda in virtue of its presumed link to the question "What is a human being?" They hold human beings to be distinctively self-knowing animals—not in the sense that we always understand ourselves soundly, but in the sense that our minds are necessarily capable of rising to some form of self-awareness, be it sound or unsound. Accordingly, they treat the philosophical analysis of self-knowledge as a contribution to understanding of our own distinctively human nature.

When seen against this backdrop, the most striking feature of contemporary work on self-knowledge is its rigorous repudiation of these ways of framing its topic. To be sure, contemporary philosophers continue to take an interest in our capacity to know our own minds, but they tend to consider this topic in an isolated form, detached from wider theses about the distinctive nature of human minds or the difference between rational and nonrational

---

[3] This is a very broad characterization, and even in this form it is contestable. I have in mind, in the case of Plato, the kind of connection he makes between, for instance, self-knowledge and the virtue of temperance.

[4] Cf. Augustine, *On the Trinity (2002)*, 10.3.5, 10.9.12.

mentality.⁵ The standard contemporary way of motivating interest in self-knowledge is rather to present it as a special problem in epistemology, on a par with the problems of perceptual knowledge, knowledge by induction, knowledge by testimony, and so on. This problem is typically introduced by contrasting our knowledge of our own mental states with the knowledge other people can have of these states. Another person can tell what I am thinking or feeling, what I believe, want, or intend, only by interpreting observable signs: my words, actions, and other behavior. But it seems that I normally do not need to observe my own behavior to know such things about myself: my knowledge of such facts seems somehow immediate. Contemporary philosophical analyses of self-knowledge tend to focus on the question how it is possible for us to know our own minds in this strikingly immediate and yet seemingly reliable way.⁶ In this way, the topic of self-knowledge is dissociated from metaphysical claims about the nature of human mindedness and framed as a discrete epistemological problem in its own right.

Moreover, even this modest, epistemological formulation of the problem has come under increasing pressure in recent years, as skeptics about human self-knowledge have raised doubts about whether we really have the sorts of immediate and reliable knowledge of our own mental states asserted in the standard story. On the contrary, these skeptics argue, we are often ignorant of or mistaken about our own mental states, and even when we are correct about them, our knowledge is not in principle more immediate than our knowledge of the mental states of other people. The skeptics often add that, if there is some limited sphere in which our knowledge of our own minds is privileged, this privileged self-knowledge is of little interest. Thus, in an influential expression of such skepticism, Quassim Cassam observes:

> What [contemporary] philosophers find interesting isn't how you can know your own character or abilities but much more mundane examples of self-knowledge such as your knowledge that you believe you are wearing socks or that you want to have ice cream for pudding. This is usually news to non-philosophers. . . . The self-knowledge which most reflective human beings tend to regard as important is substantial self-knowledge, and they expect philosophy to have something to say about its nature, scope, and value. I don't think that this is an unreasonable expectation. (Cassam 2014: vii–viii)

---

⁵ With notable exceptions: Shoemaker 1996, Moran 2001, Rödl 2007. I am indebted to each of these authors—especially to Moran and Rödl, whose perspectives on the topic of self-knowledge have been crucial to the development of my own. What I owe to them, and where I differ from them, will become clear in due course.

⁶ Shoemaker 1996, Wright 1998, Bar-On 2004, Gertler 2011, Byrne 2018, etc.

Yet, Cassam observes, with regard to "substantial" self-knowledge of our character, our deepest values, our underlying motives, and so on, we seem to have no special privilege. Indeed, other people commonly know us better in these respects than we know ourselves.

Under these sorts of pressure, the philosophical topic of self-knowledge threatens to dwindle down to a wisp. As Eric Schwitzgebel puts it in another influential defense of the skeptical position:

> Self-knowledge? Of general features of our stream of conscious experience, of our morally most important attitudes, of our real values and our moral character, of our intelligence, of what really makes us happy and unhappy . . . — about such matters I doubt we have much knowledge at all. We live in cocoons of ignorance, especially where our self-conception is at stake. The philosophical focus on how impressive our self-knowledge is gets the most important things backwards. (Schwitzgebel 2012: 197)

If we consider the topic from a broader historical perspective, I think Schwitzgebel's target will look like a straw man: the classical philosophical concern with human self-awareness was hardly an interest in "how impressive our self-knowledge is." But given the state of the contemporary debate, Schwitzgebel's attitude is understandable. For this is indeed the contemporary situation: the orthodox discussion of self-knowledge focuses on our supposed privilege in making a narrow and apparently insignificant set of judgments about our own mental states, while a growing heterodox movement denies that our knowledge of our own minds exhibits any very significant privilege at all.

This book grows out of a conviction that the topic of self-knowledge has fallen into this disreputable predicament because contemporary philosophical work on self-knowledge has become detached from its proper moorings. I want to urge a reconsideration of the classical idea that the topic of self-knowledge must be approached via a consideration of the distinctive *nature* of human minds. This does not amount merely to the suggestion that we have some sort of privileged knowledge of our own minds in virtue of the very nature of our mental states (a view about the basis of self-knowledge commonly called "constitutivism"). It amounts, rather, to a suggestion about what we should take the fundamental philosophical topic of self-knowledge to be—a suggestion about where its intellectual roots lie, so to speak, and thus about how we should understand its significance. My claim will be that this topic is misconceived when it is represented as a puzzle about how we can *know* a special range of facts. Instead, it should be regarded primarily as an inducement to reflect on the *nature* of the relevant facts themselves, and of the kind of mind of which they hold. In this way, the interest of the topic is fundamentally ontological or metaphysical rather than merely epistemological: its philosophical importance lies in the light it can shed on what our minds are, rather than just on how we come to know certain facts about them. My aim in the chapters that follow will be to bring this out, and thereby to put us in a position to see a link between debates about how we know our own minds and the sort of dark but intriguing idea about human nature that Sartre expresses in his remark (quoted in the epigraph to this Introduction) that, for a human being, "to exist is always to *assume* its being" in a way that implies "an understanding of human reality by itself."

I want to suggest that this Sartrean conception of the existential roots of self-awareness is insightful, and that we should understand both the availability of a sphere of privileged self-knowledge and the value of deeper self-understanding in terms of it. An implication of the Sartrean standpoint, as we shall see, is that our primary form of self-awareness is not an awareness *of* our own mental states, but an awareness at work *in* our manner of inhabiting the world. For just this reason, I will suggest, this primary self-awareness must be *transparent*: its focus must be, not on ourselves, but on aspects of the non-mental world presented in a way that is informed by an implicit self-awareness. Yet, as I will also seek to show, we are necessarily capable of transforming this implicit self-awareness, through *reflection*, into an explicit understanding of ourselves and our own mental states.

Both the case for these claims and the concrete development of them will have to wait for the coming chapters. The purpose of this Introduction is simply to sketch the general outlook from which this enterprise proceeds, in a way that should shed light on its governing spirit and its motivation.

I.2. Self-Knowledge and the First-Person Perspective

According to the view I will defend, the topic of self-knowledge can come into proper focus only if we recognize its bearing on metaphysical questions about the nature of human mentality. But how might debates about self-knowledge bear on questions about the nature of human minds? To clarify this idea, it will help to note some connections between these debates and broader disputes about the soundness of what is sometimes called "the first-person perspective" on a human life.

The term "first-person perspective" is, of course, a piece of philosophical jargon, not a phrase with a clear pre-theoretical meaning, and I think its philosophical meaning remains somewhat nebulous.[7] It is presumably introduced by analogy with the notion of point of view in the visual arts, and perhaps also with

---

[7] For a diverse range of conceptions of this topic, see Nagel 1986, Korsgaard 1996, Shoemaker 1996, Moran 2001, Zahavi 2005, and Baker 2013.

the idea of first-person narration in literature, but the nature of these analogies is not straightforward, and it will be a main task of the chapters that follow to give the philosophical notion a definite sense. For the present, we may simply think of the first-person perspective as the way of representing things characteristic of a subject immersed in facing the problems her life presents, as opposed to the way of representing things characteristic of someone who seeks to theorize about how that subject's representations relate to her situation. When we describe a conscious subject's life "from the first-person perspective," we describe how things present themselves *to* that subject, whereas when we describe how things look from the theorist's perspective, we bring the subject herself into the frame and think *about* her representations and the laws that govern them. The latter standpoint on human subjects is often called "the third-person perspective," and—despite some misgivings that I will mention shortly—I will adopt this terminology.

A nice example of the contrast between first- and third-person perspectives occurs in a well-known passage from Christine Korsgaard's *The Sources of Normativity*. Korsgaard is discussing how our capacity to reflect on our own desires gives rise to the idea of free will. Her remarks are worth quoting at length:

> Occasionally one meets the objection that the freedom that we discover in reflection is a delusion. Human actions are causally determined.... When desire calls we think we can take it or leave it, but in fact someone could have predicted exactly what we will do. But how can this be a problem? The afternoon stretches before me, and I must decide whether to work or to play. Suppose first that *you can predict* which one I am going to do. That has no effect on me at all: I must still decide what to do. I am tempted to play but worried about work, and I must decide the case on its merits....
>
> The freedom discovered in reflection is not a theoretical property which can also be seen by scientists considering the agent's deliberations third-personally and from outside. It is from within the deliberative perspective that we see our desires as providing suggestions which we may take or leave. You will say that this means that our freedom is not 'real' only if you have defined 'real' as what can be identified by scientists looking at things third-personally and from outside. (Korsgaard 1996: 94–95, 96).

Korsgaard suggests that, when we take the "deliberative perspective" of an agent facing the question of what to do, we necessarily presume our own freedom, at least in the minimal sense that we presume ourselves to face a choice whose outcome is not settled independently of our now selecting between different options. But she also suggests that this freedom is "not a theoretical property" visible "from outside," by which she seems to mean that the agent's right to presume, in deliberating, that she faces a genuine choice does not depend on the truth of the claim that, prior to her choice, there is no determinate fact of the matter about what she will do. Even if there is such a determinate fact, the agent still presently faces the question of (e.g.) what to do with her afternoon, and the truth of determinism does not resolve this question for her. In facing this question, she must presume "from the deliberative perspective" that what she will do is up to her to settle.

How these two "perspectives" can coexist, despite the seeming tensions between them, is a question we shall pursue more fully in the chapters that follow. But at any rate, Korsgaard's discussion vividly brings out the contrast between these two standpoints on choice, one of which articulates what the agent herself presupposes in confronting the question of what to do, while the other draws back to a theorist's perspective from which the agent's own view looks questionable, precisely because it becomes, not the lens *through* which the scene is viewed, but one element *of* a larger picture, whose relation to other elements (preceding events, present circumstances, future events, etc.) can be a topic for investigation. The first-person perspective here is the view of a choice-situation one has *as* the deliberating agent; the third-person perspective is the view one has when one considers the same situation "from sideways on," in such a way that the agent's own representations become topics for causal explanation and prediction.[8]

To call the theorist's standpoint "the third-person perspective" is somewhat misleading, for in many cases we speak about someone in the third person while treating her own perspective as presumptively correct. Thus if I ask you whether you will come to dinner on Friday, and you promise to do so, I might report to another friend, "He'll be there" (rather than merely, "He says he'll be there"). Here I speak about you in the third person, but in a way that does not treat you as an *object* of explanation or prediction, but as a fellow *subject* whose point of view on your own future action is presumptively decisive.[9] By the same token, we may sometimes think of ourselves in the first person, but step back from our standpoint as subjects to consider how we might appear to a theorist seeking to predict our thoughts and actions on the basis of general tendencies. Thus, having promised to come to dinner, but knowing my own tendency sometimes to forget such plans, I might say to myself, "Well, I did promise, so probably I'll be there." Here I treat my own future action as a topic for prediction and view my own promise as a piece of evidence supporting the view that I will come. In this way, I step outside the perspective from which, in promising, I regard it as *settled* that I will

---

[8] I believe this use of the phrase "from sideways on" is due to John McDowell. See his *Mind and World* (1994), passim.
[9] This kind of attitude toward other persons is clearly crucial to our capacity to make agreements with them, to engage in joint projects, and even to our sheer ability to learn things by having people *tell* them to us. For illuminating discussion of these connections, see Moran 2018.

come. Thus the grammatical distinction between first and third person does not really track the crucial contrast, but this terminology is entrenched, and at any rate I think the contrast itself is tolerably clear.

Indeed, once we get the hang of this contrast, we can start to see it everywhere. Thus we can contrast how a subject might explain why something made her sad or angry and how a theorist might explain this, what factors she would cite as having influenced her thinking about a given topic and what factors a theorist would identify, how she would explain her having reached a conclusion about a controversial question and how a theorist might explain this, and so on. The possibility of such contrasts seems, indeed, to be as general as the phenomenon of intentionality itself: it exists wherever a subject has some conscious representation *of*, or attitude *about*, some topic.[10] In any such case, it will be possible to distinguish between the subject's perspective on her situation and the perspective of a theorist concerned with explaining and predicting the subject's thought and action. In many instances, the explanations offered by such a theorist will differ from the explanations the subject herself would offer. But even where the theorist ultimately affirms the subject's view, her standpoint as theorist commits her to problematizing the subject's representation of things in a way that the subject, insofar as she remains immersed in her own perspective, cannot. For what the subject represents as so, simply in having a given perspective, the theorist is committed to regarding as merely the subject's representation of things, which may or may not be accurate.

The generality of this contrast between first- and third-person perspectives prompts a general question about how to adjudicate the claims of these two perspectives. On the one hand, the first-person perspective is one that all of us, as subjects, inevitably take up in one aspect of our own lives. On the other hand, experimental psychology is rapidly generating a wealth of data about how our minds perform various cognitive tasks, and these results often seem to support a picture of the causes of our thoughts and actions quite different from the one we presuppose *in* confronting these tasks as subjects.[11] Might the view from the first-person perspective present a fundamentally misleading picture of the explanation of our thoughts and actions? Or does this standpoint possess some kind of privilege that implies at least a normal presumption of truth?

This question about the soundness of the first-person perspective can be raised without presupposing that we have privileged knowledge of our own

---

[10] Cf. Moran: "A distinguishing fact about 'intentionally characterized' phenomena generally (not only states of mind, but actions, practices, and institutions, including linguistic ones) is that they admit of a distinction between inside and outside perspectives, the conception of them from the point of view of agents or participants as contrasted with various possible descriptions in some more purely naturalistic or extensional idiom" (Moran 2001: 34–35).

[11] See, e.g., Wegner 2002 and Wilson 2002.

mental states; for the issue turns, not on our knowledge of our own mental states and processes, but on things we presuppose in our unreflective engagement with the non-mental world. Even if I do not consider whether my *will* is free or whether my *judgments* are made for the reasons that I consciously accept—even if I never think about my own choosing or judging as such, but only about the non-psychological questions of what to do and what is the case—still I implicitly presuppose my ability make up my mind about what to do and what to think. Whether or not I formulate these presuppositions explicitly, I constantly take them for granted in my practice of judging and deciding: in order to decide what to do, for instance, I consider reasons for different courses of action, and thereby presuppose—even if I never explicitly think—that I can determine what I will do by deliberating about reasons.

Nevertheless, there is clearly a connection between the question of the soundness of the first-person perspective and the question of whether we have some sphere of privileged knowledge of our own minds. For whatever privilege we enjoy in knowing our present mental states is surely a reflection of our having a first-person perspective on our own lives. It is because I have some kind of special standpoint on my own perceptions as the one who experiences them, on my own desires as the one who feels them, on my own choices as the one who makes them, etc., that I can know these aspects of my mental life in a way that others cannot. When we ascribe such mental states and activities to ourselves, we characterize our first-person perspective explicitly, but even if we did not do so, we would still view the world *from* this perspective. It is our ability to make a transition from such world-directed awareness *from* a particular subjective standpoint to a reflective comprehension *of* this standpoint that links questions about the first-person perspective to questions about privileged self-knowledge.

I.3. The Stakes in These Debates

When I suggest that philosophical debates about self-knowledge might have implications for the nature of human minds, I have in mind specifically that they might bear on the question whether our first-person perspective on our own minds has some necessary presumption of correctness. Seeing this connection helps to clarify what is at stake in debates about self-knowledge. For skepticism about the soundness of the first-person perspective challenges something more basic than our mere *knowledge* of our own minds. It challenges our justification for approaching our lives in a certain way—as if we are genuinely capable of making up our own minds about what is the case and what to do, as if the grounds on which we make choices are the ones that genuinely move us, as if the reasons for which we suppose ourselves to be angry or hopeful, elated or miserable, are the genuine bases of our feelings, and so on.

The question of the soundness of the first-person perspective is thus closely connected with our warrant for conceiving of ourselves as *rational animals*, as a long philosophical tradition held us to be. In this tradition, our rationality was not taken to consist primarily in our tendency to arrive at certain preferred cognitive *outcomes*—for it has long been recognized that our human capacity to form reasonable beliefs and make optimal choices is at best very imperfect—but rather in our capacity to think and choose in a distinctively self-determined *manner*, in such a way that our beliefs and choices are determined by our conscious deliberations, rather than by forces operating automatically or "behind our backs." To be sure, this contrast needs clarification. But however the contrast between rational self-determination and merely automatic determination is to be understood, it is clearly connected with the question of the soundness of the first-person perspective. If this perspective on judgment and choice has some normal presumption of correctness, it makes sense for us to try to make our judgments and choices in the light of our own best assessment of reasons; and when we engage with other people, it makes sense to address them primarily as subjects capable of persuasion through rational discussion.

Once the soundness of the first-person perspective is called into question, however, an alternative attitude toward human cognition becomes attractive. On this other picture, our sense of conscious control over our own beliefs and choices, though perhaps explicable from an evolutionary perspective, is in fact an illusion. Perhaps in some kinds of cases we are good at identifying the factors that influence our judgments and choices, but in others we are not, and we cannot tell the difference by mere introspection. In any case, our mental processes, including the processes that occur when we consciously deliberate, are governed by laws that hold whether we are aware of them or not. We should not expect to have immediate insight into these laws, but should rather hope to learn ever more about them from experimental psychologists. Moreover, once we understand these laws, we may discover that, in many cases, the best policy to follow in judging and choosing is a strategic one: not the naïve policy of simply considering the first-order question of what is the case or what to do, but some sophisticated, second-order policy of constraining our own deliberation in a way that will tend to produce better judgment- or choice-outcomes on the whole. (In contemporary discussion, this sort of strategy for constraining one's own judging and choosing is sometimes called a "nudge" or "life hack.") In implementing such policies, we treat ourselves in something like the way Odysseus treats himself when he orders his deafened crew to keep him tied to the mast while they sail past the Sirens: we inhibit the free exercise of our "rational" capacities because we mistrust their unconstrained operation.

Only a Luddite would claim that such strategies are never useful. There is, however, a broader question at stake here: not just how we should approach particular judgments and choices, but what our general attitude should be toward our own capacities to judge and choose. We can undoubtedly sometimes be mistaken about what we really believe, what our real reasons are for a given judgment, what really motivates us to make a certain choice, etc.; but is there some general presumption of correctness that belongs to a judging and choosing subject's perspective on her own life, or at least to certain aspects of it? Can we take seriously the general picture of ourselves as rational, self-determining beings that is presupposed in the first-person perspective? Or must we be skeptical of this picture as a whole, even if we cannot avoid presupposing it in one aspect of our lives?

Philosophers have traditionally been partisans of the first-person perspective, but today it is increasingly common to find them voicing skepticism about the reliability of this standpoint. Thus, in a recent post to the *New York Times* philosophy blog "The Stone," Alex Rosenberg argues that a wide range of psychological evidence supports this conclusion:

> Our access to our own thoughts is just as indirect and fallible as our access to the thoughts of other people. We have no privileged access to our own minds. If our thoughts give the real meaning of our actions, our words, our lives, then we can't even be sure what we say or do, or for that matter, what we think or why we think it. (Rosenberg 2016, n.p.)

And similarly, in a discussion of the place of the first-person perspective in epistemology, Hilary Kornblith writes:

> [W]hen epistemologists think about deliberation, they tend to think about it from the first-person perspective.... If what I have argued here is even roughly right, then such an approach is radically mistaken.... [W]hen the phenomenon we seek to understand is one that has been studied extensively by the cognitive sciences, and when scientific advances have begun to displace our prescientific understanding of some phenomenon, we cannot simply turn our backs on the ways in which that understanding has supplanted our commonsense views. A philosophical methodology that would have us study these phenomena from the armchair, however, would do precisely that. (Kornblith 2018: 144–145)

These are radical views, but Rosenberg and Kornblith are not alone in their skepticism about the first-person perspective. This kind of skepticism is increasingly widespread, not just in philosophy, but in our intellectual culture at large.

The case for such skepticism has, indeed, become a popular theme of newspaper op-eds and magazine think-pieces, and has provided the basis for a number of "pop psychology" bestsellers. Many of their titles will be familiar to contemporary readers:

Daniel Wegner, *The Illusion of Conscious Will* (2002)
Timothy Wilson, *Strangers to Ourselves* (2002)
Malcolm Gladwell, *Blink* (2005)
Richard H. Thaler and Cass R. Sunstein, *Nudge* (2008)
Dan Ariely, *Predictably Irrational* (2009)
Jonah Lehrer, *How We Decide* (2010)
Daniel Kahneman, *Thinking, Fast and Slow* (2011)
Leonard Mlodinow, *Subliminal* (2013).

What is noteworthy about these books is not just what they say, but that they are so popular: it suggests that we—at any rate, a growing number of us—have an appetite for this sort of thought about ourselves. We are ready to be skeptical of our own pretensions to self-understanding. We feel an obscure satisfaction in seeing the mask of Reason torn away. Why this is so is an interesting question—it suggests larger forces at work—but whatever its causes, the controversy is clearly not just "academic" in the pejorative sense. It is an issue that matters, not just to scholars, but to reflective persons in general.

The fact that our privileged knowledge of our present mental states is often discussed in isolation from such controversy accounts, I believe, for the apparent triviality of this discussion stressed by writers like Cassam and Schwitzgebel. Considered in isolation, the question whether I have privileged knowledge of (to take Cassam's example) my own belief that I am wearing socks appears to focus on a variety of self-knowledge that is strikingly insignificant when compared with "substantial" self-knowledge of my deepest motivations or my true character. What is at stake in this focus stands out more clearly, however, once we recognize its connection with broader questions about how seriously to take the subject's own perspective on her life as a knower and agent. Are the things the subject takes herself to believe her real beliefs, and are they held for the reasons she supposes? Are her actions really motivated by the values she takes to guide them? And more generally, is she right in her unreflective assumption that these matters are up to her to settle? These are not questions of interest only to philosophers; they should matter to anyone who cares about how we should approach our own lives and how we should address the other people who confront us as potential partners in or obstacles to our pursuits.

I.4. Epistemic versus Metaphysical Approaches to Self-Knowledge

If it could be demonstrated that the first-person perspective is necessarily privileged in certain respects, this would show something, not merely about the extent to which we know our minds, but about the nature of the minds we know: it would show that they are *essentially* such that the subject's own perspective on them has some presumption of truth.[12] A principal aim of this book will be to defend a claim along these lines: that our first-person perspective on our own minds cannot in general be unsound, on pain of there being no psychological phenomena of the relevant kind to study from any perspective.[13]

This conception of what is at stake in debates about self-knowledge contrasts with the conception according to which the significance of these debates is primarily epistemological. On the latter conception, the task of a theory of self-knowledge is simply to explain how we can acquire a particular variety of knowledge, one whose availability is supposed to be puzzling, as our knowledge of laws of nature or truths of mathematics is commonly taken to be puzzling. This sort of approach to the topic of self-knowledge assumes a certain structure in the problem: on the one hand, there is a domain of facts (in this case, facts about our own mental states); on the other hand, a set of beliefs we hold about them. The philosopher's task is then to explain how these two realms come to stand in the right relation—whatever relation it is that must obtain for these beliefs to constitute knowledge of the facts they concern. We might call this the *Correlation Model* of self-knowledge.

Once the topic of self-knowledge has been conceived in this correlationist way, a familiar array of options present themselves. Is the required relation established by some form of inward-directed perception,[14] or by some sort of conscious or

---

[12] Such a claim is defended with great depth and power in the work of Sebastian Rödl, who argues, "It is characteristic of the empiricist tradition in epistemology and the philosophy of mind that it thinks it the highest possibility of thought to lay hold of objects that exist independently. . . . It is impossible to understand first person thought without giving up this conception of knowledge, for unmediated first person knowledge is distinguished by the fact that, here, the thing known is not a reality that is independent of the [subject's] knowledge of it" (Rödl 2007: 101).

For reasons that will emerge in due course, I think Rödl's way of putting this point fails to draw a crucial distinction between an implicit form of self-awareness that indeed is "included in the reality of the thing known" and an explicit form of self-knowledge that is not (except in special cases) included in this reality. Nevertheless, Rödl's elaboration of this point has played a crucial role in the development of my own thinking about the metaphysical significance of the topic of self-knowledge.

[13] This claim will obviously need sharpening before it becomes defensible. I will not defend the presumptive soundness of *all* our views about our own minds, but only of those that reflectively articulate an implicit awareness that belongs necessarily to the relevant first-order mental states. More will also need to be said about the relevant notion of "presumptive soundness," which is intended to capture the thought that the relevant views, though capable of being mistaken, are grounded in a way that ties them essentially to the facts they concern.

[14] E.g., Armstrong 1968.

unconscious inference,[15] or by some mechanism that reliably generates second-order beliefs corresponding to our first-order mental states?[16] Or again, does the relation hold because, under the right conditions, our being in the first-order state somehow constitutes our believing ourselves to be in this state,[17] or because our believing ourselves to be in a given mental state somehow constitutes our being in the relevant state,[18] or perhaps brings this state into being?[19] These are profoundly diverse approaches, but for all their differences, they are alike in taking the problem of self-knowledge to be that of explaining how the proper alignment is achieved between a first-order mental state and a second-order belief about that state. In this sense, they all take the structure of the problem of self-knowledge to be fixed by the general concept of knowledge, which is assumed to require some kind of correspondence between a fact and a belief about that fact. I call any account of self-knowledge that assumes this framework an *epistemic approach*.[20] Even the skeptical views mentioned earlier are, in effect, epistemic approaches: although they deny that we have any significant sphere of privileged self-knowledge, they agree in holding that such knowledge would have to consist in an alignment between a belief and a corresponding fact.

My aim will be to argue that this epistemic, correlationist approach is wrong at its foundation, and that we can achieve a satisfying perspective on the epistemological topic of self-knowledge only by seeing it as a manifestation of a more fundamental metaphysical point about the nature of human mentality. The core idea of this *metaphysical approach* to self-knowledge is that the basic form of self-awareness does not consist in a relation between a first-order mental state and a second-order belief, but rather belongs intrinsically to certain of our first-order mental states themselves. It is for just this reason, I shall argue, that our first-person perspective on our own minds cannot in general be unsound, though it can certainly be mistaken in particular cases. It cannot be generally unsound because it does not consist merely of a set of second-order beliefs we hold about the nature and explanation of our own first-order mental states and processes. It is, rather, the reflective expression of an awareness essentially involved in the existence of the relevant first-order mental states and processes themselves. Hence, although many factors can distort our reflective understanding of our own minds, it is not an accident when this understanding is sound, but merely

---

[15] E.g., Carruthers 2011, Cassam 2014.
[16] E.g., Nichols and Stich 2003. When their views are considered at a certain level of abstraction, the authors mentioned in the previous two notes could also be listed here.
[17] E.g., Shoemaker 1996.
[18] E.g., Wright 1998.
[19] E.g., Peacocke 1998.
[20] I owe the phrase "epistemic approach" to Bar-On 2004, though I use the term in a different way than she does.

the unimpeded expression of an awareness essential to the states and processes that are thereby understood.

I.5. Kantian versus Sartrean Conceptions of Self-Consciousness

In contemporary philosophy, the idea of an essential connection between rational mentality and self-awareness is most closely associated with a Kantian tradition of thinking about self-consciousness. In his *Critique of Pure Reason*, Kant famously claims that it must be possible for any human knower to "accompany [her] representations with the *I think*," on pain of these representations being "nothing to" her (KrV B131-2). In his *Anthropology*, he adds the following striking claim about the importance of human self-consciousness:

> That the human being can have the representation *I* raises him infinitely above all the other beings living on earth. By this he is a person . . . —that is, a being altogether different in rank and dignity from things, such as nonrational animals. . . . [A]ny language must think 'I' when it speaks in the first person, even if it has no special word to express it. For this power (the ability to think) is understanding. (An. 7:129)

Since Kant also characterizes the understanding as a "spontaneous" or self-determining power (KrV A50-1/B74), and since he maintains that this power distinguishes a rational mind from a nonrational one, he is often taken to hold that our capacity to think of ourselves in the first person, and to reflect on our own representations by "accompanying them with *I think*," is what makes us capable of the special kind of cognitive self-determination characteristic of a rational creature.[21]

The present project began life—I hesitate to think how long ago—as an attempt to defend this sort of Kantian perspective on the significance of self-consciousness.[22] I was moved by the thought that our capacity to think of

---

[21] I am not at all sure that this was Kant's view. His remarks on the connection between understanding and apperception are subtle, and it is not clear to me that he must be read as holding that the general capacity for understanding requires actual grasp of a first-person notion and concepts of thinking, as opposed to the mere potentiality to acquire such concepts through reflection on our own cognitive activity. If Kant held the latter view, his position is similar to my own. But at any rate, a number of influential contemporary Kantians have attributed to Kant the stronger view formulated in the text. I will use the label "Kantian" for such views without implying any claim about the position of the historical Kant.

[22] For an expression of this standpoint, see Boyle 2009. In what follows, I will reserve the term "self-consciousness" for this intellectually demanding notion of self-awareness, and will use "self-awareness" as a more generic term that applies not only to self-consciousness in the demanding sense, but also to less intellectually demanding forms of self-awareness that do not require the capacity for

ourselves in the first person and to reflect on our own representations effects a kind of liberation of our cognition from the forces that govern the cognitive processes of nonrational animals. Many recent writers have endorsed versions of this Kantian idea, but Christine Korsgaard has expressed it in an especially evocative way:

> [T]he human mind *is* self-conscious in the sense that it is essentially reflective. I'm not talking about being *thoughtful*, which of course is an individual property, but about the structure of our minds that makes thoughtfulness possible. A lower animal's attention is fixed on the world. Its perceptions are its beliefs and its desires are its will.... But we human animals turn our attention on to our own perceptions and desires themselves, on to our own mental activities, and we are conscious *of* them.... And this sets us a problem no other animal has. It is the problem of the normative. For our capacity to turn our attention on to our own mental activities is also a capacity to distance ourselves from them, to call them into question. I perceive, and I find myself with a powerful impulse to believe. But I back up and bring that impulse into view and then I have a certain distance. Now the impulse doesn't dominate me and now I have a problem. Shall I believe? Is this perception really a *reason* to believe? I desire and find myself with a powerful impulse to act. But I back up and bring that impulse into view and then I have a certain distance. Now the impulse doesn't dominate me and now I have a problem. Shall I act? Is this desire really a *reason* to act? The reflective mind cannot settle for perception and desire, not just as such. It needs a *reason*. (Korsgaard 1996: 92–93)[23]

The task of Kantians, insofar as they believe something along these lines, is to explain what self-consciousness is and why it makes this sort of difference: what sort of "distance" it gives us from our "impulses" to believe and to act, and how this distance is connected with the special form of engagement with reasons of which human knowers are (supposedly) distinctively capable. And this was what I took my project to be: to show how the proper treatment of the topic of self-consciousness intersects with more general topics in the theory of rationality in a way that vindicates the Kantian association between rationality, self-consciousness, and self-determination.

---

explicit first-person thought and explicit conceptualization of one's own representational states as such. It will be one of the burdens of this book to argue that there are such less-demanding forms of self-awareness.

[23] In addition to Korsgaard, see Pippin 1987, Shoemaker 1991, McDowell 1994, Allison 1996, McGinn 1996, and Rödl 2007.

The problem I encountered was that, inspiring as these ideas seemed to me, they did not appear to be quite true. For one thing, despite much effort, I found it difficult to reconstruct a non-question-begging argument for the Kantian claim that a rational being must be able to think of herself in the first person and reflect on her own representations as such. Doubtless a mature human being *will* normally possess a first-person notion of herself: a notion by which she represents herself as the single, underlying subject of her manifold thoughts and experiences. But *must* she possess such a notion, and corresponding concepts of various kinds of representational states, as a condition of being able to weigh reasons for belief and action? There may appear to be a quick argument for this conclusion, namely that a subject must at least possess a first-person notion and the concepts of belief and action in order to entertain such questions as:

Do I have adequate reason to believe that *p*?
Do I have adequate reason to do A?

But this argument in fact begs the crucial question, since it takes for granted that a subject who considers reasons for belief and action must consider them as reasons for *her to believe* something or reasons for *her to do* something.

If reasons for belief and action must be considered in this explicitly self-predicative mode, then certainly a rational subject must possess an understanding of the first person, of the concepts of belief and action, and of the concept of a reason itself. But it is not obvious that the capacity to consider reasons for belief and action requires such explicitness. For why couldn't a subject consider one of these simpler questions:

whether *p*
whether to do A

These questions certainly pertain to what the subject will believe or do, but their formulation does not make explicit reference to *her believing* or *her doing*. At least apparently, then, a subject might entertain one of these simpler questions without thinking of herself and her own belief or action as such: she might merely think about the *object* of her belief or action (the proposition that *p*, the deed of A-ing) without thinking of *herself* and her own *cognitive relation* to this object.[24] Still, if a subject were able to entertain such questions, and to consider grounds

---

[24] Nor, seemingly, need she think of her reasons *as reasons*. The question whether *p* can be answered by giving what are in fact reasons ("Well, *q* and *r*") without marking these considerations *as* reasons in a way that requires deployment of the concept *reason*. And so too, *mutatis mutandis*, for the question whether to A. These sorts of points have been made by a number of authors. For a forceful formulation, see Peacocke 2014.

for answering Yes or No, this would surely show "rationality" in the sense that matters: the ability to arrive at one's beliefs and actions, not automatically or instinctively, but on the basis of a consideration of reasons for believing and acting. Thus, if it is possible to weigh reasons in this non-self-ascriptive mode, it is unclear why rationality should require the capacity to think of oneself in the first person and to self-ascribe one's own representations.

Of course, someone might argue that the apparent simplicity of these questions is misleading, and that a subject who can entertain them must in fact have the capacity to think of her own mental states as such. But the preceding discussion brings out that there is no *quick* argument for this conclusion, and once the illusion of a quick argument has been dispelled, it is not easy to see what sort of argument could be offered. At any rate, I believe that many purported arguments linking rationality with self-awareness are question-begging in the manner of our quick argument: they reach their conclusion only by building an assumption of self-awareness into their characterization of the cognitive task that a rational subject must perform.[25]

Moreover, once the quick argument has been rejected, the Kantian claim that rationality requires the capacity to reflect on one's own representations looks strikingly substantive and not terribly plausible. If it is to avoid the risk of triviality, this claim must mean that a knower who can think rationally about *any* topic must have the capacity to think explicitly about certain particular topics: herself and her own representational states. But this sets an implausibly high bar for rationality. Couldn't a young child learn to consider (e.g.) the first-order, non-psychological question *whether p*—assembling grounds in favor of a given answer and responding relevantly to queries about these grounds—without having mastered the special psychological concepts that would enable her to frame the second-order questions *whether she herself believes that p* and *what convinces her* of her answer?[26] Consider what is involved in grasping the

---

[25] Though its argumentative structure is not fully clear, the recently quoted passage from Korsgaard appears to suffer from this defect: it presupposes that my "impulses" to believe and act will cease to "dominate" me only if I can entertain such questions as "Shall I believe? Is this perception really a reason to believe?" and "Shall I act? Is this desire really a reason to act?" But this builds explicit reference to oneself in the first person, to modes of psychic activity such as believing and desiring, and to the concept of a reason itself, into the very questions that a rational subject must be able to consider, and thus trivializes the argument purporting to connect the general capacity to weigh reasons with the capacity for self-conscious reflection. For similar argumentation, see, e.g., McGinn 1996 and Shoemaker 1991. For criticism of such arguments consonant with the ones raised above, see Moran 2001, Burge 2009, Kornblith 2012, and Cassam 2014.

[26] The point of this appeal to what a child could do is simply to make this issue vivid, not to invoke any special information from developmental psychology. My understanding is that developmental psychologists generally do believe young children to be capable of thinking intelligently about world-directed questions before they master the kinds of "meta-representational" concepts that would enable them to think about their own beliefs as such (cf. the well-known False Belief Test and related experiments); but I do not mean to rest my case on any empirical findings. I mean to rest it, rather, on the patent conceptual distinction between the capacity for first-order thought and the capacity for meta-representation. The former is the capacity to think intelligently about whether p; the latter, the

latter concepts: to grasp the concept *believes*, for instance, presumably requires understanding this relation as capable of holding between an arbitrary subject and an arbitrary proposition—so in order to understand the thought that *I believe that p*, I must understand the relational predicate ξ *believes that* Π, which is open to arbitrary substitutions of a person for ξ and a proposition for Π. To insist on this point is simply to subsume the present case under the broader rule that possession of a *concept* implies a general capacity, one that can figure in the explanation of indefinitely many distinct thoughts involving that concept.[27] Yet the capacity intelligently to consider first-order propositional questions surely does not require any such general grasp of the second-order concept *believes*. It simply requires the capacity to think about the question *whether p* (and to come to believe it or not), not the capacity to think thoughts *about* belief as a specific cognitive relation in which subjects can stand to propositions.

For these sorts of reasons—which I will discuss more fully in subsequent chapters—I have come to think that the Kantian claim about the connection between rationality with self-consciousness cannot be correct, inasmuch as it overintellectualizes rationality and sets the bar for possessing it implausibly high. Nevertheless, although the strong Kantian formulation misses the mark, I believe it comes near to an important truth. I will argue that, although it is not true that every rational subject must have the capacity to self-ascribe her own representational states in the first person, any such subject must have the intellectual basis for such a capacity at her fingertips, so to speak: she must be capable of framing a first-person notion of herself, and concepts of the basic modes of presentation in which she can engage, by merely *reflecting* on an implicit self-awareness already involved in her first-order thinking. Moreover, although this implicit self-awareness does *not* require the application of a psychological concept to a first-person subject, our account of it will vindicate the broader Kantian intuition of a link between rationality, self-awareness, and self-determination. In this way, I have come to think, a satisfactory account of what is insightful in the Kantian standpoint must begin by drawing a basic distinction between pre-reflective and reflective self-awareness, and must give a central place to pre-reflective self-awareness in explaining how we know our own minds and how this knowledge is linked to our rationality.

In coming to see the importance of pre-reflective self-awareness, I have been helped—much to my own surprise—by the writings of Jean-Paul Sartre. From his early essay "The Transcendence of the Ego" (1936) to the end of his

---

capacity to think explicitly about *one's own perspective* on whether *p*. The latter is, on its face, a more sophisticated intellectual achievement. A powerful argument would be needed to establish that, contrary to appearances, the former capacity in fact presupposes the latter.

[27] Cf. Gareth Evans's well-known "Generality Constraint" (Evans 1982: Ch. 4).

philosophical career, Sartre insisted on a distinction between what he called "pre-reflective" or "nonpositional" self-consciousness and "reflective" or "positional" self-knowledge.[28] Using "consciousness" as his general term for the intentional directedness of minds toward objects, Sartre claimed that any consciousness that "posits" some entity or state of affairs as its intentional object implies a correlative consciousness of this very state of consciousness. This consciousness of one's own consciousness, however, he held to be "nonpositional," meaning that it does *not* posit the conscious subject or her own state as its intentional object.[29] Moreover, he maintained that our human capacity to achieve "positional" self-knowledge, in which we *do* explicitly ascribe mental states to ourselves, depends on this more basic, nonpositional form of self-awareness. His term for the activity by which we move from nonpositional self-consciousness to positional self-knowledge was "reflection."

The contrast between these two kinds of self-awareness, one pre-reflective and the other reflective, will be a constant theme in the chapters that follow. I will argue that, whereas reflective self-awareness must involve a first-person representation of oneself and a concept of a certain type of mental state, the corresponding pre-reflective self-awareness is not subject to these requirements. Rather, such pre-reflective self-awareness is, as I shall put it, *transparent*: it primarily presents aspects of the non-mental world, but in *modes* that express an awareness of our own representational states. In the fundamental case, I will maintain, explicit self-knowledge is based upon such implicit self-awareness: it makes the mode of such transparent self-awareness into a topic for *reflection* in its own right.

It should be clear that this Sartrean conception of self-awareness amounts to what I have called a "metaphysical" approach to the topic. For Sartre's doctrine that all consciousness of the world involves nonpositional consciousness

---

[28] Appeal to this distinction is pervasive in Sartre's work, but other key invocations of it occur in *Sketch of a Theory of Emotions* (1939), *Being and Nothingness* (1943), "Consciousness of Self and Knowledge of Self" (1948), and *Search for a Method* (1957).

[29] Sartre presents these claims as characterizing "consciousness," but he also speaks of them as defining the distinctive character of "human reality." This raises a problem for interpreters: Is Sartre offering an account of all forms of consciousness, including (presumably?) the forms found in non-human animals, or does he mean to characterize a special type of consciousness distinctive of human beings? In particular, is his claim that all positional consciousness of an object implies a correlative "nonpositional" consciousness of consciousness meant to apply exclusively to the rational consciousness of human beings, or to the consciousness of all animals who have some sort of awareness of their environment? I will take no position on this issue as a question of Sartre interpretation, but I should make clear at the outset that, in my view, the philosophical importance of Sartre's notions of nonpositional consciousness and reflection lies in the light they can shed on the consciousness of rational animals: animals capable of *thinking* about what is the case and what to do, as contrasted with animals that arrive at determinations about what is the case and what to do in a merely automatic or instinctive manner. The connections between nonpositional consciousness, reflection, and rationality need a fuller discussion, however, and I will offer such a discussion in Chapter 7.

of consciousness amounts to the claim that self-awareness does not first arise when a certain relationship is established between a first-order mental state and a second-order belief about that state, but rather belongs intrinsically to certain kinds of first-order mental states. Moreover, he holds that even when we reflect on our own states of consciousness, this does not, in the basic case, involve our forming distinct, second-order beliefs about our first-order states:

> [W]e are used to representing reflection as a new consciousness, suddenly appearing, targeting the reflected consciousness and living in symbiosis with it.... But... it is completely impossible [in this way] to account for its absolute unity with the reflected consciousness, a unity which alone can render the authority and certainty of reflective intuition conceivable. (BN 218/186)

Sartre seeks to give an account of reflective self-knowledge that respects this requirement that it should constitute an "absolute unity" with the consciousness on which it reflects. The result, as we shall see, is a view on which reflection does not, in the most basic case, bring about a distinct state of awareness *of* our first-order conscious states, but transforms the character of these first-order states themselves. Moreover, Sartre sees implications in this point, not just for the nature of our mental states, but for the nature of human existence more generally. Thus, having characterized all consciousness of objects as essentially involving "nonpositional" consciousness of consciousness, he goes on to suggest that

> we can now begin an ontological study of consciousness, not as the totality of human being, but as its instantaneous kernel. (BN 117/106)

This is a dark statement, and its darkness is only compounded by a rather grandiose continental idiom, which can induce in anglophone philosophers a powerful urge to bid our goodnights and head home to bed. Nevertheless, I hope in due course that we will be able to make something of this Sartrean idea: that a study of the essential self-awareness of human mentality opens out into a study of the distinctively self-determined character of human existence. For Sartre, this idea goes hand in hand with the thought that human beings have a certain distinctive kind of being, which he calls "being for itself." For such beings, he maintains, self-awareness is not a mere cognizance of our own condition that sometimes supervenes on this condition; it is the very medium in which our lives take shape. Hence it is possible for us not merely to *know* ourselves, but genuinely to *be* ourselves in a self-aware manner—a condition Sartre calls "authenticity." And hence, too, our failures of self-awareness can constitute states, not of mere self-ignorance, but of the special kind of self-erosion that Sartre calls "bad faith."

I.6. Plan of the Chapters

I will mention Sartre frequently in the chapters that follow, but this will not be an essay in Sartre exegesis. Rather, I hope to lead us, through an independent investigation, to a standpoint from which we can recognize something insightful in a certain complex of Sartrean ideas. We will approach this standpoint in three stages.

The first part of the book, "Self-Knowledge and Transparency," seeks to lead us from the standard, epistemological conception of the topic of self-knowledge toward a more metaphysical conception, one that places this topic in the context of questions about how the very nature of our mentality gives us a special perspective on our own lives. To make a case for this reorientation, I first argue for an approach to self-knowledge that makes the so-called *Problem of Transparency* (PT) central (Chapter 1). I then turn to some prominent recent responses to this problem, considering their strengths and weaknesses, and arguing that an adequate solution to PT should explain why our normal knowledge of our own minds is not just immediate and reliable but *non-spectatorial* in character (Chapter 2). I go on to argue that only what I call a "reflectivist" account of transparency can meet this condition (Chapter 3). On the resulting, Sartre-inspired view, our entitlement to treat questions about our own mental states as transparent to questions about the non-mental world depends on the presence, in our first-order awareness of the non-mental world, of a nonpositional form of self-awareness, whose presence enables us to make explicit psychological self-ascriptions through mere reflection.

The twin notions of nonpositional self-awareness, on the one hand, and reflection, on the other, set the agenda for the rest of the book. Part II, "Self-Consciousness and the First-Person Perspective," gives more careful scrutiny to the notion of nonpositional self-awareness and its relation to the broader notion of a first-person point of view. A natural question provoked by Sartre's idea of nonpositional self-awareness is: How can there be a genuine form of self-awareness that is not awareness of one's own mental states *as such*? What could "nonpositional" self-awareness even be, and what sort of understanding does someone who possesses it have of her own subjectivity?

In response to this challenge, I distinguish two kinds of self-representation: on the one hand, explicit *self-consciousness*, which deploys a first-person representation and specific psychological concepts; and on the other hand, a more basic, implicit manner of representing the relation of given objects to one's own subjectivity, which I call *consciousness-as-subject* (Chapter 4). I show that we need this distinction, not only to solve PT, but also to make satisfactory sense of a variety of topics unconnected with self-knowledge. Moreover, this distinction enables us to give a sharper and more principled account of the difference between positional and nonpositional self-awareness, and to explicate the notion of a first-person perspective in a way that clarifies its fundamental importance for understanding our relation to our own lives as knowers and agents.

I go on to show how the distinction between consciousness-as-subject and self-consciousness sheds light on the nature and function of first-person thought (Chapter 5) and on the special, liminal form of awareness we have of our own bodies (Chapter 6). A key point here is that our comprehension of our own objective presence in a world of bodies with which we can interact, and indeed our very capacity for first-person thought, depends on an implicit or "nonpositional" awareness of our own point of view. Our capacity for explicit first-person thought about ourselves thus proves to be itself a product of reflection, indeed the essential first product of this activity, which makes all others possible.

This observation marks the transition to the third part of the book, "Reflection and Self-Understanding." Even if we grant that there is a kind of implicit self-awareness that necessarily informs our first-order mental lives, a question remains about how to understand the step from such implicit self-awareness to explicit self-knowledge. "Reflection" is the conventional philosophical term for this step, but what exactly is reflection, and how does it accomplish this transubstantiation of implicit self-awareness into explicit self-knowledge?

I begin by arguing that the kind of reflection that is relevant to this problem is a kind we must invoke much more generally to account for the characteristic cognitive powers of rational animals: the capacity to frame concepts, to judge, and to draw comprehending inferences (Chapter 7). I go on to show how our capacity for reflection enables us to frame concepts of our various modes of cognitive activity, and how it enables us to investigate the nature of the cognitive powers that underwrite them. This amounts, I argue, to a vindication of the possibility of a kind of "armchair psychology" about which many contemporary philosophers are skeptical (Chapter 8). Moreover, this account of reflection gives us the resources to offer a more general defense of our understanding of our own lives from the first-person perspective against influential criticisms brought by philosophers and psychologists (Chapter 9).

I conclude by considering the importance of reflective self-knowledge (Chapter 10). If I am right that there is a kind of implicit self-awareness that necessarily informs our first-order mental states, then it is natural to ask why the step to explicit self-knowledge matters—what difference it makes to our lives. Socrates famously said, "The unexamined life is not worth living." Did he have a point? I argue that he did, but that we can bring the point into proper focus only if we recognize how reflection can transform the character of our first-order knowing and acting, rather than merely supplying us with further information relevant to the management of such first-order activities. On the resulting view, reflection can enrich our lives rather than just equipping us to live them more successfully. Our inquiry thus helps to clarify why self-knowledge might be thought to represent a problem for human beings in a way that it does not for nonrational animals, and so why the Delphic injunction to "know thyself" can claim to state, not just an arbitrary demand placed on us by some deity, but a necessary and proper task in a human life.

PART I
SELF-KNOWLEDGE AND TRANSPARENCY

1
Transparency and Other Problems

> A child said What is the grass? fetching it to me with full hands; How could I answer the child? I do not know what it is any more than he. I guess it must be the flag of my disposition, out of hopeful green stuff woven.
> —Walt Whitman, "Song of Myself" §6

1.1. Introduction

The topic of this book will be *self-knowledge*, by which I mean, not mere knowledge one has of the person who is *in fact* oneself, but knowledge of this person grasped *as* oneself—the sort of knowledge one might express in a first-person claim of the form:

I am F.

There are familiar illustrations of the importance of this distinction. Oedipus knew that the killer of Laius had brought a curse on Thebes, and since he himself was Laius's killer, this was in a sense knowledge about himself; but, tragically, he did not grasp the object of this knowledge *as* himself until it was too late to avoid certain other unfortunate choices. Or to take a more mundane case: once, while climbing aboard a tram, the physicist Ernst Mach saw a man standing at the back of the car and thought, "That man is the very image of a shabby schoolteacher," only to discover a moment later that the man he saw was himself reflected in a mirror. From the outset, Mach took himself to look like a shabby schoolteacher, but only when he recognized the role of the mirror did he grasp this person *as* himself. Only when this realization dawned did he come to have self-knowledge in the sense that will concern us.

    A person can have self-knowledge, in this sense, of any of her properties whatsoever, provided only that she grasps the person who has these properties to be herself. Philosophical discussions of self-knowledge tend to focus, however, on our knowledge of a narrower range of properties: not our non-mental properties such as weight, hair color, parentage, or astrological sign, but our own present mental states.[1] Indeed, with some exceptions, contemporary philosophers writing on self-knowledge tend to focus even more narrowly on what is called "privileged knowledge" of our own mental states: knowledge we seem to have straightaway, without needing to observe our own behavior or draw on other sources of extraneous information (self-observation, brain scans, knowledgeable friends, general knowledge acquired from psychology courses, etc.). It seems clear that not all of our mental states are known to us in this immediate way. For one thing, there are "subpersonal" cognitive states and processes of which we normally do not have any awareness. For another, there seem to be aspects of our "personal-level" mental state of which we do not always have privileged knowledge: I may, seemingly, be anxious or angry without realizing it, may hold certain kinds of biased attitudes without recognizing that I do, may be oblivious to my own arrogance or obnoxiousness, etc. Nevertheless, there seems to be a range of mental states that we can, at least normally, know ourselves to be in straightaway, without having any specifiable grounds for this knowledge. Most of the non-dispositional mental state types recognized by commonsense psychology appear to fall within this range: belief, desire, intention, hope, fear, as well as experiential states such as seeing, hearing, touching, tasting, and feeling sensory pleasure or pain.

Contemporary discussions of self-knowledge tend to focus on this privileged knowledge of our own minds, and I will largely follow suit (though I will also discuss bodily awareness in Chapter 6 and will make some remarks about richer and less-easily-accessible forms of self-knowledge in Chapters 9 and 10). This focus needs justification, however: not merely because the extent and the interest of this kind of self-knowledge have been challenged by critics, but also simply for the sake of sharpening our sense of what falls in the relevant range and what needs explanation about it. Indeed, I believe that skeptical challenges to the extent and the interest of our privileged self-knowledge arise largely in response to unsound framings of the topic. This first chapter will therefore concentrate on the question of framing: What makes our knowledge of our own mental states, not just of personal interest to private individuals, but of theoretical interest to philosophers? What about this topic calls for understanding? What, in particular, are the *problems* that an account of privileged self-knowledge must resolve?

My aim in the first part of this book will be to motivate an approach to the topic that makes the "Problem of Transparency" central, and to argue that an

---

[1] Except where finer distinctions matter, I will use "mental states" as a generic term for the truthmakers of all kinds of psychological claims about persons. So I will not stress the distinctions between genuine states and other kinds of modifications such as events, processes, actions, passions, etc.—though of course I admit that such distinctions are real and important for many purposes. I will be concerned with mental phenomena of all these categories, however, insofar they are possible objects of self-knowledge. Lacking a better general term, I will follow the slovenly but widespread practice of calling all such modifications "states."

adequate response to this problem must move beyond the epistemological orientation characteristic of much contemporary work on self-knowledge, and toward a more metaphysical conception of the topic. Before taking up these tasks, however, it will be helpful to survey some other common ways of framing the problem of self-knowledge.

1.2. Standard Formulations

There are various standard ways of making our ability to know our own minds seem puzzling. One approach presents the difficulty as one of justification: How I can justifiably make judgments about my present mental state without looking for behavioral evidence, when I can make them about the mental states of others only on the basis of such evidence? Another approach invites us to puzzle about the deference accorded to certain sorts of assertions: Why are my claims about my own present mental states treated as having some sort of special authority that other people's claims about those states are not taken to possess? Yet another focuses on the apparent inapplicability of certain kinds of challenges to my claims about my present mental states: Why is it, for instance, that if I say, "I have a headache," it seems out of place to ask "How do you know?" when this question applies straightforwardly to many other kinds of knowledge claims? Corresponding to these different ways of framing the question are different terms for the topic: philosophers who assume that the issue concerns a special way of knowing facts often use the term "privileged access" to designate the theme of their inquiries, whereas philosophers who wish to suspend judgment about this cognitivist conception of the topic often use the term "first-person authority," which places the focus on the deference accorded to a person's claims about her own mental states, while not taking for granted that this reflects a special way of knowing independently existing facts.

Despite these differences, there is a common thread running through many contemporary formulations of the problem of self-knowledge, namely the suggestion that it arises when we draw a *comparison* between our (purported) knowledge of our own minds and our knowledge of other topics (especially of the mental states of other people, but also of other non-psychological facts). Consider these representative formulations:

> People can be variously deluded about themselves: self-deceived about their motives, for instance, or overly sanguine, or pessimistic, about their strengths of character and frailties. But it is none the less a truism that for the most part we know ourselves best—better than we know others and better than they know us.... [T]he type of case that sets our problem is that which gives rise to

the phenomenon of *avowal*—the phenomenon of authoritative, non-inferential self-ascription. (Wright 1998: 13–14)

When compared to other non-a priori ascriptions, . . . avowals [of present mental states] are much more certain, much less subject to ordinary mistakes, significantly less open to a range of common doubts, and highly resistant to straightforward correction. (Bar On 2004: 10)

Roughly: beliefs about one's mental states acquired through the usual route are more likely to amount to knowledge than beliefs about others' mental states (and, more generally, beliefs about one's environment). (Byrne 2005: 80)

[Y]ou are typically in a better position to identify your own mental states than others are. . . . To elucidate the sense in which we are authoritative about our own mental states and to explain the grounds for this authority are the principal goals of most theories of self-knowledge. (Gertler 2011b: 2–3)

In all these formulations, we are invited to consider self-knowledge from a comparative perspective. There is said to be an "asymmetry" between our knowledge of our own minds and our knowledge of the minds of other people, or we are said to be "in a better position" to know our minds than others are to know them (which is supposed to give us a special "authority" in speaking about them), or our claims about our own mental states are said to be "more secure" and "less subject to challenge," or "more likely to be knowledge," than our claims about the mental states of others. It is these contrasts with other forms of contingent knowledge that are supposed to call for explanation.

One effect of this way of framing the issue is to reinforce an epistemological perspective on it, for even as we distinguish self-knowledge from other kinds of knowledge, we nevertheless emphasize knowledge as the category in which we draw these distinctions, and so our general notions about how to understand knowledge tend to shape our inquiries into this particular topic. I have already expressed reservations about this epistemic approach to self-knowledge in the Introduction, and I will return to it below. For the moment, however, I want to press a plainer question: Is what is philosophically interesting about self-knowledge really its contrast with other forms of knowledge? If something about our knowledge of our own minds needs understanding, shouldn't it be possible to formulate the difficulty without appeal to comparisons?

After all, what do I really know about the relative "security" of claims to self-knowledge, or their tendency to receive "deference," or whatever the point of comparison may be? I cannot speak for others, but for my part, I do not have firm pre-theoretical intuitions about these matters. I certainly presume myself normally to know my own mind in various respects, but am I really sure that I know it *better* than others do? I have no firm view about this, or about when or how readily I might defer to others who reject my own sincere claims about my mental states. I do not really know how "secure" I take these claims to be, or how this compares with my sense of the security of, say, my perceptual judgments about objects in plain view. My objection is not exactly that such comparative claims are false: they certainly seem to be in the neighborhood of something significant, and if I am forced to choose between affirming and denying them, I will be inclined to affirm. But I will do so with the sense that I am affirming propositions whose grounds I do not fully understand, and that my inclination to assent to them must be a downstream consequence of my awareness of some more basic feature of self-knowledge, a feature I ought to be able to characterize in its own right.

Comparative formulations of the distinctiveness of self-knowledge invite us to step back from the perspective each of us has as someone who knows his or her own mind and to adopt the perspective of an epistemologist surveying the several forms of human knowledge. But shouldn't it be possible to see what is interesting about self-knowledge without looking to the left and right in this way? Shouldn't this be possible without departing from the perspective of a self-knower reflecting on her own specific knowledge? Consider how you would respond to such questions as these:

What are you thinking about?
How are you feeling?
Is the pain in your leg any better?
Who do you believe will win the next election?
Do you desire worldly acclaim?
What are your plans for tomorrow?

There is indeed something striking about our ability to answer such questions, but I think it is not primarily that our answers seem to be especially secure or protected from doubt, or that we take ourselves to be better able to answer such questions than other people are to answer corresponding questions about us. These things may be true, but they do not get to the intuitive root of the matter. The root, it seems to me, is that there seems normally to be no need whatsoever for me to *find out* the answers to such questions: the relevant mental states seem to be somehow present to me, just as such, in a way that enables me to answer questions about them simply by articulating things of which I am already aware. Thus it seems that, normally, all that is required for me to know that I am thinking of a certain old friend is that I in fact am thinking of that friend; all that is required for me to know that the pain in my leg is not as bad as it was is for my leg not to feel as bad as it did; all that is required for me to know my conflicted attitude toward public acclaim is for me to have the relevant ambivalent feelings about acclaim; etc. When I cannot give a determinate answer to such questions, this is normally taken to indicate, not that there might be some first-order mental state of which I lack knowledge, but that my first-order state is itself indeterminate. Perhaps I don't know what I was thinking because I was not really thinking of anything in particular. Perhaps I don't know whether I want worldly acclaim because I don't yet have a settled attitude toward acclaim: I need to make up my mind. But what I generally do not need to do, it seems, is *discover* whether I am in such first-order states: when such states obtain, there is normally no question of my needing evidence that they exist.

Philosophers sometimes express this point by saying that our normal knowledge of our own present mental states is (or at least seems) "immediate," in the sense that it does not rest on grounds distinct from the facts known. And this seems right, as far as it goes: whereas for most kinds of contingent knowledge that we possess, there is some answer to the question *how* we know the relevant facts (e.g., by perceiving them, by inferring them from specifiable indications, by being informed of them by other knowers, etc.), in the case of our own present mental states, there seems normally to be no specifiable "how" whatsoever. But this comparative characterization of the distinctiveness of such knowledge is merely negative, and does not capture what it is like, from the subject's own perspective, to be aware of such states. It comes nearer to the heart of the matter, I think, to say that I seem to know the relevant states "from the inside" or "from the first-person perspective"—i.e., in some special way that is made available simply by my being the subject who is in the relevant states. It is not merely that I am in these states on the one hand, and know that I am in them on the other, as I might be digesting and also know (perhaps immediately) that I am digesting. Being in such states seems *itself* (normally) to involve some kind of modification of my awareness. They seem to be states of which I cannot normally be oblivious, since I have a special perspective on them "from the inside."

Versions of this point apply, I believe, not only to occurrent states and activities, such as pain and conscious thinking, but also to standing attitudinal states, such as belief and intention. There are obviously fundamental differences between occurrently conscious mental states and events (which occupy determinate periods of time, can be continuous or discontinuous, and tend to capture our attention as they occur) and standing attitudinal states (which need not have sharply defined temporal boundaries and can obtain even when we are not thinking about them, or indeed when we are asleep). Nevertheless, the idea that we have a special awareness "from the inside" of our own mental states applies, *mutatis mutandis*, to states in both of these categories. It certainly holds true for occurrent states like pain, felt emotion, or conscious thought. But our standing attitudes also seem, in their own way, to modify our overall state of awareness: they modify how things non-occurrently seem to us to be—e.g., what seems to us to be true, attractive, inviting, or terrifying—whereas nothing like this could be said of states like having a low iron level or having tousled hair. So while we must certainly distinguish between how things are occurrently experienced as being and how they non-occurrently seem to be, there is a broad sense in which both sorts of seemings are modifications of our point of view on the world. In this sense, both types of states are ones of which we are aware "from the inside," and this is borne out by the fact that we appear to be capable of privileged self-knowledge with respect to both types of states.

Admittedly, these ways of expressing the point are only metaphorical: our task will be to state clearly what phrases like "awareness from the inside" are meant to mark. Since our present purpose is simply to orient our attention in the right direction, however, a metaphorical evocation will suffice for now. What is striking about our normal knowledge of our own minds, we may say, is that our being in the relevant states normally seems to involve our having a "first-person perspective" on them, an awareness of them "from the inside." This is not to deny that we can sometimes be in such states and yet fail to be aware of them, or think ourselves to be in them when we are not—the qualification "normally" is crucial—but these kinds of states seem to be ones for which the default presumption is that, when they obtain, the subject has some kind of first-personal awareness of them, whereas there is no presumption of her having awareness of her having (e.g.) a low iron level or tousled hair.

The idea that we have such a first-person perspective on our own mental states is intuitively attractive, but theoretically perplexing: it is not easy to see what it could mean for there to be states that we are aware of "from the inside," simply by being in them. For how could a mental state make me aware of *itself*? Our mental states seem, in general, to involve (purported) awareness of things *other* than themselves: my belief that *p* presents it as the case *that p*; my wish for worldly acclaim presents *worldly acclaim* as attractive; my intention to go jogging presents it as settled *that I will go jogging*; and even my feeling of pain in my leg presents *my leg* (not my mind) as in an excruciating condition. But if mental states in general make me aware of their objects, mustn't I be made aware of my own mental states by second-order states of awareness which present these first-order states as their objects in turn? Mustn't there be some second-order state of awareness that makes me aware, not of the purported fact that *p*, but of *my belief* that this is a fact; not of the attractiveness of worldly acclaim, but of *my desire* for it; not of the purported fact that I will go jogging, but of *my intention* to do this; not of my painful leg, but of *my feeling* this pain? Indeed, if the fact that I am in a mental state M is a substantive fact, whose holding differs from my merely thinking it to hold, mustn't my knowing myself to be in M consist in my being in M and also, as a distinct matter, thinking myself to be in M (on the right sort of basis, presumably)?

To respond to these questions, we will first need to sharpen our formulation of the intuition that gives rise to them. In the next section, I want to consider three classic observations about the self-ascription of mental states that we might invoke to clarify our claim about the tight connection between our being in such states and our being aware of them from the first-person perspective. Each of these observations brings out, from a different angle, what is striking about this connection, and each does so without recourse to comparisons with other forms of knowledge. Any of the three could, I think, provide the starting point for a philosophical investigation of self-knowledge. Nevertheless, I will prefer one of these starting points, and I want to say something about my reasons for this preference.

1.3. Three Observations about Self-Knowledge

Not all ways of framing a problem about knowing one's own mind rely on comparisons with other forms of knowledge. There are a number of well-known observations that highlight, in a direct and noncomparative way, the striking connection between being in certain kinds of mental states and knowing oneself to be in those states.

One such observation, originally due to G. E. Moore, is that there seems to be something paradoxical about making an assertion of the form:

(MP) p, but I don't believe that p

even though claims of this form (commonly known as "Moore's Paradox") are not contradictory and are in fact liable to be true, in the case of any given person, for a significant number of values of p.[2] This observation gives rise to a puzzle: What *is* the source of the tension in such assertions? For surely it can and sometimes is true of me that I do not believe p although it is the case that p, and it would in general be perfectly coherent for another person to say of me:

p, but he doesn't believe that p.

So why should it be problematic for me to assert the first-person counterpart of this proposition?

Many commentators have hoped that resolving this puzzle might shed light on how we know our own beliefs, and I am inclined to agree: the tension involved

---

[2] Cf. Moore 2013. Another version of the paradox would be generated by the statement: "I believe that p, but not-p."

in asserting (MP) seems, on its face, to rest on some sort of relationship between believing the first-order proposition that *p* and being in a position to recognize the truth of the self-ascriptive proposition *I believe that p*, and it seems plausible that investigating this relationship might yield insights into the basis of our privileged knowledge of our own beliefs. Nevertheless, I think reflecting on Moore's Paradox is not a promising way to begin a general inquiry into privileged self-knowledge, for at least two reasons.

First, although the apparent tension in asserting (MP) *might* reflect some relationship between believing *p* and recognizing the truth of *I believe that p*, there are other cross-cutting factors that confound the issue. In particular, since Moore's observation focuses on a problematic form of *assertion*, it invites explanations that appeal to the rational pragmatics of assertion, rather than to facts about the relationship between belief and knowledge of belief. A person who asserts (MP) *represents* herself as holding a weird conjunction of views, and it might be irrational to represent oneself in this way, given natural assumptions about the point of assertion, even if there were no special link between believing that *p* and being in a position to know that one believes that *p*. To be sure, it might be argued that such assertion-focused explanations do not explain what is paradoxical about simply believing or thinking (MP) without asserting it. But even if it were shown that simply accepting (MP) is irrational, this would not yet throw light on how we know our own beliefs: it would simply show that we should not accept this sort of conjunctive proposition, whatever our actual beliefs may be. If there is a connection between this issue and our capacity for privileged knowledge of our own beliefs, it does not seem straightforward, and I take this to be a reason to prefer a less vexed starting-point if one is available.

Moreover—and this is the second reason to think of Moore's Paradox as an unpromising starting-point—it is hard to see how this puzzle bears on our knowledge of other kinds of mental states besides belief. Some authors have argued that we can formulate counterparts of (MP) for other mental state types: "Please give me X, but I don't want X"; "How lovely it will be if you come!—but I don't hope you'll come"; "Ow!—but I'm not in pain"; etc.[3] But although there seems to be something in this, these counterparts feel strained in a way that (MP) does not: it is less obvious what must be paired with the psychological self-ascription to generate a paradox, and less obvious that whatever paradox is achieved is strictly analogous to the one that arises for (MP), since in these latter cases there are not two *propositions* that might both be true but that seem paradoxical to assert jointly. Thus, for this reason too, it seems desirable to find some more straightforward way of focusing our intuition that there is a general connection between

---

[3] Cf. Bar-On 2004: Ch. 6; Shoemaker 1996: 34ff.

being in various kinds of mental states and having a first-person perspective on those states.

We find a more general and less vexed formulation of this intuition, I think, in Sydney Shoemaker's well-known observation that what he calls "self-blindness" seems impossible.[4] Shoemaker defines a *self-blind* person as one who has normal rationality and possesses concepts of the various familiar kinds of mental states (belief, desire, intention, perception, pain, etc.), but who is able to know that she is in such states only "in a third-person way"—i.e., on the basis of the kinds of observable evidence from speech and other behavior on which another person would be able to know of her mental states. Shoemaker offers an intricate argument in support of his claim that a rational and conceptually competent person could not be self-blind, and this argument has been widely criticized. But it seems to me that Shoemaker's observation stands by itself, independent of any supporting argument, and constitutes a *prima facie* constraint on our theorizing about self-knowledge.[5] If our knowledge of our own mental states were based on some kind of inner sense or other specialized cognitive mechanism, we would expect to find cases in which the relevant mechanism breaks down while normal rationality and conceptual competence are preserved, as a blind person may have normal rationality and conceptual competence and yet be unable to classify objects on the basis of vision. The fact that we find no actual cases of self-blindness, and indeed seem unable to conceive of such a condition, strongly suggests that, in the context of normal rationality and conceptual competence, there is some kind of necessary connection between being in the relevant kinds of mental states and being in a position to know oneself to be in these states.[6] This raises the question of what it is about being in a mental state, or being rational, or being competent with psychological concepts (or some combination of these) that makes self-knowledge available in this special way. We might take it as our task to answer this question.

This seems to me a step in the right direction, but still not sufficiently focused to guide our inquiry. Shoemaker's observation invites explanation, but unlike Moore's Paradox, it does not take the form of a *prima facie* puzzle in need of resolution, and as a result it does not point us in any very specific direction. Is the ground of the impossibility of self-blindness to be sought in the general nature of rationality? In the nature of competence with psychological concepts? Or

---

[4] Shoemaker 1988, 1994.
[5] Here I agree with Byrne 2018: 158.
[6] Note that to deny that self-blindness is possible is not to deny that people may *sometimes* be unable to know their own present mental states except in a third-person way. A self-blind person would be someone who was rational and competent with psychological concepts but had no *capacity* for non-observational self-knowledge. This is a more radical deprivation than the one that affects a person who has this capacity, but cannot, for whatever reason, exercise it with respect to certain particular mental states.

simply in the nature of the first-order mental states that we know? Lacking any determinate difficulty to resolve, we may contemplate all sorts of explanations for this fact.[7] Moreover, Shoemaker's observation is not framed from the perspective of the self-knowing subject herself, and this leaves us without any determinate sense of what it is like *for her* to have such knowledge. It certainly seems true and important that, whereas other human cognitive capacities are open to local forms of impairment that do not impair our general rationality or conceptual competence, our capacity for self-knowledge is not cognitively isolable in this way. But this negative observation still leaves the self-knowing subject as a kind of black box: it does not clarify how, from her own point of view, her self-knowledge and her first-order awareness are related. This opens the door to unconstrained theorizing, whereas it would be desirable if possible to begin from some positive thought about what *is* involved in our knowing our own minds.

For these reasons, I prefer a third line of approach to the topic of privileged self-knowledge, one that focuses on the phenomenon that has come to be known as the "transparency" of mental state self-ascriptions. This phenomenon is standardly introduced by quoting a remark from Gareth Evans, who observed that we are normally in a position to ascribe beliefs to ourselves, not by seeking evidence concerning our own psychological states, but by looking to the realm of non-psychological facts:

> In making a self-ascription of belief, one's eyes are, so to speak, or occasionally literally, directed outward—upon the world. If someone asks me "Do you think there is going to be a third world war?", I must attend, in answering him, to precisely the same outward phenomena as I would attend to if I were answering the question "Will there be a third world war?" I get myself in a position to answer the question whether I believe that *p* by putting into operation whatever procedure I have for answering the question whether *p*. (Evans 1982: 225)

Although Evans himself does not use the term, the phenomenon he points out here has come to be known as the "transparency" of first-person belief ascriptions, since Evans's procedure advises us to treat the question "Do I believe that *p*?" as simply tantamount, or "transparent," to the question "Is it the case that *p*?"

Evans clearly regards this observation as demystifying our capacity for privileged knowledge of our own beliefs. It can seem mysterious how we are able to say what we believe without observing ourselves, even though we must observe another person to determine what she believes; but, Evans suggests, this should not seem strange once we recognize that a person can answer the question

---

[7] Cf. Fricker 1998.

whether she believes *p* by "putting into operation whatever procedure [she has] for answering the question whether *p*." Many subsequent writers, however, have thought of Evans's observations not primarily as providing the solution to a puzzle, but as presenting a puzzle in their own right. After all, where *p* is a proposition about the non-mental world, it is generally possible for it to be the case that *p* although I do not believe that *p*. Indeed, this is surely my actual situation for many values of *p*: I am hardly omniscient (or omnicredent, for that matter). So what *justifies* me in answering such questions about my own psychology by looking to seemingly independent facts about the world?[8]

It will not suffice, as an answer to this question, simply to point out that the contents of our beliefs are systematically related to the contents we would express in answering corresponding world-directed questions. This is certainly true, and it is part of what gives Evans's procedure its initial appeal, but it does not address the heart of the puzzle. If I reach the conclusion that there will be a third world war, I become cognizant of an apparent fact that is (in fact) the topic of a certain belief I hold. But the procedures Evans outlines instruct me to lay claim to a further item of knowledge: knowledge *that I believe* that there will be a third world war.[9] It is this psychological knowledge whose warrant is in question, and the *Problem of Transparency* is that nothing in my apparent basis seems to supply a ground for it. Nevertheless, it is widely agreed that Evans put his finger on something important about the basis for such knowledge, whose significance we need to explain.

Of the three observations we have considered, this Evansian one seems to me the most promising as a basis for our investigation: not because it highlights a fundamentally different point from the one that underlies the other phenomena we have surveyed, but because it focuses our attention on this point in the most productive way. In the first place, it focuses us on the perspective of the self-knowing subject herself: the observation is that she must take answering the question whether *p* to be a way of determining her own belief on this question. In this way, Evans's observation does not merely set an abstract, theoretical problem about the explanation of privileged self-knowledge, but confronts us with a question about the self-knowing subject's intelligibility to herself: How can *she* presume this to be a way of gaining knowledge of her own beliefs? Moreover, by raising a specific problem about this intelligibility, the Problem of Transparency sharpens our sense of what we need to understand. What Evans's observation brings out is that our capacity to know our own beliefs is linked to our capacity to consider questions about the states of affairs that are the topics of our beliefs.

---

[8] This question is pressed by Gallois 1996, Moran 2001, and Byrne 2018, among others.
[9] The difference between knowing the content of one's attitudes and knowing that one holds the attitudes is forcefully emphasized by Dretske 2003, 2012.

What we must understand, therefore, is not merely some general "privilege" that a subject has in knowing her own beliefs, or some "authority" she has in speaking about them, but how her capacity to know her own mind in a privileged way is related to her capacity to think about the non-mental world. It will emerge that this reformulation holds the key to understanding both our capacity to know our own minds and the place of this knowledge in our lives. Or so, at least, I shall argue.

It might seem, however, that there is a difficulty about generalizing Evans's observation, as there was about generalizing Moore's Paradox. Is the phenomenon of transparency confined to the case of belief, or can it provide the basis for a broader inquiry into our privileged knowledge of our own mental states? I turn to this question in the next section.

1.4. Generalizing the Problem of Transparency

Can Evans's observation be generalized? A number of commentators have suggested that the point does not extend far beyond the case of belief,[10] or that it applies only to a certain restricted class of mental states (perhaps only to attitudes about which we can deliberate),[11] or that it can be generalized only given certain special and questionable assumptions (e.g., that we represent the world only in ways that it would be rational for us to represent it).[12] And it is true that, whereas it seems easy to formulate the world-directed question to which the psychological question "Do I believe that p?" is transparent, it seems considerably less obvious what a corresponding world-directed question would be for many other kinds of mental states. Consider:

What am I perceiving?
What am I imagining?
What sensations am I feeling?
What am I thinking about?

All of these kinds of mental states are ones of which we seem normally to have some kind of privileged awareness. They are all states on which we may be said normally to have a "first-person perspective"—whatever exactly this means. Yet it is hard to see what the non-mental topic could be to which these questions might be treated as transparent. To what extent, then, does Evans's observation

---

[10] Finkelstein 2003: Postscript; Bar-On 2004: Ch. 4.
[11] Cf. Boyle 2009.
[12] Cf. Finkelstein 2012, Cassam 2014. For discussion, see Boyle 2015.

about belief suggest a more general approach to investigating privileged knowledge of our own minds?

Well, for starters, Evans himself suggests that an analogous point can be made about the self-ascription of perceptual states:

> [A] subject can gain knowledge of his [perceptual] states in a very simple way.... He goes through exactly the same procedure as he would go through if he were trying to make a judgment about how it is at this place now, but excluding any knowledge he has *of an extraneous kind*.... The result will necessarily be closely correlated with the content of the [perceptual] state which he is in at that time. (Evans 1982: 227–228)

By knowledge "of an extraneous kind," Evans means knowledge that is not based on present perception, but he thinks we can characterize this extraneous knowledge without presupposing knowledge of what one perceives. Extraneous knowledge would be (roughly) knowledge of how things are "at this place now" for which I possess some non-tautologous justification: that someone told me things here are thus-and-so, that I remember having arranged things so, that general laws imply that things must be so, etc. By contrast, perceptually based knowledge of how things are with X will be epistemically primitive (if we exclude appeal to the fact that I am presently perceiving X, as required by our project of explaining the basis of this knowledge). Evans's idea is that, whether my perception is veridical or not, what I can say in this primitive way about how things are at this place now will in fact be how things perceptually appear to me. In this way, I can answer the psychological question how things *perceptually appear to me* by treating this question as transparent to the world-directed question of how things are here now, provided that I answer the latter question while excluding extraneous information.

This proposal is obviously just a first stab at characterizing the topic to which questions about how things perceptually appear to us are transparent. Evans does not attempt to work out his proposal in detail, and even its broad outlines are contestable. Certainly more work would need to be done to explain how this proposed way of knowing how things *perceptually* appear to me can be differentiated into ways of knowing how things *visually* appear to me, how they *tactually* appear to me, etc. Nevertheless, our very ability to contest the details of Evans's proposal suggests that we are implicitly familiar with the topic he is attempting to characterize. The topic, we might say, is *how the world presents itself to a perceiver*. For it is surely clear that what perception primarily presents to us are aspects of the non-mental world. Perceiving X may in some way make me aware of the psychological fact that *I perceive X*, but what it primarily presents to me is the non-mental entity X in its various perceptible aspects: its color, its shape, its texture, etc. This is true even when my perception is not veridical: what it *purports* to present me with are not my own mental states, but non-mental things in their perceptible aspects.

Still, perception presents non-mental things to us in distinctive ways: there are only certain kinds of properties of an object that we can directly discover on the basis of perception (we can, e.g., discover its color but not its age), and our discovery of these properties takes certain specific forms (think, e.g., of the role of coming closer in the visual discrimination of properties, or of the kinds of fine-grained comparisons of properties falling on a continuum that our senses enable us to make). We might think of Evans's proposal as just a preliminary sketch of how we might implement a general program for explaining our capacity to know how things perceptually appear to us.[13] The program would be (1) to identify the characteristic ways in which the non-mental world (purportedly) presents itself to a perceiver, and then (2) to show that a perceiver can answer questions about how things perceptually appear to her by treating these questions as transparent to questions about the non-mental world, inasmuch as it is presented in these characteristic ways. This program could be—and in fact has been[14]—pursued farther than Evans pursued it, and disputes about the details of any particular account of the world-directed questions to which questions about our own perceptual states are transparent need not threaten the program as a whole.

Moreover, this program for explaining our knowledge of how things perceptually appear to us can be generalized to other kinds of representational states. Again, the project would be (1) to identify the characteristic ways in which non-mental objects are presented to a subject in states of the relevant kind and (2) to show that the subject could answer questions about her own representational states by treating them as transparent to questions about such objects, inasmuch as they are presented in the relevant ways. And I think we will find that we know at least how to make a start on doing this, if we put our minds to it. To give some rough examples: desire represents its object as attractive or appealing in some describable way; fear represents its object as terrifying; imagination represents its object as in a distinctive way present *in absentia*;[15] etc.

---

[13] Indeed, when his discussion is considered in its wider context, it seems to me clear that this is all that Evans intended: to sketch, in a couple of representative cases, a broad strategy for explaining privileged self-knowledge by relating it to an ability to make judgments about the non-mental world.

[14] See Byrne 2018: Ch. 6. I take Byrne's book as a whole to provide strong evidence of the viability of the transparency approach to self-knowledge. One may disagree with the details of his proposals, and indeed, as will emerge in the coming chapters, I have basic disagreements of principle with the way Byrne develops the transparency approach. Nevertheless, it seems to me that one cannot read his book without becoming convinced that there is a broad topic to investigate here, contrary to what many authors (including myself at an earlier moment: cf. Boyle 2009) have suggested.

[15] For elucidation of this obscure remark, see the excellent discussion in Sartre, *The Imaginary* (2004), Ch. 1.

The first task of a transparency account of self-knowledge will therefore be to characterize the specific ways in which different kinds of representational states and activities (desire, fear, imagination, thought, sensation, etc.) present their objects, where "objects" means what philosophers following Brentano have come to call "intentional objects": whatever they purport to present, whether this be a material object, a property, a state of affairs, or something of some other category. Of course, it is controversial whether all mental states of which we have privileged self-knowledge have intentional objects in this sense, and even if this were granted, it would be controversial whether there is some question about the relevant objects to which questions about the subject's own mental state could be treated as transparent. Characterizing the relevant world-directed questions would certainly be no simple task—not significantly simpler than, and closely related to, the task of giving a philosophical analysis of the relevant kinds of mental states. But the idea that such characterizations could in principle be given is at least no less plausible than the idea that, to each type of representational state, there corresponds some characteristic manner of representing aspects of the non-mental world. And this is surely an interesting idea, and not obviously a false one.

I should add that, when I speak of what our mental states represent as "the non-mental world," this is a convenient but inexact shorthand. It is obvious that our mental states can represent, not only the non-mental world, but also our own mental states and those of other people. Even in this case, however, there will be a distinction between the object *represented* (in this case, some mental state) and the *representing* of this object. What a given representational state represents is its intentional object, whatever this may be; it does not represent its own representing of this object, except perhaps in the strange and limiting case in which a representational state has itself for its intentional object. The general task of a transparency-based account of self-knowledge, as I conceive it, would be to explain how awareness of the *object* of a representational state makes possible awareness of our *representing* itself, and this task will remain even once states that represent mental states are taken into account. Having noted this, I will persist, for the sake of simplicity, in speaking of the objects of our mental states as in general "non-mental"; I will also sometimes speak, for brevity, of "the world" rather than of "the non-mental world." This again is merely a convenient shorthand: I certainly do not deny that the world broadly conceived includes our mental states. Rectifying these simplifications would not alter any of the main points I have to make.

In the chapters that follow, I will make proposals about how we might give a transparency-based account of our knowledge of various kinds of mental states, but I will not attempt to offer any general proof that this can be done for every kind of state of which we have privileged self-knowledge, nor will I be concerned to defend the specific proposals I make as the final words on their respective topics. What matters most to me is the broad plausibility and interest of the program sketched above. I hope that, taken in their totality, the coming chapters constitute a case for this program. To the extent that this case is convincing, it should commend to everyone the tasks of carrying out this program as far as it can be carried, and of getting the details right. To the extent that the case for the program is unconvincing, such tasks will of course be pointless.

In any event, no demonstration of the generality of the phenomenon of transparency, however broad, could by itself defuse the Problem of Transparency. This difficulty will arise, not just for our transparent knowledge of our own beliefs, but for any purportedly transparent knowledge of mental states of any kind. For our knowledge of our own mental states is said to be "transparent" inasmuch as we can knowledgeably answer questions about these states by attending in the right way, not to anything "inner" or psychological, but to the objects or states of affairs toward which our mental states are directed. But how can a consideration of non-mental things, whether they are present or absent, real or imaginary, be a way of gaining knowledge about our own mental states? Consider Evans's proposal about how I might determine how things perceptually appear to me: namely, by describing how things are in my immediate environment while setting aside "extraneous knowledge." Even if Evans is right that what I thus describe will in fact be how things perceptually appear to me, what sort of reason do I have for supposing this to be so? Suppose I determine that there is a gray cat here lying on a mat. This surely might be so—a gray cat might be here on a mat—even if I were *not* perceiving this situation. Hence the fact that this is so seems by itself to be no evidence whatsoever *that I perceive* it to be so. By contrast, the fact that I judge there to be a cat on the mat here on the basis of perceptual observation would of course be conclusive evidence that I perceive a cat on a mat (or at least that I seem to perceive one). But to know this, I would need already to know how things perceptually appear to me, and so our explanation of my knowledge of my own perceptual appearances as grounded in a consideration of the non-mental world would be undercut.

It is easy to generate a difficulty of this sort about any transparency-based account of how we know our own mental states. The problem arises from the general structure of the transparency approach, not from the details of any particular proposal. But we should not regret this difficulty: it will be the engine that drives our inquiry, and resolving it will turn out to shed great light on the nature of our mental states and the kind of relation in which we stand to them as their subjects.

1.5. Conclusion and Prospect

My aim in this first part of the book will be to argue for a solution to the Problem of Transparency that is inspired by Sartre's idea that all consciousness involves a form of "nonpositional" consciousness of our own consciousness. Sartre claimed, in effect, that our capacity to know our own minds is linked to our capacity to know the world because our awareness of the world constitutively involves a kind of implicit self-awareness, which we can transform, on reflection, into an explicit knowledge of our own minds. I want to suggest that this idea is the key to resolving the Problem of Transparency, and that appreciating its relevance to this problem is the key to seeing the truth in Sartre's somewhat darkly expressed point.

I came to see the importance of Sartre's notion of nonpositional self-consciousness while trying to clarify a distinction I had been led to draw, in earlier work (Boyle 2011b), between "tacit" knowledge of one's own mental states and explicit, reflective knowledge of those states. In order to bring out the motivation for Sartre's position, it will help to explain what led me to draw this distinction, and why I now think it must be clarified along Sartrean lines. So I will begin by describing how I arrived at my earlier position, and will situate it relative to three other prominent approaches to the Problem of Transparency. Seeing the strengths and weaknesses of these approaches will help us to see the point in Sartre's idea.

2
Contemporary Approaches

2.1. Introduction

To bring out the attractions of the Sartrean approach to the Problem of Transparency, it will be useful first to consider some other approaches to the problem, not just for the sake of criticizing them, but to learn from their insights, and thereby to identify some constraints on a satisfactory solution.

In this spirit, the present chapter will examine three prominent approaches to the Problem of Transparency. This is hardly a comprehensive survey of responses to the problem, but the three approaches I will discuss are among the most influential, and each is, in its own way, quite natural and attractive.[1] My aim will be to highlight what makes them attractive, while also bringing out certain basic difficulties they face—difficulties which, I shall argue, point the way toward the Sartrean approach.

An important theme that will emerge from our discussion, and that will be with us throughout the rest of the book, is that transparently known mental states are known in a distinctively immanent or "non-spectatorial" manner. This idea is crucial to Richard Moran's influential work on transparency, but we shall see that it is separable from other claims Moran makes about the basis of transparent self-knowledge. Once it has been distinguished from these other claims, I will argue, this idea from Moran can be thought of as setting a general condition of adequacy of accounts of transparency, one that provides grounds for doubt about some other influential approaches to the Problem of Transparency. Our criticisms of these approaches will, in turn, motivate the Sartrean idea that our very representation of the non-mental world must draw on a kind of "nonpositional" awareness of our own representing.

---

[1] Approaches I will not discuss include those of Fernandez 2013, Gallois 1996, O'Brien 2007. I hope my responses to the views I do discuss give some indication of how the Sartrean position I defend might respond to these other approaches.

2.2. Transparency versus Alienation: Moran

The prominence of the term "transparency" as a label for the relation between questions about one's own mind and questions about the world is primarily due to Richard Moran's work, and his account of why the question whether I believe that *p* is (normally) transparent to the question whether *p* (henceforth, "doxastic transparency") will provide us with a useful starting point, both because it is grounded in certain compelling observations about the character of transparent self-knowledge, and also because the other approaches we will consider are framed in significant part as responses to Moran's position.

Moran famously holds that doxastic transparency is explained by the fact that we normally answer the question whether *p* by exercising our capacity to determine whether *to* believe that *p*. To be sure, one cannot always determine whether one believes *p* by answering the question whether *p*: there are occasions on which we can only discover our actual beliefs by observing ourselves, much as a spectator would. These are, however, pathological situations in which we are "alienated" from our own beliefs, in the sense that we cannot regard these beliefs as governed by our conscious assessment of grounds for taking the relevant propositions to be true. When we are not thus alienated, Moran suggests, we are in a position to know whether we believe *p* by considering whether *p* precisely because such consideration settles (i.e., makes it the case) that we believe (or do not believe) *p*. It is this fact that resolves the puzzle of doxastic transparency:

> What right have I to think that my reflection on the reasons in favor of *p* (which is one subject-matter) has anything to do with the question of what my actual *belief* about *p* is (which is quite a different subject-matter)? Without a reply to this challenge, I don't have any right to answer the question that asks what my belief [about, e.g., whether it will rain] is by reflection on the reasons in favor of an answer concerning the state of the weather. And then my thought at this point is: I *would* have a right to assume that my reflection on the reasons in favor of rain provided me with an answer to the question of what my belief about the rain is, if I could assume that *what* my belief here is was something determined by the conclusion of my reflection on those reasons. (Moran 2003: 405)

Moran summarizes his proposal by saying that I am in a position to have transparent knowledge of my own beliefs just insofar as I am entitled to address the question whether I believe that *p*, not as a "theoretical" or "speculative" question about what is (perhaps unbeknownst to me) the case with me, but as a "deliberative" question about whether *to* believe *p* (cf. Moran 2001: 58, 63). In a slogan, our capacity to have transparent knowledge of our own beliefs rests on our capacity to "make up our minds."

It is hard to read Moran's work on doxastic transparency without feeling that he has put his finger on something crucial, but on closer scrutiny, it is not easy to say just what the insight is and how broadly it applies. For one thing, as a number of critics have pointed out, the phenomenon of transparency is not confined to conditions that can be brought about through deliberation.[2] As we noted earlier, questions about how things perceptually appear also seem to exhibit a kind of transparency to world-directed questions, as for that matter do questions about appetitive desire (e.g., whether I'm hungry can manifest itself in whether a cheeseburger looks delectable). These are not conditions we determine to exist on the basis of reasons: they are conditions to which the question "What is your reason for X-ing?" seems not to apply. Thus it is not easy to see, in cases like these, what it might mean for us to take a "deliberative stance" toward the relevant psychological questions, or how this idea might contribute to explaining our entitlement to treat such questions as transparent to questions about the non-mental world.

Furthermore, even in cases where we do make up our minds by deliberating about some factual question, it is not entirely clear how the idea that we take a deliberative stance toward our own beliefs explains our knowledge of what we believe.[3] Consider a case in which I deliberate about whether to believe that p and conclude: "Yes, p is to be believed." This can surely be the case although I don't actually believe p. Indeed, as an imperfect being, this is presumably often my situation: there is some belief that is the right one to hold on a factual question—some proposition that is "to be believed"—and yet I don't believe it. So it remains unclear why, in the kind of case under consideration, I am entitled to treat my answer to the question whether *to* believe that p as implying an answer to the question whether I *do* believe that p. We may grant for the sake of argument that, in concluding that p is to be believed, I make it the case that I do in fact believe that p. Still, what puts me in a position to *know* that I believe this, given that the topic about which I draw a conclusion—whether to believe that p—is in principle independent of the topic of my own belief? A problem emerges here that is analogous to the original problem of transparency: just as, in the original problem, it was unclear how a subject can rightly treat the question of whether she believes a given proposition as transparent to the seemingly independent question of whether p, so here it is unclear how the subject can treat this question as transparent to the seemingly independent question of whether p is to be believed.

For these reasons, Moran's response to the Problem of Transparency seems not fully satisfactory as it stands.[4] Nevertheless, I believe it has at its foundation a compelling observation of which we should not lose sight. As we have seen,

---

[2] Cf. Byrne 2005: 85; Finkelstein 2003: Postscript; and Bar-On 2004: Ch. 4.
[3] Cf. O'Brien 2003.
[4] I should emphasize, however, that my aim here is not to deny the connection Moran proposes between doxastic transparency and the deliberative stance, but simply to highlight some problems

Moran contrasts the relation in which we stand to our own mental states when we can know them transparently with an alienated, "spectatorial" relation to those states. He puts this point—focusing, as usual, on the case of belief—by observing that we can have transparent self-knowledge only of our conscious beliefs, and

> to call something a conscious belief says something about the *character* of the belief in question. It is not simply to say that the person stands in some relation of awareness to this belief. . . . I see myself in this belief; my conscious belief forms the basis for my further train of thought about the thing in question. (Moran 1999: 188)

Moran goes on to argue that it is possible to know immediately and without observation that one holds a certain belief, and yet not *consciously* to hold the relevant belief. As an example, he asks us to consider an analysand who has so perfectly internalized the perspective of his psychoanalyst that he knows immediately what beliefs his analyst would attribute to him, and (rightly) ascribes those beliefs to himself, but does not consciously hold the beliefs in question.

I think there is an important point here, though Moran's example may be unnecessarily contentious. Whatever we think of the possibility of psychoanalytic knowledge of unconscious beliefs, we should admit that consciously believing *p* requires more than merely knowing, without observation or inference, that one believes *p*. To know that one believes (e.g.) that there will be a third world war requires only that one takes *one's own belief-state* to be of a certain kind. A person who *consciously believes* that there will be a third world war, by contrast, does not merely know herself to have this belief; she consciously inhabits the relevant viewpoint, in the sense that, when she thinks about the world-oriented question whether there will be a third world war, it seems to her that there will. Moran's insight is that transparent self-knowledge of a mental state is available just when the relevant mental state is conscious in this sense: the point of view one ascribes to oneself is the very one that one consciously inhabits, in such a way that the question of what one believes and the question of what is so fuse into one.

It seems to me that this point embodies an insight that is independent of Moran's more specific claims about the explanation of doxastic transparency. The insight is that transparent self-knowledge is not merely knowledge that can be had immediately and without self-observation; it is knowledge grounded in consciously inhabiting the relevant point of view, and as such contrasts with the knowledge of a spectator. A spectator might know that I believe *p*, but it is one thing for her to know this about me and another for *her* consciously to see the

---

that a satisfactory account of transparency should resolve. Moran offers his own responses to some of the difficulties I have raised in Moran 2012.

world from the perspective of *p*-believer. If unconscious belief is possible, then it is also possible for me to stand in this sort of spectatorial relation to one of my own beliefs: I can know myself to believe that *p*, and yet not consciously inhabit the perspective of a *p*-believer. But at any rate, for a person who *consciously* believes that *p*, being aware of her own belief and seeing the world from the perspective of a *p*-believer are just two aspects of the same condition. Such a person does not merely have a point of view on the world, on the one hand, and know of its existence, on the other. She consciously holds the relevant point of view, and can thus express both *belief that p* and *knowledge that she believes that p* in a single act, by saying "I believe that *p*." We can thus say that she knows her own belief from the perspective, not of a spectator, but of an inhabitant of the relevant point of view.

This point can be accepted even by philosophers who reject Moran's idea that the primary alternative to a "spectatorial stance" toward oneself is a "deliberative stance." It may be that Moran overestimates the closeness of the tie between being able to know one's mental states "transparently" and treating those states as open to deliberation. Perhaps this opposition characterizes only certain kinds of attitudes. Be that as it may, it remains true in general that our relation to mental states we can know transparently is not spectatorial. Perception can again serve as an example. People with normal perceptual awareness can, as Evans observed, have transparent knowledge of their own perceptual appearances. But consider a person with the kind of cerebral damage that produces "blindsight."[5] Blindsighted subjects do not consciously see what is presented in the "blind" region of their visual field, but when prompted, they are able to perform perception-dependent tasks (for instance, making guesses about the features of objects in the blind field) with a better-than-chance rate of success. We may thus say that a blindsighted subject stands in an alienated, spectatorial relation to her own seeing: she can say what she perceives only by drawing inferences from her own behavior (including her dispositions to make guesses about what is present in a certain region). But our normal relation to our visual appearances is not like this: it is not merely that we can know how things visually appear to us with an immediacy that is unavailable to blindsighted persons; we consciously experience *the world* as containing objects with specific features, whereas she does not. Our knowledge of how things perceptually appear to us is thus not spectatorial: we are aware of these states *by inhabiting their perspective*, inasmuch as we consciously perceive the world around us to be a certain way.

---

[5] For purposes of making my point, I rely on the simplified understanding of the blindsight commonly discussed by philosophers of perception. For an account of the phenomenon in its full complexity, see Weiskrantz 1986.

At the same time, our knowledge of how things perceptually appear to us is obviously not deliberative: if we could deliberate about whether *to* have specific perceptual appearances, perception would not be the kind of cognitive power that it is. Moran's insight—that the availability of transparent self-knowledge marks a distinctively non-spectatorial mode of awareness of one's own mental states—thus applies more broadly than his emphasis on opposition between spectator and deliberator might lead one to suppose. I believe this insight sets a condition of adequacy on accounts of transparent self-knowledge. I now want to argue that it is a condition some other influential accounts of transparency fail to meet.

2.3. Transparency as Inference from World to Mind: Byrne

We noted earlier that there is a crucial gap in Moran's account of our warrant for moving from the judgment that *p* to the judgment *I believe that p*: How does the former justify the latter? In seeking to fill this gap, there are two natural routes to explore. On the one hand, we might argue that our warrant derives somehow from what we consider: some (seeming) feature of the non-mental world. On the other hand, we might propose that it derives, not from what we consider, but from our consideration itself: some conscious mental state or process that occurs when we take up the relevant world-directed question. Each of these routes has in fact been explored, and I want to examine a prominent representative of each approach—not simply for the sake of surveying the literature, but because I think that each approach has significant attractions, but that each also misses something crucial.

The first approach I will consider seeks resolutely to defend the idea that, when one has transparent self-knowledge, the basis on which one ascribes a mental state to oneself is not any kind of awareness of one's own mind, but merely a purported awareness of a fact about the non-mental world. As we have noted, this idea is not easy to accept, for it is hard to see how such a step could be warranted. Nevertheless, if such an approach could be defended, it would provide an elegant solution to the Problem of Transparency, since it would explain our capacity for non-observational self-knowledge without appealing to any special faculty of introspection or preexisting form of self-awareness. It would thus clarify Evans's attractive idea that the relevant knowledge can be acquired simply by looking "outward," rather than "inward" toward our own mental states.

An approach of this sort has been forcefully defended by Alex Byrne (2005, 2011, 2018). Byrne's account rests on a simple idea: that we can acquire transparent self-knowledge by making an "inference from world to mind" (Byrne 2011: 203). In general, Byrne holds, our capacity for inference is a capacity to make rule-governed transitions between acceptance of some set of propositions and acceptance of some further proposition. The problem of transparency is that the relevant inferences—for instance, the *doxastic schema*

    BEL: p
    ————————————
    I believe that p

look on their face as though they cannot yield knowledge, since their premises neither entail nor evidentially support their conclusions. But, Byrne suggests, this sort of objection to an inference-schema can be overcome if we can show that (1) inferring in accordance with the relevant schema reliably produces true beliefs and (2) such inferences are "safe" in the technical sense that drawing this conclusion would not have produced false belief in any nearby possible world. If we could show this, and if we had no reason to suppose that BEL is *not* knowledge-conducive, we would, Byrne argues, be entitled to show deference to the view presupposed in our ordinary practice: that making such transitions is a way of coming to know what one believes.[6]

Byrne's project is thus first to identify inference-schemata corresponding to the kinds of mental states we can know transparently, and then to show that these schemata are "neutral" (i.e., that their premises do not presuppose knowledge of the relevant mental states), reliable, and safe. If this can be shown, he holds, the problem of transparency will be solved, for we will have explained why the relevant inferences are, in spite of appearances, normally knowledge-conducive. Moreover, we will in the process have accounted for the fact that we can speak with special authority about the relevant mental states, and we will have given an attractively economical account of this authority: one that does not appeal to any special introspective faculty, but only to general cognitive capacities required also for other kinds of cognition.

In the case of belief, the relevant inference-schema is plainly BEL, and it is easily shown that this schema is safe and reliable. A subject will be in a position to infer according to BEL only if she accepts the premise: p. But this amounts to saying that she will be in a position to apply the rule only if she believes that p, and this ensures that her conclusion will be sound, whether her premise is true or false. In other cases the relevant inference-schema is less obvious, and the argument to its reliability and safety is less direct; but suffice it to say that Byrne makes a forceful case for the claim that, when their application is appropriately restricted, inferences such as the following are neutral, reliable, and safe:

---

[6] Cf. Byrne 2005: 96–98; Byrne 2011: 206–207.

SEE:	$[\ldots x \ldots]_v$ & x is an F	INT:	I will ϕ
	I see an F[7]		I intend to ϕ[8]

By demonstrating that such analyses can be given in a wide variety of cases, Byrne (2018) seeks to show that the "inference from world to mind" approach applies wherever transparent self-knowledge is possible.

Although I believe there is a great deal to be learned from Byrne's analyses of particular relations of transparency, I think his general account of the basis of such transparency implies an unacceptably alienated, spectatorial picture of the subject's relation to her own mental states. To bring this out, I will raise two objections, which highlight different but related aspects of this problem.

First, it seems to me that Byrne's approach does not explain the rational intelligibility of these world-to-mind inferences from the subject's own standpoint. Our capacity for (personal-level) inference is a capacity to arrive at new beliefs in virtue of seeing one or more (seeming) facts as supplying some sort of *reason* to accept some further proposition as true. The conclusions we reach through inference are not just beliefs that appear unaccountably in our minds; they are convictions for which we take ourselves to have a reason, and this is what makes them sustainable in the face of the capacity for critical scrutiny that belongs to rational subjects as such. What makes Byrne's BEL-inference problematic, it seems to me, is not merely the concern that it would be unreliable or unsafe, but a concern about how a subject who draws such inferences could herself understand them to be reasonable. I cannot see how Byrne's account speaks to this problem.

Suppose for the sake of argument that a subject concludes that she believes p by inferring according to BEL. Let her now ask herself what her grounds are for accepting that she believes p. Citing the ostensible fact that p sheds no light: this has no tendency to show that she believes that p, as Byrne admits. What would support the subject's conclusion, of course, is the fact that she is prepared to treat p as a premise from which to draw inferences. But to represent *this* as her ground for accepting that she believes p would be, in effect, to presuppose that she already knows her own mind on the matter, and thus would undermine Byrne's account, which requires the premise of the BEL-inference to be neutral.

---

[7] Byrne 2012. "$[\ldots x \ldots]_v$" is supposed to be a "v-proposition": a proposition ascribing to x only properties characteristically available to vision (shape, orientation, depth, color, shading, movement, etc.).

[8] Byrne 2011. The INT-rule is supposed to be defeasible, and the subject must refrain from inferring according to it if he believes that he will ϕ on the basis of what he takes to be good evidence that he will ϕ. For a related proposal, see Setiya 2012.

So Byrne's approach appears to face a dilemma: either it represents the subject as drawing an inference that she should find rationally unintelligible, or else it requires her to have a kind of ground that would undermine the basic idea of the approach.[9]

Moreover—and this is my second objection—reflection on particular cases of transparency suggests that the cognitive transitions we make are not in fact transitions from *sheer* propositions about the world to propositions about the subject's own mental states. To see what I mean by saying that they are not "sheer" propositions about the world, consider the transition from

---

[9] Byrne himself is unmoved by this objection. He replies that people who draw inferences are not necessarily aware of the basis of their inferences, and that even if I am aware that I infer *I believe that p* from *p*, and aware that the fact that *p* does not support the proposition *I believe that p*, this does not necessarily give me a reason to give up my belief in the latter proposition. After all, although the premise of the BEL-schema does not rationally support its conclusion, BEL is (so Byrne has argued) a knowledge-conducive pattern of reasoning. Moreover, many writers on self-knowledge assume that our privileged knowledge of our own mental states is groundless, so, Byrne suggests, the fact that his account presents such knowledge as unsupported is not obviously an objection to it (cf. Byrne 2018: 122–124).

This reply depends on a conception of inference that is very different from mine, but let me grant it for the sake of argument. (For some indications of how my own conception differs, see Chapter 7.) My objection remains that Byrne's interpretation of the Transparency Method does not make the self-knower's basis for holding a belief about her own mental state intelligible to this person herself. It is true that many philosophers, in introducing the problem of privileged self-knowledge, suggest that these beliefs about our own present mental states are "groundless," but I take this to be not a satisfactory resting point, but an observation that raises a *prima facie* puzzle on which a philosophical account of self-knowledge should shed light. I do not deny that we may rationally hold various types of belief without specifiable support, but I think that, as philosophers, we should want, for each of these types of belief, an account of its subject-matter, on the one hand, and of our own cognitive capacities, on the other, that clarifies how a subject with such capacities could reasonably take herself to know things of that type without grounds.

What Byrne offers, it seems to me, is not an account of how the self-knowing subject could take herself to be reasonable, but rather an account why it would be reasonable for onlookers to approve of her thought process. On his interpretation, the BEL-schema gives the subject a method for reliably arriving at true beliefs about her own mental states, and if we grant for the sake of argument that a person could be disposed to make cognitive transitions according to this schema, then I suppose that such a subject could come to appreciate Byrne's case for the claim that her inferential disposition is reliable and safe, and could thereby come to have a kind of second-order approval of her disposition to draw the BEL inference. But this would be a *post hoc* approval, not an understanding in virtue of which the subject makes the relevant transition. The structure of Byrne's account requires that the basic transition be from a proposition sheerly about the world to an unrelated proposition about the subject's mind, and this appears to require that the subject's disposition to make this transition must be automatic, not rational.

We might compare Byrne's case for the goodness of the BEL inference with the kind of case for my being able to jump over a chasm that is made by a sports psychologist who tells me, "You should believe you can do it, since if you believe this, you'll be able to do it." Suppose I know the sports psychologist to be right that if I believed I could jump over the chasm, I would be able to. This still leaves me with a problem about how rationally to come to believe that I can jump over the chasm. If I did believe this, then, by hypothesis, it would be true. But in order rationally to come to believe it, I must see it as true on some basis independent of whatever truths would be brought into being by my holding this belief. Perhaps people can be trained to form such beliefs automatically, and from the standpoint of chasm-jumping, this tendency would doubtless merit our approval. But this does not explain its reasonableness from the subject's own perspective.

(1) I will φ

to

(2) I intend to φ.

I think Byrne is right that if a person judges (1), on a certain sort of basis, this also warrants her in judging (2). This would constitute a vindication for Byrne's approach, however, only if her grounds for so judging were neutral, in the sense that their availability did not presuppose an awareness of her own intentions. Now, (1) is superficially neutral: it does not refer explicitly to the subject's present mental state. But if we think carefully about the kinds of circumstances in which someone might, on the basis of thinking (1), be warranted in thinking (2), we will see that there is reason to doubt this apparent neutrality.

Let us stipulatively define a special "intention-based" sense of "will," "will$_I$," whose use in joining a subject with an action-verb expresses a present intention so to act. We can distinguish "will$_I$" from a "will" of blank futurity ("will$_{BF}$"), which merely asserts that the subject will at some future time do something, leaving it open what makes this the case. In the "will$_I$"-sense, it might be true that *I will walk to work tomorrow* (as I now intend), but false that *I will trip and break my leg tomorrow*, even if these propositions are both true when "will" is read in the "will$_{BF}$"-sense. Now we can ask: In cases where one can move transparently from (1) to (2), is the "will" in (1) "will$_I$" or "will$_{BF}$"? Certainly the step is warranted if the "will" is "will$_I$": in this case, (2) just unpacks what the subject is already committed to, in accepting that she will φ. But the step looks much harder to understand if her basis is simply a conviction that she will$_{BF}$ φ. Suppose I believe I have been subjected to hypnotic suggestion, and that as a result, when a bell rings, I will$_{BF}$ begin to cluck like a hen. It would be strange to infer from this that I now intend to cluck; and surely it would be even stranger if my premonition that I will$_{BF}$ cluck were groundless. Yet it looks as though, in such a case, Byrne's INT-schema would encourage me to infer: I intend to cluck like a hen.

The INT-schema thus does not distinguish between convictions about my own future grounded in present intention and premonitions about my future that are simply groundless. Once we recognize this, I think the INT-inference looks much less attractive. A plausible hypothesis about what grounds its initial appeal is that we are disposed to read its premise in the charitable way, as

(1a) I will$_I$ φ.[10]

---

[10] Note that, although the English verb "will" is ambiguous between will$_I$ and will$_{BF}$, we have verbal forms that strongly favor the former reading. If a person declares either "I am going to φ," this normally expresses a present resolution to φ. I submit that Byrne's INT-schema is initially attractive precisely because we are inclined to read the premise as tantamount to *I will$_I$ φ*.

But if my normal basis for judging that I intend to φ is a conviction that (1a), then although my basis is superficially neutral, it is not genuinely neutral: it presupposes an implicit awareness on my part of what I intend to do. I am, we might say, presupposing that this aspect of my future is mine to decide. Thus my basis for this self-ascription is a judgment about the world, but not a judgment *sheerly* about the world. It is, rather, a judgment about my future that presupposes something about my own cognitive relation to this future.

A plausible story about some of my beliefs about my own future is this: I hold them precisely because I *consciously intend* to make them true. These beliefs express "practical knowledge" (or at any rate, practical conviction) about my own future: they do not involve a spectatorial or predictive attitude toward my future, but a consciousness of this aspect of the future as mine to determine in virtue of my power to choose what I will$_I$ do. Byrne's account, however, posits the contrary order of epistemic dependence: on the basis of a sheer belief about what what I will$_{BF}$ do, I reach a conclusion about what I now intend to do. It seems to me that this would leave me with a knowledge of my own intentions that was palpably self-alienated. For such knowledge would be grounded, not in my seeing a certain act as in my power and regarding it as the thing to do, but simply in my supposing that it will in fact come to pass that I so act. Even if we grant for the sake of argument that an inference to what I intend on this sort of basis could give me knowledge that I intend to φ, it seems clear that it would not supply me with me an *agent's perspective* on my future φ-ing: I would not be in a position to see the matter as settled *because* I so settle it.

I believe versions of these problems can be raised in every case to which Byrne applies his account. Both problems arise from the same basic feature of his approach: his resolute insistence that, when we transparently ascribe mental states to ourselves, we do not rely on any awareness of our own minds, but only on a sheer (purported) awareness of facts about the non-mental world. The result of this insistence is, first, that the subject is left without a satisfactory understanding of the rational connection between her self-ascription and its basis; and second, that her relation to the mental state she ascribes is rendered alienated and spectatorial. Thus, even if she could know *that* she is in the certain state in this way, she could not know this *from an inhabitant's perspective* (as we put it in our discussion of Moran): she would take the world to be a certain way and on this basis *suppose* herself to be in a certain mental state, rather than consciously experiencing her mental state *in* the way she takes the world to be.

To avoid such alienation, it seems that we must reject Byrne's uncompromising insistence on a transition from sheer awareness of the non-mental world to awareness of the subject's own mental state, and allow instead that the subject's basis for self-ascribing a mental state itself draws on some sort of preexisting awareness of her own mind. The next view I want to consider seeks to account for transparent self-knowledge in this way.

2.4. Transparency as Inference from Judgment to Belief: Peacocke

If transparent self-knowledge cannot be satisfactorily explained by an inference from a sheer proposition about the world, it seems that it must draw on some preexisting awareness of our minds. To focus once again on the case of belief: the idea must be that although the question on which the subject reflects is whether p, her transition to the self-ascription *I believe that p* depends not merely on (seeming) awareness that p, but on some sort of awareness of her own consideration of the question. Christopher Peacocke (1998, 2008) has defended such a view of transparent self-ascriptions of belief. As we will see, however, the way Peacocke conceives of this approach generates a form of alienation no less problematic than the one we found in Byrne's view. Seeing this problem will sharpen our sense of what sort of self-awareness a satisfactory solution must invoke, and how this awareness must relate to the subject's "outward-looking" awareness of the world.

According to Peacocke, a subject's ability to determine whether she believes that p by considering whether p rests on her awareness of her own act of *judgment* in response to the latter question. Judgment, Peacocke holds, is a phenomenally conscious act.[11] Hence when a subject judges that p, she will be conscious, not merely of the (apparent) fact that p, but also of her own act of judging that p. This consciousness will in turn warrant her in self-ascribing a belief that p, since the act of judging that p normally expresses belief that p (if such a belief already exists) or produces belief that p (if it does not yet exist). Peacocke admits, however, that these connections do not hold universally: sometimes a conscious act of judgment does not express or produce a standing belief. Nevertheless, he maintains, consciousness of judging that p is a normally reliable indicator that one believes that p, so when a subject has no special reason to doubt that her situation is normal, she may justifiably self-ascribe a belief that p on this basis. Moreover, provided that her self-ascription is true, she may thereby come to know what she believes.[12]

---

[11] Peacocke suggests that it is specifically an "action awareness" (Peacocke 1998: 88, elaborated in Peacocke 2008), but this will not be crucial for the issue that concerns us.

[12] Cf. Peacocke 1998: 71–73, 88–90. Peacocke goes on to acknowledge that there may be cases in which a subject self-ascribes a belief without an intervening act of conscious judgment, but he holds that, even in such cases, the subject's warrant will rest, not sheerly on her belief that p, but on the fact that she would have consciously judged that p if she had considered the question (cf. the "requirement of first-order ratifiability" discussed at Peacocke 1998: 93–94). This complication will not matter for our purposes.

This seems to me a natural alternative to Byrne's interpretation of doxastic transparency. It rejects the idea that the subject's basis for self-ascribing a belief is sheer awareness that p, and holds instead that her basis is awareness of a mental event: *her judging that p*.[13] This is certainly a possible interpretation of the phenomenon Evans described: it might be that I learn what I believe *by* considering a question about the non-mental world, but that this "look outward" warrants me in self-ascribing a belief only because it makes me conscious of my own act of judgment. This indeed is how Peacocke sees the matter: he holds that his account "should not be regarded as in competition with" the method described by Evans, since, just as Evans says, it is by "putting into operation my procedure for answering the question whether p" that I come to have a basis for self-ascribing a belief (Peacocke 1998: 72–73).

Yet, in spite of its naturalness, I think this account mischaracterizes something crucial about our cognitive relation to our own beliefs. We can see what is odd about it by once again considering the matter from the standpoint of a subject trying to understand her own reason for taking herself to believe that p. What can she say to herself?

It is essential to Peacocke's account that the step from consciously judging that p to knowing oneself to believe that p be a step from one item of awareness to another, distinct item of awareness. For his view, as we have seen, is that awareness of judging is a normally reliable indicator of belief that p, but one that can sometimes occur in the absence of such an underlying belief.[14] Now, I am skeptical of the intelligibility of this notion of conscious judgment. After all, not just any event of consciously entertaining the content that p is a case of judging that p. If I entertain the notion that p merely for the sake of argument, or in a counterfactual spirit, I have not thereby expressed conviction in the truth of p, and so presumably I have not judged. Judging that p requires, not merely inwardly affirming that p (whatever that might mean), but affirming p *in the conviction that p is true*. And it is hard to see how this can mean anything less than: it requires inwardly expressing one's belief that p. But then it is hard to see how my consciousness of judging that p can provide me with an independently available ground for believing that I believe that p. If I am fallible about whether I believe that p, then for the same reason I am fallible about whether I (genuinely) judge that p: my warrant for the latter must include my warrant for the former, whatever it may be.

Let us suppose, however, that there is such a thing as the characteristic phenomenology of judgment: a phenomenal profile distinctive of judging that p,

---

[13] Nico Silins has defended a similar view, which he explicitly contrasts with Byrne's approach in this respect. Cf. Silins 2012: 304, fn. 12, and 306, fn. 17.

[14] Cf. Silins 2012: 309, fn. 20.

which can be present even when a corresponding belief is absent. Could the presence of such phenomenology give me a reason to self-ascribe the belief that p? My grip on this idea is not firm enough for me to argue with confidence that it could not; but I want to suggest, at any rate, that if it did, it would at best put me in a position to have an alienated, spectatorial knowledge of my own belief. To see this, consider a case of knowing that I believe that p by judging that p, and suppose for the sake of argument that Peacocke's analysis of this case is sound. I consider whether p and make the judgment that p. So some part of me has taken an affirmative stance toward p—call him 'MB *qua* judger.' But by hypothesis, there is another part of me, 'MB *qua* believer,' whose stance on p might yet differ. We seem to have two points of view here: one which accepts that p, another which may or may not accept it. Now, such a division can arise within a person: what I judge when I consciously consider whether p can come apart from the attitude toward p reflected more broadly in my behavior. But Peacocke's account builds such a division into its characterization of even the most unproblematic case of attitudinal self-knowledge. It does not matter that the stance on p expressed in judgment may for the most part *coincide* with the stance embodied in belief. The point is that, even when the judging subject has settled on an answer to the question whether p, there is still (in principle) another question for her to settle, namely whether she actually believes that p.

Many contemporary philosophers endorse this sort of inferentialist picture of the epistemic relation between judgment and belief, but I think on reflection it should strike us as strange. Focusing on a case in which the subject expresses her judgments aloud helps to bring out its strangeness.[15] Let the subject consider whether p and express her conclusion by saying:

(1) Yes, p.

Now let her infer her own belief from this 'external prompting,' and again express her conclusion aloud:

(2) I believe that p.

Assuming the subject is not alienated from her own belief, we would ordinarily take (2), like (1), to express *belief that p*. On Peacocke's analysis, however, this cannot be right. Whereas (1) may express belief that p, (2) relates to this belief only indirectly: it merely expresses the subject's belief *that she believes that p*,

---

[15] I consider verbal expressions of thought for vividness, but I do not think anything turns on this. The subject's private thoughts about her own attitudes would stand in an equally uncanny relation to her attitudes; imagining these thoughts uttered in a conversational situation just focuses our attention on what is missing.

which is based on the evidence that she verbally affirmed that *p*, but is not itself an unmediated expression of her first-order belief. So her assertion of (2) expresses, not an endorsement of *p* as true, but a (no doubt very well-founded) hypothesis about herself. If she were fully clear about her own epistemic situation, she really ought to say to herself: "Yes, *p*, and so it is extremely likely that I believe that *p*, since my beliefs coincide with my verbalized judgments in most cases, and I've no reason to think that this is an exception." If I received this sort of report on someone's beliefs, I should demand to speak to the believer herself, not just to her biographer, however well-informed the latter might be.

In locating my ground for self-ascribing a belief in a fallible indicator of belief, Peacocke's account thus drives a wedge between my consciously judging *p* to be true and my knowing that I believe *p* (which I infer from, but am not entitled to identify with, my conscious judgment that *p*). What I can acquire by this method is, if anything, a bit of information about myself, not a consciously held belief on the question whether *p*. If this is right, then Peacocke's account has failed to meet the condition we identified in our discussion of Moran: it has not explained the non-spectatorial character of transparent self-knowledge. For this reason, I think Peacocke's approach loses hold of the true spirit of Evans's observation, even if it fits the letter of his account. Genuinely transparent self-knowledge is not merely arrived at *by* considering whether *p*; it remains a mode of knowing *in* which I (self-consciously) look outward. This, I believe, is the deeper sense in which our knowledge of our own minds can be transparent: not merely that it can be *based* on a consideration of the world, but that it can simply *consist* in a self-conscious attitude toward the world, not an independent knowledge *of* one's holding such an attitude.

2.5. Transparency and Expression: Finkelstein and Bar-On

Before closing, I want to comment on one other approach to the topic of self-knowledge, the "neo-expressivist" approach championed by David Finkelstein (2003, 2012) and Dorit Bar-On (2004, 2015).[16] This is not generally presented as an account of transparency, but it bears important relations to this topic and to the issues about alienation that have loomed large in our discussion.

Neo-expressivists take their inspiration from a suggestion made by Ludwig Wittgenstein: that we might learn to use sentences that self-ascribe mental states to *express* the relevant states, in a sense of "express" comparable to the one we

---

[16] Finkelstein and Bar-On's views differ in many ways, of course, but they are similar in treating the idea that self-ascriptions of mental states can express these states as the key to a satisfactory account of self-knowledge. My characterization of the neo-expressivist position will focus on this point of agreement.

invoke when we say that these states are expressed by certain facial expressions, cries, movements, etc.[17] Thus a child might learn to say, "It hurts!" or (later) "I'm in pain," as an expressive substitute for crying out in pain. If this is how we learn to say that we are in pain, then—Wittgenstein appears to suggest—the philosophical question of how one *knows* that one is in pain is in an important way misconceived: my capacity to say, "I am in pain," when I am in pain does not rest on an ability to discern whether I am in pain and then make a self-ascription; making such self-ascriptions is simply something I acquire a disposition to do when I am in pain, as I was already disposed to wince and cry out and tend to the painful area. Our capacity to make privileged, non-observational self-ascriptions of pain thus does not depend on any preexisting knowledge of the fact that I am in pain; it simply depends on my non-cognitive capacity to express pain. Nevertheless, neo-expressivists argue, when such an expression is informed by an understanding of what "I am in pain" means, it can also express (not preexisting but collateral) knowledge that one is in pain. Moreover, if this conception of the basis of mental state self-ascriptions can be generalized to other mental states, as neo-expressivists suggest that it can, then the problem of explaining how we can have immediate and authoritative knowledge of our own mental states appears to be avoided, or at least greatly reduced.

I have discussed neo-expressivism elsewhere, and I will not repeat my criticisms here.[18] I want, rather, to emphasize a point of contact between the neo-expressivist position and the idea from Moran that has guided our discussion in this chapter. The idea from Moran was that, when we know our minds immediately and authoritatively, this is characteristically because we know them, not as spectators, but "from an inhabitant's perspective"—i.e., in such a way that the point of view we ascribe to ourselves is the very one through which we consciously view the world. When we know our own minds in this way, I suggested, we are characteristically able to express, in the very same self-ascription, both our knowledge of being in a certain first-order state and that first-order mental state itself (e.g., both knowledge that I believe that p and my belief that p itself). Now, this is just the point that neo-expressivists emphasize: that we can have immediate and authoritative knowledge of our own mental states just when we can express those very states by self-ascribing them. I accept this point, and indeed I have presupposed it in criticizing Byrne and Peacocke (though it seems to me more illuminating to state the point as a connection between the subject's representing the world in a certain way and her being aware of her own mind as being in a certain state, rather than indirectly as a point about the connection

---

[17] Wittgenstein 1973: §244 (and cf. §§290, 404).
[18] See Boyle 2009 and 2010.

between her *expressing* a certain mental state and her *expressing* awareness of that mental state).

We should not, however, confuse a condition of adequacy on an account of self-knowledge with the account itself. I accept that an adequate account of self-knowledge must validate this proposition:

(E) When a subject S can know her own mental state M immediately and authoritatively, S can express M itself in self-ascribing M.

But if (E) is put forward as the crux of an *account* of how we know our own mental states, I reject it as insufficient. For it leaves unexplained the very fact for which we have been seeking an explanation, namely that S can characteristically treat the question whether she is in M as transparent to some corresponding question about the world.[19] This fact concerns the relationship, from S's perspective, between two topics, one pertaining to the world and another pertaining to her own mind (e.g., whether p and whether she believes that p). Explaining this relationship requires explaining how it can be reasonable, from S's own perspective, to treat these two questions as connected, even though S can be presumed to understand the profound difference between p being *true* and p being *represented* as true by some subject. The truth-conditions of p and the truth-conditions of S believes that p are fundamentally different, and anyone who understands the meaning of "S believes that p" must understand this. Yet the assertability-conditions of "S believes that p" appear to coincide with those of "p" when the former is asserted in a first-person, present tense form. This is the connection we need to understand, and we need to understand it, above all, from the standpoint of the subject who makes the connection: How does she herself understand the relationship between these two topics?

As far as I can see, the neo-expressivist's emphasis on (E) leaves this question untouched. Suppose S is taught to assert "I believe that p" just when she was formerly disposed sincerely to assert "p." Assuming that S's asserting "p" in such circumstances expresses her belief that p, this will ensure that S satisfies (E) with

---

[19] Both Finkelstein and Bar-On respond to this explanatory demand in part by denying that the explanandum is generally true. They grant that the transparency point may hold in the case of knowledge of one's own beliefs, but they argue that, for many other kinds of privileged self-knowledge, there is no world-directed question to which the psychological question is plausibly transparent. Thus, they claim, no plausible transparency account is available for knowledge of one's own passing thoughts (Finkelstein 2003: Afterword; Bar-On 2004: Ch. 4; and Bar-On 2015), for knowledge of one's feelings of pain or one's general mood (Finkelstein 2012), for knowledge of one's "unbidden desires" (Bar-On 2015: 139), etc. I will not attempt to develop a transparency account for every one of these cases—each raises its own problems—but I hope that the next chapter will indicate a general strategy for approaching them, and some of the particular cases will be touched on in subsequent chapters. Finkelstein and Bar-On fail to see that a transparency approach to such cases is possible, I think, mainly because they presuppose a too-narrow conception of the transparency approach.

respect to the mental state of believing that *p*. But this fact provides us with no insight into S's own understanding of this situation. Even if a neo-expressivist informs S that she is disposed to assert "I believe that *p*" in a way that expresses her first-order belief that *p*, this will not clarify how, from her standpoint, the one question bears on the other. We may assume that S is a thinking being, not a parrot or a robot: How then does she understand the connection between the question whether *p* and the question whether she believes that *p*, which differ in general but intersect at just this point?

The views we have considered in earlier sections offer responses to this question, but although neo-expressivists emphasize the very point that needs to be explained, it seems to me that they do not actually explain it. They attempt, rather, to short-circuit the Problem of Transparency by denying that the subject need have any insight into the rational relationship between her being in a certain mental state and her being ready to self-ascribe this state, any more than she has insight into the relationship between her feeling of sharp pain and her urge to cry out.[20] Since I take there to be a genuine problem here—one whose resolution yields insight into the general relationship between our understanding of the world and our understanding of our own minds—I cannot accept this response. The most compelling reasons to side with me in this dispute, however, will come into view once we see that a more satisfying response to Problem of Transparency is possible; and we shall see this in the next chapter.

2.6. Conclusion

Setting aside neo-expressivism for the present, then, let us return to Peacocke and Byrne and ask why, for all their differences, their approaches to transparency encounter versions of the same difficulty. Is there some shared feature in virtue of which they each yield, at best, an alienated form of self-knowledge?

What these two views have in common, I want to suggest, is their fundamentally inferential structure: they represent the step to transparent self-knowledge as a rule-governed transition from one item of (purported) awareness to another, distinct item of awareness. For Byrne, the initial item of awareness is (in the

---

[20] For instance, Finkelstein writes:

> Why is it that I seem to require no behavioral evidence when I avow, e.g., that I'm afraid? No evidence is called for when I smile or wince either. Mental state self-ascriptions are not, typically, reports. They require no more evidence than do smiles (2003: 101).

I think focusing on the question of whether I need *evidence* to self-ascribe a present mental state is a red herring. The difficulty is not to understand what grounds I have for ascribing a mental state to myself, but what makes it reasonable for me to treat two questions, one about my mind and another about the world, as coinciding from my perspective.

simplest case) a sheer proposition about the non-mental world. For Peacocke, it is an awareness of my own act of judgment. But for both, it is an awareness distinct from the one expressed in the resultant judgment about my own mental state. It is this inferential structure, I believe, that generates the difficulty. So long as self-awareness is achieved by this sort of step, the judgment self-ascribing an attitude will express a view of the world distinct from the attitude of which it is an awareness, rather than expressing the very view of the world that it self-ascribes. Hence this sort of self-awareness will not be "from an inhabitant's perspective": it will not be a self-awareness *in* having which I regard the world in the very way that I ascribe to myself. I may in fact regard the world in the relevant way—my self-ascriptive judgment may be true—and I may endorse this attitude. Nevertheless, my self-awareness will be one mental state, and the first-order attitudinal state of which it is an awareness will be another: my self-ascriptive judgment will express a mere view about myself, not than a consciously held attitude.

In the next chapter, I will argue that, in order to account for the non-spectatorial character of transparent self-knowledge, we must conceive of it as achieved by a different kind of step: not an *inference* from one item of awareness to another, but a *reflective* transition from a form of self-awareness that is present but merely implicit to a form that is explicitly self-ascribed. Our next task will be to clarify this "reflectivist" approach to the Problem of Transparency.

3
The Reflectivist Approach

> [T]he mode of existence of consciousness is to be self-consciousness [*conscience de soi*] ... [But] this consciousness of consciousness—except in the case of reflective consciousness, on which we shall dwell shortly—is not *positional*, which is to say that consciousness is not for itself its own object. Its object is by nature outside it.
> —Sartre, *The Transcendence of the Ego* (1962), 40–41/23–24

3.1. Reflectivism and Its Problems

In the last chapter, I objected to Byrne's idea that a subject's basis for transparent self-knowledge is a *sheer* proposition about the world, and also to Peacocke's idea that her basis is some conscious event that serves as a mere *indicator* of her own mental state. For different reasons, I argued, each of these proposals could at best provide a subject with an alienated knowledge of her own mind. Nevertheless, I believe there is an insight worth preserving in each approach: Byrne is right in his resolute insistence that transparent self-knowledge must look outward, while Peacocke is right to think that the basis of this knowledge must not be a sheer awareness of the world, but some sort of awareness that implies something about the subject's own state of mind. But can there be a kind of awareness that satisfies both of these demands?

In earlier work (Boyle 2011b), I tried to argue that there can. The interpretation of transparent self-knowledge I proposed, which I called "reflectivist," holds that we are warranted in self-ascribing mental states on the basis of a consideration of the world because there is already a kind of self-awareness implicit in the relevant ways of representing the world. I put this by saying that the existence of the relevant mental states (perception, belief, intention, etc.) itself involves the subject's "tacit knowledge" of their existence, so that all the subject needs to do to achieve explicit knowledge of these states is to *reflect* on what she already knows. On this view, the subject's step is not, as Byrne suggests, an inference from a sheer fact about the non-mental world to a fact about her own psychology; nor is it, as Peacocke proposes, a transition from awareness of one mental event to knowledge of another, distinct mental state. It is not an acquisition of new information, but a reflective articulation of an awareness that was already involved in the subject's regarding the world in a certain way.

I continue to think that only an approach along these lines can satisfactorily explain transparent self-knowledge, but I am no longer satisfied with my earlier account of reflectivism. The crucial problem lies in making sense of the idea of tacit knowledge. For on the one hand, if a subject already *knows* (e.g.) that she believes that *p*, mustn't this involve her taking it to be true that she believes that *p*? But then in what sense can this knowledge be "tacit," other than the inconsequential sense that she has not yet verbally expressed it? And on the other hand, if the subject's knowledge that she believes *p* is truly *tacit*, in the sense that she does not yet have any attitude toward the proposition *I believe that p*, in what sense can she be said already to know this? States of knowledge are standardly thought to be individuated by their propositional contents. If a subject does not yet know "explicitly" that she believes that *p*, what can this mean but that she does not yet possess this particular item of knowledge? The notion of tacit knowledge thus appears to be in internal tension with itself. Yet appeal to this notion is crucial to the reflectivist position, for only in this way do reflectivists capture the cognitive difference between a subject who has the mere potential to reflect on one of her own mental states and a subject who has actually reflected.

The reflectivist claim that belief involves tacit knowledge of belief is also problematic for another reason. Knowledge is commonly assumed to be subject to the following Concept Possession Requirement (CPR):

A subject can know that *p* only if she possesses the concepts necessary for understanding the proposition that *p*.

If the tacit knowledge invoked by reflectivism were subject to (CPR), then the reflectivist would be committed to holding that a subject can have beliefs only if she possesses the concept of belief. But this is an implausibly strong intellectual requirement on belief. The *concept* of belief seems to be a fairly sophisticated attainment, the first step toward a theoretical understanding of what it is to believe, whereas it seems that quite unreflective persons, not to mention young children and nonhuman animals, can have beliefs and act intelligently on the basis of them. So it seems the reflectivist should hold that our "tacit knowledge" of our own beliefs is not subject to (CPR). But if we sever the link between ascribing knowledge that one believes that *p* and ascribing grasp of the concept *belief*, we make it much less clear what this ascription comes to. Just what does it mean to say that the subject "tacitly knows" this?

3.2. Sartre and Reflectivism

The reflectivist thus faces formidable challenges, but he is not alone in his predicament. Jean-Paul Sartre's distinction between "positional" and "nonpositional" consciousness, which we encounter in the epigraph to this chapter, grew out of an attempt to respond to a structurally similar set of challenges. Some might wonder how much help can be expected from this sort of companion, but I will argue that Sartre's distinction is in fact of great value in responding to the problems just noted.

The positional/nonpositional distinction belongs to Sartre's broader enterprise of characterizing "consciousness" (*conscience*), the mode of being characteristic of the entity he calls "the for-itself." We can introduce his distinction by explicating four fundamental propositions about consciousness asserted in the Introduction to *Being and Nothingness*:

(S1) "[A]ll consciousness . . . is consciousness *of* something. In other words, there is no consciousness that is not a *positing* [*position*] of a transcendent object" (BN 9/17).

(S2) "[E]very knowing consciousness [*conscience connaissante*] can only be knowledge [*connaissance*] of object" (BN 10/18).

(S3) "[A]ny positional consciousness of an object is at the same time a nonpositional consciousness of itself" (BN 11/19).

(S4) "[N]on-reflective consciousness [*conscience non-réflexive*] is what makes reflection possible" (BN 12/19).

(S1) is a point that Sartre credits to Husserl: it expresses Husserl's idea that the defining trait of the psychic aspect of our existence—"consciousness" being Sartre's generic term for the mode of being of the psychic—is its intentionality, its being *of* or *about* some object distinct from the relevant state of consciousness itself.[1] In this sense, consciousness "transcends" itself to posit a realm of being beyond itself. "Positing" is Sartre's term for the relation of consciousness to its object (i.e., that which we would specify in specifying what it is a consciousness of: an "object" in the broadest sense). Consciousness is said to be "positional" inasmuch as it is of or about an object.[2]

---

[1] I will follow the common practice of speaking of "states" of consciousness, though Sartre himself would reject this mode of expression as implying a kind of passivity that is foreign to consciousness (cf. TE 61–68/45–51 and 109n/15n). It will be useful to have some common noun designating the sort of thing exemplified when a subject is conscious of something, and I think the term "state" is innocuous once its potentially misleading connotations have been flagged.

[2] As we noted in the Introduction, it is natural to ask whether Sartre's characterizations of "consciousness" are meant to apply to all animals that are capable of some form of awareness of their environment, or only to some special form of awareness of objects that is distinctive of human consciousness. My purposes here do not require me to settle this as an interpretative question, but in the

Sartre does not think that all positional consciousness consists in knowing an object—there are other modes of positing, such as imagining, desiring, and so on—but he does regard knowing as a species of positional consciousness: it is a kind of relation in which consciousness stands to some posited object. That object, and only that object, is what the relevant consciousness is knowledge of. This is the thought expressed in (S2).

The crucial point for our purposes is (S3): that all positional consciousness of an object involves nonpositional consciousness of that very state of consciousness. "Nonpositional" consciousness is supposed to be a mode of awareness that does *not* posit that of which it is aware as its intentional object. This may sound paradoxical: how can there be a consciousness *of* something that does not "posit" that thing, if to posit something just is to relate to it in such a way that one is conscious *of* it? To avoid outright paradox, Sartre places the "of" in parentheses when he speaks of "nonpositional consciousness (of) consciousness," as a way of indicating that nonpositional consciousness does not give us awareness *of* its object in the positional sense (cf. BN 12/20). But this maneuver is obviously of no help without an explanation of this other mode of awareness, the one signified by "(of)."

Sartre claims not only that there is such a thing as nonpositional consciousness of consciousness, but that there must be such nonpositional consciousness if there is to be positional consciousness of objects:

> [T]he necessary and sufficient condition for a knowing consciousness to be knowledge *of* its object is that it should be conscious of itself as being this knowledge. It is a necessary condition: if my consciousness were not conscious of being conscious of the table, it would thereby be conscious of the table without being conscious that it was so, or, alternatively, it would be a consciousness that did not know itself, an unconscious consciousness—which is absurd. It is a sufficient condition: my being conscious of being conscious of the table suffices for me in fact to be conscious of it. (BN 10/18)

Sartre thus holds that to deny the existence of nonpositional consciousness of consciousness is absurd: this would be to posit an "unconscious consciousness," which is a contradiction in terms.

I suspect most contemporary philosophers would not be impressed by this argument. They would reply that the notion of an "unconscious consciousness" may sound self-contradictory, but if it just consists in consciousness of an *object*

---

ensuing discussion I will assume that Sartre has in mind human consciousness first and foremost, in a way that permits him to say things about consciousness that apply properly only to our (rational) consciousness. I discuss this issue in greater depth in §7.7.

without some sort of consciousness of *that very state of consciousness*, then there is really no contradiction. To insist otherwise is to beg the question. I sympathize with this response, but I think it is possible to make a more forceful case for (S3) than Sartre does here. I will turn to this task shortly. First, however, a brief remark about (S4). We have seen that Sartre holds positional consciousness of an object to depend on nonpositional consciousness (of) consciousness. (S4) adds that *reflective* consciousness of our own mental states, in which we "posit" these states as objects of knowledge in their own right, is made possible by the presence, prior to reflection, of another kind of self-awareness: a nonpositional consciousness that belongs intrinsically to the relevant conscious states. Sartre holds that, when we reflect, it is this nonpositional consciousness that we draw on and make explicit.

My "reflectivist" approach resembled Sartre's view in that I also held our capacity for explicit, reflective knowledge of our own mental states to be grounded in another, more basic mode of self-awareness. I called this more basic self-awareness "tacit knowledge," but I have come to think it better to follow Sartre in calling it "nonpositional consciousness," reserving the term "knowledge" for the kind of explicit awareness that posits what it is aware of. To suggest that (e.g.) belief involves *knowledge* of belief raises all the difficulties noted earlier, and adding that the relevant knowledge is "tacit" does not make clear how to avoid them. Characterizing the relevant awareness as "nonpositional consciousness" does not by itself provide the needed clarification, but it at least marks the spot where clarification is needed. I now want to argue that we can begin to clarify the nature of such nonpositional consciousness by connecting it with the problem of transparency.

3.3. Nonpositional Consciousness and Transparency

As a first illustration of how the notion of nonpositional consciousness might bear on the problem of transparency, consider again transparent knowledge of one's own intentions, which we discussed earlier in connection with Byrne.

Byrne plausibly observes that a person can sometimes be warranted in answering a question about whether she intends to φ simply by treating it as transparent to a question about her own future: whether she will φ. I argued, however, that if such a transition is to give a person non-alienated knowledge of her own intention, she must, in answering the question whether she will φ, already think of her future in a distinctive manner, the one we introduced the expression "will$_1$" to mark. Her true basis for ascribing an intention to φ to herself will thus be a thought to this effect:

(1a) I will$_I$ φ.

(1a) is a specific way of thinking that it will be the case that I φ, namely one that (as we theorists may put it) presents the relevant future action as settled by my present intention to φ. Nevertheless, thinking (1a) is not equivalent to thinking

(1b) I will$_{BF}$ φ in virtue of the fact that I now intend to φ.

If thinking (1a) amounted to thinking (1b), then only subjects who possessed the concept of intention and the concept of whatever relation is signified by "in virtue of" could think (1a). But this would be an implausible intellectual requirement: surely a person may think about her own future in the special manner characteristic of someone who intends to do something before mastering special psychological concepts that mark her relation to the relevant future acts. Moreover—and this seems to me the deeper objection—(1b) does not capture the distinctive stance toward one's future φ-ing that is expressed in (1a). For (1b) simply asserts a connection between two facts, one about the present (that I presently intend to φ) and another about the future (that I will$_{BF}$ φ). But it is clearly possible for me to think that such a connection holds without thereby expressing the intention to *determine* my own future expressed by (1a). (1a) does not merely posit, from a spectatorial standpoint, that a present mental state of mine will cause me to φ; it expresses a practical intention to φ. No mere claim about the relation between my present and my future, however complex, can express this sort of distinctively practical attitude unless it represents this aspect of the future in the distinctive practical manner expressed by "will$_I$."[3]

Thus, when I think (1a), I do not explicitly ascribe an intention to myself; rather, I think that I will φ in a manner that implicitly presupposes such an intention. The fact that I now intend to do this is, we might say, expressed "nonpositionally" in (1a): the fact that I intend to φ is not made explicit in my thought, but it is also not something to which I am oblivious. My awareness of it will come out in the specific kinds of grounds I consider for propositions like (1a), and the specific kinds of consequences I draw from them. My grounds will

---

[3] This is true even if we add a self-referential device to the reformulation, as in

(1c) I will$_{BF}$ hereby φ because I now intend to φ (cf. Setiya 2012).

Adding "hereby" marks the fact that my now representing this causal connection will contribute to making the relevant connection obtain, but it is clear that even this more complex thought might express a disengaged observation about the causal relationship between various facts, rather than a practical intention to make things so. (On a different reading, perhaps, the "hereby" would itself express what we have been using "will$_I$" to express: that I resolve to make things so. But if this is what "hereby" expresses, it does not contribute to an account of the intention-expressing "will$_I$" in terms of independently intelligible materials; it is simply an alternative marker of the relevant mode of presentation.)

speak primarily to the desirability of φ-ing, rather than to the evidential question whether it will be the case that I φ. And I will draw consequences, not about what I am likely to do, but about what else I must do in order to φ and how my φ-ing should affect my other plans. I will, in short, treat such propositions in ways which indicate that I understand them to express decisions rather than mere predictions. But this understanding will be expressed, not in my explicitly thinking *I intend to* φ, but in my distinctive manner of thinking of my future φ-ing. I hope this example begins to clarify what, concretely, it could mean for positional consciousness of some aspect of the world (in this case, an aspect of my own future) to involve nonpositional consciousness of one's present state of consciousness.

Now consider a person who makes the transition from

(1a)   I will$_i$ φ

to

(2)   I intend to φ.

The reasonableness of this transition is evident. A person who thinks (1a) already thinks of her future φ-ing in a way that implies a present intention to φ: her judging (2) just makes this implication explicit. What she must understand in order justifiably to make the transition from (1a) to (2) is simply that the way of thinking of her future involved in (1a) implies a present intention to φ. But this is to say that she does not need any further information about her present psychological state beyond what is already contained in (1a). All she needs is a grasp of the conditions of the first-person application of the concept *intention* itself.

Where this is the case—where a subject's manner of thinking of the world is such that she requires only general competence with a certain psychological concept in order to know, on this basis, that she is in a certain psychological state—I will say that the subject is in a position to know her own psychological state by *reflection*. A reflective transition is not an inference from premises that are "neutral" in Byrne's sense: accepting the relevant premises presupposes a kind of awareness of one's own psychological state, but this is a *nonpositional* awareness, which does not involve the application of a psychological concept. Nevertheless, such awareness can warrant a psychological self-ascription, for the application of the relevant concept just makes explicit a consciousness that was already implicit in the corresponding way of thinking of the world.

Turn now to transparent knowledge of one's own perceptions. Consider a subject who makes a transition from the world-oriented observation:

(3) This cat is purring

to the reflective thought:

(4) I perceive a purring cat.

How can this be a reasonable transition, given that it is one thing for a cat to be purring and another for me to perceive it? Well, consider the way the cat is represented in (3): it is presented in a distinctive manner, which we express with a "this." Now, an object is available to a given subject for this sort of demonstrative reference only in specific kinds of circumstances. Although a cat may be purring, I cannot successfully think of it as *this cat* when it is miles away, or hidden behind a screen, or known to me only by hearsay. Philosophers commonly call such a "this" a "perceptual demonstrative" precisely because it expresses a mode of presentation of an object that is available just when the relevant object is perceived.

A subject will have the capacity to refer to objects in this way only if she is sensitive to the obtaining of the kind of relationship to an object that makes such thoughts possible: namely, that she presently perceives the object in question, in a way that enables her to keep track of it and distinguish it from other objects.[4] Nevertheless, a subject who thinks (3) on the basis of perceptual consciousness does not think *that she perceives* the relevant cat: the only object she thinks about is the cat. Nor is her way of thinking of the cat reducible to a proposition about her own mental state conjoined with a sheer proposition about her environment, as in:

(3b) There is a purring cat here and I perceive it.

(3b) does not capture the distinctively singular mode of presentation of a cat expressed by "this cat": it represents the subject as having a nonsingular, merely existential thought of a cat that satisfies a certain description. By contrast, a subject who thinks (3) thinks *de re* about a particular cat, but in a manner which presupposes that she perceives it. We might therefore say that her perceptual relation to the cat is expressed "nonpositionally" in her thought: it is not posited, but it is a presupposition of the soundness of what is posited.

So again, we have a mode of consciousness of the world that is possible only in virtue of nonpositional consciousness of one's own consciousness. Hence, if the subject goes on to think the reflective thought:

---

[4] Cf. Evans 1982: Ch. 6, esp. pp. 170–176 and 192–196.

(4) I perceive a purring cat

she will be making explicit a psychological state whose presence was already presupposed in her world-directed representation of the cat.[5] To acquire knowledge of her own perceptual state in this way, a subject need only understand the relationship between this special demonstrative mode of presentation of non-mental objects and her own perceptual state. Provided that she grasps the first-person application-conditions for the concept *perceives*, then, such a subject will thus be in a position to know her own perceptual state through mere reflection: she will not need to draw on any further information about her present psychological state beyond what is already contained in (3). What justifies her reflective step, however, is not the sheer fact that a certain cat is purring, but her *nonpositional* consciousness of her own manner of apprehending this fact, which is expressed in her manner of thinking of the cat.

Consider finally the case of belief. Suppose I wonder whether there will be a third world war and reach the alarming conclusion that:

(5) There will be a third world war.

(5) is clearly a proposition about the non-mental world, but my manner of representing this proposition differs from the way I would represent it if I were merely supposing (5) for the sake of argument, imagining a possible world in which it holds true, etc. Moreover, subjects who can deliberate competently about factual questions must have an implicit awareness of their own manner of representing such propositions. For such subjects must be able to distinguish between propositions represented in the mode of belief and those represented in other modes. In particular, they must be able to distinguish between a factual question being open and its being closed: between the attitude toward *p* involved in considering whether *p* and the attitude involved in settling this question one way or another.

Now consider the kind of openness and closure that are at issue here. Suppose a person regards it as an open question whether there will be a third world war. In what sense does she regard this matter as unsettled? Not in the sense that she must regard the truth of the question as metaphysically indeterminate: she may suppose that there is a perfectly determinate fact of the matter, which she aims to discover. The sense in which she regards the question as open is rather

---

[5] The presupposition of her thought may of course be false: her representation *this cat* may express a merely apparent awareness of a perceptually presented cat. More would need to be said in a full account of our warrant for self-ascriptions of factive and non-factive perceptual states. More would also need to be said to account for the ways in which we can acquire reflective knowledge of the specific sense modality involved in a given perception, of which properties are perceived, etc. I say more about these topics in Chapter 8. Here I am just trying to illustrate the basic Sartrean strategy in accounting for transparent knowledge of one's own perceiving.

an epistemic one: she regards it as still open *for her*, i.e., a question to which *she* possesses no determinate answer. This is not to say that she must think of herself and her own epistemic situation as such: she need only think the proposition *p* in an interrogative mode, as it were. But her manner of thinking of this proposition distinguishes between a kind of openness which is in fact an openness from her epistemic standpoint and a contrasting form of closure which is in fact closure from her standpoint. When things go well, the latter mode of presentation amounts to her knowing whether *p*; but whether things go well or not, representing the question as closed implies that her own belief on the question is settled.

The point here is not merely that the subject's answer to the question whether *p* expresses a belief she holds, but that she herself already implicitly distinguishes between this mode of presentation and a contrasting non-committal mode. She might mark this distinction by using modal verbs in a way that expresses epistemic possibility, so that:

(5) There *will be* a third world war

expresses closure of the question from her standpoint while

(6) There *might be* a third world war

expresses openness. But however she marks it, this is a distinction that she will, as a competent deliberator, implicitly recognize. We might therefore say that, in concluding that there will be a third world war, she expresses a *nonpositional* consciousness of her own belief: an awareness that figures, not as the object of her thought, but as the necessary background of her thinking rationally about the question of whether there will be a third world war.

Hence, if the deliberating subject goes on to think the reflective thought:

(7) I believe that there will be a third world war

she will simply be making explicit an awareness that was already implicit in her world-directed representation of the likelihood of a third world war. To acquire reflective knowledge of her own doxastic state in this way, she need only understand the relationship between a certain mode of presentation of a worldly state of affairs and her own state of belief. And again, what justifies her reflective step will be, not the sheer thought that there will be a third world war, but her nonpositional consciousness of her own stance on this question. Moreover, although we have developed this point with reference to an example in which a subject deliberates, it should be clear that the occurrence of deliberation is not essential to this account. What is crucial is that the subject's believing involves nonpositional awareness of holding a question to be closed. In a subject capable of considering propositional questions, such awareness will characterize all beliefs, even those about which the subject does not deliberate.

3.4. The Structure of the Sartrean Account

Let us now step back to consider the general structure of this Sartrean approach to transparency. The approach has two main elements: first, the idea that any consciousness of the world (in the broad Sartrean sense of "consciousness": any form of contentful awareness, whether occurrent or stative) involves *nonpositional consciousness* of itself; second, the idea that this nonpositional consciousness can be transformed, through an act of *reflection*, into explicit knowledge of one's own representational state. It is our ability to bring our nonpositional consciousness to reflective articulacy, I claimed, that explains our capacity for transparent self-knowledge.

In the last section, I showed how this Sartrean analysis can be applied to a few widely discussed cases of transparency: transparent knowledge of our own intentions, perceptions, and beliefs. In each case, I argued that what justifies our reflective self-ascription is a preexisting awareness of the relevant mental state that is expressed, not explicitly in the content of our first-order representation, but implicitly in what we may call the "mode of presentation" of this content. Moreover, I claimed that grasp of the relevant mental state concepts will involve an understanding of the connection between such modes of presentation and the applicability of corresponding mental state concepts, and hence that a subject who grasps concepts such as *intention*, *perception*, and *belief* will be in a position to make a corresponding self-ascriptive judgment simply by reflecting on the objects of her intentions, perceptions, and beliefs.

It would take further work to show how this analysis can be applied to other types of mental states, but the general strategy should be clear from these examples. On the Sartrean view, nonpositional consciousness of our own representational states is not simply a further awareness superadded to our consciousness of the worldly objects of these states; it is implied in the very mode of presentation of the relevant objects. In this way, nonpositional consciousness (of) our own consciousness is integral to our first-order representational states themselves. Moreover, this necessary nonpositional consciousness explains how a subject who possesses concepts of the relevant mental state types can achieve positional knowledge of her own mental states through mere reflection.

Several notions involved in this Sartrean approach to transparency are plainly in need of further clarification. In the first place, more needs to be said about the notion of a mode of presentation. This notion is most familiar from Frege's invocation of it in solving his famous problem about how there can be informative identity-statements connecting terms with the same referent, but my use of the notion differs from Frege's. Fregean modes of presentation differentiate presentations of the very same object, but I am interested in a more generic sort of difference, one that differentiates, not presentations of a particular object, but general types of presentation.[6] Thus our capacity for perception presents us with indefinitely many particulars (objects, qualities, events, etc.), but it presents all these particulars in a general mode that is characteristic of perception as such: viz., as *this*-es. Similarly, our capacity to act intentionally allows us to consider and undertake an indefinitely wide array of possible actions, but it considers these actions in a general mode that is characteristic of the practical thought: viz., as things the agent *will₁* do, as we have put it. But when exactly does a feature of a represented content count as a mode of presentation in this sense?

I count a feature of a representation as belonging to its *mode* of presenting its object, rather than to the content presented, when this feature expresses some aspect of the subject's cognitive relation to the represented object, but in a way that cannot be captured by starting with a generic type of representational content and adding further specifications bearing on the subject's cognitive relation to this object. Perceptually representing *this cat*, for instance, involves a specific mode of presentation of a cat, namely one that (as we theorists may put it) presents the relevant cat as perceived; yet perceptually representing *this cat* is not equivalent to representing *the cat I presently perceive*. For one thing, as we have already noted, it is surely possible for a subject who does not possess the concept of perception to represent *this cat*, whereas someone who represents *the cat I presently perceive* must possess this concept. The more fundamental point, however, is that no such definite description would capture the distinctive mode of presentation expressed by a perceptual demonstrative. To think of a cat only as *the cat I presently perceive* is, in an important sense, not yet to clarify *which* cat satisfies the relevant description, whereas to think of *this cat* is to identify the cat in question. For the former representation singles out the unique cat, if any, that satisfies a certain description (viz., "cat I presently perceive"), whereas the latter does not single out a cat by description: it is an irreducibly singular, non-descriptive mode of presentation.[7]

---

[6] My use of the notion of a mode of presentation in this way is inspired by Recanati 2007. He credits it to Searle.

[7] One way to bring this out is to observe that I might know that there is a unique cat that I presently perceive, and thus might be in a position to think with warrant about *the cat I presently perceive*, and yet might not be in a position to think demonstratively of it as *this cat*. Suppose, for instance, that I am reliably informed that there is a single cat visible from here, but that its coloring makes it blend into the background against which I see it. I may know that, when I look in a certain direction, I am in fact perceiving a unique cat, but not yet have discriminated it in the way that would enable me to think of it as *this cat*.

Similarly, thinking of a possible A-ing in the manner we have marked with "$will_I$" is a specific mode of thinking of one's own future A-ing, namely one that (as we theorists may put it) presents the relevant future action as settled by my present intention to do A. Nevertheless, thinking *I $will_I$ do A* is not equivalent to thinking *I $will_{BF}$ do A because I now intend to do A*. Again, one indication of this is that a person who does not possess the psychological concept of intention can think *I $will_I$ do A*. But the more fundamental point is that no such reformulation would capture the distinctive way of presenting a future action expressed by *I $will_I$ do A*. For any such reformulation would merely make a claim about the causal connection between a present fact and a future fact: e.g., that I will in future do A because I now intend to do A. But, as we have seen, *I $will_I$ do A* does not merely posit that a present intention of mine will cause me to do A; it expresses a practical resolution so to act. No claim about the relation between my present and my future, however complex, could express this sort of distinctively practical attitude unless it contained some element like "$will_I$," which expresses the distinctively practical *mode* of the relevant thought. Thus, like the perceptual demonstrative *this*, the intentional $will_I$ does not add further content to some generic kind of representation of a future action, but expresses an irreducible and distinctive mode of presentation of an action as to-be-done.

Our Sartrean reflectivist approach to transparency claims that, for any representational state of which we can have transparent self-knowledge, there is some mode of presentation of objects that is distinctive of the relevant type of state. Moreover, it claims that the subject's capacity to represent objects in this mode expresses a nonpositional consciousness of her own state, and that this nonpositional consciousness can be transformed, through reflection, into an explicit, positional knowledge of this state. Like the notion of a mode of presentation, the notions of nonpositional consciousness and reflection will need further clarification. The preceding discussion has made it plausible, I hope, that these notions have an important role to play in solving the Problem of Transparency. But it is one thing to see the need for such ideas, another to achieve a systematic understanding of them. We will need, on the one hand, to give a sharper and more rigorous account of what nonpositional consciousness is and how it is connected with our having, even prior to reflection, a "first-person perspective" on our own lives. And we will need, on the other hand, to clarify the role of reflection in transforming our nonpositional self-awareness into positional self-knowledge. These will be the tasks, respectively, of the two remaining parts of this book.

3.5. Conclusion

Before closing this part of the discussion, let me note some advantages of this Sartrean approach to the Problem of Transparency.

In the first place, the approach allows us to reconcile what is attractive in Byrne's idea that transparent self-knowledge is grounded simply in a consideration of the world, on the one hand, and Peacocke's thought that such knowledge must draw on some sort of awareness of our own psychological state, on the other. Sartre's idea of nonpositional consciousness is the key to this reconciliation: it shows how a look outward can itself presuppose awareness of one's own psychological state without foregrounding this awareness in a way that severs the link between the subject's awareness of her own mental state and her first-order perspective on the world.

By the same token, the Sartrean approach explains why Moran is right to insist that transparent self-ascriptions of mental states express a non-spectatorial knowledge of these states. For on the Sartrean view, as we have seen, transparent mental state ascriptions simply make explicit a mode of awareness that was already implicit in the corresponding outward-looking awareness of the world. Hence transparent self-knowledge does not leave open the question whether the world is as one represents it to be; even as it self-ascribes a mental state, it continues to look outward.

Finally, the Sartrean approach enables us to address the concern that reflectivism imposes implausibly strong intellectual requirements on belief, perception, intention, etc. We can admit that a subject might (e.g.) believe that p without possessing the concept of belief, for on our Sartrean view, the consciousness of believing involved in belief does not take the form of a *positional* representation of oneself *as* believing, but of a nonpositional awareness implicit in a certain mode of presentation of a worldly state of affairs. This nonpositional awareness does not itself "posit" the believer herself as a topic of knowledge or represent her condition as being of a certain kind, but provided that she possesses the relevant concepts, it enables her to make a warranted self-ascriptive judgment when she reflects. Once we recognize this point, we see the need for a new kind of inquiry into self-knowledge: not an investigation of how we are in a position to know our own minds at all, but an inquiry into the nature of the reflective act by which we transform a necessary nonpositional self-consciousness into an explicit *knowledge* of ourselves.

Sartre's *Being and Nothingness* is, among other things, an extended investigation of this topic, and it is worth noting how the distinction between nonpositional self-consciousness and reflective self-knowledge is connected with another great Sartrean theme, the perpetual threat of self-alienation that characterizes our lives as conscious subjects. A major source of resistance to approaches that represent our minds as essentially self-aware, I think, is the sense that they cannot do justice to the depth and ubiquity of this threat. But precisely because it distinguishes between nonpositional self-consciousness and reflective self-knowledge, Sartre's approach can readily acknowledge the many ways in which our reflective self-understanding can distort the reality of our psychic lives, both in the more prosaic sense that it can fail to appreciate the facts, and in the more profound sense that it can involve a kind of "bad faith" in which there is no stable fact to know. We shall return to this topic in Chapter 10, where we will consider how our capacity for reflection is the ground both of the possibility of bad faith and also of the conceivability of a project of authenticity.

PART II
SELF-CONSCIOUSNESS AND THE FIRST-PERSON PERSPECTIVE

4
Consciousness-as-Subject

> When I run after a streetcar, when I look at the time, when I am absorbed in contemplating a portrait, there is no *I*. There is consciousness *of the streetcar-having-to-be-overtaken*, etc., and nonpositional consciousness of consciousness. In fact, I am then plunged into the world of objects; it is they which constitute the unity of my consciousnesses; it is they which present themselves with values, with attractive and repellant qualities—but *me*, I have disappeared. . . . And this is not a matter of chance, due to a momentary lapse of attention, but happens because of the very structure of consciousness.
> —Sartre, *The Transcendence of the Ego* (1962), 48–49/32

4.1. Introduction

The Sartrean thought we are pursuing holds that all positional consciousness of an object involves a correlative nonpositional consciousness of this very state of consciousness. By "positional consciousness of an object," we mean any form of representational awareness, whether occurrent or stative, with any kind of intentional object whatsoever, be it a concrete individual, a property or relation, an event or process, a state of affairs, etc. By "nonpositional consciousness of consciousness," we mean a kind of awareness that does *not* have our own mental state as its intentional object, but that is nevertheless a genuine awareness of this state in some other sense. As we saw, Sartre sometimes marks the nonpositional character of this latter awareness by putting parentheses around the "of" in "nonpositional consciousness (of) consciousness." But however we mark it, this idea obviously needs further clarification. What exactly is "nonpositional consciousness (of) consciousness"?[1] In what sense is it, and in what sense is it not, an awareness of one's own mental state?

---

[1] Having noted this need for clarification, I will henceforth drop the Sartrean parentheses. If we come genuinely to understand the sense in which nonpositional consciousness (of) X can be said to make us aware of X, then parentheses should not be necessary. If we fail to understand this, adding parentheses will not help.

The task of this second part of the book will be to give more careful consideration to the notion of nonpositional consciousness. The preceding chapter sought to motivate this notion by appeal to cases, but we must now give a more systematic account of it. In particular, we will need to address two questions. First, in what sense is nonpositional consciousness of consciousness a genuine form of awareness of one's own mental states?[2] We have proposed that nonpositional consciousness of one's own state of consciousness is expressed in the characteristic mode of presentation of the object posited by the relevant state of consciousness. Thus, we said, one is nonpositionally conscious of *perceiving* a cat in being aware of a cat in the distinctive manner that one would express with a perceptual demonstrative "this," and one is nonpositionally conscious of *intending* to go to the beach in thinking that one will go to the beach in the decisive manner that I have marked with "will$_1$." But even someone who granted that there are modes of presentation characteristic of different types of representational states might still doubt that these modes express awareness of the relevant mental states. For certainly it is not universally true that, where B covaries with A, B expresses awareness of A. It may be true, for instance, that my experience of strangers as inviting and agreeable varies with my state of drunkenness, and yet my experiencing strangers as increasingly inviting and agreeable surely need not express an awareness that I am increasingly drunk, even if drunkenness is in fact the cause of my experience. In what sense, then, do the modes of presentation we have identified express *awareness* of the mental states that give rise to them?

Secondly, even someone who grants that the modes of presentation of objects characteristic of different types of mental states express some kind of awareness of these states might wonder in what sense they express awareness of the relevant states *as my own*. It is, after all, a familiar observation that a person can be aware of what is in fact her own state and yet not be aware of it *as* her own state. Recall the case of Ernst Mach, mentioned in Chapter 1. While looking unknowingly at a mirror, Mach saw a figure who was in fact himself and thought:

> That man looks like a shabby schoolteacher.

Mach's case shows that it is possible to be aware of a state that is in fact one's own (in this case, one's looking like a shabby schoolteacher), and yet fail to be aware of this *as* one's own state. To be sure, the states of which we have "nonpositional

---

[2] My former colleague Susanna Siegel raised this question about an early version of this material. The present chapter attempts to respond to her concern.

consciousness" are states of a quite different kind, and our awareness of them has a quite different character, from the ones at issue in this example. Still, we should want an account of nonpositional consciousness that explains why it is apt, on reflection, to express the content of such consciousness in the first person, as in

> I perceive X / I believe that p / I intend to do A / etc.

If nonpositional consciousness of my own consciousness warrants such specifically first-personal forms of ascription, it might seem that the relevant forms of nonpositional consciousness must themselves present the relevant states of consciousness *as mine* in some sense. Yet we shall see that it is *not* attractive to think of nonpositional consciousness of perceiving as involving awareness of the subject who perceives—not even in the etiolated sense in which it involves awareness of perceiving. This will help us to understand what Sartre means when he says that "there is no I" in pre-reflective consciousness; but it will leave us with the problem of understanding the relation between this subjectless pre-reflective consciousness and the subject-involving knowledge that we achieve on reflection.

This second question about how nonpositional consciousness of consciousness relates to explicit subject-involving knowledge will occupy us in Chapter 5. In the present chapter, we will focus on the first question: the one about the sense in which nonpositional consciousness is a genuine form of *awareness* of our own mental states at all. My aim will be to show that there is a form of awareness of our own mental states that is fundamentally different from, and more basic than, positional self-knowledge. I will call this more basic form of awareness "consciousness-as-subject," and will introduce some concepts and distinctions that will help us to analyze its nature and differentiate it from positional self-knowledge.

To introduce the notion of consciousness-as-subject, it will help first to consider a more general contrast between representation-*as*-subject and representation *of* a certain subject (§§4.2–4.4). Once we understand this general distinction, we will be in a position to see that the distinction between consciousness-as-subject and positional self-knowledge is a special case of it (§4.5), and to bring the more specific distinction to bear in analyzing how transparent self-knowledge depends on nonpositional consciousness (§4.6). In the process, we will also arrive at a more definite understanding of the intuitive notion of a "first-person perspective" to which we appealed in our preliminary characterizations of our topic in the Introduction.

4.2. Imagining-as-Subject

To introduce the topic of representation-as-subject, it will help to consider a contrast between two kinds of imagining drawn by Zeno Vendler in his essay "Vicarious Experience" (1979):

> We are looking down upon the ocean from a cliff. The water is rough and cold, yet there are some swimmers riding the waves. "Just imagine swimming in that water" says my friend, and I know what to do. "Brr!" I say as I imagine the cold, the salty taste, the tug of the current, and so forth. Had he said "Just imagine yourself swimming in that water," I could comply in another way too: by picturing myself being tossed about, a scrawny body bobbing up and down in the foamy waste. (Vendler 1979: 161)

As further instances of the intended contrast, Vendler mentions the difference between (a) imagining eating a lemon (sour taste) and imagining yourself eating a lemon (pinched face) and (b) imagining being on the rack (agony) and imagining yourself being on the rack (distorted limbs). He refers to the contrast exemplified in these cases as the distinction between "subjective" and "objective" acts of imagination.

In subjective acts of imagination, we might say, a person imagines a given scenario "from the inside" or "from the first-person perspective." Or again, we might say—using the terminology I will employ in this chapter—that she imagines the situation "as subject." But these are clearly just sophisticated labels for a kind of imagining our basic understanding of which derives from our familiarity with the contrast between imagining such things as:

(1a) being F
(1b) doing A
(1c) undergoing P

and imagining such things as

(2a) S's being F
(2b) S's doing A
(2c) S's undergoing P.

To speak of imagining *myself* being F (etc.) is ambiguous between these two varieties of imagining: it may be understood as merely a formal, somewhat pompous way of expressing the sort of imagining involved in (1a), or as a special case of the sort of imagining in (2a): one in which I imagine a scene in which I myself am the person who is F.

In the sort of imagining evoked in (1a)–(1c), by contrast, one's "imaginative project"—to use Bernard Williams's (1973) felicitous phrase—does not on the face of it involve imagining a certain person at all. This comes out not only in the naturalness of using a subjectless verb phrase to express the topic of such imagining, but also in the outward-directedness of what is imagined. In an objective act of imagining, I might imagine *myself swimming in the ocean*, as seen from a vantage point high above on the cliff; but when I perform the subjective act of imagining *swimming in the ocean*, what I imagine is not *myself* but certain things I might experience: the chill of the water, the salty taste, the tug of the current, etc.[3] Such experiences must, of course, have a subject, so when I imagine having them, what I imagine in some sense presupposes the existence of a subject; but no such subject falls within the scope of what is imagined. This is evident if we ask ourselves what attributes the subject who has these experiences is supposed to have. The difficulty we face in answering this question is not just that the relevant subject is imagined hazily; the problem is that we simply draw a blank, except insofar as imagining the subject to have certain attributes (e.g., a waterproof wristwatch visible on his right wrist) belongs to the project of imagining the experience of swimming itself. Setting such complications aside, we may say that what is imagined in subjective acts of imagination is imagined *as subject*, but not *as having a certain subject*. This is not to say that one imagines these experiences to occur subjectlessly, of course. One simply does not undertake to imagine any subject who has them, not even oneself.

4.3. Representing-as-Subject in General

Vendler focuses on the contrast between subjective and objective acts of imagination, but my interest in this chapter will be in a general structure of representation of which this is just one case. To see the generality of the topic, consider the contrasts between:

(3a) anticipating being F   (3b) anticipating S's being F
(4a) wanting to do A   (4b) wanting S to do A
(5a) caring about suffering P   (5b) caring about S's suffering P.

---

[3] But might I not, at least, imagine myself in the sense that I might imagine the increasing feeling of fatigue in my arms, the pounding of my heart, etc.? Properly understood, I think these kinds of imagination do not falsify the point made in the text: that when I am imagining the situation as subject, I do not imagine myself but certain things I experience. I will not be in a position fully to clarify this point, however, until we discuss bodily awareness in Chapter 6.

In each of these pairs, we find a contrast between a "subjective" and an "objective" form of a given attitude. In the objective forms, the topic is a possible state of affairs involving some individual's being, doing, or undergoing something, a topic naturally expressed using a full subject-verb structure. In the subjective forms, the topic is a mode of being, doing, or undergoing conceived "from the inside"—a topic it is natural to express using a subjectless (infinitive or gerund) verb phrase. These examples suggest that Vendler's contrast between subjective and objective acts of imagination is a special case of a more general distinction.

In objective acts of anticipating, wanting, or caring, one represents the relevant case of being, doing, or undergoing as having a certain subject. By contrast, in the corresponding subjective acts, it at least *seems* that one does not represent the being, doing, or undergoing *as* having a particular subject. This way of describing the matter is contentious, however, for many contemporary philosophers and linguists would insist that, even in their subjective forms, the true objects of such attitudes' ascriptions are full subject-verb structures.[4]

On this view, although the verbal objects of attitudes (3a)–(5a) do not include an explicit subject term, there is in fact an implied subject that forms part of the content represented. This subject need not be indicated in the verbal formula because competent speakers tacitly know rules for moving from subjectless verb phrases used in such contexts to associated subject-verb structures, such as the rule that

(6a) S wants to do A

is tantamount to

(6b) S wants herself to do A

or, as contemporary linguists tend to write it,

(6c) S wants PRO to do A

where "PRO" is an unpronounced pronoun that is "controlled" by the attitude verb, so that it refers to the subject of that verb, S.[5] Given this interpretation of the syntax of (6a), it is natural to suppose that the semantic value of the infinitival clause "to do A" is in fact a full (albeit untensed) proposition: that S herself does

---

[4] For a contemporary defense of this sort of position, see, e.g., Stanley 2013: Ch. 3. There is also an important tradition of opposition to this sort of analysis, to which I am indebted. For different forms of such opposition, see, e.g., Perry 1986, Recanati 2007, and Musholt 2015.

[5] More precisely, this pronoun must refer to S in a specifically "*de se*" way, so that S could express what she wants by saying: "What I want is: *myself* to do A." More about this shortly.

A.[6] And then the difference between subjective and objective attitudes looks less deep than I have suggested: although the subjective forms differ superficially from the objective ones, at a deeper level of analysis they are both attitudes toward propositions whose content is that a certain subject performs a certain action.

Now, I am not a linguist, and I am not in a position to dispute the prevailing linguistic analysis of subjectless verb clauses. To integrate the treatment of such clauses into a systematic linguistic theory, it may be necessary to represent their syntax in the way (partially) indicated in (6c), and to treat the semantical objects of such clauses as propositions. But whatever the advantages of such a regimentation, they should not blind us to the palpable difference between (3a)–(5a) and (3b)–(5b). It is true that if S wants to do A, then her want is satisfied only if S herself does A; but if we insist on reading the whole of this satisfaction condition into the content of S's want, we will be forced to recognize an ambiguity in wants with the content:

(6d) S herself does A.

For consider (e.g.) a person who wants to quit smoking (because this would be good for her health), but who does not want to take the steps that quitting would require (because it is torment to go through the day without cigarettes). Of such a person we might naturally say that she wants it to *be the case* that she quits, but she does not actually want to *do* it. But if the true object of the desire *to quit smoking* is the one displayed in (6d), then making sense of this distinction will require us to recognize two ways of wanting *that I myself do A*: the objective way that merely implies wanting it to be the case that I do A, and the subjective way that implies actually wanting to do A.[7] Similar examples could be constructed for anticipating and caring.

What such examples show, I submit, is that attitudes like anticipating, wanting, and caring about can have, as the focus of their intentionality, either an objective state of affairs consisting of someone's being/doing/undergoing something, or a mere being, doing, or undergoing, considered *from the standpoint* of

---

[6] Though some linguists interpret the semantics of PRO-constructions differently. See, e.g., Chierchia 1989.

[7] Note that what is at issue here is not simply the contrast between a form of concern for myself that is "immune to error through misidentification" (IEM) and a form that is open to error through misidentification. It is true that, if I want to do A, it does not make sense to suppose that this might consist in my wanting someone to do A, but mistakenly taking myself to be the person whose doing of A I desire. So wanting *to do A* passes the standard test for being IEM. But so too do some forms of wanting it to be the case *that I myself do A*. If I simply form the desire that I myself do A, without identifying some individual (e.g., the person in the mirror) as myself, then this "objective" want is also IEM.

the subject who is, does, or suffers it.[8] I would want to maintain this even if our best semantic theory of such attitude ascriptions assigned them uniformly propositional objects. For even if this were so, I would argue—and will argue in more detail in the next section—that there are crucial differences between holding an attitude toward the relevant proposition considered objectively and holding an attitude toward it considered from the standpoint of its subject.

If this is right, then however we may go on to regiment attitude ascriptions like (3a)–(5a) for the purposes of semantic theory, we should recognize a difference between subjective attitudes like (3a)–(5a) and objective attitudes like (3b)–(5b). Nothing prevents us from marking this difference by distinguishing two senses of wanting "that I myself shall do A" (cf. anticipating that I myself will be F, caring that I myself will suffer P). But it is more perspicuous, I would suggest, to avoid ambiguity by stipulatively reserving talk of wanting "that I myself do A" for the case in which the subject has an "objective" desire for it to be the case that she herself does something, i.e., a desire of the form

(4b)   wanting S to do A

where she herself is the S whose doing of A she wants. We can then express the contrasting "subjective" desire in the ordinary way, using the (at least superficially) subjectless form

(4a)   wanting to do A.

I will observe these stipulations in what follows, and for any attitude Ψ that admits of a contrast between a subjective form like (4a) and an objective form like (4b), I will refer to the subjective form as Ψ-ing *as subject*, and the objective form as Ψ-ing *concerning a certain subject*.

---

[8] It does not matter, for my purposes, whether every verb phrase that can appear in such contexts gives rise to a subjective/objective contrast. Perhaps there is no real difference between, e.g., imagining being related to Grover Cleveland and imagining that I am related to Grover Cleveland. That is, perhaps there is no such thing as imagining being related to Grover Cleveland "as subject," as contrasted with merely imagining a world in which a certain fact holds true of the person who is in fact myself. Be that as it may, it remains true that a range of possible beings, doings, and undergoings give rise to a palpable subjective/objective contrast, which we can recognize even in the absence of a grammatical test by which to distinguish the relevant verb phrases. I have attempted to bring out this contrast by connecting it with a distinction between two kinds of attitude ascriptions that we can make in English, but even if this difference in grammatical structure does not always give rise to the relevant contrast, I would still want to claim that there are cases in which the contrast is palpable. It is such cases that will concern us going forward.

4.4. Subjective versus Objective Attitudes: Some Contrasts

The important point for present purposes is that, for any attitude Ψ that admits of a subjective/objective contrast, Ψ-ing as subject is not just a special case of Ψ-ing concerning a certain subject, but a distinct type of attitude requiring a separate investigation. A person who wants to do something, for instance, does not simply want it to be the case that she herself does something. She does not simply hold an attitude toward a state of affairs of which she is the subject, regarding this state of affairs, as it were, from a God's-eye point of view. Rather, she desires the relevant doing "from the first-person perspective," as philosophers say. But what does this mean? What is it to anticipate, want, or care about something "as subject," if it is not simply to anticipate, want, or care about the obtaining of a state of affairs involving oneself? Let us consider some examples.

Suppose I want to go to Kansas City: How does this differ from merely wanting it to be the case that I go to Kansas City? A natural first characterization of the difference is this: whereas the former desire is *engaged*, the latter is *detached*. If I want it to be the case that I go to Kansas City, I simply want a certain fact to hold true of myself; but if I actually want to go to Kansas City, the primary object of my desire is not that something should hold true of me—though of course, if my desire is fulfilled, it will be true that I have gone to Kansas City. Still, the primary object of my desire is: to go to Kansas City. This is not a state of affairs consisting of someone's doing something, but an action, something any number of people might do. Wanting to go to Kansas City will involve seeing this action as attractive, and what makes it attractive need not show *my going there* to be a desirable state of affairs. According to a song in the musical "Oklahoma":

> Everything's like a dream in Kansas City,
> It's better than a magic lantern show.

If these lines are true, then everyone has a reason to want to go to Kansas City, not because *his or her* going there is desirable—that is quite another question—but simply because *going there* is desirable, given the remarkable attractions of the place.

More generally, wanting to do A is made intelligible by considerations that show *doing A* to be desirable, and such considerations need not show the state of affairs in which I do A to be desirable. Wanting to learn to play Chopin's *Nocturnes*, for instance, is perfectly intelligible, because the *Nocturnes* are beautiful, but this does not show that it is desirable—even from my own point of view—for me to realize the state of affairs in which I become one more mediocre interpreter of Chopin's *Nocturnes*. Whether this state of affairs is desirable is not the point: the relevant question for me is not whether it is a desirable state of affairs that I learn to play Chopin's *Nocturnes*, but whether learning to play the *Nocturnes* is a desirable thing to do. We may sum this up by saying that, in contrast to wanting it to be the case that one does A, wanting *to do A* is outward-looking in its perspective on what is desirable: it focuses on what one proposes to do, not on one's own doing of it.[9]

A person who merely wants it to be the case that she goes to Kansas City, by contrast, wants something to hold true of herself at some point in the future: that she has gone to Kansas City. She wants this fact to be a part of her life story, as it were. There is something palpably self-involved about this sort of wanting: one wants, not primarily to *do* something, but for it to *be the case of oneself* that one does it. If one tries to imagine the kind of attitude toward life that would make sense of such a desire, it is natural to think of a kind of second-order desire to "live one's life to the fullest" or to check items off what is sometimes (hideously) called one's "bucket list." It is certainly possible to desire things in this mode, but when one does so, one stands, as it were, one step back from the standpoint of the ordinary practical desire. One is concerned, not primarily with the desirability of going to a certain city, but with the desirability of one's being someone who goes there. In this sense, one's attitude is detached from the standpoint of first-order agential desire.

Moreover, there is a certain passivity about one's attitude toward the state of affairs one wants. One wants it to *come about* that one goes to Kansas City, of course, but this does not imply any commitment about the role this desire must play in *bringing about* this state of affairs. After all, wanting it to be the case that I go to Kansas City is structurally analogous to wanting it to be the case that my friend Sally goes to Kansas City, and the latter desire clearly does not imply any

---

[9] I do not mean to suggest that the question whether one desires X can in general be identified with the question whether one takes X to be desirable. My claim is simply that the distinction between the desirability conditions of *doing A* and the desirability conditions of *my doing A* shows that these constitute distinct objects of desire, even though fulfillment of my desire to do A implies my doing A. Note that it is consistent with this point to admit that facts about my own nature and situation may affect the desirability *for me* of doing A. If my hands are severely arthritic, for instance, there may be less to be said, from my standpoint, for learning to play Chopin than there would be if this activity were considered from a more favorable standpoint. But this kind of relativity of the desirability of doing A to an individual standpoint is a relativity in the desirability of *doing A*, which remains a different topic from the desirability of the state of affairs in which *I do A*. We can mark this difference by drawing a scope distinction between

(a) the desirability for me of doing A

and

(b) the desirability of my doing A.

In these formulations, only what appears to the right of "of" characterizes the object whose desirability is under consideration. So the "for me" in (a) falls outside the scope of the desirability function, as it were: it merely relativizes the desirability of *doing A* to a certain person, whereas in (b), the fact that it will be I who does A belongs to the object whose desirability is considered. Thus, even where my own standpoint affects what it is desirable for me to do, the *object* whose desirability is considered may remain an action, not a state of affairs in which I do something.

particular commitments about what role my so desiring should play in bringing this about. It may be true that, inasmuch as I want Sally to go to Kansas City, I must be disposed to take steps which (I believe) will lead to her going. But if she just goes without my taking any such steps, then my desire will be fully satisfied, for what I want is simply that a certain state of affairs should obtain, not that my so desiring should play some specific role in making it obtain. So too if I want it to be the case that I go to Kansas City: in this case, *what* I want is that I myself do something, but again, my desire is simply that this should come to pass, not that my so wanting this should play some particular role in bringing it about. In this sense, too, my desire is detached, even though what I desire is that I myself do something.

If I want *to go to Kansas City*, by contrast, what I want is not the sort of thing that can come about independently of my so wanting. An action is a type of thing to do, and to want to do it is to want in virtue of this very state of desire to bring about an instance of doing it. Hence to want to go to Kansas City is necessarily to be concerned with the problem of how to realize this aim:

> I might take a plane, I might take a train,
> But if I have to walk I'm going to get there just the same.

These reflections from Wilbert Harrison's 1959 hit "Kansas City" express the kind of open-ended engagement with the question of how to perform an action that is characteristic of wanting to do A. Such engagement cannot be reproduced through any mere specification of what one wants it to be the case that one does: for however specifically we describe what the subject wants herself to do, this remains merely a description of a state of affairs concerning which she has a detached desire that it should obtain. A subject who wants *to do A*, by contrast, looks upon the prospect of her own doing A, not from a perspective of transcendent approbation, but from the standpoint of the agent who must see to it that A-ing is accomplished. Her interest in doing A is not an abstract interest in a certain outcome, but an engaged concern with a practical problem.

This sort of agential interest in doing A will inform a person's apprehension of her surroundings in characteristic ways: things will present themselves as opportunities or obstacles in relation to her aim. This outward-looking orientation of practical desire is emphasized in Sartre's *The Transcendence of the Ego*, which has been an important source of inspiration for this chapter:

> I feel pity for Peter and I come to his aid. For my consciousness, one thing alone exists at that moment: Peter-having-to-be-helped. This quality of 'having-to-be-helped' is to be found in Peter. It acts on me like a force. . . . At this level, the desire [to help Peter] is given to consciousness as centrifugal (it transcends

itself, it is the thetic consciousness of 'having-to-be' and the non-thetic consciousness of itself) and impersonal (there is no *me*: I am faced with the pain of Peter in the same way I am faced with the color of this inkwell). There is an objective world of things and actions that have been performed or are going to be performed, and actions come to adhere like qualities to the things that summon them. (TE 56/39)[10]

I hope the foregoing reflections help us to see a point in these intuitively appealing but somewhat wild remarks. The point concerns what it is to want something "as subject": it is to be focused, not on oneself, but on problems and opportunities presented by one's environment. These problems and opportunities are there to be perceived only insofar as one wants to do A, but they are represented as characteristics of the environment itself, not as aspects of one's attitude toward it.

These features of wanting-as-subject have counterparts in the case of other subjective attitudes. In the first place, the object of such attitudes is characteristically not a certain subject's being, doing, or undergoing something, but simply: being, doing, or undergoing something. As we have seen, to imagine swimming is not, except incidentally, to imagine *oneself* swimming. Similarly, to anticipate being hit on the head is not to anticipate oneself being hit on the head—though of course, if what one anticipates comes to pass, it will be one's own head that is hit. Still, the object of one's anticipation is not a state of affairs in which a certain person (namely, oneself) is hit, but an undergoing whose logical type can be expressed using Church's lambda notation:

(7) $(\lambda x)(x\text{'s head is hit})$.[11]

When I anticipate (7), *what* I anticipate is something that might happen to anyone—being hit on the head. I do not anticipate *that* this will happen to me. The fact that it will be I who receive the blow follows, not from what I anticipate, but from the fact that it is I who anticipate it: it follows, that is, from my being the holder of the relevant attitude, not from the sheer content of the attitude I hold.[12]

---

[10] I take Sartre's "thetic"/"nonthetic" contrast to be simply an alternative vocabulary for the positional/nonpositional contrast. Some commentators suggest that Sartre speaks of "thetic" consciousness where he has in mind consciousness *that p* and "positional" consciousness where he is thinking of consciousness *of O* (cf. Gardner 2009: 45); but while this would be a natural distinction to draw, I do not know of any specific textual basis for this interpretation.

[11] Church's notation is useful because it allows us to mark the fact that the object anticipated is not a proposition but something predicable of the thinking subject. Care is needed, however, in interpreting this predicable element. If we read (7) as "the property of being someone who is hit on the head," we build the idea of being a particular person into the content the subject anticipates. To avoid this, we should simply read (7) as "the property of being hit on the head."

[12] Of course, any normal self-conscious subject will understand that, when she experiences a blow to the head, a particular person receives a blow. So if she anticipates being hit on the head, she will be in a position also to anticipate that a certain person, namely she herself, will be hit. But she will

Secondly, there is a certain outward-directedness that characterizes all subjective attitudes. In the case of imagining swimming, the mark of this is that what I imagine is not a certain person (namely, myself) doing something, but certain perceptible features of the situation I would encounter: the chill of the water, the tug of the current, etc. In the case of wanting to do A, the mark is that my desire to do A is expressed, not in my having a favorable attitude toward the state of affairs in which *I* do A, but in my seeing *doing A* as attractive, and so seeing things in my environment as problems or opportunities relative to this purpose. And in the case of anticipating being hit on the head, the mark is that I anticipate something that will happen *to* me (being hit), not the event of its happening to *me* (my being hit). In all these cases, my perspective on the relevant state, action, or passion is, as we might put it, immanent rather than transcendent: the focus of my concern (where "concern" is used as a generic expression ranging over various possible attitudes) is not on *my* being, doing, or undergoing something; it is on aspects of the situation I confront, regarded in a manner characteristic of the attitude I hold.

4.5. Consciousness-as-Subject and Self-Knowledge

We have been exploring a contrast between two forms of representation of a situation: an immersed form of representation from the standpoint of a subject *in* the situation and a detached form of representation *of* the total situation, including the subject's own place in it. But our ultimate interest is more specific: we want to examine a (purported) contrast between two forms of *awareness of our own mental states*, one of which "posits" these states as such, while the other makes us aware of them without positing them. I now want to argue that we can clarify the latter contrast by relating it to the former.

To bring this out, it will help to return to a thought from Richard Moran that figured prominently in Chapter 2. As we saw, Moran claims that the standard, epistemologically oriented way of framing the topic of self-knowledge is distorting. Contemporary philosophical discussions of self-knowledge standardly set out from the observation that we seem to know our own minds in a special and privileged way. My knowledge of my own present mental states of mind seems normally to be distinctively *immediate*—not based on specifiable

---

anticipate this, not primitively, but in virtue of anticipating *being hit on the head* and having a general understanding of how subjective experiences are related to objective states of affairs. Yet surely it is possible to anticipate being hit on the head without possessing such an understanding: a dog, for instance, might anticipate being hit on the head, and take evasive action, though it is not obvious that dogs comprehend themselves as objective particulars. If this is right, anticipating being hit on the head need not itself involve having any idea of *someone's* being hit on the head—and so *mutatis mutandis* for other subjective attitude forms.

grounds—and distinctively *authoritative*—there seems to be some default presumption that I am in a position to know my own mind, whereas no such presumption is afforded to my claims about the mental states of other persons. According to Moran, however, this way of framing our topic leaves out something crucial.

What is distinctive of our knowledge of our own minds, Moran claims, is not merely that we have specially immediate and authoritative access to information about our own mental states; it is that we normally relate to these states in a nonspectatorial way. I do not merely know *of* my present mental states with special ease and assurance; I know them "from the first-person standpoint," in a way that contrasts with a spectatorial knowledge of those same states. It would be possible, Moran argues, for a person to have immediate and authoritative knowledge of her own attitudes and yet remain in a spectatorial relation to them:

> [T]he conditions so far specified could still apply to a case where, say, I had immediate awareness of my attitude (perhaps in the way one has immediate awareness of the disposition of one's limbs), but where the attitude was one of which I could make no sense, whose reasons were opaque to me.... [I]f the attitude in question [were] a belief, it would then be a belief I was conscious *of*, but it would not have any of the first-person character that is indicated by referring to something as a conscious belief. (Moran 2001: 33)

When we ask how we know our own beliefs, Moran suggests, what should really interest us is the kind of awareness we call "conscious belief." But, he argues, the standard way of framing the topic encourages us to overlook the distinctive character of this awareness and to focus simply on the immediacy and authority of the relevant knowledge. In this way, we are led to think of self-knowledge as a kind of privileged access to facts about oneself, whereas in fact it is a different form of awareness altogether, one with a distinctively "first-person character."

Moran's distinction between "conscious beliefs" and beliefs we are merely "conscious of" is intuitively attractive, but what exactly does it mean to believe something consciously, in such a way that one's awareness of one's own belief has a "first-person character"? I want to suggest that Moran's point comes into clearer focus if we connect it with our distinction between a subjective and an objective form of awareness. To see this, notice first that, like wanting, imagining, and anticipating, cognitive states such as knowing and being aware of admit of a distinction between subjective and objective forms:

(8a) being aware of V-ing (8b) being aware of S's V-ing
(9a) being conscious of V-ing (9b) being conscious of S's V-ing
(10a) knowingly V-ing (10b) knowing S to be V-ing.

It is easiest to draw the contrast in the case of verbs like "to be aware of" and "to be conscious of," where the same cognitive verb can take both a subjectless verb phrase and a full subject-verb structure as its object. By contrast, the English verb "to know" requires a full subject-verb phrase as its complement. This seems, however, to be a superficial feature of English usage: there are other languages that allow "know" to take a subjectless verb phrase in a manner akin to "be aware of," and even in English we can ascribe the subjective variety of knowledge by using the adverbial form "knowingly," as in (10a).[13] For present purposes, at any rate, any semantic distinctions between knowing, being conscious, and being aware of something will be unimportant: what will matter is the distinction between the subjective and objective forms of these states. So in what follows I will speak interchangeably of "knowing," "being conscious," and "being aware," using whichever term is grammatically convenient in context.

Once again, the importance of this subjective-objective contrast will be clearest if we consider a case in which I myself am the topic of both kinds of awareness. So consider, for instance, the contrast between

(11a) being aware of believing p (11b) being aware of myself believing p.

As usual, there is a reading of (11b) on which it is just a formal, somewhat pompous way of expressing the sort of awareness ascribed in (11a): the "myself" in (11b) may simply be read as emphasizing the contrast with being aware of another person's believing p, without implying the positive presence of an idea of myself in the content of my awareness. There is, however, another reading of (11b) on which it expresses a kind of awareness quite different from the one ascribed in (11a). For example, an employer who discovers that he consistently responds more favorably to the dossiers of male applicants than to the dossiers of similarly qualified female applicants might (arguably) become aware of *himself believing that male applicants are superior*, although he is not aware of *believing that male applicants are superior*.[14] That is, he might become *conscious that* he himself has the property of believing male applicants are superior, though he

---

[13] For discussion of the possibility of knowledge-ascriptions involving subjectless verb phrases in other languages (with special reference to Italian), see Chierchia 1989: 20. Note also that, like knowing, consciousness can be predicated adverbially. Rather than speaking of

(9a) being conscious of V-ing

we may speak of

(9a′) consciously V-ing.

The difference between (9a) and (9a′) seems to be that (9a′) more strongly suggests that the subject has *mere* consciousness-as-subject of V-ing, whereas (9a) may be read either as ascribing either mere consciousness-as-subject or explicit self-knowledge grounded in consciousness-as-subject. These distinctions will be clarified shortly in the main text.

[14] I adapt this example from Peacocke 1998. Some readers may object that such a person does not really *believe* that male applicants are superior, although he has an unconscious bias in favor of them.

does not *consciously believe* that male applicants are superior. When he reflects on the latter proposition, he may find it dubious or outright false: it may not express his conscious view about the qualifications of different job applicants. Nevertheless, he may be forced to admit that his decision-making reflects his at some level accepting that male applicants are superior. In this way, he might become aware that he himself believes something that he is not conscious-as-subject of believing.

Although Moran does not put the point in these terms, I would suggest that the distinction he draws between consciously believing something and merely knowing that one believes something is best understood in terms of our distinction between a subjective and an objective form of awareness. The special "first-personal" awareness of belief Moran emphasizes has just the features we noted in other subjective attitude forms: (i) its focus is not on a fact about me (that I believe p), but on a condition any subject might be in (believing p), and (ii) its perspective on this condition is not the transcendent standpoint of someone asking whether a certain person believes p, but the immanent, outward-looking standpoint of someone considering whether the proposition that p is credible. When I am aware of believing p in this subjective way, I *consciously* take p to be true. This does not consist in my being aware of a fact about myself, but in my seeing the proposition that p as convincing. Not every subject who believes that p does so consciously in this sense: for instance, the employer who (unconsciously) believes that male applicants are superior does not. When a subject consciously believes p, her consciousness of believing p is not a further cognitive state distinct from her believing p, but a characteristic manner of believing p, as is neatly captured in the adverbial formulation, "*consciously* believing p."[15]

When I speak of *consciousness-as-subject* of a state, action, or passion, it is this sort of immanent awareness that I have in mind. Being conscious-as-subject of believing p does not imply knowing that one believes p, for one may consciously believe p without holding any attitude toward the proposition *I believe that p*. Moreover, as we observed in the case of the biased application reviewer, it seems possible for someone to know that he himself believes p without having consciousness-as-subject of believing p. So if we call the explicitly self-ascribed

---

I sympathize with the sense that talk of "belief" has its proper home in characterizations of conscious attitudes toward propositions, but the point I want to make does not really hang on the application of this term. At any rate, it seems possible for a person to have an unconscious bias favoring male applicants over female applicants. If a person discovers himself to have such a bias, he may be said to become *conscious of his own bias*, but still he is not *consciously biased* in favor of male applicants (as he would be if he consciously believed that male applicants are superior). It is the existence of this distinction between two types of consciousness/awareness/knowledge, one objective and the other subjective, that is crucial for my argument here.

[15] Cf. Moran 2001: 31.

kind of knowledge *self-knowledge*, we must distinguish between having consciousness-as-subject of a state, action, or passion and having explicit self-knowledge about it.

4.6. Consciousness-as-Subject and Nonpositional Consciousness

With this distinction in hand, we can return to the topic of nonpositional consciousness. Recall that we took nonpositional consciousness of our own mental states to be expressed, not in the specific representational contents of these states, but in the modes of presentation via which different types of mental states characteristically present their contents. My Sartrean claim can now be stated as follows: these modes of presentation supply us with consciousness-as-subject, but not explicit self-knowledge, of our own mental states. When I say that these modes give us "nonpositional" consciousness of our own mental states, this is what I mean.

But is this a genuine form of awareness of our own mental states? At the beginning of this chapter, I mentioned a possible doubt about this claim: that even if there are modes of presentation characteristic of different types of representational states, it does not follow that these modes express awareness of the relevant mental states. Thus, we observed, my experience of strangers as inviting and agreeable might vary with my state of drunkenness, and yet it does not follow that my experiencing strangers as increasingly inviting and agreeable expresses awareness—even "nonpositional" awareness—that I am increasingly drunk. To show that the modes of presentation characteristic of different types of mental states express nonpositional awareness of these states, then, it does not suffice merely to show that these modes of presentation vary with the subject's mental state. It is necessary also to justify the claim that this variation expresses a genuine form of awareness of the relevant states.

I think we are now in a position to respond to this challenge. We can make three points. First, we have seen that it is possible for a subject to be in a given mental state without having consciousness-as-subject of this state. This possibility is exemplified in one way by our biased application reviewer, who does not consciously believe that male applicants are superior, but who does, as we say, believe this "at some level." It would be exemplified in a different way by a blindsighted subject who does not consciously see anything in a certain region of her visual field, but who is nevertheless visually aware of things in this field "at some level." And it would be exemplified in a third way by a person who does not consciously feel angry at a friend's unthinkingly belittling remark, but whose conduct following the remark expresses the presence, "at some level," of persisting anger at this remark. Now, the point to notice about these cases is that, when a subject lacks consciousness-as-subject of her own state, the object of the relevant state is *not* presented to her in the corresponding mode. Her friend's remark is not presented to her as infuriating (though she is in fact infuriated by it); the object in her blind field is not available to her as a "this" (though she is in fact visually aware of it); and the world is not presented to her as one in which male applicants are superior (though she—or more probably he?—does at some level so regard it). What this shows, I suggest, is that awareness of objects under such modes of presentation expresses a relation to one's mental states that stands in contrast to sheer unconsciousness of these states. This relation is not one of explicit self-knowledge, but it is one of inhabiting the relevant states *consciously*, in a sense that contrasts with the kind of unconsciousness exemplified in the aberrant cases just described. To just this extent, these modal features of our representational states do express a genuine form of awareness of these states, albeit one that differs structurally from positional self-knowledge in the ways I have tried to describe.

Secondly, we have seen that, although nonpositional consciousness of a mental state M does not require explicit representation of oneself as in M, it does require a certain intelligent responsiveness to what is in fact one's being in M. Thus, as we observed in the last chapter, a person who is capable of representing her own future in the way we have marked with the expression

$$\text{I will}_1 \phi$$

will think of such aspects of her future as settled in ways that reflect an understanding of them as her own choices (e.g., as to be determined by her consideration of the desirability of doing ϕ, as having implications for what else she must do, etc.), rather than merely as predictable facts about her own future that are not up to her. Similarly, a person who is capable of representing an object in her environment in the way we have marked with the expression

$$\text{this O}$$

will show, in her manner of thinking about such objects, an intelligent sensitivity to the satisfaction-conditions required for her to perceive them: she will not represent objects in this mode except when they are perceivable by her; she will be disposed continuously to represent an object as "this" only so long as she can keep perceptual track of it; she will seek to gain information about such an object in certain specific ways that are made possible by perception; etc. In these and similar ways, such modes of presentation do not merely covary with the subject's mental state, but express her pre-reflective understanding of the specific nature and significance of this state. So on this ground, too, we are justified in conceiving of these modes as expressing genuine awareness of the states they mark, even though the subject does not conceptualize these states as such.

Finally, consider the relationship between nonpositional consciousness of being in M and explicit self-knowledge that one is in M. We have said that the former does not entail the latter, yet there is clearly an intimate relationship between these two forms of awareness. For, as we have seen, a person who has nonpositional consciousness of being, doing, or undergoing something can acquire self-knowledge proper, not by acquiring some new piece of information, but simply by *reflecting* on what she already knows.[16] Indeed, as I argued in Chapter 3, it is our possession of such nonpositional consciousness of our own mental states that warrants us in treating questions about our own mental states as transparent to corresponding questions about the non-mental world.

Nonpositional consciousness of one's own mental state is not, however, merely a basis for *acquiring* explicit self-knowledge of that state, but a precondition of the continued existence of such knowledge. For consider a person who acquires self-knowledge by reflecting on a belief of which she has nonpositional consciousness, but who then ceases to have nonpositional consciousness of the relevant belief. That is, she falls into a condition like that of the biased application reviewer, in which she holds a belief that p but cannot ascribe it transparently, by reflecting on whether p is true. Surely the thing to say about such a person is that she no longer *knows* whether she believes that p. She may remember that she *did* believe that p at some time in the past, but the fact that this belief still persists in her is not known to her—unless she comes to know it on some other basis, such as self-observation. So her nonpositional consciousness of her belief not only puts her in a position to acquire explicit self-knowledge of that belief, but is a condition of her retaining the normal kind of knowledge of her own belief state. As soon as she ceases to have nonpositional consciousness of the relevant belief, any knowledge she may have of it becomes at best a form of *alienated* self-knowledge: knowledge *that* she believes something not grounded in consciously *believing* it.

Nonpositional consciousness of believing p is thus the essential precondition of non-alienated self-knowledge that one believes that p. Since what

---

[16] My conception of reflection is indebted to Recanati (2007 and 2012), who also uses the term "reflection" to refer to an activity in which features of a subjective mode of presentation are made explicit topics of thought (cf. Recanati 2012: 192ff). Recanati offers an example that provides a useful illustration of the idea. Suppose I am proprioceptively aware of standing. The content of this awareness, according to Recanati, is not that *I* am standing; it is simply the existence of standing, presented in a characteristically "internal mode." The step to the judgment *I am standing* consists in my reflectively recognizing that this way of being presented with standing is a mode of being presented with *my* standing. Mastering the ascriptive application of the concept *standing* on the basis of proprioception involves mastering this kind of transition. I am suggesting that we make a similar transition in moving from consciousness-as-subject of believing p to explicit self-knowledge that I believe p.

differentiates knowledge that *p* from mere true belief that *p* must be some linkage of the relevant belief to a mode of awareness that *p*, it follows that what we have called "nonpositional consciousness of believing *p*" is a mode of awareness of one's belief that *p*. And the same kinds of points we have made about belief could also be made, *mutatis mutandis*, about other types of mental states. Thus, although nonpositional consciousness of one's own mental state does not involve explicit self-representation, it does amount to a form of self-awareness—namely, the form we have called "consciousness-as-subject" of our own states, an awareness whose distinctively "first-personal" character our inquiries have helped us to understand.

5
Self-Consciousness

> [I]t is not said to the mind: "Know thyself," as it is said: "Know the Cherubim and the Seraphim!" For they are absent, and we believe what we have been taught concerning them. ... Nor as it is said: "Know the will of that man!" It is utterly impossible for us to perceive or to understand his will unless he makes it known by some corporeal signs, and even then we would believe rather than understand. Nor as is it said to a man: "Look at your face!" This can only be done by means of a mirror. ... But when it is said to the mind: "Know thyself," it knows itself at the very instant in which it understands the word "thyself"; and it knows itself for no other reason than that it is present to itself.
> —Augustine, *On the Trinity* (2002), 10.9.12

5.1. Introduction

In the two preceding chapters, I argued that, in order to explain our capacity for transparent self-knowledge, we must recognize a form of self-awareness more basic than the knowledge we express in explicit self-ascriptions of mental states. In this more basic form of self-awareness, I claimed, the knowing subject does not represent herself or her own mental states as such, but merely represents non-mental objects in modes that express an implicit or "nonpositional" awareness of her own mental states. In the previous chapter, we saw how this implicit awareness amounts to a kind of *consciousness-as-subject* of our own condition, and why this consciousness must be sharply distinguished from explicit *self-knowledge*. Nevertheless, I suggested that we can normally achieve explicit self-knowledge by merely *reflecting* on this more basic consciousness-as-subject.

By now, I hope the attractions of this Sartrean reflectivist approach to transparent self-knowledge are starting to become apparent. In order fully to understand the reflectivist proposal, however, we need to achieve a more abstract and theoretical understanding of reflection and how it allows us to move, with warrant, from a form of awareness in which we do not represent ourselves and our own mental states to a form in which we do. We shall see that this transition raises a number of conceptual problems, which we will need to resolve in order fully to comprehend the role of reflection in self-knowledge and in our cognition more generally.

I will defer several of these problems until Part III of this book, when we will examine the activity of reflection in detail and trace its role in supplying us with a conceptual understanding of our own mental lives. There is one problem, however, that cannot be deferred if we are to achieve even a preliminary understanding of the step from nonpositional consciousness to positional self-knowledge: namely, the problem of understanding how nonpositional consciousness of various particular mental states can ground knowledge that these several states belong to a single *subject*. For it seems clear that, in explicit self-knowledge, each of us ascribes his or her mental states to a single subject, whom s/he designates with the term "I." To know my own mind, I must become aware of such facts as these: that *I* feel a pain in my shoulder, that *I* am thinking about tomorrow's lecture, that *I* believe it is going to rain, etc.; and these ascriptions seem to commit me to the idea that these various states belong to a single knowing subject. Yet if my knowledge of such facts is grounded in a "nonpositional" consciousness of psychological states in which I myself am not presented, then the emergence of the first person in these reflective self-ascriptions can look mysterious. Where exactly does this "I" come from, and how is its introduction justified?

I mean this question to evoke a famous dispute about the content of self-awareness, which we might call the *Egoist/Anti-Egoist Controversy*. As is well known, Descartes and St. Augustine, the archetypal Egoists, claimed that my awareness of thinking gives me indubitable awareness that I, the thinker, exist.[1] They also share a subtler thought about the significance of this Cogito argument: that my indubitable awareness of thinking not only assures me *that* I exist, but also gives me an understanding of what *sort* of thing I am, namely a mind. This is what Augustine means when he says, in the epigraph to this chapter, that the mind "knows itself at the very instant in which it understands the word 'thyself.'" In understanding the Delphic injunction to "Know thyself," I understand that I am commanded to know *myself*; and Augustine claims that, in understanding this, I already have everything I need to fulfill the injunction, since my understanding of the first person contains an understanding of what I, *qua* mind or thinking subject, essentially am. And Descartes makes a similar point when, reflecting on the lesson of the *Cogito*, he writes that

> I am, then, in the strict sense only a thing that thinks; that is, I am a mind, or intelligence, or intellect, or reason—words whose meanings I have been ignorant of until now.[2]

---

[1] Cf. Descartes, *Meditations on First Philosophy* (1986), II, and Augustine, *City of God* (1984), XI.26.
[2] Descartes, *Meditations on First Philosophy* (1986), II (AT VII: 27).

Both Augustine and Descartes thus accepted that (1) my awareness of thinking supplies me with an awareness of a thinker whom I call "I" (or "myself"), and (2) my awareness of myself as "I" supplies me with a general concept of a subject or mind as the sort of thing that thinks.

This tradition of thought about the content of self-awareness stands in striking contrast to an Anti-Egoist tradition that denies that our awareness of our own thoughts supplies us with knowledge of a subject who thinks. Thus Hume famously remarked:

> For my part, when I enter most intimately into what I call 'myself', I always stumble on some particular perception or other, of heat or cold, light or shade, love or hatred, pain or pleasure. I never can catch myself at any time without a perception, and never can observe any thing but the perception.[3]

Hume's suggestion seems to be that our awareness of our own conscious states does not by itself equip us with any notion of an entity that is the bearer of these states. Perhaps I may found a notion of "myself" on some other basis, but my awareness of my own *mental* life presents only conscious states, not any "self" who is their bearer. Hence, Hume concludes, our awareness of our own mental activities gives us no genuine conception of "the mind" as a locus in which these states inhere. This is part of the significance of his notorious "bundle theory" of the self:

> The mind is a kind of theatre, where several perceptions make their appearance; pass, re-pass, glide away, and mingle in an infinite variety of postures and situations. There is properly no simplicity in it at one time, nor identity at different.... The comparison of the theatre must not mislead us. They are the successive perceptions only, that constitute the mind; nor have we the most distant notion of the place, where these scenes are represented, or of the materials, of which it is composed.[4]

Hume's doubts about whether our awareness of our own mental lives supplies us with a concept of a subject or mind are echoed with variations by a variety of other figures, notably Lichtenberg and Wittgenstein.[5] Kant occupies an interesting middle ground, holding on the one hand that our apperceptive awareness of our own thinking entails awareness of an "I" in which our thoughts are united,

---

[3] David Hume, *Treatise of Human Nature* (2000), 1.4.6.
[4] Ibid.
[5] Cf. Lichtenberg 2000, K 18, and Moore "Wittgenstein's Lectures in 1930–33" (1959).

while denying (rather darkly) that our awareness of this unifying "I" by itself constitutes knowledge of a substantial *thing* that thinks.

All this is very familiar, of course, and has been extensively discussed in debates about the nature of the self and the meaning of the first person. I want to suggest, however, that it is also relevant to our problem about the basis of transparent self-knowledge. The fact that I am able to answer the question (e.g.) whether I believe that p by treating it as transparent to the question whether p is puzzling, not merely because the latter question appears to have no bearing on my own state of belief, but also (*a fortiori*) because it has no bearing on my existence as a representing *subject*. Yet each of us readily assumes that the psychological question s/he can answer by determining whether p is rightly formulated as:

Do *I* believe that p?

rather than merely as:

Does there exist belief that p?

That is, each of us assumes that s/he is entitled to ascribe transparently known beliefs to a knowing subject, namely him- or herself. It is of course eminently natural to assume this, but we shall see that the basis for this assumption is not easy to understand. To explore its basis is, in effect, to explore the connection between *consciousness-as-subject* of various representational states and explicit *self-consciousness*—i.e., consciousness of oneself *as the subject* of these states. It is to explore the connection between having a "first-person perspective" and being able to think of oneself in the first person.[6]

The aim of the present chapter will be first to show why this connection needs clarification, and then to sketch an account of it. In earlier chapters, I argued that a satisfactory solution to the general Problem of Transparency must recognize that our first-order awareness of the world already contains an implicit awareness of our own mental states, and that the step to propositional self-knowledge consists in a reflective articulation of this implicit awareness. Here I want to suggest that this approach can be extended to address the Anti-Egoist Challenge to the inclusion of "I" in ascriptions of self-knowledge. This should presumably count as a point in favor of the reflectivist approach; but quite apart

---

[6] I reserve the term "self-consciousness" for the kind of self-awareness possessed by someone with the capacity to think of herself as herself in the special way that is expressed with the first person. This usage is stipulative: I do not assume that all self-awareness requires the capacity to think explicit first-person thoughts. Indeed, as should be clear from the preceding chapters, this is the very contrary of my view. Nevertheless, I take the cognitive step that a subject takes when she learns to think in the first person to be significant, inasmuch as it constitutes the cornerstone of all explicit self-representation. It is the warrant for this step that I explore in the present chapter.

from its dialectical interest, I think the extension throws a valuable light on the nature and significance of first-person thought. The result will be a somewhat different approach to the first person from those prevalent in recent philosophy, but I hope to show that this nonstandard approach sheds a helpful light on some more standard issues and controversies.

5.2. The Anti-Egoist Challenge

Hume is not alone in suggesting that the "I" to whom we ascribe self-knowledge is somehow absent from the field to which we look in making such ascriptions. There is also, for instance, this famous remark from Wittgenstein's *Tractatus*:

> If I wrote a book called *The World As I Found It*, I should have to include a report on my body, and should have to say which parts were subordinate to my will, and which were not, etc., this being a method of isolating the subject, or rather of showing that in an important sense there is no subject; for it alone could *not* be mentioned in that book. (Wittgenstein 1961: 5.631)

My first order of business will be to rouse sympathy for this sort of Anti-Egoist remark. My purpose in doing so, however, is not to join the Anti-Egoists in disputing our entitlement to include "I" in our ascriptions of self-awareness, but to sharpen our sense of what the nature of this entitlement must be.

For this purpose, it will help to consider Lichtenberg's famous criticism of Descartes, which presents the Anti-Egoist challenge in a particularly simple and direct form. Descartes of course claimed that his awareness of thinking provided him with indubitable proof of his own existence, by way of the argument *Cogito ergo sum*, "I think, therefore I am." Lichtenberg replied that, if we possess an indubitable awareness of thinking, its content is properly rendered, not as "I think," but rather as "There is thinking" (*Es denkt*), on the model of "There is lightning" (*Es blitzt*).[7] His remark is somewhat gnomic, but his point seems to be that the awareness we conventionally express with "I think" is really only an awareness of *thinking*, not an awareness of a particular *subject* who thinks. If he is right, then Descartes was mistaken to reason *Cogito ergo sum*, since his conclusion ("I exist") follows only given an over-strong reading of his premise.

How much force is there in Lichtenberg's criticism? On first inspection, it might seem that our entitlement to say "I think" on the basis of our awareness of thinking is beyond question. Suppose I am consciously thinking about whether it will rain tomorrow. It seems that nothing else is needed to warrant me judging

---

[7] Lichtenberg 2000: K 18.

I am thinking about whether it will rain besides my consciousness of *thinking about whether it will rain*.[8] For mustn't any thought have a thinker? And whose thought could I be directly conscious of but my own? Certainly it seems to make no sense for me to think, on the basis of such awareness, "*Someone* is thinking about whether it will rain, but is it I?"[9] If I were in a state of radical amnesia, I might have no idea who I was, yet surely even then I would know in thinking that I, the thinker, exist. Thus it can seem indisputable that our awareness of thinking includes awareness of a thinking subject, the being to whom "I" refers.

On further reflection, however, the inclusion of "I" in "I am thinking of whether it will rain" can seem to assert too much. By hypothesis, what I am aware of is: thinking about whether it will rain. But to ascribe this activity to a subject is to assert more than the mere existence of thinking. It is, seemingly, to assert the existence of a being to whom this thinking belongs, an agent of this activity or bearer of these states. Moreover, the fact that I ascribe many mental states and activities, including ones occurring at different times, to this selfsame "I" appears to commit me to claiming that there is a *single, enduring* being to whom all such mental states and activities belong. Yet how could sheer awareness of thinking (or any other mental state or process) inform me of the existence of such a unified, enduring being? Certainly the claim that there is such an entity does not seem indubitable in the way our non-observational awareness of thinking is indubitable. To doubt the latter awareness is incoherent, since to doubt that one thinks is itself to think something, as Descartes famously pointed out. But it is not obviously incoherent to doubt that there is a subject who performs this act of thinking; for even if the existence of the act is indubitable, the existence of a subject who performs it is not, inasmuch as the latter is presumed to exist in a way that transcends this act. It is not clear how awareness of a present act of thinking, however indubitable, could by itself justify positing this more expansive sort of entity.[10]

Perhaps it will be replied that it is simply a necessary truth that any act must be performed by a subject. But even if this is granted as a general metaphysical principle about acts, do we really have apperceptive awareness that thinking

---

[8] And similarly, *mutatis mutandis*, for other kinds of self-knowledge: I seem, e.g., to need no further warrant for judging *I feel pain* beyond awareness of *feeling pain*.

[9] Thus such uses of "I" are said to be "immune to error through misidentification." See Shoemaker 1968, and Evans 1982: Ch. 7.

[10] Doubtless the *contents* of our thoughts will sometimes presuppose that we are enduring beings: for instance, if I think *I will meet him at the restaurant this evening*, I presuppose that I am a single, enduring being who not only thinks the present thought but will be able later to meet someone at a restaurant. But the fact that the content of my thought *presupposes* this does not show that my awareness of thinking *proves* it. The question is whether I could establish the existence of such a subject simply on the basis of my awareness of thinking, and the problem is that it is not obvious how I could.

is an "act" in the sense of which this metaphysical principle holds? Not every process requires a bearer: there can be thunder or lightning without any subject that thunders or "lightens." Does our apperceptive awareness of thinking *by itself* make clear that thinking cannot occur subjectlessly in this way? Someone who raises this sort of question need not deny that, when we take a broader view of things, we can readily identify a thinker of the relevant thoughts. Of course we all know, or anyway assume, that acts of thinking have subjects, and when we are not in the grip of skeptical doubts, we generally take ourselves to have a tolerably clear idea of what sort of beings these subjects are: space-occupying, flesh-and-blood human beings. Lichtenberg was presumably not denying that this is so, but merely questioning whether its being so can be appealed to in a certain dialectical context: one in which our task is to characterize what can be known solely on the basis of the pure awareness of thinking to which Descartes drew attention. We must, as it were, put on special Cartesian blinders and then assess whether this supposed entity, the thinking subject, continues to be visible.

Once we abide by this restriction, I think it is far from clear that any such entity remains in view. For the Cartesian procedure requires us to restrict our attention to what we are aware of *simply in being aware of thinking*. But to ascribe this activity to a subject seems to involve ascribing it to an entity presumed to transcend the present act of thinking, an entity conceived as capable of performing indefinitely many such acts. How could awareness of thinking by itself warrant us in positing such a being? It is doubts of this sort, I believe, that lead Anti-Egoists such as Hume and Lichtenberg to query the aptness of including "I" in the basic formulation of what a self-knower knows. If they are right, then Descartes was wrong to suppose that each of us can prove to himself that he exists simply by attending to his own thinking, for our awareness of thinking does not itself support the ascription of this thinking to a subject. Rather, when we ascribe our thoughts to a subject, we include a claim whose warrant must lie elsewhere.

Yet if the inclusion of "I" in the statement of self-knowledge is not warranted by our apperceptive awareness of our own thinking (where "thinking" is understood in the broad, Cartesian sense, as including all the states and activities that belong to conscious mentality), it is not easy to see how it could be warranted at all. For could it be warranted by, e.g., the visible presence of my body, perhaps seen from the characteristic standpoint depicted in Ernst Mach's famous illustration (Figure 5.1)?

It should be clear that what I can see from this perspective does not by itself settle the question of the existence of a *subject* of this experience. Certainly what I see shows me that a particular person exists, but to think *I am that person* is to think that this visible person is in fact the subject who has this very experience, which presupposes that this experience has a subject. What my visual experience

Figure 5.1. Ernst Mach, *Self-Portrait from the Left Eye* (Mach 1886: 14).

presents does not demonstrate the truth of this presupposition; it can have probative value only if the latter question is already settled.

It is thus possible to sympathize with Wittgenstein's idea that, although I can find my body in the world, I cannot find *myself*—the *subject* of these various thoughts and experiences—there. The point of this cryptic claim is that mere awareness of an object—even a human body which I can see from the characteristically Machean perspective, and whose limbs I can move at will—cannot ground the thought that I exist, since the fact that *this body* exists could demonstrate that *I* exist only if I am this embodied person, which is an intelligible proposition only if it is already presupposed that I—the *subject* who sees this body—exist.[11] If the latter point can be established at all, it seems that it must be demonstrated, not by my awareness of any object, but by my awareness of myself *in* perceiving, thinking, wanting, willing, etc. Yet, as we have seen, it is not easy to understand how it could be demonstrated in this way.

This kind of Anti-Egoist challenge has not received much attention in contemporary discussions of the first person, presumably because most contemporary philosophers take it as axiomatic that "I" refers, on any occasion of use, to whoever uses it, and they take it that the users of "I" are flesh-and-blood human beings, whose existence is plain enough.[12] And indeed this is plain if we approach the matter from an onlooker's perspective; but this does not answer the Anti-Egoist challenge. If I hear a human being say "I," then indeed, I know that this use of "I" refers to the human being who uttered it. But if I look at a human body from the characteristically Machean perspective and think to myself "Am I that person?," I do not merely want to know, of some particular tokening of "I," whether this person produced it. I want to know whether this person is the locus of the stream of conscious experience that I know from inside, by being its subject.[13] But to make sense of this question, I must make sense of how this knowledge "from inside" can ground the idea of a subject who has this awareness. It is our entitlement to introduce "I" on this basis that the Anti-Egoist calls into question.

In earlier chapters, I argued for what I called a "reflectivist" approach to the Problem of Transparency, according to which we are justified in treating questions about our own mental states as transparent to questions about the non-mental world because there is, necessarily, a kind of self-awareness already implicit in the relevant forms of thinking about the world. In what follows, I want to argue that the Anti-Egoist challenge can be resolved in an analogous way. For this strategy to work, we will need, first, to identify a form of awareness which does not present the representing subject as such, but which does contain an implicit reference to this subject in its mode of presentation of the non-mental

---

[11] The fact that I have a privileged perspective on a certain body—that I perceive it from a special standpoint, am aware of its states with a special immediacy, and can move its limbs at will—may explain why I should think of it as in *my possession*, but it does yet not make clear why I should think of it as *myself*. As P. F. Strawson puts it in a famous discussion, these sorts of special connections to a body

> provide a good reason why a subject of experience should have a very special regard for just one body, why he should think of it as unique and perhaps more important than any other.... [T]hey even might be said to explain why, granted that I am going to speak of one body as mine, I should speak of this body as mine. But they do not explain why I should have the concept of myself at all, why I should ascribe my thoughts and experiences to anything (Strawson 1959: 93).

[12] See, e.g., Strawson 1974c and Perry 2000. The idea that "I" is an expression that *refers* to its user is widely accepted, but is famously disputed by Anscombe 1975. I accept the more standard view, but I take Anscombe's view seriously and will return to it in due course.

[13] Cf. Nagel 1986: Ch. IV.

world. And we will need, second, to explain how it is possible for a thinker to be warranted by such implicit awareness in reflectively "accompanying her representation with *I think*" (to borrow a famous phrase from Kant). These will be our next two tasks.

5.3. Egocentric Thought: Monadic versus Relational

It is a familiar observation that certain of the ways in which we represent objects reflect our own relations to them. When I perceive something as on the *left* or the *right*, as *ahead* of or *behind* me, as *up* or *down*, as *here* or *there*, the significance of these modes of presentation must be explained by appeal to facts about my own relation to the perceived object. To be presented as on the left, for instance, is to be presented as located in a certain direction *relative to my orientation*; to be presented as here is to be presented as *where I am*; etc. Hence these modes of presentation are often called "egocentric," inasmuch as they characterize things and places in terms of their relation to the subject. I want to suggest that such egocentric modes of presentation give us a model of how a consciousness of oneself as a single subject might be implicit in aspects of the mode of presentation of objects in the non-mental world.

To bring this idea into focus, we must note a few points about such egocentric modes of presentation. The first thing to observe is that, although the import of descriptions like "here," "there," "to the left," and "to the right" must be explained by reference to a relation between the object and the representing subject, the descriptions themselves need not be explicitly relational. It is possible, of course, to formulate explicitly relational egocentric descriptions: I can describe something as, e.g., "where I am" or "to the left of me." But egocentric descriptions can also be *monadic*: they can simply ascribe a property to an object (being here, being to the left), rather than relating this object to the subject.[14] In such cases, the connection to the subject will appear, not in the content of the property ascribed, but in what must be said to explain the nature of this property: for instance, *being to the left* is a property that something can have only with respect to a subject facing a particular direction; and to explain, in a given context, what makes a certain direction *the left*, we must refer to the subject's orientation.

It might seem that such monadic egocentric descriptions must be elliptical, and that understanding them requires filling in the missing relatum in thought. But in fact, there are strong reasons to think that it is possible to represent one's environment in ways aptly expressed in monadic egocentric terms without

---

[14] The application of the relational/monadic contrast to egocentric descriptions is due to Campbell 2002: 184. I am indebted to Campbell's discussion at several points in what follows.

possessing the conceptual resources needed to comprehend the corresponding relational properties. Consider, for instance, the monadic/relational pair *being here* vs. *being where I am*. To understand the relational term in this pair, a subject must understand how a general notion of being in the vicinity of an individual (*being where α is*) combines with the notion of a particular individual (*I*) to yield the notion of a particular place. But this presupposes intellectual abilities that are not plausibly required for understanding the monadic notion *being here*. To suppose that such abilities are required for possession of the monadic notion would be, in effect, to demand that a subject who can represent something as here must possess a general understanding of what it is for something to be in the vicinity of an arbitrary individual. But the latter surely requires a more sophisticated form of understanding than what is needed simply to represent something as here.

To be able to represent something as *here*, one must have the capacity to represent objects in a distinctive way in virtue of *being* in their vicinity. To be able to represent something as *where I am*, by contrast, requires the capacity to think *about* the relation between individuals and objects in their vicinity: it requires comprehension of the general notion *where α is*. The latter sort of representation involves a more abstract understanding of spatial relations: not merely a practical ability to keep track of (what are in fact) spatial relations to oneself, but a detached, general understanding of a way one thing can relate to another in space. Surely a small child or a nonhuman animal might represent certain objects as *here*, and others as *over there*, without possessing a general understanding of what it is for an object to be in the vicinity of an arbitrary individual. And what holds of children and nonhuman animals holds also of human adults: although cognitively mature human beings are normally capable of representing the relational property *being where α is*, and thus of recognizing that something located *here* is located *where they themselves are*, it is not plausible to suppose that their very capacity to represent things as *here* depends on their capacity for such a sophisticated, relational form of egocentric representation.[15]

Moreover, relational egocentric descriptions seem to overstate the content of ordinary egocentric experience. If, like Macbeth, I see a dagger hovering before

---

[15] The argument in the text turns on considerations of plausibility, but I believe there is also an objection of principle to the idea that understanding the monadic notion *being here* requires understanding the relational notion *being where I am*. For understanding the latter notion requires making sense of the idea that I am located at a particular place, and it is arguable that we would not be able to make sense of this idea if we were not capable of making judgments about where we are located on the basis of knowledge about what is *here*. If this is right, the capacity to represent things as being here is a precondition of the capacity to think about one's own location, and cannot be explained in terms of it. (For argumentation in support of these claims, see Evans 1982: Chs. 6–7, esp. §§6.6 & 7.3. Evans does not, however, draw my conclusion that the capacity to represent things as here is cognitively more basic than the capacity to represent things as where I am: he takes these two capacities to be equiprimordial. I think this is a mistake, for reasons that should be clear from the larger argument of this chapter, but it would overburden an already complicated discussion to enter into this issue.)

me, I do not—except in special cases—see its relation to my own location: I see *it* but not *myself*, and so it would be an exaggerated description of what I see to say that the dagger visually appears to be *where I am*. The dagger appears to be *there*, hovering in the air, and of course Macbeth takes it to be *before him*, since he understands that what appears to be there is in fact before him. Nevertheless, this relational formulation surely goes beyond what *appears* to Macbeth in the strict sense: he sees the dagger *from* his vantage point, but he does not see himself, and so does not *see* the relation between himself and the dagger.

Monadic egocentric descriptions characterize objects in our environment; they do not assert relations between those objects and the experiencing subject. Nevertheless, such descriptions characterize objects in a distinctively egocentric *mode*, one that *presupposes* specific relations to the representing subject. A person who represents a certain object as *here*, for instance, represents something true just if the relevant object is in her vicinity, i.e., the vicinity of the very subject who represents it as here. Indeed, "here" belongs to a *system* of egocentric spatial notions, which express systematically interrelated ways of representing places relative to a subject. As Gareth Evans puts it:

> To understand how 'here'-thoughts work, we must realize that they belong to a system of thoughts about places that also includes such thoughts as 'It's *F over there*', 'It's *F up there to the left*', 'It's *F a bit behind me*'. 'Here'-thoughts are merely the least specific of this series. We may regard this as an *egocentric* mode of thought. (1982: 153)

It is apt to call this mode of thought "egocentric" not merely because the significance of monadic egocentric descriptions must be explained by appeal to relations to the thinking subject, but also because the subject occupies a privileged position in the relevant system of places. The location of the subject, namely *here*, is the *center* of the egocentric framework; other positions are ordered by their relation to this position.

Moreover, this ordering is not merely a set of relations to an arbitrary geometrical point of origin. Each egocentric mode of presentation has a characteristic kind of cognitive and practical significance. To understand something as *here* is to understand it as immediately available for perception and action; things are grasped as *farther away* in proportion as they are less immediately available, and the different axes of the space are understood to have specific forms of significance for perception and action. This point is nicely brought out, for the up-down axis, in the following remark from Charles Taylor:

> Our perceptual field has an orientational structure, a foreground and a background, an up and a down. . . . This orientational structure marks our field as

essentially that of an embodied agent. It is not just that the field's perspective centers on where I am bodily—this by itself doesn't show that I am essentially an agent. But take the up-down directionality of the field. What is it based on? Up and down are not simply related to my body—up is not just where my head is and down where my feet are. For I can be lying down, bending over, or upside down; and in all these cases 'up' in my field is not the direction of my head. Nor are up and down defined by certain paradigm objects in the field, such as the earth or sky: the earth can slope for instance. . . . Rather, up and down are related to how one would move and act in the field.[16]

Similar remarks could be made about the relation between the forward-backward dimension and our differential capacities to interact with things in front of vs. behind us, and about the relation between the left-right axis and our capacities to turn and move toward things.

In these and similar ways, monadic egocentric modes of presentation are connected with capacities to engage, perceptually and practically, with objects in one's environment. A subject who can perceive things in her environment in such modes will be able to do such things as *turn toward* a sound that presents itself as coming from *the left*, *reach for* a handle that presents itself as *there*, etc.[17] Indeed, as Gareth Evans nicely observes, if a person did not know straightaway which direction is to the right, but needed to think of "right" as the direction associated with his writing hand, then "to the right" could function, for him, as a basic description of how things and places are perceptually presented (Evans 1982: 155). Egocentric descriptions only function as expressions of modes of presentation of objects insofar as they are immediately connected with perception and action in such ways.[18] Nevertheless, as we have seen, the capacity to represent things in

---

[16] Taylor, "The Validity of Transcendental Arguments" (1979), quoted at Evans 1982: 156.

[17] In making this point, I do not mean to suggest that any particular set of capacities for perception or action is necessary for perception in egocentric modes. Perhaps there could be, e.g., a spherical creature whose entire surface functioned like a single, omnidirectional eye and which could not engage in directed movements or actions, but only in nondirected responses to its environment like expelling a poisonous gas or a cloud of ink (cf. Peacocke 1992: 65, and Hawthorne and Scala 2000: 199–200). I do not deny that such a creature is possible, or that it might have its own set of egocentric modes for representing perceived objects (though these might be more along the lines of *near* and *far* than *this* and *that*). My point is just that whatever perceptual and practical capacities a creature possesses will normally be integrated with its capacities for monadic egocentric representation.

[18] Indeed, if we broaden our focus, we can see that a variety of other ways in which we represent objects have an implicitly egocentric character. For instance, representing objects as possessing so-called "affordances" (e.g., as *graspable*, or *movable*, or *within reach*) characterizes them in terms that are implicitly relative to one's own capacities for action, while representing them as *desirable*, *valuable*, *appealing*, etc., arguably presupposes a relativity to one's own conative and evaluative capacities. Once we recognize the diverse ways in which such modes of awareness of objects imply a relativity to our own cognitive, evaluative, and practical capacities, we can begin to see the point in a theme stressed by writers in the phenomenological tradition: that objects in our environment are characteristically given, not merely as "present-at-hand," in a way that leaves open the question of our own

egocentric modes does not require the capacity to *represent* the relations between objects in one's environment and one's own powers of perception and action. If a subject could engage perceptually and practically with X, but did not represent her own relation to X as exemplifying some general relation such as α *is near* β, this would suffice for egocentric orientation with respect to X: she would know where X was in the sense that would allow her (e.g.) to turn her attention to it or reach for it. By contrast, if a subject merely knew *that* she stood in a certain spatial relation to X, but did not possess the ability to engage perceptually and practically with X, this would *not* suffice for egocentric orientation: she would know a certain fact about the relation between X's location and her own location, but this knowledge would not enable her to *locate* X in the sense expressed by remarks like "Here it is!" or "It's right over there." It is thus the capacity to engage with objects in virtue of *being* a located perceiver and agent, rather than the more sophisticated ability to frame representations *of* one's own spatial relation to objects, that is fundamental for monadic egocentric representation.

5.4. Consciousness-as-Subject versus Self-Consciousness

With these observations in hand, we can return to the Anti-Egoist challenge. The problem was to explain our warrant for including "I" in the formulation of self-knowledge, when our basis for such ascriptions does not seem to include any presentation of a subject. I suggested that we would be in a position to respond to this challenge if (1) we could identify a form of awareness that contains an implicit reference to this subject in its mode of presentation of the non-mental world, and (2) we could show how positing a thinking subject can be warranted by mere reflection on this implicit awareness. We have now taken the first of these two steps: we have identified a form of awareness of objects in our environment that presents these objects in an egocentric mode but does not require any explicit conception of myself as the subject who possesses the relevant awareness. Our next task will be to explain what warrants the step from such modally egocentric awareness to explicitly self-ascriptive awareness.

We can focus this question by considering a subject who is aware of objects in her environment, in a manner whose apt expression would require the use of monadic egocentric descriptions, but who does not yet possess an explicit understanding of herself as the subject of this awareness. What does she need to learn in order to understand these monadic egocentric modes of presentation

---

relations to them, but as "ready-to-hand," i.e., in modes that presuppose our own presence in and engagement with the world. I say more about this topic in Chapter 6.

as reflecting *her own* relation to the presented objects? What is involved in her thinking, for instance, not just

>X is here

but

>X is where I am

and what would justify this re-conception of her situation?

It is worth remarking on how this question about the first person differs from the one that has been the primary focus of discussion in recent decades. The more standard question has been how a thought expressible with the first person differs from a thought that singles out the same person in some other way.[19] Such discussions typically begin by observing that it is possible for me to think about the person who is *in fact* myself and yet not think of this person *as* myself in the distinctive way expressed by the first person. Thus Oedipus was (in fact) thinking of himself when he thought that the killer of Laius had brought a curse on Thebes, but he did not at first think of this person *as* himself: he did not realize what he would express by saying, "I have brought a curse on Thebes." And thus John Perry was (in fact) thinking of himself when he thought that there was a shopper in the market with a torn bag of sugar in his cart, but because he did not realize that he himself was the shopper in question, he was not in a position to think: I have a torn bag of sugar in my cart. In each case, of course, the relevant realization made all the difference—in the former case as tragedy, in the latter as farce. Recent work on the first person has generally focused on what a person comes to understand when s/he makes this special kind of cognitive transition.

The kind of cognitive step illustrated by the cases of Oedipus and Perry is undoubtedly important, but I believe that a too-exclusive focus on it has often led to the conflation of two different cognitive achievements. We certainly need to recognize the difference between

>(1) awareness that S is F / S is doing A / S is undergoing P

where "S" is an expression that singles out an individual without employing the first person (e.g., a proper name, demonstrative expression, definite description, etc.), and

>(2) awareness that I am F / I am doing A / I am undergoing P.

---

[19] Shoemaker 1968, Anscombe 1975, Perry 1979, Evans 1982, etc.

But we must also distinguish the kind of awareness expressed by (2) from

(3) awareness of being F / doing A / undergoing P

where the variable positions in these expressions range over such things as *being here, going forward, being struck from the left,* etc. Using the terminology introduced in Chapter 4, we can call the type of self-awareness ascribed in (3) *consciousness-as-subject,* by contrast with the explicit *self-consciousness* ascribed in (2). Any subject who is aware of the world in a mode that reflects her own relation to it may be said to be conscious-as-subject of the relevant relations, even if she does not possess the intellectual resources to formulate the proposition *that* she herself stands in these relations. For consciousness-as-subject is a kind of consciousness that is essentially *from* a subjective perspective, but that does not conceptualize this relation-to-a-subject as such.

Treatments of the first person that focus exclusively on the difference between (1) and (2) tend, I think, to over-intellectualize ordinary self-awareness by blurring the distinction between self-consciousness proper and consciousness-as-subject.[20] Framing the topic in our way allows us to consider, not just the difference between being disoriented with respect to a situation and locating oneself in it, but also the difference between an implicit and an explicit form of orientation. A person who thinks of a table as *here* but cannot yet think *I am in the vicinity of that table* is not, after all, disoriented with respect to the table. She does not have a merely abstract knowledge of the table's existence without a practically relevant understanding of her own relation to it, as Perry knows of the existence of the shopper with the torn bag of sugar without having a practically relevant understanding of his own relation to that shopper. As we have seen, there is a sense in which a person who simply thinks of a table as here *is* aware of her own relation to it; but her awareness is implicit rather than explicit: she has the kind of awareness we have called "consciousness-as-subject" even if she does not explicitly think that she herself is in the vicinity of the table.[21]

---

[20] Although I believe the dominant strand of discussion has been guilty of this over-intellectualization, points related to the one I am making have been noted by a number of authors, notably Recanati 2007, Peacocke 2014, Musholt 2015, and (in later writings) Perry himself (cf. Perry 1986).

[21] This point is also relevant to the interpretation of the much-discussed "Mirror Test" of self-awareness (cf. Gallup, Anderson, and Shilito 2002). In this test, an animal is familiarized with how mirrors work and then is marked in a way not visible without use of a mirror (typically, by rendering it unconscious and then putting a dab of lightweight, odorless red paint on its forehead). If the animal, upon seeing the reflection of this mark in a mirror, spontaneously proceeds to investigate the marked part of its body, this is taken to show that it can recognize the figure in the mirror as itself, and thus is capable of self-consciousness. It turns out that many kinds of primates (and also dolphins and a growing list of other animal species) can pass this test, though there are also many other species of primates that cannot.

This is not the place for a full treatment of the topic, but it is worth remarking on how our distinction between consciousness-as-subject and explicit self-consciousness might contribute to clarifying

Once we draw this distinction, we can see a need for caution in drawing conclusions from cases like those of Oedipus and Perry. For though it is true that, for both Oedipus and Perry, grasping a proposition of the form *I am the F* brings about a crucial change in their cognitive situation, it is not obvious that the relevant sort of change *requires* grasping a first-person proposition. Perry, for instance, was at first aware only that

(4) S has a torn bag of sugar in his shopping cart.

Later, he became aware of the torn-bag-of-sugar situation "from the subject's point of view." We might put this by saying he became aware of

(5) having the torn bag of sugar *here* in *this* cart.

Now, given that Perry has mastered the use of the first person, he can also formulate his realization in a first-person proposition:

(6) *I* have the torn bag of sugar in *my* cart.

But even someone who lacked the capacity for explicit first-person thought could in principle make the transition from (4) to (5), since this is fundamentally a transition from abstract awareness of the obtaining *of* a certain situation to oriented consciousness-as-subject *in* the relevant situation, and we have seen that the latter is in general possible even in the absence of a capacity for self-consciousness proper. An awareness of (5) would suffice for the crucial shift, the one that makes it reasonable for the subject to stop trying *to find S and make him stop making a mess* and to try instead simply *to stop making a mess*.

It would certainly be odd for a person to be capable of thinking all this while not possessing the capacity for explicit first-person thought, but however farfetched such a case may be in practice, it is worth considering when we are

---

the issue in dispute. It is certainly plausible that an animal which passes this test exhibits the capacity to make a link between information about a perceived individual (the animal in the mirror) and its own condition. As we have seen, however, there are two different ways of having information about *one's own condition*: having consciousness-as-subject of the relevant information, and having explicitly attached the relevant information to a first-person notion of oneself. A subject who possesses a first-person notion can make the link between the figure in the mirror and itself by thinking the thought whose colloquial (if slightly ungrammatical) expression is: *That's me*. But even a creature which lacks a first-person concept can in principle learn to translate perceptually gathered information about the properties of a figure in the mirror into consciousness-as-subject of the holding of the relevant properties. For instance, it may simply learn to associate seeing that a certain figure in the mirror has a mark on its forehead with having consciousness-as-subject of having a mark on its forehead. On the face of it, there is no reason why this transition *must* be mediated by the thought *That's me*: it might simply be the result of a learned associative disposition unmediated by any identity judgment.

seeking a theoretical understanding of the first person. For focusing on this kind of case allows us to ask why it matters, not merely to be oriented with respect to one's situation, but to bring one's orientation to explicit self-consciousness. What does explicit self-ascription of the relevant relations add? What is its cognitive significance?

5.5. Introducing the First Person

What, then, would a subject need to learn in order to advance from an understanding of monadic egocentric claims to an understanding of explicitly relational self-ascriptive claims? For concreteness, let us consider the difference between these monadic egocentric claims:

(7) There is a table here
(8) The door is to the left

and their relational counterparts:

(7′) There is a table near me
(8′) The door is to the left of me.[22]

(7′) and (8′) differ from (7) and (8) in that they express the subject's orientation in an explicitly self-ascriptive form. So by asking what a subject must learn to understand thoughts like (7′) and (8′), we may hope to isolate the specific intellectual contribution of the first person to self-awareness.

The transition to claims like (7′) and (8′) might initially seem straightforward. Couldn't a person who was capable of making claims like (7) and (8) learn to formulate corresponding self-ascriptive claims by merely applying a series of simple transformation rules? For instance, one such rule would be that if there is warrant for claiming

---

[22] My approach to this topic is inspired by Evans. See his remark that

[n]othing more than the original state of awareness—awareness, simply, of a tree—is called for *on the side of awareness*, for a subject to gain knowledge of himself thereby. But certainly something more than the *sheer* awareness is called for: the perceptual state must occur in the context of certain kinds of knowledge and understanding on the part of the subject. (Otherwise, we might say as before, the 'I think' which accompanies the subject's perceptions is purely formal, or *empty*.) No judgment will have the content of a psychological self-ascription, unless the judger can be regarded as ascribing to himself a property which he can conceive as being satisfied by a being not necessarily himself—a state of affairs which he will have to conceive as involving a persisting subject of experience (Evans 1982: 231–232).

X is *here*

there is also warrant for claiming

X is *near me*.

Similar rules could be formulated for transitions from other kinds of monadic egocentric claims to corresponding relational claims involving the first person. In this way, a person capable of assessing claims like (7) and (8) could learn to transform her capacity to assess such claims into a capacity to assess claims like (7′) and (8′) without needing to acquire any independent information about herself and her own place in the world.

This, however, would be too quick an account. Merely mastering such transformation rules would not yet supply a person with an *understanding* of the relevant first-person propositions. By learning such rules, she could learn to assert the relevant claims when they are in fact true; but it is one thing merely to be able to assert what is true, another to understand what one is saying. To comprehend what claims like (7′) and (8′) mean, over and above what is signified by claims like (7) and (8), the subject would need to come to understand the relevant self-ascriptions ("X is near me," "X is to the left of me," etc.), not as mere forms of words applied by rote, but as semantically complex expressions whose composition she understands. In particular, she would need to understand how, when she asserts (e.g.), "There is an X near me," her assertion is the product of two meaningful elements: a two-place relational expression ("α is near β") and an expression specifying herself as one of the relata ("I"). These two elements would need to become semantically significant parts of her assertion, rather than just elaborate verbal window dressing on what was still, for her, merely an alternative way of saying, "There is an X here."[23] So our question should be: What sort of understanding must a subject possess in order to employ the first person comprehendingly?

A first point to observe is that the subject's understanding of her situation must come to involve a certain generality. On the one hand, understanding the relational concept *α is near β* will involve understanding this relation as capable of being exemplified by *any* two spatially located individuals. This generality is what is marked by placing two variables, α and β, at the poles of the relational

---

[23] It has been convenient to develop this point by focusing on a verbal assertion, but a similar point will hold, *mutatis mutandis*, for the thought the subject thereby expresses: in order to distinguish itself from the simpler thought *Here is an X*, the thought *I am in the vicinity of an X* must become intelligible as the result of the joint exercise of two distinct conceptual capacities embodying two different kinds of understanding: an understanding of the relation *x is in the vicinity of y* and an understanding of *oneself* as a possible relatum.

expression: these signify that the relevant relation is understood as capable of exemplification by any ordered pair of individuals of the appropriate type. And on the other hand, understanding *oneself* as a relatum will involve a different but related sort of generality. For in order to count as thinking of herself as standing in a certain relation, the subject's so thinking must be the product of two distinct capacities: on the one hand, the capacity to think of the relevant relation as holding, and on the other hand, a capacity to think of herself as such. But if a person's capacity to think of herself is to be distinct from her capacity to think of the obtaining of this particular relation, she must be capable of exercising her capacity to think of herself in other contexts, by thinking of herself as bearing other states, standing in other relations, etc. Only if her capacity to think of herself in the first person acquires this sort of independence from any particular thought-context do the materials which were, so to speak, fused together in the predicate *is here* disentangle themselves into a capacity to think first-personally of oneself, on the one hand, and a capacity to think of a certain relation as holding, on the other.

These observations bring out a crucial aspect of what is at stake in the transition from monadic egocentric awareness to explicit self-consciousness of one's own location in an egocentric framework: it is a transition to the recognition of a single *topic* on which all monadic egocentric representations bear, albeit in diverse ways. This is precisely what is achieved in transforming our system of monadic egocentric representations into a set of concepts of relations to a common bearer. To predicate an attribute of a first-person subject is to think of that attribute as borne by a single bearer of this and potentially many other attributes. Only insofar as I possess the capacity to think in the first person can I represent this topical unity: this is a crucial aspect of the intellectual advance that a person makes when she comes to possess, not mere egocentric consciousness-as-subject, but explicit self-consciousness.

Having made this point, however, it is also important to emphasize the radical distinctiveness of this topical unity. It will be true of any singular thought-element that it represents a potential bearer of indefinitely many predicates. Any such element will define a topic about which information can be gathered, concerning which questions of identity be posed, whose attributes must respect the law of non-contradiction, etc. Some philosophers have denied that the role of "I" is to express such a singular element of thought, but I see no convincing reason to doubt that understanding "I" involves understanding it to introduce a single topic for thought in this way.[24] To attach various predicates to a first-person subject is surely to understand all these predicates as bearing on *one and the same*

[24] I have in mind the tradition, following Wittgenstein 1958 and Anscombe 1975, of denying that "I" is a "referring expression." For further discussion, see §5.8.

topic—namely, myself. Nevertheless, this is a topic of a quite special sort: not one more *object* we represent, but the very *subject* who does the representing.

It is easy to say this, but harder to appreciate the depth of the point. A useful way to bring this out will be to employ a stratagem famously used by Elizabeth Anscombe in her landmark essay on the first person: that of contrasting "I" with another expression, "A," that refers to the very person who uses it but *not* in such a way as to express self-consciousness. We need not rehearse the details of Anscombe's own "A"-language, which depend on the intricacies of her own dialectic. Instead, we may focus on the way we have introduced the first person here: as part of a sophisticated reformulation of the content of monadic egocentric thoughts, in which we replace monadic egocentric predications such as

X is here / over there / to the left / to the right / etc.

with relational self-predications such as

X is where I am / where I am attending / to my left / to my right / etc.

Now, just as it is possible to define a system of monadic *egocentric* descriptions that characterize an object in ways that depend on its relation to the representing subject, so it is also possible to define a system of monadic *allocentric* descriptions (as we may call them) that characterize an object in ways that depend on its relation to an arbitrary person A, as in:

X is shmere / over shmair / to the shmeft / to the shmight / etc.

An object X will count as "shmere" just when it is in the immediate vicinity of A, "over shmair" when it is a remote object of A's attention, "to the shmeft" when it is on A's left-hand side, etc. In this way, we could introduce monadic allocentric expressions that characterize objects in terms of their spatial relations to an arbitrary individual without making explicit reference to that individual. And we could go on to introduce explicitly relational counterparts of these expressions, as in:

X is where A is / where A is attending / to A's left / to A's right / etc.

Yet the cognitive significance of "I" and "A" would clearly be radically different— even if I myself were A, and knew this about myself. This is the difference we need to understand.

To bring this difference into focus, it helps first to reflect on the difference between monadic egocentric descriptions like "here" and monadic allocentric descriptions like "shmere." To determine whether an object X was shmere, shmair, etc., I would need to determine its spatial relation to a certain person, namely, A. This would hold true even if I learned to use such descriptions before learning a name for the relevant person. Still, in order to determine whether X is "shmere," I would need to determine its spatial relation to A, and so would need to locate (the person who was in fact) A, even if I had no special term for this person.[25] By contrast, I do *not* need first to determine my own location in order to determine whether X is *here*. Rather, I must simply locate X: if it falls in a given region of space—roughly, the region presented to me as immediately available for perception or action—then it is here; otherwise not.[26] But again, when I say that this region is presented to me "as immediately available for perception and action," I do not mean that I must explicitly represent the region as standing in this relation to my perceptual and practical capacities. As we saw in §5.3, *being here* is a primitive way for things to be presented as located: one that is in fact characteristic of a certain relation to my own perceptual and active powers, but whose apprehension does not require that I represent this relation as such.

My purpose in stressing these points is to bring out a crucial difference between the basis on which we introduce "A" and the basis on which we introduce "I." One determines whether X is shmere by determining whether it is in the vicinity of A. Hence, even if the name "A" were introduced only subsequent to monadic allocentric descriptions like "shmere," this name would perforce be introduced as a term for an object with which the users of such descriptions were already acquainted, an object of whose location they already kept track. By contrast, one determines whether X is here, not by determining whether X is located in the vicinity of a certain person, but by *being* located somewhere and locating X *from* this position. Hence the introduction of "I" in a relational reformulation of monadic egocentric judgments does not require preexisting acquaintance with some orienting object. Its introduction serves a different purpose: not to *designate an object* in the field of things represented, but to *posit a subject* of this very act of representing. Thus when I reformulate

---

[25] This point would hold even if I myself were A, and knew this about myself. If I knew that I were A, I could establish A's location simply by applying the rule that A is where I am (viz., here); but even so, my capacity to determine that X is shmere (etc.) would depend on my capacity to determine the location of A.

[26] This is obviously a simplification. "Here" can be used to designate a wider or narrower field, and indeed to designate different kinds of location, in ways that depend on context. For instance, in certain conversational contexts, I might intelligibly say "We don't drive on that side of the road here," meaning by "here" the United States—a field which is not in any straightforward sense available to my immediate perception and action. Clarifying the role that context plays in determining the meaning of "here" would require a separate investigation, but I do not think that such an investigation would affect the main point made in the text: that the representation of something as *here* does not depend on a prior identification of the location of the representing subject.

(9) X is here

as

(10) X is near me

I introduce "me" as a term, not for another object of which I am aware, but for the subject of this very awareness, and I re-frame "here" as, in effect, a characterization of the content of this awareness: I am aware of X in such a way as to be aware of its falling in the region directly accessible to me. In this way, "X is near me" expresses a spatial relation known "from the inside": known, not by *apprehending* the two relata, but by *being* one of the two relata and apprehending the other from that point of view.

The point that we have been exploring in the special case of egocentric spatial thought is expressed in an elegant and general form by Gareth Evans when he writes that

> 'I'-thoughts are thoughts in which a subject of thought and action is thinking about him*self*—i.e. about a *subject* of thought and action. It is true that I manifest self-conscious thought, like 'here'-thought, in action; but I manifest it, not in knowing which object to act upon, but in acting. (I do not move myself; I myself move.) (Evans 1982: 207)

Evans's point is not merely that the function of "I" is to serve as a means by which the subject who thinks and acts can designate herself, but more specifically that its function is to express the special "inner" perspective that a subject has on her own cognitive and practical activities: the kind of awareness of being a thinker one has *in* thinking, as opposed to a merely abstract awareness that I am a being who thinks; the kind of awareness of being a self-mover one has *in* oneself moving, as opposed to a merely abstract awareness of one's own body as something that can be moved; etc. Using the term introduced in Chapter 4, we may say that "I" is a tool for making explicit our *consciousness-as-subject* of our own states and activities, a consciousness in whose primary, implicit form we do not represent ourselves as such, but merely represent the non-mental world in modes that reflect our own relations to it.

We can now see more clearly what is at stake in the introduction of "I" into relational egocentric claims like (7') and (8'): it plays a specific role in transforming our nonpositional consciousness-as-subject into positional self-consciousness. This transformation requires, on the one hand, a singular term to mark the common subject of these various states of consciousness, and on the other hand, a range of predicative expressions to make explicit the significance of their several modes. "I" plays the former role, and a person who employs it thereby recognizes that her various conscious states belong to a single subject. Employing it comprehendingly does not, however, require awareness of some worldly object that "I" designates, for its fundamental role is not to designate something *of* which we are aware, but to posit a certain unity among our states of awareness themselves: it serves to represent these states as diverse modifications of one consciousness, one subjectivity.

The thought that the locus of these various conscious states is in fact an embodied person is certainly one whose warrant we will need to understand, and I will turn to it in the next chapter; but we should not build this idea into our account of the very meaning of "I."[27] For as we saw in §5.2, the thought *I am an embodied person* makes a substantive claim about the relationship between the *subject* of consciousness and a possible *object* of consciousness. Even if there are grounds for this identification internal to our consciousness-as-subject—and we will see in the next chapter that there are such grounds—taking the identification for granted will only impede our understanding of the special cognitive role of the first person. Its primary role is to make it possible to express consciousness-as-subject in what Sartre would call a "positional" form: as a topic of cognition in its own right, rather than merely as a modality through which we cognize extramental objects.[28]

We could think of this transformation of nonpositional consciousness-as-subject into positional self-consciousness as a kind of reversal of the polarity of consciousness. In its primary form, our consciousness posits what Sartre calls "transcendent objects": things other than consciousness itself. But this positing of transcendent objects (as real or imaginary, present or absent, extant or to-be-achieved, etc.) is made possible, as we have seen, by a correlative nonpositional consciousness through which we are implicitly aware of our own states of consciousness. When we reflectively self-ascribe these states of consciousness, we transform this nonpositional self-awareness into a topic for cognition in its own right, and the first person plays a special role in this transformation: it identifies the underlying subjectivity whose various states of awareness we go on to characterize. We might say that, whereas in the unreflective consciousness our topic is some transcendent *object* of consciousness ("it"), in reflective self-consciousness our topic is not a transcendent object but the very *subject* of this consciousness

---

[27] As Strawson 1959 and Evans 1982 do, for instance. For related criticisms of their view, see Longuenesse 2017: Ch. 2.

[28] This is not to deny, of course, that once we possess the term "I," we can also use it to self-ascribe states and activities of which we are not conscious-as-subject, as in "I have gray hair in my beard" or "I weigh 185 pounds." But the function of "I" in such contexts is to link these attributes to the being of whose life the speaker is conscious-as-subject in certain crucial respects, whereas its use in articulating consciousness-as-subject anchors the term and gives it its special significance. For versions of this point, see Shoemaker 1968, Evans 1982, McDowell 1998, Perry 2002.

("I"). And whereas, in unreflective consciousness, self-awareness figures only nonpositionally, as the mode through which transcendent objects are posited, in reflective self-consciousness, it is rather our awareness of transcendent objects that figures nonpositionally, inasmuch as it serves, not to present worldly objects, but to characterize the contents of our own states of consciousness. Thus when sight makes me conscious of

> this gray cat

I am aware of an object, the cat, in a distinctive perceptual mode marked by "this," but when I go on to reflect that

> I see a gray cat

I re-conceive of this state of awareness as informing me about my own subjective state, and reference to the gray cat now appears in a characterization of this state.[29] This is what I mean when I say that explicit self-consciousness reverses the polarity of consciousness: it rearranges the same materials so that they converge on the opposite pole of the relation *X is conscious of Y*. The cognitive focus is now not on Y ("it"), but on X ("I").

In Chapter 3, I introduced the term "reflection" to designate the intellectual activity by which we transform nonpositional conscious-as-subject into positional self-consciousness. The upshot of the preceding discussion is that the first person bears a special relation to this activity. "I" designates the fundamental topic of reflective awareness, the subject of whom any reflective self-knowledge is predicated. As such, it expresses the first and most basic act of reflection: the one by which we recognize our own consciousness as a topic for cognition at all.

5.6. The Reflectivist Approach to the First Person

In making these observations about the cognitive significance of the first person, we have not yet answered the question of what justifies the introduction of such a representation. As we have seen, this step is not trivial, even if we prescind from

---

[29] Since seeing is a veridical state, the thought *I see a gray cat* posits the cat as really existent. Nevertheless, the primary role of reference to a gray cat here is in characterizing my own representational state, while the cat itself is posited only in virtue of the factive nature of this state. The fact that reflective self-ascriptions refer to objects primarily in order to characterize the subject's own state explains how such ascriptions can refer to objects that are *not* posited as really existent, as in *I seem to see a gray cat*.

the question whether "I" refers to an embodied person. For even in the absence of this further thesis, the claim that

> I am conscious of X

adds a substantive commitment to the claim that

> There is consciousness of X

namely that this consciousness has a *bearer* which can bear other states of consciousness as well. To present consciousness-as-subject in such a subject-predicate form is, in effect, to impose the structure of positional knowledge on the analysis of subjectivity: it is to understand consciousness-as-subject as presenting manifold determinations of a single *subject* in the logical sense: a single bearer of various properties. But what can justify the imposition of this structure? This, I believe, is what Hume meant to challenge when he denied that there is such a thing as "the mind" or "the Self": he did not doubt that his several perceptions were causally connected with the vicissitudes of a single *object*, David Hume; what he disputed was that his consciousness of these perceptions itself gave him reason to posit a single *subject* (a mind) of which they were attributes. What can we say to this Anti-Egoist challenge? Nothing is more familiar than this step from a representation of the egocentrically known world to an ascription of this representation to a knowing subject; but when we consider it carefully, nothing is less straightforward.

It is at just this point that it is useful to recall our reflectivist approach to the Problem of Transparency. In that case, our problem was that nothing seemed more evident than that one can answer the question whether one believes *p* by considering whether *p*, yet nothing in our field of view when we consider *p* seems to warrant that claim "I believe *p*." Our present difficulty is strikingly analogous. Nothing seems more evidently justified than the step from monadic egocentric claims like

(7) There is a table here

to self-ascriptive claims like

(7′) There is a table near me

yet nothing in our field of view seems to justify this step. Now, the reflectivist approach to the Problem of Transparency was to suggest that our warrant for this sort of step lies, not in *what* we represent, but in the mind-implicating *mode* in which we represent. Might something analogous apply here? The point could not be exactly the same, since what is now in question is our warrant, not for ascribing particular psychological predicates to ourselves, but for thinking in the first person at all. If our mode of representing the non-mental world can justify this, the relevant mode must somehow pertain, not to how things are presented on some particular occasion, but rather to how things are always presented. For though our thoughts and experiences may vary, our justification for thinking of ourselves as the subject who has these thoughts and experiences does not.

But in fact we have already seen a feature of monadic egocentric modes of presentation that is invariant in the required way: the *centering* of such modes on a subject whose location gives them their order and significance. Objects are presented as egocentrically located in diverse ways: as here or there, up or down, ahead or behind, near and far, etc. But these ways are not merely diverse: they are all related to one another systematically in virtue of the fact that they depend on relations to a single representing subject. Thus, whether an object counts as *ahead* or *behind* depends on its relation to the orientation of the representing subject, and whether it counts as *near* or *far* depends on its distance from her, etc. These oppositions are all defined in relation to the representing subject, and have their several forms of significance in virtue of their relations to her position, orientation, and so on. Moreover, there is clearly a sense in which a subject who represents in egocentric modes must keep track of these relations, for she must represent objects in ways that systematically depend on their relation to her own location, and she must stand ready, as we have seen, to exercise her perceptual and practical powers in ways that depend on these relations. Thus, although the subject does not represent herself in monadic egocentric thought, the form of her representation presupposes her own presence on the scene—not in the sense that it presupposes the existence of an *object* at the center of the egocentric framework, but in the sense that it posits this center as the point *from* which objects are presented.[30] So when a subject shifts from representing her environment in monadic egocentric terms, as in (7), to making explicitly relational egocentric ascriptions, as in (7'), her positing a subject to whom all such objects are related does not represent a new discovery, but merely makes explicit a presupposition of her former, monadic mode of presentation of her environment: the presupposition of a single representing subject in relation to whom these diverse representational states are possible.

---

[30] For the sake of simplicity, I assume there is only a single egocentric framework, but it would not undermine the points I have to make if there were multiple such frameworks (e.g., one centered on the subject's hand, another on her head, etc.). To be sure, if there were multiple egocentric frameworks, there would be a question about how the subject integrates her several modes of presentation into a single, coherent representation of her environment. I cannot take up this topic here, but I hope the argumentation of this chapter as a whole suggests a strategy for approaching such questions.

The fact that this subject must stand at the center of a system of spatial positions is of course a special feature of egocentric representation, which is not relevant to our basis for positing a single subject of (e.g.) our various thoughts and feelings. Nevertheless, I believe considerations broadly analogous to the ones just sketched apply in these other domains. In the case of egocentric thought, our case for introducing the first person turned on the observation that the diverse modes of egocentric representation all presuppose relations to the standpoint of a single representing subject. We could mount a more general form of this case if we could show that a single representing subject is presupposed by the diverse modes of presentation in virtue of which we are presented with objects of perception, belief, intention, and so on. And in fact we can mount such an argument by appealing to a more abstract notion of a point of view.

To see how this might work, consider a subject who holds the time-honored belief:

(B) The cat is on the mat.

In Chapter 3, I argued that a subject who believes (B) can know her own belief transparently because she can recognize on reflection that the cat is presented as on the mat in a way that already implies an attitude of belief on her part. For in representing the cat as on the mat, she represents a certain factual question as closed, and this closure stands opposed to an openness that is not metaphysical but epistemic: if she regards a factual question as open, she need not suppose that the fact itself is *indeterminate* (that there is no fact of the matter about whether the cat is on the mat), but merely that the answer to this question has not yet been *determined*. Any subject who is capable of thinking about factual questions must, I claimed, understand this distinction between a question's being (epistemically) closed and its remaining open, even if she does not yet possess the concept of belief. But in recognizing this distinction, she already in effect recognizes the difference between decidedness and undecidedness from her own point of view.

Now, it is natural to use the phrase "from her own point of view" in formulating this point, but what exactly does this phrase mean? Certainly it does not mean: from the spatial position she occupies—for she would have this point of view even if she moved to a different position, whereas another occupant of this position would not count as having this point of view. The phrase must rather mean: from her *epistemic* point of view—that is, from the standpoint on factual questions constituted by the body of beliefs she holds about the world. Moreover, this epistemic standpoint has a certain interconnectedness. For if this point of view involves commitment to the truth of the propositions $\{p, q\}$, then the relevant subject would be right also to believe:

(C) $p \& q$

whereas (C) would not be right for any subject to believe if p and q were each believed in a distinct point of view.[31] In this way, the propositions held true as parts of a single point of view are held true *together*, even before the holder of this point of view thinks any explicitly conjunctive thought about them: they are held true as parts of a single total outlook on what is the case, and stand in rational relations to one another in virtue of this.

What I am suggesting, however, is not merely that beliefs bear rationally on one another in virtue of belonging to a single epistemic point of view, but that a nonpositional awareness of the unity of this standpoint is presupposed in our believing. When we recognize a factual question as open or closed, we implicitly recognize it as undecided or decided *from the epistemic standpoint in which this question is posed*. This standpoint is such as to involve responses to many distinct factual questions, and our responsiveness to each of them shows that we understand these responses to be rationally related to one another. This will be shown, for instance, by my readiness to treat the conjunctive proposition (C) as closed when I regard the questions whether p and whether q as closed. This readiness shows that I regard the closure of these questions as interdependent, and as we have seen, the notion of "closure" that is relevant here is epistemic: it concerns what is (taken to be) known, even though I do not explicitly think about what I myself know (or believe) but merely about the questions whether p, whether q, and whether $p \& q$. In such ways, our capacity to consider factual questions presupposes a nonpositional awareness of our own epistemic standpoint as constituting a single overall outlook on the world, one that is determinate in some respects and indeterminate in others.

Now consider the relevance of these points to our warrant for ascribing beliefs to a believing subject. We have observed that the claim

I believe that p

adds a substantive further commitment to the claim

There is belief that p

namely that this belief is a state of a subject who is also capable of holding other beliefs. But this further commitment is not a reckless addition to what is given in

---

[31] Similar points could be made, of course, about other kinds of logical relations between propositions: they carry implications for what else it is right to believe only insofar as the relevant beliefs all belong to a single epistemic point of view. I have been helped here by Bernard Williams's discussion of Lichtenberg's challenge in Williams 1978: 79ff.

consciousness of believing *p*, as Anti-Egoists suggest. It is rather a reflective articulation of something presupposed in our consciousness-as-subject of believing itself. To be sure, Hume could rightly say that "when I enter most intimately into what I call 'myself,' I always stumble on some particular [belief] or other.... I never can catch myself at any time without a [belief], and never can observe any thing but the [belief]."[32] That is, he could rightly insist that I am only conscious of believing (e.g.) that the cat is on the mat, and not of some subject who believes this and other things. No such subject is presented in my consciousness-as-subject of believing, but we must distinguish between what is presented and what is presupposed. In consciously believing that *p*, I *presuppose* that this belief belongs, with others, to a single epistemic standpoint on the world. Even though I am not presented with any entity who holds this standpoint, I am necessarily conscious-as-subject of the unified standpoint *from* which this belief is held, and it is this unified standpoint that I posit when I reflectively ascribe this belief to *myself*.

Each of us will have a purely reflective justification for ascribing her manifold representations to a single representing subject insofar as her various ways of representing the world already make implicit reference to such an overall point of view. I will not attempt to argue for this proposition in its full generality.[33] Nevertheless, I hope the sketch just offered gives an indication of how such an argument might proceed. The key would be to show that the several modes in which we represent aspects of the non-mental world—as true, as desirable, as to-be-hoped-for or to-be-feared, etc.—involve, not just a nonpositional consciousness of corresponding mental *states*, but also a nonpositional consciousness of the membership of these states in a single representational *point of view* on the world. If we could show this, we would thereby show that a subject who reflects on such nonpositional consciousness has grounds for ascribing these manifold representations to a single representing subject. In positing herself as such a subject, she would not assert her identity with some *object* in the knowable world; she would merely posit herself as a single consciousness *of* objects. Still, she would make a substantive claim about the nature of this consciousness—that its various determinations are grounded in a unity—and her basis for this claim would rest on mere reflection on something already presupposed in her consciousness-as-subject of her various mental states.

---

[32] Compare Hume, *Treatise of Human Nature* (2000), 1.4.6, quoted above.
[33] Descartes famously found it to be self-evident:

[W]hen I consider the mind, or myself in so far as I am merely a thinking thing, I am unable to distinguish any parts within myself; I understand myself to be something quite single and complete.... As for the faculties of will, understanding, sensory perception and so on, these cannot be termed parts of the mind, for it is one and the same mind that wills, and understands, and has sensory perceptions (*Meditations on First Philosophy* (1986) VI, AT VII: 86).

A full exploration of our reflective warrant for positing such a unity would, of course, need to consider the nature of this unity in greater detail. The unity that we posit in ascribing our mental states to a single subject evidently has two dimensions: a *synchronic* dimension that enables us to represent diverse mental states occurring at one time as borne by a single subject, and a *diachronic* dimension that enables us to represent mental states occurring at different times as belonging to the same subject. Hence a full account of our warrant for positing such a unity would need to show how we are warranted in positing, not just a synchronic subjective unity, but a diachronic subjective unity. My aim here, however, has been merely to sketch a strategy for approaching such questions, so I will be satisfied if the reader comes away from this discussion convinced that these are real challenges and that a reflectivist approach to them is not unpromising.

5.7. The First Person and Others

The foregoing description of the basis of first-person thought might seem still to leave out something crucial. We said that understanding the first person consists fundamentally in comprehending the unity of a subjective point of view on the knowable world. I acknowledged that this leaves us with a problem, which we will take up in the next chapter, of explaining our warrant for thinking of ourselves, not as mere points of view *on* the world, but as embodied beings located *in* it. But isn't there, so to speak, a wholly other dimension of first-person thought, one that requires grasping oneself as one of a possible manifold of conscious subjects? This was, famously, P. F. Strawson's view: he held that "[o]ne can ascribe states of consciousness to oneself only if one can ascribe them to others" (Strawson 1959: 100), and thus that understanding the first person requires understanding "I" to signify one of potentially many conscious persons. Many other philosophers agree with Strawson in affirming this *Multiplicity Thesis*, as we may call it:

(MT) Understanding "I" requires understanding it to signify one of a potential multiplicity of conscious subjects.[34]

But does our account of the reflective basis of first-person thought validate (MT)?

---

[34] For three very different accounts of first-person thought that nevertheless agree in affirming (MT), see Evans 1982: Ch. 7; Rödl 2007: Ch. 6; and Musholt 2015: Ch. 6. The thesis that self-consciousness requires consciousness of others also has important roots in the history of philosophy, of course, notably in the "Self-Consciousness" chapter of Hegel's *Phenomenology of Spirit*, which is widely taken to defend a thesis akin to (MT).

It does not validate (MT), but I do not apologize for this. It is one thing not to validate a thesis, another to rule it out. Our account of the reflective basis of first-person thought explains what would warrant each of us in thinking of their various representations as belonging to a unified point of view, and thus gives us the materials needed to respond to the Anti-Egoist Challenge; but it does not explain what warrants a subject in thinking of her point of view as constituting one of potentially many points of view belonging to different subjects. Note that the latter is a stronger claim than merely that her own point of view might have been different (that she might have perceived the world from a different location, might have held different beliefs, etc.). To understand that *my* point of view might have been different is not yet to understand that there might be *another* point of view, a locus of consciousness other than my own. Our reflectivist account of the basis of first-person thought does not explain our warrant for the latter thought, but it also does not rule out our having such a warrant, and of course I believe that we human beings do have one. Each of us thinks of themself as *one* subject among others, and we are surely warranted in doing so. Moreover, this is arguably not merely something we think about ourselves, but something that is implied in our very understanding of the first person: that it stands over against other possible subjects who might figure as "you"s to my "I."

We should be cautious, however, about demanding that an account of the nature of first-person thought should validate this understanding. Let us grant for the sake of argument that an understanding of the opposition between "I" and various potential "you"s is implied in our human understanding of ourselves as conscious subjects. Is it *impossible*, though, that there might be a conscious being which grasped the unity of its own subjective point of view but did not comprehend that there might be other such points of view, other subjectivities? I do not claim that such a solipsistic self-consciousness is possible, just that the claim that it is impossible looks on its face like an ambitious and interesting philosophical thesis, one we should defend through argument rather than building by stipulation into our account of the meaning of the first person. On the face of it, our actual understanding of the first person has two dimensions: on the one hand, an understanding of how I as conscious subject stand over against any *object* of which I am conscious (call this the *"I-It" dimension* of self-consciousness); and on the other hand, an understanding of how I as subject differ from any other conscious *subject* (call this the *"I-You" dimension*). It is a substantive question how these two dimensions of self-consciousness are related. One can imagine various views about this: that the two dimensions are independent, that they are necessarily interdependent, that the I-It dimension is a precondition of the I-You dimension, that the I-You dimension is a precondition of the I-It dimension, etc. I think the question of the relation between awareness of the unity of my own subjectivity and awareness of the possibility of other subjects is a rich and fascinating one. To prevent the present inquiry from bursting its boundaries, however, I propose to set this topic aside here. This is not, to repeat, because I judge it to be unrelated to our present inquiry, but because I judge the question of its relation to our inquiry to be a matter that is complex enough to merit reserving for another occasion.

Sartre, of course, did not reserve the topic of the relation between self-consciousness and consciousness of others for another occasion: he treated it at length in the part of *Being and Nothingness* on "Being-for-the-Other." Nevertheless, I think of my insistence on distinguishing the "I-It" dimension of self-consciousness from the "I-You" dimension as having a Sartrean provenance. Sartre introduces the distinction between nonpositional consciousness of consciousness and reflective self-knowledge in connection with his general analysis of consciousness, whose mode of being he calls "being-for-itself." He treats the topic of being-for-itself in Part II of *Being and Nothingness*, before turning to being-for-the-Other in Part III. Commenting on this transition, he writes:

> [B]eing-for-the-Other is not an ontological structure of the for-itself: we cannot expect, in fact, to derive being-for-the-Other from being-for-itself, in the way we can derive a consequence from a principle; nor, conversely, can we derive being-for-itself from being-for-the-Other. Doubtless, it is a requirement of our human reality that it be simultaneously for-itself and for-the-Other, but our present investigation does not aim to constitute an anthropology. It would not perhaps be impossible to conceive of a for-itself who was wholly free of any for-the-Other and able to exist without even suspecting the possibility of being an object [of the Other's Look]. Only this for-itself would not be 'man'. What the *cogito* reveals to us here is simply a *factual* necessity: it happens—and this is indubitable—that our being, in connection with its being-for-itself, is also for the Other. (BN 384/321–322)

Sartre's view thus seems to be that being-for-itself does not necessarily entail being-for-another, although we human beings can know ourselves, with the kind of certainty supplied by the Cogito, to be cases of *both* being-for-itself and being-for-another. Sartre calls this knowledge of a "factual necessity," meaning that, although it is not a necessary truth that, in every case, being-for-itself is accompanied by being-for-another, still we know it to be essential to our own nature that we possess both of these forms of being. In the terms of the present discussion, we could restate this by saying that Sartre leaves open the possibility that the "I-It" dimension of self-consciousness might in principle exist without the "I-You" dimension, but holds that our human self-consciousness knows itself essentially to involve both dimensions.

This is not the place to explore these Sartrean thoughts in detail, but I hope the parallels with the present discussion are clear. I grant that it is a deep and interesting fact about human self-consciousness that each of us understands themself to exist as one subject among others, and indeed I think, following Sartre, that our awareness of other subjects does not consist in mere cognizance that they exist, but in a fundamental orientation toward their points of view on us, one that pervasively transforms our experience. I do not, however, take it for granted that any possible self-consciousness must be oriented toward other subjects in this way—not because I affirmatively think it possible for a solipsistic self-consciousness to exist, but because I am uncertain about the matter and think that ruling out this possibility would require an argument that I do not possess. These topics deserve their own investigation, which I will not undertake here.

Throughout this book, then, I will confine myself to investigating the general relation between nonpositional consciousness of consciousness and reflective self-knowledge, without considering what relation, if any, these topics have to our consciousness of other subjects. Yet because my examples are drawn from familiar forms of *human* experience, and because human self-consciousness *is* (so I believe) essentially social rather than solipsistic, there will be many moments at which my discussion contains loose threads which, if they were followed out, would lead us beyond the boundaries of our present inquiry and toward an inquiry into our awareness of other subjects. The fact that these threads are not pursued constitutes a limitation of our discussion, but for the reasons just given, I do not regard it as a defect in our inquiry, which has its own proper topic. I hope to take up questions about the relation between self-awareness and other-awareness in future work.

5.8. Implications

To draw together the strands of our argument, and to bring out its wider significance, it will help to note its bearing on some contemporary debates. I will conclude this chapter with some remarks on its relevance to three controversies about first-person thought: the debate about whether "I" is a referring expression, the debate about whether first-person thought plays an essential role in the explanation of intelligent cognition and action, and finally, the Egoist/Anti-Egoist controversy with which we began.

5.8.1. Referentialism versus Anti-Referentialism

It is natural to think that the semantic role of "I" is to refer to a particular person, namely the person who uses it, whether in speech or in mere thought. As Sydney Shoemaker observes in a classic discussion:

> If we consider the logical powers of first-person statements and the role played by the first-person pronoun in communication, nothing seems clearer than that in all first-person statements, ... the word "I" functions as a singular term or singular referring expression. Statements expressed by the sentence "I feel pain" have it in common with those expressed by sentences like "He feels pain" and "Jones feels pain" that they contradict the proposition "Nobody feels pain" and entail the proposition "Someone feels pain." In these and other ways "I feel pain" behaves logically as a value of the propositional function "X feels pain." Moreover, in all first-person statements, including "psychological" or "experience" statements, the word "I" serves the function of identifying for the audience the subject to which the predicate of the statement must apply if the statement is to be true (what it indicates, of course, is that the subject is the speaker, the maker of the statement). And this is precisely the function of a referring expression. (Shoemaker 1968: 555)

A number of philosophers have, however, forcefully challenged this referentialist interpretation of "I." Thus Wittgenstein famously distinguished between a use of "I" "as object" and a use of it "as subject," and he appeared to suggest that, when "I" is used as subject, its function is not to refer to a particular person.[35] And this view has been defended more systematically in Elizabeth Anscombe's famous paper "The First Person" (1975), which maintains that "I" is "not a referring expression," not merely in certain uses, but in general.[36]

It is a delicate question how to understand this anti-referentialist position about "I." Anscombe grants that a statement of the form "I am F" is true just if the person who asserts it is F. What then is she denying in denying that "I" refers to this person? It is most illuminating, I believe, to understand her as rejecting a specific logical analysis of "I am F," one on which, when a person S thinks what she would express by saying "I am F," her situation can be represented as

(11)   S | thinks | SELF is F

where the vertical bars separate distinct elements of the analysis. Thus, (11) would assert a relation (thinking) between a person (S) and a proposition (SELF

---

[35] Thus Wittgenstein writes

> To say 'I have pain' is no more a statement *about* a particular person than moaning is.... The difference between the propositions 'I have pain' and 'He has pain' is not that of 'L. W. has pain' and 'Smith has pain'. Rather, it corresponds to the difference between moaning and saying that someone moans (Wittgenstein 1958: 67–68).

[36] In her most direct statement:

> 'I' is neither a name nor another kind of expression whose logical role is to make reference, *at all* (Anscombe 1975: 32).

is F), in which S herself, referred to via a special first-person mode of presentation (SELF), is thought of as falling under the concept *x is F*. But on Anscombe's view, the proper analysis of the situation is rather along the lines of

(12)   S | self-thinks | being F

where (12) asserts, not a generic relation of thinking that connects a person to a *proposition*, but a special and primitive relation of self-thinking that connects a person to a *concept* that she self-applies. On this interpretation, the semantic function of "I" in "I am F" (and also of the first-person form of the verb "to be") is not to present the subject of the proposition *SELF is F*, but simply to indicate the special way in which S applies the concept *x is F*: she does not apply it to a certain person whom her thought singles out as the subject of a singular proposition, but rather self-applies it, where this is not reducible to her thinking any proposition to be true. In this way, the thinker's relation to a concept she self-applies is, as Anscombe puts it, "unmediated" by any conception of herself.[37]

Anscombe's thesis is often treated as incredible, but understood in this way, I think it represents a powerful and interesting philosophical idea about the analysis of self-consciousness, one that parallels ideas expressed to less opprobrium by other philosophers.[38] Indeed, it is an idea that, in some respects, coheres well with the point of view developed here. For on our view, too, it might be said that "I" is not a referring expression, inasmuch as it does not designate some object of which we are conscious, but merely makes explicit the unity of our conscious point of view itself. If a referring expression is one whose function is to identify which object in "the universe of discourse" is said to have a certain property, then we too should deny that the basic role of "I" is to refer, for on our view the primary function of "I" is not to single out some given object *of* which we are conscious, but to posit the conscious point of view *from* which objects are presented as constituting a unity.[39] In these respects, we should find Anscombe's anti-referentialism congenial.

Nevertheless, we should hesitate to endorse her position if it is construed as denying that someone who asserts "I am F" expresses any specifiable

---

[37] On "unmediated conceptions," see Anscombe 1975: 34. My account of Anscombe's position is indebted to Michael Thompson's unpublished lecture "I and You," which has been crucial to my understanding of Anscombe's view. For a brief synopsis of this material, see Thompson 2013.

[38] For dismissal of Anscombe's position as unacceptable, see, e.g., Evans 1982, Burge 1998, and McDowell 1998. For parallel ideas, see Lewis 1979.

[39] As we noted in §5.5, this is consistent with allowing that this point of view in fact belongs to an embodied person. Indeed, we shall see in the next chapter that our very self-awareness contains the basis for such an attribution. Nevertheless, I take this to be a piece of substantive knowledge about ourselves, not grounded in the very meaning of the term "I."

understanding of the topic of this predication. I do not think Anscombe intended to deny this, but she may be faulted, at least, for not making the positive significance of her position fully clear. In explaining her view, she writes that

> these I-thoughts [viz., thoughts such as "I am sitting," "I am writing," "I twitched"] are examples of reflective consciousness of states, actions, motions, etc., not of an object I mean by "I", but of this body. [They] are unmediated conceptions (knowledge or belief, true or false) of states, motions, etc., of this object here, about which I can find out (if I don't know it) that it is E.A. (Anscombe 1975: 34)

It is certainly a desirable result that if E.A., who is an embodied person, says or thinks, "I am sitting," she expresses consciousness of a state of the embodied person E.A. But how, on Anscombe's view, does E.A. herself understand the topic of her thought? A state, action, or motion must be a state, action, or motion of *someone*, and E.A. can be presumed to know this; but what is E.A.'s understanding of which "someone" is in question? As Anscombe recognizes, E.A. may fail to know that the relevant individual is called "E.A.," and may even doubt that this individual is an embodied being. Such a doubt is made far-fetched, of course, by Anscombe's chosen predicate, "__ is sitting" (contrast, "__ is thinking of the Middle Ages"). But we should distinguish between the understanding of the subject implied by a given *predication* and the minimal understanding of the subject required to think any "I"-thought whatsoever. Our question concerns this minimal understanding: What sort of "someone" *must* E.A. suppose her predication to concern?

We may agree with Anscombe that E.A.'s conception of her state is "unmediated" by a conception of its subject if this means that this subject is not singled out via some distinct notion of the being who is the topic of the relevant predication. For on our view, too, "I" does not by itself express a conception of which *being*, which object in the world, is the subject of this predication, but merely makes explicit something implicit in our awareness of the state we predicate. Be that as it may, the commitment it makes explicit is substantive, namely that this state pertains to a single point of view of which other representational states may be predicated. This, as we have seen, is what minimally differentiates

>I am F

from

>There is F-ing.

A person who has learned to ascribe states of which she is conscious-as-subject to a first-person subject has therefore made a genuine intellectual advance: she has understood the relation of these states to a single point of view. We may leave to logicians the question of how best to represent first-person thought, and specifically whether it is to be represented as possessing a propositional structure or as a primitive form of self-application of a concept; but we should insist at any rate that it implies such understanding. To this extent, we should sympathize with the thought that motivates referentialists, even if we reject the details of their analysis.

5.8.2. Essentialism versus Inessentialism

A different question about first-person thought concerns whether it plays an *essential* role in explaining how intelligent cognition and action are possible. Classic papers by Perry (1979), Lewis (1979), and others convinced many philosophers that the capacity for so-called *de se* representation—representation of oneself as oneself, in a manner whose linguistic expression would require the first person—is in some way crucial to our cognition and action. The nature of this alleged essentiality was never fully clear, however, and recently a number of philosophers have challenged the idea that the capacity for *de se* representation is really essential for thought or action at all.

The most thorough defense of this *Inessentiality Thesis* is offered by Herman Cappelen and Josh Dever in their *The Inessential Indexical* (2013), which offers a comprehensive survey and systematic criticism of claims about the essentiality of *de se* representation.[40] Cappelen and Dever grant that a subject may know that

(13) S is F

where "S" is any non-first-person term or description referring to the subject, and yet may fail to know that

(14) I am F

and they grant that in some circumstances this gap in S's knowledge might lead her to miss something important about what she should think or how she should act. But, they observe, this is just a special case of a general and widely recognized point about co-referring expressions: they are not freely intersubstitutable in

---

[40] For other criticisms of the Perry-Lewis idea, see Millikan 1990 and Magidor 2015.

knowledge-attribution contexts. As Frege famously pointed out, it is true of *any* two co-referring expressions, A and B, that a subject S may know A to be F and yet not know B to be F; and with respect to any such discrepancy, it will be possible to imagine circumstances in which this gap in S's knowledge leads her to miss something important about what she should think or how she should act. By itself, this does not show that the capacity for *first-person* representation is specially essential to intelligent thought or action. What would be needed, over and above the observation that no other expression is intersubstitutable with "I" in knowledge-attribution contexts, is an argument demonstrating that a subject cannot think or act intelligently unless she knows some first-person propositions. Cappelen and Dever maintain that no clear argument has ever been offered for this claim, and that the claim is not plausible on closer consideration. When John Perry has a torn bag of sugar in his shopping cart, why couldn't the thought that tips him into appropriate action (or makes it rational for him to so act) be *John Perry has a torn bag of sugar in his cart* rather than *I have a torn bag of sugar in my cart*?

This challenge raises questions about the role of *de se* representations in cognition and action that I cannot take up here, so my aim will be, not to answer Cappelen and Dever's anti-essentialism outright, but simply to bring out the bearing of our discussion on their question about what makes first-person thought special. On the view developed here, the primary function of "I" is to play a special role in enabling us to transform nonpositional consciousness-as-subject into positional self-knowledge: namely, the role of specifying the topic of such knowledge, the single subject whose point of view is characterized by various reflectively ascribed predicates. To be sure, mastery of "I" also enables us to self-ascribe states and activities of which we are not conscious-as-subject, as in "I am bald" or "I weigh 185 pounds." But the function of "I" in such ascriptions is presumably to link the relevant states and activities to the standpoint from which the speaker is conscious-as-subject: knowing that *I weigh 185 pounds*, for instance, links this information to my sudden desire (of which I am conscious-as-subject) *to run across this frozen pond*, making it a relevant question for me whether the ice will support 185 pounds. By itself, the desire to run across the pond is one that I might have without thinking of myself as such: the open expanse of ice might simply beckon like Sartre's "streetcar-having-to-be-overtaken," and the reflective thought that *I want* to cross it might be far from my mind. Nevertheless, inasmuch as I understand the equivalence between this way of thinking of a frozen pond and the self-ascriptive thought *I want to run across that pond*, I will be in a position to recognize the bearing of the fact that *I weigh 185 pounds* on this desire, whereas the knowledge that *MB weighs 185 pounds* will stand at a greater rational distance from my desiring consciousness, one that must be bridged by knowledge that *I am MB*.

Does this show that the capacity for first-person thought is essential for intelligent action? On the contrary: I have granted that a person might want *to run across the ice* without framing the self-ascriptive thought *I want to run on the ice*; and if she could have this desire, then presumably she could act on it, too, taking suitable means to her end (scrambling down the embankment, avoiding the fallen tree, etc.). Or again, she could notice that the ice looks thin and decide to hold back—all while merely representing the situation "as subject" rather than engaging in explicit self-representation. Nevertheless, it is obvious that we often do integrate information about ourselves *not* known as subject into our thinking about what to do, and I have suggested that "I" has a special function in this integration: it is precisely the term that effects a link between consciousness-as-subject and knowledge about the objective person one is. Hence we may say that, if consciousness-as-subject is essential to intelligent cognition and action, then the first person has at least a crucial role to play in linking this consciousness with one's awareness of the properties of the objective person who is in fact oneself. It is beyond the scope of this chapter to demonstrate the antecedent of this conditional, and Cappelen and Dever might dispute it. But even this merely conditional conclusion should sharpen our sense of the distinctive role of the first person in cognition and action.

In any case, although integrating objective information about ourselves into our perspective as conscious subjects is a core function of the first person, this is not its most basic cognitive function. On the view developed here, it has an even more basic role in enabling each of us to express our recognition of the *unity* of our own subjective point of view. Even if we set aside the role of "I" in linking consciousness-as-subject to knowledge about the objective person one is, its role in making this unity explicit would remain, and we have seen that this by itself represents a genuine intellectual advance.

The importance of this advance is brought out in another nice remark from Gareth Evans. Having observed that a person can learn to make transparent self-ascriptions of belief simply by following the rule that whenever she is in a position to assert that p, she is *ipso facto* in a position to assert "I believe that p," Evans goes on to observe that mastery of this rule is not sufficient for understanding the meaning of "I believe that p." To understand the meaning of this claim, the subject must come to appreciate how it differs in significance from the bare assertion "p," and Evans makes the following remarks on this difference:

> "I believe that p" admits of a distinction between internal and external negation. "It is not the case that I believe that p" can be the expression of an open mind. This enables us to express one side of the central notion of objectivity—the idea that truth transcends my knowledge or belief: it may be that p, it may be that not-p; I do not know, and have no belief on the matter. A connected point is that the

prefixing of a sentence "*p*" with "I believe that" means that my claim does not have to be withdrawn in the circumstance that it is not the case that *p*. Such a state of affairs—expressible in the past tense by "I believed that *p*, but it was not the case that *p*"—cannot be believed to obtain currently, but its possibility makes sense. This is the other side of the idea of objectivity: although I believe that *p*, it may be the case that not-*p*. In short, learning the difference between "I believe that *p*" and "*p*" involves learning the different ways in which the two sentences embed under various operators: crucially negation, modality, and the past tense. (Evans 1982: 226, n. 36)

Similar points could be made about other transparent mental state ascriptions: coming to understand them involves learning how their truth-conditions differ from the truth-conditions of the non-psychological propositions to which they are transparent, and thus learning to make a conceptual distinction between how the world is and how the subject represents it to be. And while the psychological predicates involved in these ascriptions will vary, the constant factor will be the first person, which expresses the very idea of a representing subject, the possessor of a point of view, who can represent the world in indefinitely many ways. Coming to grasp this idea allows the subject to reflect explicitly upon the distinction, and the possibility of a difference, between how things are and how she represents them as being. And this would hold true even if the subject did not identify herself with some objective entity *in* the world she knows.[41]

---

[41] For this reason, I must disagree with Perry when he suggests that

> For many purposes we don't need notions of ourselves at all. . . . The success of sticking one's hands under the faucet, as a response to the sight of one's own dirty hands, depends on a number of identities that are usually architecturally guaranteed. When one sees dirty hands in a certain way, it is the perceiver's hands that are dirty. When one washes hands in a certain way, it is the agent's hands that get clean. And when a perception of the first sort causes an action of the second sort in a more-or-less direct way, the subject of the perception is the agent of the action. *We don't really need a self-notion to handle any of this. We will need one when we start to get information about ourselves in ways that are not normally self-informative* (Perry 2002: 208–209, my emphasis).

I agree that for many purposes we do not need an explicit notion of ourselves at all, since much of our cognition and action can remain at the level of consciousness-as-subject. But if Perry is suggesting that one needs a first-person notion of oneself *only* when one begins to acquire information about the objective person one is, I believe this overlooks the Evansian point noted above: that the first person allows us to articulate the very idea of a point of view, and that this idea by itself can make a rational difference to our thinking. Whether we "need" a first-person notion for this purpose will depend on whether we need to grasp the very idea of a point of view, and I'm not sure what it would mean to claim that we *need* to grasp this. But at any rate, it represents a real intellectual advance, one that is rationally prior even to our grasp that our point of view belongs to an objective person.

5.8.3. Egoism versus Anti-Egoism

Let us return, finally, to the Egoist/Anti-Egoist controversy with which we began. The position at which we have arrived can be thought of as representing a qualified—but only a qualified—victory for Egoism. It is a victory inasmuch as we have endorsed the Egoist claim that the content of reflective self-knowledge can be expressed as

I think that...

rather than merely as

There is thinking that...

since reflective awareness of thinking (where "thinking" is understood in the broad Cartesian sense as including all kinds of representing) includes awareness that a given representation belongs to a single, overarching point of view to which all of my representations belong. It is only a qualified victory, however, inasmuch as we have rejected the further claim, endorsed by classical Egoists like Augustine and Descartes, that the awareness expressed in "I think that..." necessarily implies the existence of a *being* who is the possessor of the relevant point of view. On the contrary, we have maintained that the awareness expressed by "I think" does not per se imply the existence of any possible *object* of conscious awareness who thinks. It implies only the existence of a *subject* who thinks, which is to say, a conscious point of view that this act of thinking partly characterizes. This conscious point of view is posited through mere reflection on our consciousness-as-subject of thinking, and so does not imply the existence of any objective entity who possesses this point of view, though it also does not rule out the existence of such an entity.

In these respects, our position bears comparison with the position Kant takes in his famous chapter on the Paralogisms of Pure Reason. Kant claims that, when we accompany our representations with "I think," this "I think" "serves only to introduce all thinking as belonging to consciousness" (KrV A341/B400), and thus is "not even a representation distinguishing a particular object, but rather a form of representation in general, insofar as it is to be called cognition" (KrV A346/B404). The "form of representation" he has in mind, I believe, is the form in virtue of which various representations belong to the *unity* of single interconnected point of view. He takes our warrant for accompanying our several representations with "I think" to lie in our awareness that they essentially belong to such a unity; but he denies that we can draw from this awareness any metaphysical conclusions about what kind of objective being, if any, underlies this unity. To draw any such conclusion, he maintains, would be to mistake "the logical exposition of thinking in general" for "a metaphysical determination of the object" (KrV B409). Just so, we have claimed that, when a subject accompanies a thought of which she is conscious-as-subject with "I think," she recognizes this thought as implying relation to a single conscious point of view, whose unity she expresses by ascribing her thought to a first-person subject. On our view, this "I" does not by itself designate any object of which she is aware, but merely posits the subjective unity that is essential to her consciousness as such. So we too can say that the error of the kind of "rational psychology" practiced by Augustine and Descartes is to seek to draw metaphysical conclusions about the objective being that I am from my awareness of this subjective unity.

Still, we should acknowledge a sound point in the Augustinian/Cartesian identification of "I" with the mind. If we think of "I" as most contemporary philosophers do, simply as an indexical term that refers, in any context, to its user in that context, then the suggestion that "I" must refer specifically to the mind will seem strange—perhaps the residue of some dualistic conception of the relation between mind and body. But the real source of the identification, I believe, lies not in the opposition of mind to body, but in that of subject to object. Augustine and Descartes take "I" to express our idea of the mind because they take "I" to signify the single subject of whom various conscious states (or activities) are predicated, and they think of "the mind" as the conventional term for the bearer of these states.[42] This does not yet settle how we should think of the relation between the bearer of these states and the bearer of bodily states like being bald or weighing 185 pounds: perhaps "I" refers to a Strawsonian "person," who is the unequivocal bearer of both mental and physical properties, rather than to a Cartesian "thinking substance" that is "really distinct" from any body.[43] But recognizing the essential link between "I" and the articulation of consciousness-as-subject makes the question of the relation between myself and my body at least intelligible: if "I" fundamentally signifies the *subject* of consciousness, and bodies are essentially possible *objects* of consciousness, then there is a real question about how these two topics are related. It is to this question that we will turn in the next chapter.

---

[42] This need not imply that *only* conscious states are mental states. The claim that the connection to consciousness-as-subject anchors the concept of mind need not imply that it exhausts this idea.

[43] Cf. Strawson 1959: Ch. 3.

6
Bodily Awareness

> [P]recisely because the body is inapprehensible [*insaisissable*], it does not belong to the objects of the world—i.e., to those objects that I know and use. And yet, on the other hand, since I cannot be anything without being conscious of what I am, it must be given in some way to my consciousness.
>
> —Jean-Paul Sartre, *Being and Nothingness*, 440/368

6.1. Introduction

In the previous chapter, I stressed the deep difference between positing oneself as the *subject* of conscious awareness and identifying oneself as an *object* of such awareness, and I argued that our basic form of self-consciousness, expressed in our use of the first person, is an awareness of our own subjectivity. It might seem, however, that this leaves out something crucial. For we are plainly *embodied* beings, not mere points of view, and surely we are aware of ourselves as such. Yet how does the conception of self-consciousness that we have been developing accommodate this point? How does it allow us to move beyond knowledge of ourselves as the unified subject *of* our various representational states to awareness of ourselves as embodied beings who are physically present *in* the world we represent? If our reflectivist approach to self-consciousness cannot account for this, it has surely left out something crucial. I want to argue, however, that our approach can account for this awareness of our own embodiment, and indeed, that the notion of nonpositional consciousness is crucial to accounting for it. To bring this out, it will help to begin by considering a classic problem about the relationship between awareness of oneself as the subject who thinks and awareness of oneself as a bodily being (§6.2) and Sartre's somewhat puzzling response to this problem (§6.3). Unraveling the meaning of Sartre's response will open a new perspective on bodily awareness (§§6.4–6.5), and this in turn will transform our conception of what it is to be aware of ourselves as embodied beings (§§6.6–6.7).

6.2. The Subject-Object Problem

After completing his famous argument for the "real distinction" between mind and body, Descartes acknowledges that certain sorts of experience can lead us to overlook this distinction:

> There is nothing that my own nature teaches me more vividly than that I have a body, and that when I feel pain there is something wrong with the body, that when I am hungry or thirsty the body needs food and drink, and so on. . . . Nature also teaches me, by these sensations of pain, hunger, thirst and so on, that I am not merely present in my body as a sailor is present in a ship, but that I am very closely joined and, as it were, intermingled with it, so that I and my body form a unit. If this were not so, I, who am nothing but a thinking thing, would not feel pain when the body was hurt, but would perceive the damage purely by the intellect, just as a sailor perceives by sight that his ship is broken.[1]

A philosopher who rejects Cartesian dualism might want to resist some of Descartes's formulations here: perhaps we already concede too much to dualism if we ask what sensations of pain, hunger, and thirst teach us about how we are "present in our bodies." Be that as it may, something in Descartes's observation seems right. My own body seems to be known to me in a specially intimate way in which other worldly bodies are not. In experiencing sensations of pain, hunger, and thirst, I do not merely come to *know about* the condition of my body, as a sailor might come to know about the condition of his ship. I *feel* the condition of my own body, in such a way that damage to my body is experienced as damage *I* suffer, and its needs are experienced as *my own* needs. Descartes calls such experiences "confused modes of thinking" because they mix together presentations of the condition of the thinking subject with presentations of the condition of a material body. A more neutral statement of the matter might be that such awareness gives me *prima facie* grounds for doubting that there are two things presented here. My bodily sensations seem to give me awareness of my body, not "from the outside," as if I were *observing* a certain object, but "from the inside," as if I *were* the object in question. They present a condition of my body as if it were a condition of my very self.

Yet though it is natural to express the import of bodily awareness in this way, the meaning of this idea is not easy to make clear. In feeling a pain in my arm, I seem to learn, through sensation, about the condition of a certain arm—perhaps that it is injured, at any rate that it is causing me pain. How does this differ in principle from the perceptual relation in which a sailor might stand to

---

[1] René Descartes, *Meditations on First Philosophy*, §VI (AT VII: 81).

the hull of his ship when he sees that it is damaged, or at any rate that it looks to be so? Might our capacity to "feel" the condition of our bodies be just one more sense modality, differing from the five familiar senses in that it is directed exclusively toward a single object, and perhaps involving some distinctive phenomenology that marks out the relevant object as specially significant to me, but still presenting what are fundamentally *perceptions* of this object? A significant number of contemporary philosophers endorse this sort of view: they hold that our capacity for bodily sensation, and also—something Descartes does not mention—our capacity for "proprioceptive" awareness of the positions of our limbs, are specialized perceptual capacities, differing from our external senses in important ways, but sharing with them the basic structure in virtue of which a subject is informed of the condition of an object by experiencing sensory impressions normally caused by this object.[2]

At any rate, whether or not it is correct to think of bodily awareness as a kind of perceptual awareness, it seems inevitable that we must conceive of it as some sort of awareness of an object. After all, our bodies surely are material objects, so what can bodily awareness be but an awareness in which these objects are presented to us? And if this is right, then making sense of Descartes's observation seems to require understanding how there can be an awareness that presents a material object, not merely as one more entity encountered by the knowing subject, but as the subject herself. We might call this the *Subject-Object Problem*: what can it consist in for the knowing subject to be presented as something *in* the world? What features of the presentation of an object could mark it out as the knowing subject herself?

Once the problem of bodily awareness has been framed in this way, further choice-points come into view. Is there perhaps some special "phenomenology of ownership" that singles out a certain body as my own? Does my sense of a certain body as my own arise, not from some separable element of phenomenology, but from a recognition of general connections between certain kinds of information about this body and my own capacities for perception, sensation, and voluntary movement? Each of these positions has been defended in recent work on bodily awareness, but a point on which both sides generally agree is that bodily awareness involves a presentation of a certain body that is somehow marked as a presentation of myself.[3]

---

[2] Prominent philosophical advocates of this sort of view include Armstrong 1962, O'Shaughnessy 1995, and Bermúdez 1998. The view is also widespread among psychologists and neuroscientists. For different kinds of opposition, see Anscombe 1962, Brewer 1995, Gallagher 2003, and McDowell 2011.

[3] For different views about the basis of our "sense of ownership" of our bodies, see, e.g., Brewer 1995, Martin 1995, Bermúdez 2005, de Vignemont 2007 and 2013.

6.3. Sartre's Enigmatic Intervention

In a well-known passage of *Being and Nothingness*, Sartre suggests that this way of formulating the problem of bodily awareness sets us on the wrong path from the start. At the beginning of his chapter on "The Body," he remarks that, if I begin by conceiving of my body as an object of which I am aware, the problem of how my consciousness relates to this body will prove insoluble:

> [I]f, after having apprehended 'my' consciousness in its absolute interiority, through a series of reflective acts, I try to unite it with a certain living object constituted by a nervous system, a brain, some glands, some digestive, respiratory, and circulatory organs, whose very matter is capable of being analyzed chemically into atoms of hydrogen, carbon, nitrogen, phosphorus, etc., then I will encounter insurmountable difficulties. But these difficulties stem from the fact that I try to unite my consciousness, not with *my* body, but with the body of *others*. In fact the body which I have just described is not *my* body such as it is for *me*. (BN 409/342)

This passage is often quoted, and it has served as an inspiration for important work on bodily awareness.[4] Yet it is undeniably obscure, and even authors inspired by Sartre's remark have, I think, often failed to grasp its point.

To see the obscurity, consider that my body surely *is* a "living object" (or better, the material body of a certain kind of living animal) consisting of a nervous system, glands, digestive organs, etc. Any account of bodily awareness that does not explain how it can make me aware of this sort of thing does not, we might think, address the crux of the Subject-Object Problem: it does not explain how a certain material being can be presented to the conscious subject as her very self. And in any case, even if we grant that there is some other mode of presentation of my body which does not present it *as* a material body with organs, glands, etc., surely the crucial question is whether the object of which my bodily awareness makes me aware is *identical* to a certain material body. But questions of identity turn, not on agreement in modes of presentation, but simply on the identities of the things presented. The Morning Star and the Evening Star have quite different modes of presentation; still they may be the very same celestial body, presented in different ways. If I *am* a certain bodily being, why should acknowledging this fact create "insuperable difficulties" for an account of "my body as it is for me"?

---

[4] For discussion of Sartre's views on bodily awareness, see Evans 1982, Brewer 1995, Cassam 1997, and Longuenesse 2017.

Perhaps moved by such concerns, some authors have sought to extract a more straightforward point from Sartre's discussion. Commenting on the passage quoted above, for instance, Gareth Evans remarks:

> [I]n one way [Sartre's claim] is correct: I can identify myself with a bit of matter only if I know that bit of matter 'from the inside'—so that a groundwork for the identification is laid in the ordinary self-ascriptive statements I learn to make. But what this constitutes a groundwork for is an ability to identify myself with an element of the objective order—a body for others, if you like—unreservedly. (Evans 1982: 266)[5]

Evans takes Sartre's good point be to this: I can identify an "element of the objective order" as myself only because I have immediate, first-personal awareness of certain facts about that body, such as that my legs are bent (on the basis of proprioception), that I am leaning to the left (on the basis of my vestibular sense), that I am standing in front of a table (on the basis of visual observation of the table, seen from a certain characteristic perspective). These are modes of awareness that

I am F

for some range of values of F that are indisputably properties of tangible bodies in space, and yet they are known *immediately* in that I can know these first-person propositions to be true without needing to infer them from independent knowledge that

X is F & I am X.

On Evans's reading, Sartre's good point is that, if we did not have such immediate, first-personal awareness of certain of our own bodily properties, we would be unable to identify ourselves as elements of the objective order. But, he holds, admitting this need not require us to deny that bodily awareness presents me with the condition of a certain object, the one to which I refer when I say "I."

I think what Evans offers as a more circumspect statement of Sartre's point misses Sartre's real insight. Sartre's claim is more radical: that bodily awareness does not, in the first instance, present *me* or *my own condition* as such. My aim in

---

[5] The quoted text was composed by Evans's editor, John McDowell, summarizing notes that Evans was not able to integrate into the finished text before his untimely death. For similar reactions to Sartre's view, see Cassam 1997: 72, and Bermúdez 2005.

this chapter will be to clarify this idea by connecting Sartre's remarks on bodily awareness with another Sartrean idea with which we are already familiar: his distinction between "positional" and "nonpositional" consciousness. Sartre's main point, I want to suggest, is that our primary form of bodily awareness is a kind of *nonpositional* consciousness. I will argue that he is right about this, and right to think that recognizing this point is crucial to understanding what it is for something to be my body. At the same time, I hope that the following discussion will throw further light on the nature and importance of the positional/nonpositional distinction.

6.4. Positional versus Nonpositional Consciousness Again

It will help first to remind ourselves of the distinction between positional and nonpositional consciousness. As we saw in Chapter 3, Sartre introduces this distinction by making the following claims:

(S1) "[A]ll consciousness . . . is consciousness *of* something. In other words, there is no consciousness that is not a *positing* of a transcendent object" (BN 9/17).

(S2) "[E]very knowing consciousness can only be knowledge [*connaissance*] of object" (BN 10/18).

(S3) "[A]ny positional consciousness of an object is at the same time a nonpositional consciousness of itself" (BN 11/19).

(S4) "[N]on-reflective consciousness is what makes reflection possible" (BN 12/19).

To see the attraction of these claims, I suggested, it helps to think of the idea that certain questions about our present mental states are normally "transparent" to corresponding questions about the non-mental world. If I want to know how things in my environment visually appear to me, it seems that I can simply ask myself to describe my environment, while restricting my description to certain kinds of features (color, shape, movement, etc.) and setting aside other extraneous information. If I want to know whether I intend to do A, it seems that I can simply ask whether I am going to do A, while restricting the grounds for my answer to the latter question in certain specifiable ways. And if I want to answer the question whether I believe that *p*, it seems that I can simply ask myself whether *p*. In each case, I answer a question about my own mental state, not by observing myself, either outwardly or through some "inner sense." Rather, I address a question about some aspect of the non-mental world and treat my answer as settling a corresponding question about my own mental state.

In all these cases, my "positional" consciousness of some aspect of the nonmental world seems to supply a basis for a reflective consciousness of my own state of consciousness. But how does the positional consciousness warrant the reflective consciousness? Suppose I am perceptually conscious of a cat lying on a mat. *What* I am conscious of—what my consciousness "posits"—is a worldly state of affairs (the cat's being on the mat) that might obtain even if I were not perceptually aware of it. So how can my perceptual consciousness of *it* give me knowledge of my own perceptual state?

Sartre's doctrine of nonpositional consciousness earns its keep by enabling us to solve this problem. The doctrine, to repeat, is that all positional consciousness of an object involves nonpositional consciousness (of) this very state of consciousness, and that reflection simply articulates the significance of this nonpositional consciousness. As an illustration of this structure, consider once again the situation in which I have perceptual consciousness of a gray cat lying on a mat in front of me. What I am "positionally" conscious of is: a gray cat lying on a mat. But I am conscious of the cat in a particular mode, one it would be natural to express by saying "*This* is a gray cat lying on a mat," where "this" is what philosophers commonly call a "perceptual demonstrative." A person who says, "This is a gray cat lying on a mat" on the basis of perceptual consciousness does not say that *she perceives* the relevant cat: the only objects she makes claims about are the cat and the mat. But her *manner* of speaking about these objects presupposes that she perceives them. The fact that she perceives the cat and the mat is expressed, we might say, "nonpositionally" in her assertion: it is not asserted, but it is a presupposition of the soundness of what is asserted.

Moreover, the same points apply, *mutatis mutandis*, if we shift our attention from the verbal formula with which the subject expresses her perceptual consciousness to her perceptual consciousness itself. What this consciousness "posits" is simply: a cat lying on a mat. But again, it presents the cat and the mat in a specific manner, one that it would be apt to express with a perceptual demonstrative. So what holds true of the assertion used to express this consciousness also holds true of the consciousness itself: it presents its object in a mode whose applicability presupposes that the relevant object is perceived. The subject's perceptual consciousness is certainly not *of* herself, but it posits the cat and the mat in a way that presupposes that she perceives them. Hence, a subject who understands the relationship between this mode of presentation of non-mental objects and her own perceptual state would be in a position, on reflection, to ascribe perceptual consciousness to herself. She would, that is, be in a position to know her own perceptual state through mere reflection. Her basis for this reflective self-knowledge would be an already present *nonpositional* consciousness (of) perceiving implied in the special "haecceitical" mode of her consciousness of the cat and the mat.

I argued that this general structure will apply wherever transparent self-knowledge is possible. Such knowledge simply makes explicit the significance of a preexisting nonpositional consciousness, where nonpositional consciousness (of) our own consciousness is not a further state of awareness over and above positional consciousness of an object, but an awareness implied in the very mode of presentation of the relevant positional consciousness.

6.5. Nonpositional Bodily Awareness

The interesting point for present purposes is that, according to Sartre, the primary form of *bodily* awareness is also nonpositional. But what would it mean for me to have nonpositional consciousness (of) my own body?

It might seem that, if I am to be aware of my own body, this awareness must be positional. After all, bodies seem to be quite different sorts of entities from states of consciousness. There is indeed some attraction in the idea that our primary awareness of our own states of consciousness does not "posit" them as such. Consciousness seems to be, as G. E. Moore put it, "diaphanous" (Moore 1903: 446, 450): it seems to have no proper content of its own, but to consist wholly in the presentation of some consciousness-transcendent object. But whatever the attractions of this idea in the case of consciousness, it might seem conspicuously unattractive in the case of bodies. A human body is something concrete and tangible—and tangible, it seems, not just to other persons, but to the subject whose body it is. For don't I have an experience that "posits" my own body when I feel (e.g.) pressure applied to my skin, or when I experience pains, itches, or tickles as located in particular places in my body? And doesn't my proprioceptive sense make me aware of the position and arrangement of my limbs? My body seems to be the intentional object of all this awareness: *it* is presented as being thus-and-so. Such consciousness is undoubtedly distinctive: it is awareness of an object "from inside" in a sense that needs clarification. But is it not still awareness *of* an object? What else could it be?

Sartre does not deny that we can, on reflection, describe our bodily awareness in such terms, but he denies that such descriptions express the primary form of bodily awareness. He holds that our primary mode of awareness of our own bodies is analogous to our primary mode of awareness of our own states of consciousness: it is a "transparent" awareness in which we are positionally conscious of extra-bodily objects, and only nonpositionally conscious (of) our own bodies. Indeed, he would suggest that even bodily sensation and proprioception are not fundamentally modes of positional awareness of one's own body. Let me say something about each of these points.

First, concerning the idea that our primary awareness of our own bodies is analogous to our primary awareness of our own states of consciousness, Sartre makes a point that has also been noted by a number of thinkers: that even when I am conscious only of non-bodily things in my environment, this consciousness is informed by an implicit reference to my own body and its powers. This is a point we already noted, in the previous chapter, with respect to "egocentric" modes of presentation of space such as "here," "there," "up," "down," etc. Sartre holds, however, that a version of this point applies not just to our ways of apprehending space, but to our ways of apprehending things in space:

> Objects are disclosed to us within a structure of equipment in which they occupy a determinate *place*. This place is not defined by pure spatial coordinates but in relation to axes whose reference is practical reference. 'The glass *is on the tray*': that means that we must take care not to knock the glass over if we move the tray. The packet of tobacco *is on* the mantlepiece; this means you have to cross a distance of three meters if you want to go from the pipe to the tobacco while avoiding certain obstacles—small tables, armchairs, etc.—which are placed between the mantlepiece and the table. In this sense, there is no distinction at all between perception and the practical organization of existents into a *world*. (BN 431–432/361)

The idea that our primary apprehension of objects in our environment presents them as "ready to hand" for us, and as characterized by "affordances" whose nature must be specified by reference to our own bodily powers, is by now a familiar thesis of phenomenological philosophy. What Sartre adds is that this apprehension of things under body-relative modes of presentation must itself be understood as resting on a nonpositional form of bodily awareness. Like the awareness of perceiving expressed in thinking of *this cat*, the awareness of my own body expressed in thinking of objects as *here* or *there*, *up* or *down*, etc., is an awareness in which my body is not posited as such, but in which an implicit bodily awareness makes possible a specific mode of awareness of extra-bodily things. I apprehend my environment, Sartre says, as a "structure of equipment," and my body itself does not appear in this field (or does so only contingently, as when I look down and see my hands). In the normal and basic case,

> [f]ar from its being the case that our body is *for us* what is first and discloses things to us, it is the equipmental-things which, in their original appearance, indicate our body to us. (BN 436/365)

In such awareness, my body appears, not as an object of awareness, but, so to speak, as the transparent medium *through* which the world around me is presented.

But what about my awareness of my body through bodily sensation and proprioception? Surely these forms of awareness "posit" my body as an object! And mustn't our awareness of the things in the world under body-relative modes of presentation presuppose such body-positing awareness? After all, how can I learn, through touch, about the tangible properties of the table if I am not already aware, through bodily sensation, of the sensory impressions that touching the table produces in my finger? And how can I be aware that (e.g.) the cup over there is *within reach* if I am not already aware of the location of my hand?

Sartre argues that this account of the relation between bodily awareness and awareness of one's environment is the very reverse of the truth. The representation of bodily sensation and proprioception as forms of positional awareness of one's own body is, he maintains, a secondary, reflective representation of these modes of consciousness. They are primarily forms of consciousness in which I posit, not my own body as being in some condition, but rather extra-bodily things as determined in ways that presuppose nonpositional bodily awareness. Here are a few of Sartre's illustration of this point: nonpositional consciousness of eye fatigue expressed by experiencing the book I'm reading as hard to take in, its words blurry, its meaning intelligible only with effort;[6] nonpositional consciousness of exertion, pressure, etc., expressed in experiencing extra-bodily objects as heavy, resistant, etc.;[7] nonpositional consciousness of fatigue expressed in experiencing the road I am walking down as interminable, the slopes increasingly steep, the sun ever more burning, and so on.[8]

---

[6] "[T]his pain may itself be *indicated* by objects in the world, i.e., by the book I am reading: it may be more difficult to drag the words away from the undifferentiated ground that they constitute; they may tremble or flicker.... It is incontestable that pain contains information about itself: it is impossible to confuse a pain in the eyes with a pain in one's finger or stomach. However, the pain is wholly lacking in intentionality.... [W]e are not considering pain from a reflective point of view; it is not being related to a body-for-the-Other. It is eye-pain or sight-pain, and is not distinguished from the way in which I apprehend the transcendent words. We have called it 'pain in the eyes' for clarity in our exposition, but it is not named within consciousness, because it is not *known*" (BN 445/372).

[7] "We never have the sensation of our effort, but nor do we have the peripheral, muscular, skeletal, tendinous or cutaneous sensations which have been proposed in its stead: we perceive the *resistance* of things. What I perceive when I want to lift this glass to my mouth is not my effort, but its *heaviness*, i.e., its resistance to entering into a structure of equipment that I have brought to appear within the world" (BN 435/364).

[8] "[F]atigue is only ... the way in which I exist my body. In the first instance, it is not the object of a positional consciousness, but my consciousness's very facticity.... Yet to the extent that I apprehend this countryside with my eyes, which unfold distances, with my legs, which climb the slopes and thereby cause new scenes and new obstacles to appear and disappear, with my back, which carries the knapsack—to this extent I have a nonpositional consciousness (of) this body—which regulates my relations with the world and signifies my engagement in the world—in the form of fatigue. Objectively and correlated with this non-thetic consciousness, the roads are revealed as interminable, the slopes as *more difficult*, the sun as more intense, etc." (BN 595/498–499).

Some of these reformulations may seem forced. Sometimes, perhaps, eye fatigue inflects my experience of reading a book, but don't I sometimes just feel a shooting pain in my skull? Sartre can admit this, however, while maintaining the point that is crucial for his purposes: that the primary, unreflective mode of bodily sensation is nonpositional. For he can say, plausibly enough, that in cases like this, I experience a bodily sensation so acute that it disrupts my unreflective engagement with the world and throws me into a state of reflective preoccupation with my own condition. This does happen, and not infrequently, but it does not show that the primary form of bodily awareness posits our own body as an object. The latter is a question, not about the frequency with which we attend to our own bodies as opposed to our environment, but about the aspect of such awareness that is epistemologically primary. Sartre claims that the epistemologically primary aspect is the one in which bodily awareness inflects our mode of awareness of the world. For the moment, my aim is merely to clarify the meaning of this claim: I will turn to Sartre's arguments in support of it in the next section.

Before turning to this topic, however, we must say something about the other, "proprioceptive" dimension of bodily awareness. All the preceding examples concern bodily sensation; Sartre does not directly address the topic of proprioception. But this very oversight points to something worth noticing: awareness of the position of my own limbs is not, except in special cases, part of my lived experience at all. When I wake up before dawn and reach out in the dark to grope for my glasses on the bedside table, my discovery of them as being in a certain place clearly depends on some sort of my awareness of the location of my hand; but it would be poor phenomenology to describe me as presented in the first instance with the location of my hand and only thereby with the location of my glasses. On the contrary, what I primarily experience is the discovery of my glasses in a certain place. The awareness of the location of my hand comes into focus only when I engage in a kind of reflective reformulation of this worldly awareness (compare the transition from being tangibly aware of the hardness of the table to being aware of the feeling of pressure that touching the table causes in my finger). Nor is there any reason why the underlying epistemology must take another shape. Why shouldn't I simply discover that my glasses are *there* (where the significance of this place-designation must, to be sure, be explained by relating it to the location of my hand) without needing first to be aware of *my hand* being there? The appearance of an argument for the contrary view disappears on closer inspection.

Indeed, I think these reflections cast doubt on the very classification of proprioception as a sense. In his evocative essay "The Disembodied Lady," the neuroscientist Oliver Sacks calls proprioception "our hidden sense," and marvels at the fact that, whereas our other five senses are "open and obvious," this sense was first noticed by a neuroscientist in the 1890s (Sacks 1970: 43). But if proprioception is a sense, why should it so easily remain hidden, while our other senses stand out unmistakably? Sacks, in the company of many other writers, appears to assume that we overlook this sense simply because it is in some way "recessive" in relation to other forms of sensory awareness. Our discussion, however, suggests a different moral: the reason this supposed sense "remains hidden" is not that it is overshadowed by other sensory awareness, but that it does not consist, in the first instance, in a sensory presentation *of the subject's own body* at all. The subject does not "proprioceive" the arrangement of her own limbs; she *perceives* things and places in her environment *under body-relative modes of presentation*. On reflection, she can make explicit the body-implicating dimension of this awareness, but what this reformulation expresses is not something presented by a distinct channel of perceptual awareness, but simply a kind of shadow cast by her body-mediated awareness of extra-bodily things.

It might seem to speak against this interpretation that people can, as a result of damage to their nervous systems, lose their proprioceptive awareness while retaining their capacity to perceive the world around them. Sacks describes a patient, "Christina," who suffers from such "deafferentation."[9] Physiologically speaking, what Christina loses is a kind of feedback by which her nervous system informs her brain about the position and movements of parts of her body, and Sacks vividly describes how, without such feedback, she becomes incapable of standing, controlling her posture, or performing routine actions without painstaking observation of her own movements. It might seem that the facts of this case—that Christina's disabilities result from a loss of somatic feedback, and that she can learn to compensate for this loss, to an extent, by relying on what is incontestably visual perceptual awareness of her own body—show that proprioception itself must be a form of perceptual awareness of our bodies, even if this mode of perception is conspicuous to us only in its absence. Moreover, the fact that Christina remains capable of perceiving objects in her environment even when she loses proprioception might be taken to show that her ability to perceive the world around her does not, after all, depend on the availability of nonpositional bodily awareness.

I believe, however, that these conclusions are unwarranted. The fact that the abilities Christina loses depend on somatic feedback does not show that they depend on a capacity for sense-perception whose *object* is her body. This is a question about how to conceive of the personal-level cognitive capacity that somatic feedback supports. On the present view, it is a capacity to perceive and engage with her environment under body-relative modes of presentation, rather than a capacity to perceive her own body and experience *it* as such. It is perfectly consistent with this view, and indeed to be expected, that our capacity to perceive

---

[9] For more detailed discussion of the phenomenon of deafferentation, see Cole and Paillard 1995.

and engage with our environment makes use of somatic feedback: this does not show that our bodies themselves are presented to us in a distinct channel of perceptual awareness. And the fact that Christina can compensate for her deafferentation by watching her own movements does not show this either: it might simply indicate that some of the things she could formerly do *without* relying on positional awareness of her own body can also be achieved, more cumbersomely, by relying on such awareness.

Christina's loss of proprioception diminishes her capacity to perceive and engage with her environment under body-relative modes of presentation, but it does not undermine this capacity altogether. This stands to reason: although proprioception is a vitally important dimension of our bodily awareness, it does not exhaust such awareness. Christina retains the ability to perceive things as *on her left*, *on her right*, *above her*, *below her*, etc., simply on the basis of vision, which presents the world around her in an egocentric framework that has her body at its center. She also retains the ability to initiate voluntary movements whose aims must be characterized in body-relative terms: stepping *forward*, reaching for the glass *over there*, etc. Her loss of proprioception diminishes her ability to execute these movements successfully, but her ability to represent her environment in such terms is supported by a lifetime of perceptual and practical engagement with the world around her, and does not simply disappear when somatic feedback is cut off. That she remains able to engage with her environment in these ways does not show that this ability is independent of bodily awareness; it simply shows that this awareness is more robust, and more diverse in its sources, than we might at first suppose.

6.6. The Primacy of Nonpositional Bodily Awareness

So far, my aim has been simply to shed light on what nonpositional bodily awareness could be. As we have seen, however, Sartre claims not only that there is such awareness, but that it is primary, whereas "positional" awareness of one's own body is secondary. But what sort of primacy is at issue here? Is this just a "phenomenological" claim about how things seem? Or are there reasons of principle why the nonpositional awareness must be primary? I'll close this chapter with a few words about this issue.

If the primacy of nonpositional bodily awareness were merely phenomenological, a philosopher like Evans might admit the point without making any substantive revisions in his position. Bodily awareness, he might say, has two aspects: it presents extra-bodily things in ways inflected by consciousness of our own bodies, and at the same time, it presents our own bodily condition as such. It may be true, Evans could concede, that the former aspect tends to predominate or to be the primary focus of our attention. There may indeed be good reasons for this: excessive attention to our own bodies might interfere with world-directed action.[10] But it does not follow that "nonpositional" bodily awareness is primary in any deeper sense, or that our bodies are *not* presented as objects in primary bodily awareness. The other aspect might be there all along, whether we attend to it or not.

Sartre's case for the primacy of nonpositional bodily awareness is indeed partly phenomenological, but he also offers principled arguments for his position. His primary strategy is to argue that the opposing view leads to a regress:

> [T]he only action that I am able to *know* at the same time that it is taking place is the action of Pierre. I see his movement and I determine his goal at the same time: he is drawing a chair up to the table *in order to* be able to sit near this table and to write the letter that he told me he wanted to write. In this way I am able to grasp all the intermediate positions of the chair, and of the body which moves it, as instrumental organizations: they are means in order to reach a goal that is pursued. Here, therefore, the other's body appears to me as an instrument in the midst of instruments.... If therefore I conceive of *my* body in in the image of the Other's body, it is an instrument in the world that I am obliged to handle delicately and which is like the key to the handling of other tools. But my relations to this special instrument can themselves only be technical ones, and, in order to handle this instrument, I need an instrument, which places us in an infinite regress. (BN 430–431/360–361)[11]

Sartre's general idea here seems to be that, if my body is presented to me as an object, it must be presented as something I can act upon, an "instrument" to which I stand in "technical" relations. But, he assumes, my capacity to act on any object itself presupposes bodily awareness: for, as we have seen, Sartre holds that the objects we act upon must be presented under body-relative modes of presentation, whose availability depends on our awareness of our own bodies. But if this presupposed bodily awareness also presented my body as an object—something whose states I must be aware of by sense perception and which I must act on to move—this would in turn require another, yet-more-basic form of bodily awareness, and so on ad infinitum. So although it is possible for me to act on my own body (e.g., by picking up my left arm with my right), I can do this only because I have a more basic nonpositional awareness of my body that enables me to perceive and to act on bodies at all: one in which my own body figures, not as an object in my sensory and practical field, but as the locus of my consciousness itself.

---

[10] For discussion, see Dreyfus 2007.
[11] Sartre's focus in the passage is on the bodily awareness drawn on in action, but he makes a parallel point about the role of awareness of my own sensory impressions in sense perception (BN 417ff/349ff).

A defender of Evans might reply that the notion of awareness of something "as an object" employed in this argument is tendentious. If awareness of my body "as an object" means awareness of it as something I must perceive and act upon, then it would indeed be implausible to claim that all bodily awareness presents my body as an object. But this point can be granted—an Evansian might argue—without prejudice to the thought that there are unreflective modes of bodily awareness that present my own body as an object in a more neutral sense. Suppose I have proprioceptive awareness that *my left leg is bent*, or what action theorists call "practical knowledge" that *I am walking*. These are forms of awareness of my own bodily states and activities that I may have without needing to observe or act upon myself. Nevertheless, they seem to have what we might call "body-positing intentionality": they involve representations *of* my body as being in a certain condition. So they are representations of my body as an object in the *logical* sense: they make my body a topic of reference and predication. And my body is, of course, a tangible thing in space. That these modes of awareness do not present my body as something I must perceive and act upon is irrelevant.

I think this Evansian response focuses the debate on the crucial question: whether our primary mode of bodily awareness presents our bodies as objects in what I have called "the logical sense." I take Sartre to deny that it does. For the reasons just given, Sartre's official argument for this claim is inconclusive, but I think we can reformulate his point in a way that responds to the Evansian objection just outlined. The Evansian objection insists that it is possible to have various forms of non-observational awareness of oneself as an object, and surely this is correct. We must inquire, however, into the preconditions of this kind of self-awareness. Proprioceptive awareness that *my leg is bent* and practical knowledge that *I am walking* may not depend on self-observation, but they do presuppose an understanding of myself as a material object, a tangible occupant of objective space. What are the preconditions of such understanding?

Well, as we saw earlier, Sartre holds that our understanding of material objectivity presupposes bodily awareness, since material objects in our environment must be given to our consciousness primarily under body-relative modes of presentation, as here or there, up or down, within or out of reach, etc. If this point is sound, it should apply not just to extra-bodily objects, but to our own bodies themselves: to *understand* them as material objects located in space requires understanding them as things we might encounter and act upon.[12] This point holds even if, in a given case, I am aware of a certain fact about my own body without self-observation: still my *comprehension* of this fact presupposes

---

[12] I think Evans would accept this: it is implied in his remarks on the need for our Ideas of ourselves to meet the "Generality Constraint," and on the role of what he calls "the fundamental level of thought" in allowing our self-thoughts to meet this constraint.

a grasp of my body as something that can be encountered and acted upon. And if Sartre is right, this comprehension in turn presupposes the kind of awareness that enables me to represent objects in my environment as here or there, within or out of reach, etc. But we have argued that these latter modes of awareness of objects themselves presuppose bodily awareness.

A revised version of Sartre's regress argument is now available. It would run as follows: Any awareness of my own body *as an object* requires understanding it to be a material object located in space; but such understanding presupposes a more basic kind of bodily awareness. If this awareness, too, presented my body as an object, it would again presuppose a more basic kind of bodily awareness. But then, on pain of regress, the epistemically basic mode of bodily awareness must not posit my body as an object. So it must be a *nonpositional* bodily awareness. Hence any positional bodily awareness presupposes nonpositional bodily awareness, and cannot be coeval with it.

On this revised version of the Sartrean argument, the sense in which my body is not presented "as an object" in primary bodily awareness is the logical sense: my body is not an object of reference and predication in such awareness. Thus I am inclined to say—though I am not sure Sartre would accept this way of putting it—that Sartre's claim that my body is not given as an object should be understood logically rather than ontologically. A human body is certainly a material object, but it is not an *object in the logical sense* in primary bodily awareness. If, in seeking to understand how our bodies are presented to us, we consider only states of consciousness in which our bodies are posited as such, we will be unable to comprehend the foundation on which rests the very idea that some body is *mine*. This is what I take Sartre to be saying in the famous passage quoted at the beginning of §6.2.

When I have nonpositional bodily awareness, I am of course warranted in making corresponding positional self-ascriptions if the question arises. Consider for instance a state of visual consciousness in which I am presented with a looming door. If the door occupies a progressively increasing portion of my visual field in a certain characteristic way, I may have the warrant for thinking, on reflection, *I am approaching a door*, a judgment in which I posit myself as a bodily presence in the scene.[13] This judgment may require nothing more in the way of *warrant* than what I have in being conscious of a looming door: I need not

---

[13] For the sake of simplicity, I set aside some issues that would need to be discussed in a full treatment of such examples. By itself, an experience of a looming object does not differentiate between a situation in which I am approaching the object and a situation in which the object is approaching me. It is clear, however, that our experience of movement in our environment normally contains features that disambiguate between these alternatives. Accounting for this should raise no difficulties for my Sartrean account of the role of bodily awareness provided that the relevant features can appear primarily as modes of presentation of objects in the environment, rather than as presentations of my own movement as such.

observe my own body or perceive it in some other way. But the judgment does require something more in the way of *understanding* than what is presupposed in consciousness of a looming door: it requires an understanding of myself as a material object in space. And now two points should be noted.

First, it does not seem obvious that the capacity for consciousness of a looming door itself requires such understanding. There is surely a difference in content between consciousness of *a looming door* and consciousness of *my approaching a door*: the latter draws on more sophisticated intellectual resources than the former. Psychologists have shown that human infants react in appropriate ways to looming presences in their visual field, to "visual cliffs," etc. But surely infants might react in such ways without yet possessing an understanding of themselves as material objects in public space. They might simply respond appropriately to looming presences without relying on any general understanding of their own location in space.[14] So, it seems, they might possess consciousness of a looming door without having consciousness of themselves approaching a looming door.

Second, if the thought *I am approaching a door* is to make genuine reference to a concrete individual, it must imply:

$(\exists x)(x$ is approaching a door$)$

where x ranges over material objects in space. But if Sartre is right, our general understanding of what it is for something to be a material object in space presupposes nonpositional bodily awareness. Hence nonpositional bodily awareness must be more basic than any positional awareness of my own body as such, and cannot be coeval with it.

6.7. Conclusion

Where does this leave the Subject-Object Problem? I think it should make us hesitant to frame this problem, as many contemporary philosophers do, as a question about what accounts for my "experience of ownership" of a body with which I am presented. For the upshot of our reflections is that what grounds our most basic experience of embodiment is not some way in which *our bodies* are presented to us. If Sartre is right, then there is not some special experience of ownership, at least not if this means some mode in which *our bodies themselves*

---

[14] I say they *might* do this because I do not want to make any claims about the actual facts of human cognitive development. Whether human infants have a general understanding of space and their location in it is, I take it, a question for empirical psychology. I do not claim to be able to answer to this question a priori; my claim is merely that, as a conceptual matter, such understanding is not obviously *required* as a precondition of the ability to be conscious of looming presences.

are experienced. Our most basic mode of bodily awareness is not one in which we experience our own bodies per se, but one in which bodily awareness figures, as I have put it, as the medium that informs our consciousness of the world around us. It is our experience of the world *from* a certain bodily standpoint, rather than any particular experience *of* this body, that grounds our awareness of being *in* the world, rather than being some kind of transcendent spectator upon it.[15]

I have only scratched the surface of this material. I have not discussed Sartre's intriguing discussion of how my consciousness of myself as an object for *another* consciousness transforms my understanding of my own embodiment (BN 453–468/379–391), or his remarks on what it is to perceive consciousness in another person (BN 468–478/392–400). Nor have I considered in detail how reflection on our nonpositional bodily awareness might contribute to our understanding of ourselves as embodied persons. My purpose in this chapter has simply been to take the first steps toward making this Sartrean perspective on bodily awareness available for consideration by clarifying the meaning of his idea that our primary awareness of our own bodies is nonpositional. If Sartre is right, our bodies, like our states of consciousness themselves, are fundamentally "transparent" to us. They are, as Sartre says, fundamentally "*lived* and not *known*" (BN 435/364):

> [M]y body cannot be transcendent and known for *me*. . . . Rather, we should say, using the verb 'exist' transitively—that [consciousness] *exists its body*. (BN 441/369)

My aim has been to show that, if we are to understand what it is for a person to "experience a certain body as her own," we must begin by coming to grips with this fundamental Sartrean thought.

---

[15] One main argument for the existence of a distinctive "phenomenology of ownership" is that it is possible to induce in people an illusion of ownership of limbs that are not actually theirs. In the so-called "Rubber Hand Illusion," a subject sees a prosthetic hand in front of her being stroked with a feather while her own hand, which is held out of view, is stroked in synchrony (for a review, see Slater et al. 2009). Subjects who undergo this procedure report experiencing sensations as if *in* the rubber hand, and they show other physiological signs of regarding that hand as if it were their own (for instance, they exhibit characteristic physiological threat responses when a sharp blade is brought toward the rubber hand). They commonly describe the experience as one in which the rubber hand is experienced as their own. Do such experiments show that there is some distinctive "phenomenology of ownership" that normally characterizes our experience of our own bodies, but that can, in special circumstances, be induced in respect of an appropriately placed prosthetic hand? If Sartre is right, it would be more correct to say that they show we can be induced to experience an illusion of feeling *the touch of that feather* (viz., the one seen to be stroking the prosthetic hand). The subject can reformulate this awareness, on reflection, as involving an illusion that their sentience extends to the rubber hand, but in its more fundamental aspect, the illusion is of experiencing the world *from* the standpoint of that hand, not of experiencing the hand itself. Hence there is no need to posit an experience *of the hand* with some special phenomenological character.

PART III
REFLECTION AND SELF-UNDERSTANDING

7
Reflection and Rationality

[T]he human mind *is* self-conscious in the sense that it is essentially reflective. I'm not talking about being *thoughtful*, which of course is an individual property, but about the structure of our minds that makes thoughtfulness possible. A lower animal's attention is fixed on the world. Its perceptions are its beliefs and its desires are its will. It is engaged in conscious activities, but it is not conscious *of* them. That is, they are not the objects of its attention. But we human animals turn our attention on to our perceptions and desires themselves, on to our own mental activities, and we are conscious *of* them. That is why we can think *about* them.
—Christine Korsgaard, *The Sources of Normativity* (1996), 92–93

7.1. Introduction

The notion of reflection has played an important part in our inquiry, but we have not yet made it an object of sustained theoretical attention in its own right. I have used the term "reflection" to name the activity by which we make a transition from nonpositional self-consciousness to positional self-knowledge, and I have illustrated this transition with a series of examples, which I hope lend plausibility to the claim that we can make transitions of this kind. But it is one thing to recognize *that* we can make such transitions, another to understand *how* we do so. So far, I have simply said that the cognitive step from nonpositional self-consciousness to positional self-knowledge is warranted by reflection. But what *is* reflection, and how does it supply us with this warrant? This question—call it the question of the *nature* of reflection—is clearly one we must address.

The notion of reflection is also of interest for another, more general reason. A long philosophical tradition sees a connection between our capacity for reflection and our rationality, the trait that is supposed to distinguish our human cognitive power from the cognitive capacities of lower animals. The above-quoted passage from Christine Korsgaard's *The Sources of Normativity* is an influential recent expression of this idea. According to Korsgaard, our capacity for reflection liberates us from a merely automatic or instinctive responsiveness to our environment and delivers us into the kind of free and distanced relation to grounds for belief and action that is characteristic of a rational animal, one that can think about the reasons for its own attitudes and choices.

Is the notion of reflection invoked by Korsgaard the same one at issue in our claims about the transition from nonpositional self-consciousness to positional self-knowledge? They certainly seem related. Korsgaard is concerned with our capacity to "back up" from mental states that would directly determine the beliefs and actions of a nonrational animal, and she conceives of this step back as implying the formulation of thoughts *about* the relevant mental states. Although she does not say so explicitly, it seems clear that she has in mind, not mere speculation about what these states might be, but a kind of thinking grounded in immediate awareness of our own mental states. She does not, to be sure, take for granted our Sartrean theory of reflection, and she relates the question of reflective self-knowledge to normative questions that lie beyond the scope of our inquiry. Nevertheless, her intended topic surely overlaps with ours. This invites the question whether our account of reflection can shed light on the importance that Korsgaard—in the company, as I have said, of a long philosophical tradition— assigns to the human capacity to reflect. Can we explain, not only what reflection is and how it is warranted, but why it makes an important *difference* to our cognition, and exactly what kind of difference it makes? We may call this the question of the *significance* of reflection.

The aim of the present chapter will be to address these two questions. With regard to the nature of reflection, I will argue that it involves a *sui generis* cognitive step in which we transform a capacity to represent *in* certain modes into an awareness *of* the relevant modes of presentation themselves. To understand the warrant for this step, I will suggest, it is crucial to see that, in the basic or "pure" case, reflection does not change the topic of our thought but merely alters our manner of thinking it: what we had formerly represented in an unreflective manner we now represent *reflectively*. Nevertheless, this alteration fundamentally transforms our relation to our own representational activity, and we shall see that this helps to explain the significance of reflection, and to vindicate the traditional association between reflection and rationality.

7.2. A Budget of Difficulties

To sharpen our thinking about these issues, it will help to begin by noting a range of difficulties we confront in seeking to answer our two questions.

Consider first the question about the nature of reflection. We said that this is a step in which the subject "makes explicit" something of which she was already "implicitly" or "nonpositionally" aware. It is not easy, however, to understand the nature of this step. For is the subject already aware of the relevant fact, or isn't she? If she is, it is hard to see what kind of contribution "reflection" could make to her cognition. If it is simply a matter of her putting what she already knows into words, how could this represent a real cognitive advance? Putting knowledge into words presumably involves exercising one's linguistic abilities to *express* some known fact in speech or articulate thought; but what is thus expressed must, by hypothesis, already be known, so the step to articulation will not itself add to one's knowledge, except perhaps in the uninteresting sense that it may add recognition that the relevant fact can be expressed in such-and-such words.[1] We are interested, however, in a kind of "articulation" that does not merely bring something one knows to verbal expression, but that somehow advances one's comprehension of the known fact itself. It seems, then, that there must be a sense in which the subject is *not* yet fully cognizant of this fact until she reflects.

Yet to the extent that she is not cognizant of the relevant fact, how are we to understand the warrant for her act of reflection? If reflection is to be, not a kind of groping in the dark, but a form of thinking that is guided by an antecedent awareness, this preexisting awareness must be rich enough to justify what the reflecting subject thinks. But it is hard to see how it could meet this condition without being so rich as to render the act of reflection cognitively superfluous.[2]

Whatever reflection amounts to, it certainly seems quite different from other familiar forms of cognitive transition. On the one hand, it seems fundamentally unlike the act of *inference*, in which a subject begins from belief in some set of propositions Π and, by recognizing a rational relation between these propositions and some further proposition p, comes to believe that p. For, as I have repeatedly emphasized, the *content* of the first-order mental state on which a subject reflects does not in general stand in any determinate rational relation to the content of her reflective thought.[3] If I believe that it is raining, for instance, the sheer proposition *It is raining* does not entail or evidentially support the thought *I believe that it is raining*; and similar points hold, *mutatis mutandis*, for the contents of other kinds of mental states on which we can reflect. The step from first-order mental state to reflective self-ascription thus does not seem to be an inference. Yet on the other hand, reflection also seems fundamentally different from the kind of cognitive transition exemplified by *perceptual judgment*, in which a subject

---

[1] Compelling oneself to articulate one's thoughts may of course sharpen one's thinking: in seeking to bring a thought to articulacy, one may discover that the point is not easy to state clearly, or raises questions that one did not foresee. Having to resolve these difficulties may bring determinacy to a thought that was initially vague or muddled. This kind of sharpening of one's thinking can certainly represent a cognitive advance, but it is not relevant to our problem: we are concerned with a kind of case in which, by hypothesis, the relevant knowledge is *not* vague or muddled, but merely "implicit." Our problem is to understand what this can mean, and what kind of cognitive advance "articulation" of such implicit knowledge can involve.

[2] A related difficulty is developed in Alshanetsky 2019. Alshanetsky's problem and his approach to solving it are in important ways different from mine, but I have been helped by his formulations.

[3] Nor need the reflecting subject suppose it to stand in some such rational relation.

begins by perceiving an object, and, on the basis of this perceptual relationship, forms a belief about what this object is like. Perceptual judgment has in common with reflection that it brings conceptual articulation to an awareness that is not in the first instance articulated: just as I can have "nonpositional" awareness of perceiving a gray cat without judging *myself to perceive* a gray cat, so I can perceive (what is in fact) a gray cat without judging it to be *gray* or a *cat*. But whereas in making the perceptual judgment

> This is a gray cat

I bring my classificatory abilities to bear on the object I have in view, in making the reflective judgment

> I perceive a gray cat

I seem to classify something that I do *not*, in any straightforward sense, have in view. What I see, after all, is the cat, not myself or my own perceiving; and again, similar points hold, *mutatis mutandis*, for other kinds of mental states on which we can reflect. What sort of cognitive step, then, can reflection be, and how does its ground rationalize its conclusion?

We may add to these difficulties a final question about the state of awareness that the reflecting subject comes to possess. A subject who is in a mental state M, and who exercises her capacity to reflect on this state, comes to be aware that:

> (R)   I am in M.

But is her awareness that (R) a further, distinct mental state over and above the state M on which she reflects? For instance, suppose M is my feeling of repulsion at the large and many-legged centipede that I have just discovered in my bathtub. If I reflect and think

> I feel repelled by that bug

does this just consist in my forming a distinct second-order belief about my first-order mental state, so that my feeling of repulsion is one state and my belief that I feel repulsion is another?

If reflective awareness of our first-order mental states just consisted in our holding second-order beliefs about ourselves, it is hard to see how it could amount to an awareness *from an inhabitant's perspective* in the sense characterized in Chapter 2. In that chapter, we drew the following moral from Richard Moran's discussion of transparency: transparent self-knowledge of our own mental states is available to us only if the point of view we ascribe to ourselves is the very one we consciously inhabit. A person who consciously inhabits a point of view, we said, does not merely have some first-order mental state, on the one hand, and a second-order belief that she is in this state, on the other. Rather, her point of view on herself and her point of view on the world fuse into one, in such a way that she can express her first-order point of view *in* thinking herself to be in the corresponding mental state. For instance, when she reflectively says or thinks:

> I feel repelled by that bug

this very thought can express her *repulsion at the bug*, not just her second-order belief *that* she feels repelled. In general, where a subject is capable of becoming aware of a given mental state by reflection, she will be able to express her first-order mental state by explicitly self-ascribing the state in this way.[4]

This appears to require, however, that the subject's reflective awareness that:

> (R)　I am in M

not be a distinct mental state over and above the first-order state that it makes explicit, but somehow an aspect of this first-order state itself. For how could the subject's thinking (R) express her first-order state of being in M if her belief that (R) were a distinct state from her first-order state of being in M?[5] Yet this idea—that a subject's being *in* a certain mental state might itself involve her being reflectively aware of that state—at the very least needs clarification. What kind of change in a subject's mental state does reflection bring about if it is not just the formation of a distinct second-order belief but some kind of transformation of her first-order state itself? How does the dawning of reflective awareness modify the first-order state on which the subject reflects? And if reflective awareness is not distinct from the state on which it reflects, how are we to maintain our grip on the idea that reflection can give us *knowledge* of our own mental states. Doesn't the very idea of knowledge imply *some* kind of distinction between a known state of affairs, on the one hand, and a representation of this state of affairs, on the other?

---

[4] This is the insightful point stressed by writers like Finkelstein and Bar-On. See §2.5 for discussion.

[5] I take it that an activity can only *express* some mental state M if it is somehow directly caused by M, not by a distinct mental state N that is in turn caused by M. The notion of direct causation at issue here needs further clarification, of course, as does the notion of expression itself. In the present context, however, these notions need only bear enough weight to allow us to formulate our problem about the relation between a first-order mental state and our reflective awareness of it. For this purpose, it will suffice if we are persuaded that the phenomena of expression and direct causation are real.

The task of explaining the nature of reflection thus presents special challenges that prevent us from assimilating this act to some more familiar model of cognition. In the preceding chapters, we responded to these challenges in particular cases, but our task now is to respond to them abstractly and in general. What *is* reflection such that it can justifiably take us from awareness of the world to a thought about ourselves? In what way does it draw on preexisting self-awareness, and how are we to understand what it adds? How can we understand the relationship between reflective self-awareness and its object so as to respect their essential interdependence without collapsing the distinction between them?

Turn now to our second question about the cognitive significance of reflection. Strong claims have been made about the importance of our capacity to reflect. Korsgaard suggests that it is because we humans have this capacity that the very question of *reasons* for belief and action arises for us:

> [O]ur capacity to turn our attention on to our own mental activities is also a capacity to distance ourselves from them, to call them into question. I perceive, and I find myself with a powerful impulse to believe. But I back up and bring that impulse into view and then I have a certain distance. Now the impulse doesn't dominate me and now I have a problem. Shall I believe? Is this perception really a *reason* to believe? I desire and I find myself with a powerful impulse to act. But I back up and bring that impulse into view and then I have a certain distance. Now the impulse doesn't dominate me and now I have a problem. Shall I act? Is this desire really a *reason* to act? (Korsgaard 1996: 93)

This passage appears to imply that the capacity to consider reasons for belief and action depends on the capacity to reflect on one's own mental states: in a slogan, that rationality requires self-consciousness. And similar claims have been made by several other recent authors.[6] A common argument for such claims is that only a subject who can reflect on her own attitudes can make rational adjustments to them, since only such a subject can consider the justification for her attitudes, their consistency with one another, and so on.

As a number of commentators have pointed out, however, this kind of argument rests on shaky foundations.[7] It may be true that only a subject who can reflect on her own attitudes can consider the consistency of her attitudes, or the adequacy of the reasons for them, *as such*, but it does not follow that only such a subject can consider the consistency of or warrant for the propositions that form the *contents* of her attitudes. If *p* and *q* are two propositions I believe, why can't

---

[6] Cf. Shoemaker 1991, McDowell 1994, McGinn 1996. Burge 1998 holds a subtler but related position.

[7] Cf. Moran 1999, Cassam 2014, Peacocke 2014.

I simply consider the consistency of *p* and *q* without needing to think about the consistency of *my believing p* and *my believing q*? And why can't I simply consider whether it is genuinely evident that *p*, rather than thinking about whether *my perception* gives me a genuine reason *to believe* that *p*? Korsgaard's rhetoric suggests that our capacity to reflect on our own attitudes is a precondition of our capacity to query our own beliefs and choices in a way that releases us from a merely automatic or instinctive responsiveness to perception and desire. But although there is something attractive in this idea, its appeal as an argument seems to trade on an ambiguity in the notion of "reflecting on an attitude." It is plausible that, in order to transcend the condition of merely instinctive responsiveness to its own representations, a creature must be able to reflect on the *contents* of its own attitudes, but it does not follow that such a creature must be able to reflect on its attitudes *as such*—i.e., to formulate self-ascriptive thoughts about its own attitudes and ask itself whether these *attitudes* are reasonable to hold. So is there a genuine connection between rationality and the capacity for reflection, and if so, how can this connection be demonstrated in a way that does not beg the question?

7.3. Rationality and the Taking Condition

At the root of all these difficulties is a fundamental unclarity about the relationship between rationality and reflective self-awareness: about how our capacity to reflect on our own mental states contributes to our rationality, on the one hand, and how the step to reflective self-awareness can itself be rational, on the other. A crucial first step in responding to these difficulties will therefore be to give closer scrutiny to this relationship. I want to suggest that the issue that interests us—the relationship between rationality and our capacity to reflect on our own mental states—is in fact a special case of a more general linkage between rationality and reflection. To bring out this more general connection, it will help to begin with a particular variety of rational activity and then generalize the point. So I will focus in the first instance on the capacity to draw inferences, a capacity commonly regarded as distinctive of rational creatures.

When I speak of the capacity to draw inferences, I mean the capacity to make cognitive transitions from a given set of propositions to a further proposition in virtue of some sort of (presumed) *understanding* of the rational connection between the former and the latter. Today, the term "inference" is often used in a broader way, especially in the cognitive sciences, where it is frequently applied to any non-accidental transition from a set of given representations to some further representation, provided that this transition is governed by a mechanism that in general produces outputs that are in fact rationally related to their corresponding inputs. In this broader sense, we may speak of inferences into which the inferring subject has no insight—indeed, of inferences that occur entirely at a "subpersonal" level, so that the subject is aware at most of their output, not of the inputs that give rise to them. Thus we are sometimes said to draw "inferences" from proximal patterns of retinal stimulation to features of distal objects, or from rudimentary acoustical data to an interpretation of spoken words, although we have no insight into the bases of these inferences or the principles that govern them. This is a perfectly acceptable way to use the term "inference," as far as it goes, but it differs from the classical usage in philosophy, in which the term is reserved for cognitive transitions that happen at the "personal level" (i.e., such that the representations involved are all ascribable to the person herself, rather than to some module or system in her), and that occur in virtue of the subject taking there to be some rational connection between the propositions that figure as her premises and the proposition that expresses her conclusion. How to understand this notion of "taking there to be a rational connection" will be our next question, but for now I will simply stipulate that, when I speak of "inferences" in what follows, I have in mind this sort of personal-level, *comprehending* step from premises to conclusions, whatever exactly such comprehension amounts to.

The problem of what such comprehension can amount to has been a topic of intensive recent debate since the publication of Paul Boghossian's influential article "What Is Inference?" (2014). Boghossian raised the question what relation must hold between a subject's belief in some set of premises and her belief in some further proposition in order for her to count as having *inferred* the latter from the former. For example, suppose a subject S draws a simple deductive inference such as:

(1) It is raining.
(2) When it rains, the streets get wet.
So (3) The streets are getting wet.

What sort of relation must there be between S's beliefs in (1), (2), and (3) for her to count as having *inferred* (3) from (1) and (2)?

As Boghossian points out, it clearly does not suffice for S first to believe (1) and (2) and then come to believe (3): she must come to believe (3) *because* she believes (1) and (2). But not just any "because"-relation will do: a person's believing (1) and (2) might cause her to believe (3) in some "deviant" way, and might thereby bring her to hold a belief that is in fact rationalized by (1) and (2), but all this might occur without her seeing in (1) and (2) a reason to accept (3). She might, for instance, have been subjected to a form of Pavlovian conditioning that causes her automatically to believe (3) whenever she believes (1) and (2), even in the absence of any insight into the connection between them.

As a way of capturing what is missing from such deviant cases, Boghossian proposes the following *Taking Condition* on inference:

(TC) A rational subject S who infers some conclusion C from some set of premises Π must come to believe C because she *takes* Π to support C.[8]

(TC) is intuitively attractive: it seems simply to spell out the psychological significance of the "so" that connects the subject's conclusion to her premises. A subject who draws a personal-level inference does not just move automatically from certain extant beliefs to a further belief; she makes this transition in virtue of some (purported) *understanding* of the connection between her premises and her conclusion. She takes her conclusion to *follow* from her premises, or at any rate to be rationally supported by them in some less stringent way (e.g., by their providing good evidence for this conclusion).

The difficulty, however, is that it is far from clear what "taking" one's premises to support one's conclusion can consist in. When we try to clarify this idea, we appear to confront a dilemma. On the one hand, if (TC) is interpreted as requiring that S *believe* something like:

(4) (1) and (2) support (3)

then we must be prepared to explain what role this additional belief plays in bringing about her transition from believing (1) and (2) to believing (3). The requirement cannot be that (4) should figure as a further premise of S's reasoning, for then (TC) will also require her to take it that:

(5) (1) and (2) and (4) support (3).

And now (5) too will need to be added to her premises, and we will be on our way to an infinite regress. But then how exactly does a subject's believing (4) contribute to her inferring (3) from (1) and (2)? In denying that the subject's belief in (4) functions as a further premise of her inference, we set aside the only well-understood model of how beliefs function in generating rational thought and action, and thus relinquish whatever gain in understanding the introduction of (TC) was supposed to provide.

Moreover, we should remember that we introduced (TC) to capture what is missing from deviant forms of connection between S's believing (1) and (2) and

---

[8] My formulation of (TC) is briefer than Boghossian's, but not different in essentials (cf. Boghossian 2014: 5). For a more general attempt to characterize rationality as a capacity to act on considerations *taken as* reasons, see Korsgaard 2018.

her believing (3). If the "taking" mentioned in (TC) is just another propositional belief, it is hard to see how it could accomplish this. If S's believing (1) and (2) can deviantly cause her to believe (3), so too, presumably, can S's believing (1), (2), and (4). So even if S's belief in (4) does not function as a premise in her reasoning, it is not clear how adding it to the background of her inference helps to solve our problem.

Yet if we reject the identification of taking with believing, how are we to understand it? The intuition underlying (TC) was that, in a genuine inference, the subject's coming to believe her conclusion must occur, not just automatically, but in virtue of her having some (purported) insight into the rational connection between her premises and her conclusion. But if we eliminate the doxastic element in our interpretation of (TC), it is not clear what remains for us to make of this idea. S may presumably be *disposed* to believe (3) in the presence of beliefs (1) and (2) without having any insight into the connection. (TC) says that the mere operation of such a disposition does not suffice for inference; S's coming to believe (3) must reflect her having some understanding of the (purported) relationship between (1), (2), and (3). But what can this mean if not that she holds some belief about this relation?

In the light of our interest in the relationship between nonpositional self-awareness and positional self-knowledge, we should be struck by the curiously liminal character of this "taking" one's conclusion to follow. It seems that such taking must be something less than an explicit belief in a proposition like (4), but something more than a blind disposition to proceed from given premises to rationally related conclusions. It must be some kind of (purported) awareness of a rational relationship, something that contributes to the subject's *understanding* of her reason for drawing her conclusion, yet it must somehow figure in the background rather than the foreground of her thinking. Indeed, it is plausible that a person can take her conclusion C to follow from her set of premises Π in the relevant sense without holding any attitude toward the proposition:

(I)   C follows from (or is rationally supported by) Π

and indeed without having framed for herself the general concepts of *implication* or *rational support* as such. The usual arguments apply here: it seems plausible that a child, for instance, could draw rational inferences without yet having formed such sophisticated concepts. It would be sufficient if she were able to defend her conclusions when queried by appealing to the corresponding premises, which would not require her having framed any general concept of the *kind of relation* she thereby asserts to hold between these propositions. Having a general concept would permit her to frame general thoughts *about* implication or rational support: it would put her in a position, for instance, to think generally about what implies what in a way that points, at its limit, toward the project of giving a general theory of logical implication. But surely it is possible, given some premises, to think about what else must be so, without having framed any general notion of the relation of implication (or any other rational relation) as such.

In its puzzlingly intermediate position between explicit belief and mere obliviousness, "taking a conclusion to follow" from given premises is strikingly analogous to the "nonpositional" awareness of our own mental states that has been our focus. Here the topic of nonpositional awareness—if we allow ourselves to speak this way—is not some property of the subject's own mental state, but a (purported) relation between propositions, which need not themselves concern a psychological topic. In spite of this difference, however, parallel issues arise in the two cases: there is, on the one hand, a puzzle about the nature of this pre-reflective taking and, on the other hand, a question about its relation to the kind of proposition that we can formulate on reflection, viz.:

(I)   C follows from Π.

Moreover, once we have seen how these puzzles arise in the case of inference, we can recognize that other kinds of rational activity raise analogous problems.

Two brief illustrations will help to bring this out.[9] Consider first a claim Philippa Foot makes about the difference between rational and nonrational agency. Nonrational agents certainly pursue ends, she admits: for instance, sheep may move to a certain part of a field to graze on the attractive grass located there. Nevertheless, she maintains—elaborating on some remarks in Thomas Aquinas—that sheep do not pursue their ends "as ends," as we rational animals do: we rational animals do not merely pursue what is in fact our end (e.g., desirable grass), but comprehend what we pursue *as* our end (Foot 2001: 54). To bring out the parallel with Boghossian's claim about rational inference, we might express Foot's claim by saying that rational agency is subject to a *Practical Taking Condition*:

(PTC)   A rational subject S who pursues some end E must do so because she *takes* E to be an end worth pursuing.

Again, there is something intuitively attractive about (PTC), but there is a difficulty about how to understand the relevant taking. For it would surely over-intellectualize rational agency to suggest that every act of a rational agent must be guided by an explicit motivating representation of the form:

---

[9] I am indebted to Doug Lavin for many conversations about this topic. The illustrations I give below are also discussed in Lavin 2011.

(M)   E is an end worth pursuing.

Surely one can act for the sake of particular ends, in a manner rationally responsive to considerations that make these ends worth pursuing, without having framed the general concept of an *end worth pursuing* as such.[10] But if (PTC) does not mean that rational agents must act in virtue of some thought like (M), what exactly does it mean?

Consider, finally, this claim Brian O'Shaughnessy makes about the difference between rational and nonrational knowledge:

> [A]nimals know truths, but not their truth. A dog knowing it is about to be fed, does not know it is true it is about to be fed. It could do so only if it could *compare the thought* 'I am about to be fed' with the reality that makes it true.... And this in turn requires the knowledge that one has that thought, together with the capacity to contemplate its denial as a possibility that is here in fact not realized. But because 'animal thought' (if one may call it that) is essentially categorical-practical, animals cannot relate in this way to their 'thoughts', which are essentially modes of practical involvement in their surrounds.... In this special sense animals may be said to be *immersed* in the world in a way thinking beings are not. (O'Shaughnessy 2003: 111)

Like Foot's claim about rational agency and Boghossian's claim about rational inference, O'Shaughnessy's claim about rational thought is contentious, but let us set aside controversy and simply consider how O'Shaughnessy's idea parallels these other claims about the nature of rationality. O'Shaughnessy claims that rational animals know "under the aspect of truth" (2003: 111), but he surely does not mean that all their beliefs must take the form:

(B)   *p* is true.

---

[10] I believe it would also be possible to raise a regress problem for this proposal, similar to the regress problem that threatened the view that taking one's conclusion to follow consists in believing that it follows. In the practical case, the starting point for the regress would be the observation that a person can accept (M) without thereby being motivated to pursue the relevant end. So it seems that in order for an attitude of form (M) to constitute a *motivating* representation of an end, the relevant attitude would have to be held in some special, "practical" mode. But if an agent's accepting something in a practical mode requires that she explicitly represent it as an end worth pursuing, then it seems as though the agent must also hold some attitude like

(M')   It is worth acting in light of the fact that (M).

But (M') too can surely be accepted in a non-practical mode, so it seems that yet another higher-order representation (M'') would be needed to ensure practicality the practicality of (M'), and so on, *ad infinitum*.

He means rather to bring out something about what is involved in their simply believing p: in so believing, a rational subject somehow thinks of the proposition that p as corresponding to the fact of the matter.[11] Once again, we could express this by saying that rational belief is subject to a *Doxastic Taking Condition*:

(DTC) A rational subject S who believes p must do so because she *takes* it to be true that p.

But whatever such "taking" consists in, it cannot in general require a further thought of form (B), for all the now-familiar reasons.[12]

It thus comes naturally to appeal to some kind of non-doxastic "taking," not just in characterizing inference, but also in characterizing other aspects of rationality. Indeed, I believe the need to appeal to such non-doxastic takings is pervasive in the characterization of rational cognition, for it arises from an intuitive and general requirement on rationality: namely, that rational activities be performed, not just blindly or automatically, but with a certain understanding. Whatever this understanding amounts to, it is implausible to think of it as consisting in the subject's holding a further belief about the topic of her cognition (that it follows from her premises, that it is an end worth pursuing, that it is true, etc.). We may call propositions that make essential use of concepts such as *follows from*, *is true*, and *is an end worth pursuing* "second-level propositions." These propositions characterize the rational significance *of* the objects a subject thinks about ("objects" in the broad sense: foci of intentional directedness, which may be concrete individuals, ends, states of affairs, etc.), whereas *first-level propositions* merely characterize these objects themselves.[13]

---

[11] O'Shaughnessy in fact goes further: he holds that, for a rational subject, believing p implies "knowledge that one has that thought, together with the capacity to contemplate its denial." I think this demand for knowledge of one's own thoughts is needlessly contentious. A weaker but still substantive claim would be that, in a rational subject, believing p implies understanding p to be a proposition that might or might not correspond to the facts. This formulation would preserve a distinction between mere "animal immersion" and the truth-oriented character of rational belief, but it would avoid requiring knowledge of one's own thoughts as a precondition of rational belief. It would thus leave room for our project of accounting for how a rational subject might come, through reflection, to understand herself as holding certain beliefs.

[12] Again, it seems plausible that the capacity to take p to be true is more basic that the capacity to believe p *is true*, which requires grasp of a general concept of truth as a property of propositions. And again, if rational belief that p requires belief in a proposition of form (B), then it seems that by the same principle rational belief in (B) should require belief in a proposition of the form

(B') (p is true) is true.

And so on, *ad infinitum*.

[13] I call these contents "first-level" and "second-level" because I have used "first-order" and "second-order" to mark the distinction between the (generally world-directed) contents *of* our mental states and thoughts *about* our mental states themselves. As I will use these expressions, second-*level* propositions characterize the rational significance of the *topics* of our mental states (things, properties, relations, purported facts, etc.), whereas second-*order* propositions characterize *our own mental states* as such. I will allow myself to speak also of the special "second-level (/

The implausibility of identifying rational understanding with a belief in some second-level proposition can be brought out in various ways: for instance, by emphasizing that such beliefs require concepts not plausibly possessed by unsophisticated but nevertheless rational subjects, or by showing that this way of characterizing rational understanding would lead to a regress. But these are just subtle ways of bringing out what is really a simple flaw. The point of saying that rational animals regard their ends "as ends," their beliefs "as true," or their conclusions "as following" from their premises, is not to identify some further *content* that such animals can represent, but to gesture toward something distinctive about the *manner* in which they represent any content whatsoever: they do so, as it were, comprehendingly. The general problem we face in seeking to understand rationality is the problem of characterizing this pre-doxastic comprehension and its relation to the reflective knowledge it makes possible. I want to suggest that our problem about the nature of reflective self-knowledge is a special case of this more general problem.

7.4. Taking and Reflection

Once we see them against this broader background, our difficulties about reflective self-knowledge take on a different aspect. In some respects, they are problems about a special topic: knowledge of our own minds. In other respects, however, they are plausibly seen as manifestations of a more general feature of rational cognition: that it involves understanding in a way that implies the possibility of reflection on its own operations. We might express this point by saying that, inasmuch as we are rational beings, all the operations of our cognitive power have a double aspect: on the one hand, they make possible some item of first-level cognition (drawing a particular conclusion from certain premises, forming a belief in some particular proposition, practical orientation toward some particular end, etc.); on the other hand, they essentially involve the *potential* for reflection on these operations and their rationale as such. I will first examine the general point about rational cognition and then return, in the next section, to the special case of reflective self-knowledge.

To bring out the general point, it will be useful to consider a famous problem about inference raised by Lewis Carroll in his essay "What the Tortoise Said to Achilles" (1895). Carroll has the tortoise ask Achilles why acceptance of the two propositions:

---

second-order) concepts" that figure essentially in such propositions, the "second-level cognition" we have of such propositions, etc. I hope the meaning of these uses of "second-level" and "second-order" will be clear enough in context.

(A) Things that are equal to the same are equal to each other.
(B) The two sides of this triangle are things that are equal to the same.

requires him to infer that

(Z) The two sides of this triangle are equal to each other.

Achilles naturally answers that, as a matter of logic,

(C) If A and B are true, Z must be true

and the tortoise says he is happy to accept this and add it to his stock of premises, of which Achilles is to keep a list in his notebook (since "whatever Logic is good enough to tell me is worth writing down"). But now of course the tortoise can raise an analogous question: Why does acceptance of A, B, and C require him to infer Z? The proposition that

(D) If A, B, and C are true, Z must be true

can be accepted and added to the notebook too, but this will still leave open an analogous question, and so on *ad infinitum*.

The moral of this parable is often said to be that acceptance of a relation of implication cannot just consist in acceptance of a further premise, and this leads to a question about what it *can* be to accept such a principle—for the tortoise is surely right that it is possible to doubt that a conclusion follows from given premises, and if it is possible to doubt this, it seems that someone who draws the inference must presumably accept it. Pursuing this question would, I think, lead us back to our problem about the nature of the non-doxastic "taking" that undergirds inference. For present purposes, however, it is useful to emphasize a point that is less often noted in discussions of Carroll's problem: that even if acceptance of a principle of inference must be something other than mere belief in a proposition, it is surely important that the inferring subject *can* formulate the relevant principle as a proposition. If Achilles had no insight into the connection between A, B, and Z—if he just found himself believing Z when he thought of A and B, without any idea of a rational connection between these propositions—then he would not be making a comprehending *inference* from A and B to Z. For as we have already observed, such comprehension is what sets genuine inferences apart from merely automatic transitions from representational inputs to rationally related representational outputs. And although this comprehension cannot *consist* in mere belief in a further proposition, it is equally true that we would not ascribe such comprehension to someone who could not, on reflection, recognize that her grounds for accepting Z are A and B, from which she takes Z to follow.

Carroll's parable invites us to puzzle about what it can be to take a conclusion to follow, if this isn't just accepting the proposition that it follows. But we should also feel a converse puzzlement at the fact that a subject who takes a conclusion to follow can so readily formulate a corresponding proposition, if this is not what her taking her conclusion to follow consists in. I believe these two puzzles must be solved simultaneously. The key is to recognize that, on the one hand, the propositional formulation of the implication is merely the reflective, second-level expression of an understanding whose more fundamental mode of operation consists in linking acts of first-level cognition: the subject's believing A and B and her believing Z. But on the other hand, the *potential* for reflection is essential to this mode of understanding: it is only because the subject can reflect on the rational background of her inference that her cognitive transition is genuinely inferential at all. Hence a rational subject will be able to formulate the principle of her inference in a proposition like (C), provided that she grasps appropriate concepts (at a minimum, the conditional structure *if—then—*and the concept of truth). But even if she does not grasp such second-level concepts, we will expect her to be able to appeal to A and B when asked about why she accepts Z, and to defend the connection between these propositions against relevant challenges.

Once we recognize these points, our puzzlement about what it is to take one's conclusion to follow should begin to dissipate. On the one hand, it is not puzzling what can keep the subject's "taking her conclusion to follow" from collapsing into a mere disposition to move from representational inputs to related outputs, since its status as a genuine form of comprehension is secured by the fact that the subject *can* articulate it on reflection. And on the other hand, it is not surprising that the subject is able, on reflection, to formulate her pre-doxastic understanding in a proposition, since even before she reflects, her understanding consists in an ability to draw a conclusion, not just automatically, but in a way that involves the ability to give (what are in fact) her reasons and defend them against relevant criticisms. These two aspects of taking one's conclusion to follow—the fact that it can govern a first-level inference and the fact that it can provide the basis of an explicit claim about what follows from what—are two different manifestations of the very same understanding, one primary and the other secondary. The primary expression of such understanding consists in the ability to draw a conclusion in a way that is rationally conditioned by one's belief in corresponding premises, where by "rationally conditioned" I mean conditioned in a way that is not just automatic but open to consideration and challenge. The secondary expression is the ability to articulate a second-level proposition about what follows from what, which a subject capable of the primary expression will be able to do by merely reflecting, provided that she possesses appropriate second-level concepts.

An important consequence of these points is that, when such a subject reflects on the relation of her premises to her conclusion, she does not come to recognize something of which she was previously unaware. Rather, she merely expresses an already existing taking-to-follow in a new, reflective form. Thus, when her articulation of the second-level proposition *C follows from Π* expresses a genuine taking-to-follow, it is not a distinct cognitive state over and above her readiness to draw the relevant first-level conclusion from the corresponding premises: it is the same cognitive state expressed in a different way. The problem with Carroll's tortoise, we might say, is that his assent to such second-level propositions never expresses a genuine taking-to-follow in this sense; rather, it expresses mere belief in a further proposition whose inferential significance remains to be determined.[14]

Similar points hold for our other cases of rational "taking." Although taking *p* to be true does not consist fundamentally in holding an attitude toward the second-level content

(B) *p* is true

it is plausible to regard a subject S's attitude toward *p* as a taking-to-be-true only if S has the capacity to formulate (B) on reflection, provided she grasps the second-level concept *is true*. And when a subject who has this capacity does formulate (B), she does not form a further distinct belief over and above her belief that *p*, but merely gives reflective expression to the very same taking-to-be-true that is expressed unreflectively in her believing the first-level proposition *p*. Similar points apply to the relationship between taking E to be worth pursuing and holding an attitude toward the second-level proposition

(M) E is an end worth pursuing.

But let me emphasize again that I do *not* mean to suggest that S can engage in the relevant forms of first-level rational activity (drawing an inference, taking a proposition to be true, pursuing an end she takes to be worthwhile) only if she already grasps the second-level concepts *follows from*, *is true*, and *is worth pursuing*. As I said earlier, I think this would impose implausible intellectual requirements on rational but conceptually unsophisticated subjects, and would miss the crucial point about such "takings": that they consist, not in the subject's being able to think thoughts with some special second-level *content*, but in her being able

---

[14] Whether a subject who genuinely understands such propositions, and genuinely accepts them, can actually maintain such a detached attitude toward them is a question we can set aside here.

to engage in the relevant first-level activities in a distinctively comprehending *manner*.

Nevertheless, although a subject who can engage in such first-level rational activities need not actually grasp corresponding second-level concepts, she necessarily has them, so to speak, right at her fingertips. For even if she does not yet possess these concepts, she already possesses the ability to consider specific kinds of *questions*: questions about whether p, why C, or whether to pursue E. A child who has not yet mastered the general concepts of truth, entailment, or being an end worth pursuing must nevertheless, inasmuch as she is capable of making rational judgments, inferences, and choices, be capable of thinking critically about such questions. She will, for instance, manifest her understanding of the grounds of her inference from the propositions in Π to C by understanding the question "Why C?," and being able to respond relevantly by citing the propositions in Π and discussing their relevance to C. In responding to such questions, she will manifest her understanding of what follows from what, not by affirming the second-level content

(I) C follows from Π.

but in the way she thinks about the first-level proposition C itself, and how she relates it to the first-level propositions in Π.

Yet this very understanding will also enable her to acquire the second-level concept *follows from* in a special way: simply by *reflecting* on what she already understands. For she could frame this concept simply by introducing a term for the link she presupposes between a proposition C and a set of propositions Π when she is prepared to answer the question "Why C?" by appealing to the propositions in Π. Doubtless we typically learn the second-level concept *follows from* from our conceptually more sophisticated peers, but in principle none of us needs to learn it in this way, nor need we acquire it by observing some perceptible relation that can hold between states of affairs. For any of us who can respond to the relevant sort of why-question, the concept *follows from* will be merely an articulation, in the form of second-level concept, of an understanding we already exercise in thinking about first-level propositions.[15] And once any of us has grasped such a concept, they will be in a position, through mere reflection, to affirm a proposition of form (I) whenever they in fact take some proposition C to follow from some set of propositions Π.

---

[15] Indeed, even if we do acquire the concept *follows from* by learning it from our peers, it is clear that we will understand it only insofar as we grasp the link between its application and the meaning of a why?-question that we already understand.

Indeed, given the ease with which a rational subject can frame such second-level concepts, some readers may doubt that there is really a deep distinction between merely being capable of considering a conclusion in the light of some premises and grasping a corresponding second-level concept.[16] Doesn't a subject who can respond intelligently to the question "Why C?" already demonstrate grasp of the concept *follows from*, even if she doesn't possess a special term for this concept? Well, I have granted that, in one significant sense, she shows an understanding of what it is for a conclusion to follow from given premises; but the kind of understanding she exhibits, which we may call *applicative understanding*, is crucially different from the *conceptual understanding* exhibited by a subject who can think thoughts involving the corresponding second-level concept. A subject possesses applicative understanding of the relation of implication insofar as she can respond intelligently to queries about the grounds on which she accepts particular first-level propositions. She need not think *that* the relevant relations of implication obtain; she need only think about first-level propositions in a way that is intelligently responsive to such relations. Her understanding is thus exercised in her activity of *relating* first-level propositions to one another, rather than in thinking second-level thoughts *about such relations*.

The capacity to think such second-level thoughts makes the manner in which propositions are to be related into a topic of consideration in its own right, rather than merely expressing an understanding of the relevant relations in the subject's thinking about particular first-level propositions. This development makes possible forms of generality that would not be available to someone who possessed a merely applicative understanding of implication. It enables the subject to think, for instance, about such questions as which propositions belong to the set of propositions that *follow from* a given set of propositions Π, whether everything that *follows from* Π has a certain property, and what is required, in general, for one proposition to *follow from* others. Such questions would not be formulable by a subject who had a merely applicative understanding of implication: it requires making implication a topic of thought in its own right, not merely the governing principle of one's thinking about first-order topics. Since grasp of a concept is generally supposed to explain the capacity to think thoughts involving this concept, I reserve the label "conceptual understanding" for the kind of understanding of implication exhibited by a subject who can think thoughts that themselves involve the concept *follows from*. To claim that possession of such conceptual understanding is a precondition of an applicative understanding of implication is surely to put the cart before the horse: the more basic ability is to *draw* inferences intelligently, not to think *about* relations of implication as such.

---

[16] I am responding here to a doubt that has been pressed in conversation by my colleague Matthias Haase.

Similar points can be made about our other second-level propositions (B) and (M): they too make reflectively explicit modes of rational significance of which the subject already exhibits an applicative understanding in her ability to respond to specific kinds of queries about particular propositions or ends. In all these cases, the step from applicative understanding to conceptual understanding involves what we may call *reflective ascent*: an understanding that in the first instance functions as the governing principle of a certain kind of first-level thinking (thinking about whether p; or whether C given Π; or whether to pursue E) becomes a topic for thought in its own right in virtue of becoming the content of a general concept *of* the relevant form of rational significance. And the important point about such ascent is that it does not require the acquisition of new knowledge beyond what is already exercised in the relevant acts of first-level cognition. It does not constitute a new discovery, but merely the reflective articulation of an understanding already at work.

7.5. Self-Reflection

Having noted these points about the general relationship between reflection and rationality, we can return to the special case of *self-reflection*, in which we reflect, not on the rational significance of the *objects* of first-level cognition, but on the nature of the *subjective* mental states in virtue of which we cognize such objects.

We could think of such self-reflection as beginning from the same place as *object-oriented reflection* (as we may call it), but proceeding in the opposite direction. Object-oriented reflection ascends from the first-level consideration of objects to the second-level consideration of their rational bearing on a given cognitive question. Thus the second-level predicate *is true* classifies first-level propositions in a way that bears on the question whether p; the second-level predicate *is an end worth pursuing* characterizes a possible object of pursuit in respect of its relevance to the question what to do; and the second-level predicate *follows from* addresses the question whether C given Π. I call these predicates *object-oriented* because they apply to the objects of first-level cognition, rather than to the knowing subject.[17] Nevertheless, they are second-level predicates, inasmuch as they characterize these objects, not in themselves, but exclusively in terms of their rational bearing on cognition: in terms that pertain to how it is *sound* to think of a given object in the context of a certain cognitive project (forming true beliefs, drawing sound inferences, pursuing worthwhile ends). Self-reflection too ascends from the first-level consideration of objects, but its orientation is

---

[17] To repeat: I use "objects" in the broad, intentional sense, as a generic term for the *topics* of first-level cognition, be they concrete individuals, properties, propositions, sets of propositions, etc.

different. Instead of characterizing the rational bearing of objects on thought, it characterizes the actual relation of thought to its objects, specifying whether a given object is a topic of belief, perception, desire, intention, imagination, etc. The predicates of self-reflection are thus second-*order* predicates rather than second-*level* predicates: they characterize states of the knowing *subject*, rather than the rational significance of the known *object*.

In spite of these contrasts, it should now be clear that object-oriented reflection and self-reflection raise analogous difficulties. In both cases, it is attractive to explain the possibility of such reflection by appeal to a pre-reflective awareness of the points that reflection merely makes explicit. In both cases, it is plausible to think that this pre-reflective awareness is possible even in the absence of the subject's holding an attitude toward the corresponding second-level/order propositions, and even in the absence of a grasp of the second-level/order concepts that would permit her to formulate such a proposition. In both cases, however, the "nonpositional" character of this pre-reflective awareness prompts questions about what such awareness can amount to and how it can warrant the knowledge arrived at on reflection.

In our consideration of object-oriented reflection, we identified a general approach to these questions. The approach depended on recognizing an interdependence between the pre-reflective "taking" that makes possible a certain form of first-level cognition and the reflective articulation of this taking in the form of a second-level proposition. On the one hand, it is only because of the essential role of such pre-reflective takings in first-level cognition that the reflective articulation of such second-level propositions is possible. But on the other hand, it is only because the subject *can* reflect on the rational background of her first-level cognition that she counts as genuinely cognizant of her grounds for inference at all, even in a pre-reflective form. When a subject reflects on such a pre-reflective taking, we said, she does not form a new belief over and above this taking; rather, she simply expresses this same taking in a new, reflective manner. Her act of first-level cognition (for instance, drawing a conclusion from certain premises) and her reflective articulation of the rational background of this act (for instance, affirming a proposition of form (I)) are thus not expressions of two distinct cognitive states, but two expressions of the very same cognitive state, one primary and the other secondary.

Once we see this, I suggested, we can make unproblematic sense of what a pre-reflective taking is and how it warrants a subject in advancing to a reflective articulation of the principle of her own inference. For what initially appeared to be an elusive form of awareness turns out to qualify as such in virtue of its link to a kind of awareness that everyone recognizes as genuine, and the step to such reflective awareness turns out to be, not a mysterious step from ignorance to knowledge, but merely a redeployment of the very same understanding in an explicit, conceptual form. To describe this awareness as initially "pre-reflective" is to offer a merely negative characterization of it: it is to describe it in terms of what it is not, viz., a propositional belief about (e.g.) what follows from what. A more positive and less mysterious characterization would be that it is the awareness that governs a certain type of first-level cognition: for instance, the taking-to-follow that enables me to believe a certain conclusion C given preexisting belief in some set of propositions in Π. When I make this taking reflectively explicit, I bring to bear a widely recognized capacity of rational animals, the capacity to frame and apply concepts, but in a special way that makes the rational background of my first-level cognition into a topic for thought in its own right.

In the next chapter, I will show in some detail how this model of reflection is applicable to the case of self-reflection, and how it explains our capacity to frame concepts of our own cognitive states and to acquire a body of general knowledge about the relevant cognitive capacities "from an armchair" (i.e., by merely reflecting on what we already understand in virtue of possessing minds with the relevant cognitive capacities). Here I simply want to say a few words, in closing, about how our account of reflection would allow us to respond to the difficulties we raised in §7.2, and about the general conception of rationality that forms the background to our discussion.

7.6. Responses to Difficulties

Our difficulties were these. First, how can the reflective "articulation" of nonpositional awareness be a real cognitive advance and yet be justified, not a mere groping in the dark? Second, what is the nature of the cognitive transition that a reflecting subject makes, and how does it differ from inference on the one hand and perceptual judgment on the other? Third, how is the subject's reflective awareness related to her first-order mental state? Fourth, why should rationality require the capacity to reflect on our own mental states, rather than merely on their contents?

We are now in a position to shed some light on these matters. We can begin with the question about how reflection can be grounded in a pre-reflective awareness and yet be a real cognitive advance. Our distinction between applicative and conceptual understanding gives us a framework for thinking about this special sort of step. A subject who can engage with the *objects* of which she is aware in a way that is intelligently responsive to her mode of awareness of them— who can, for instance, reserve a special way of representing an object, as *this*, for occasions on which she presently perceives it—already has an applicative understanding of her perceptual relation to this object. To grasp the concept *perceives*, however, requires more than this: it requires that she transform her implicit familiarity with perceptual awareness into an explicit, conceptual understanding of perceiving as a relation in which an arbitrary subject can stand to an arbitrary object. Only insofar as she makes this transition from an applicative understanding of her own perceiving to a conceptual understanding of perceiving as a general mode of relation of subjects to objects does she acquire the capacity to think, of herself, that her condition exemplifies this general mode of awareness. And just as the reflective acquisition of the concept *follows from* enables a subject to consider questions that someone with a merely applicative understanding of implication could not formulate, so the reflective acquisition of the concept *perceives* enables a subject to consider questions that could not arise for someone whose understanding of perception was merely applicative: questions, for instance, about the conditions that must obtain for an object *to be perceived*, about what kinds of properties are *perceptible*, and so on.

Thus—to turn to our second difficulty—when a subject moves from perceptual consciousness of some object O, a consciousness she could express simply by thinking about

> this thing

to reflective awareness that

> I perceive this thing

this is, in one important sense, not an advance in knowledge: there is no circumstance of which the subject was formerly unaware and now is aware.[18] Rather, the difference is in the kind of understanding she brings to bear on her awareness of the relevant circumstance. Her thought of the object as *this thing* already expressed a nonpositional awareness of perceiving the object in question, but it did not connect this awareness with a general understanding of perception as a form of consciousness, and of herself as an enduring subject of manifold states of consciousness, whereas her reflective thought *I perceive this thing* expresses her awareness in a way that brings these general forms of conceptual understanding

---

[18] This is a point emphasized by Sartre in his discussion of reflection. He puts the point by saying that reflection is "recognition" (*reconnaissance*) rather than "knowledge" (*connaissance*—which might here be translated as "cognition" to bring out the verbal relationship):

> In the case of knowledge of a transcendent object, the object is effectively *disclosed*—and the disclosed object may deceive or astonish us. But reflective disclosure posits a being that was already a disclosure in its being. The reflection confines itself to making this disclosure exist for itself; the disclosed being is not revealed as something given, but with the character of having 'already been disclosed'. Reflection is *recognition* rather than knowledge. It implies a pre-reflective understanding of what it aims to retrieve as the original motivation for that retrieval (BN 224/191).

to bear. In this sense, she makes a genuine cognitive advance: she comes to recognize her own condition as exemplifying a general mode of awareness, perceiving, in respect of this particular object. But she needs no new *warrant* for this step beyond her warrant for thinking of O as *this thing*: the same relation to O that justified that unreflective thought justifies this reflective one as well. For the step of reflective ascent does not consist in the acquisition of new information, but merely in the application of new forms of understanding. As such, it requires no distinct ground, and this explains its fundamental difference from perception on the one hand and inference on the other.

These points also bear on our third difficulty: how the state of reflective awareness is related to the first-order mental state on which it reflects. Consider again our example of the subject who feels repelled by a bug and reflectively thinks:

(R) I feel repelled by that bug.

We said that awareness of this feeling "from an inhabitant's perspective" requires that the subject's reflective thought (R) be capable of expressing, not a mere belief *about* her feeling of repulsion, but her feeling of repulsion itself. Our difficulty was to understand this: How can a thought *about* my feeling of repulsion express my repulsion itself?

Again, our discussion of object-oriented reflection gives us the resources to respond to this challenge. In the object-oriented case, we said that there are not two distinct cognitive states, the pre-reflective "taking" that governs an act of first-level rational cognition and the reflective awareness expressed in affirming a second-level proposition. Rather, these are two expressions of a single state of awareness, which operates primarily in first-level rational activity, but is also capable of being brought to reflective articulation.

We can make an analogous point about the relationship between feeling repulsion at a bug and reflectively thinking:

(R) I feel repelled by that bug.

Suppose (in keeping with our hypothesis throughout this book) that the first-order state of feeling repelled by a bug involves the bug's being presented in a distinctive mode—"as repulsive," as we theorists may put it. I emphasize that this is a characterization from the theorist's perspective because, once again, there is no requirement that the subject who feels repelled should have an attitude toward the proposition *That bug appears repulsive* or *I feel repelled by that bug*, nor need she even grasp any concept like *repulsive* or *repelled*. She need only be conscious of the bug itself in a certain characteristic mode. Yet because her mode of representation of the bug is not just automatic but intelligent and open to consideration, she will in principle be able to frame such concepts and formulate such propositions by mere reflection on her first-order awareness of the bug. And now the important point is that, if such a subject does reflectively formulate the thought (R), she will be expressing the very same state of awareness—repulsion at the bug—in a different way. Her awareness *that* she feels repelled by the bug will be, not a distinct cognitive state over and above her feeling of repulsion, but merely a secondary, reflective expression of this same feeling, inasmuch as it is linked with the kinds of general understanding embodied in a first personal representation of herself and a relational concept of the form *X feels repelled by Y*.

There are in fact two different ways in which this reflective awareness might relate to the first-order state on which it reflects. In one kind of case, it might be simply a transient expression of this state, an expression in which the subject can engage whenever the question occurs to her, but whose production does not alter her first-order mental state in any fundamental way. Here we might say that she *reflects on* her feeling of repulsion, but that this feeling does not itself become *reflective*. There is also, however, another possibility: that the understanding exercised in her reflective awareness transforms her first-order mental state itself, so that this state comes to have a reflective character. To stay with the example of repulsion at a bug, this first-order feeling of repulsion might change in character when the subject comes to think *I feel repelled by that bug*: a repulsion that she formerly felt unreflectively might come to be felt *reflectively*, where this adverbial formulation marks the fact that her state of repulsion itself comes to be informed by a conceptual understanding of her own condition, so that she now feels repelled by the bug in a thoughtful and potentially self-critical way.

I will not discuss this latter possibility further here, but we will return to it in Chapter 10 when we consider the value of self-knowledge. For now, the crucial point is the one that applies to both transient and transformative cases of reflection: that the reflective thought that one is in a certain mental state expresses, not a cognitive state distinct from the first-order state on which it reflects, but an awareness that was already involved in the first-order state itself. The reason for this, as we have seen, is that, even before reflection supervenes, the relevant first-order state involves a non-positional understanding of itself. This resolves our third difficulty.

Consider finally our fourth difficulty about how the capacity to reflect contributes to rationality. Korsgaard seems to suggest that our capacity to reflect on our own mental states and their reason-giving force is what liberates us from merely automatic or instinctive responsiveness to perceptions and desires. We found it difficult, however, to see why rational consideration of the *contents* of perception and desire should require consideration of these mental states *as such*. In light of our discussion, what should we say about this?

We should begin by admitting that some of Korsgaard's formulations suggest a simpler connection between rationality and self-reflection than our discussion supports. For instance, when Korsgaard writes that

> our capacity to turn our attention to our own mental activities is also a capacity to distance ourselves from them, and to call them into question. I perceive, and I find myself with a powerful impulse to believe. But I back up and bring that impulse into view and then I have a certain distance. Now the impulse doesn't dominate me and now I have a problem. Shall I believe? Is this perception really a *reason* to believe? (Korsgaard 1996: 93)

This way of putting things suggests that the relevant sort of rational "distance" is achieved only when I "back up" to attend to my own perceptions as such. Our discussion, however, supports only the weaker claim that, as rational beings, we must have the *capacity* for reflection, and that one application of this capacity, *self-reflection*, enables us to consider our mental states as such (while another, object-oriented reflection, enables us explicitly to consider the rational significance of their objects).

This certainly does not imply that our mental states cease to "dominate us" (i.e., to act on us regardless of our rational assent) only when we attend to these states as such. For in the first place, it is possible to call into question the things we are disposed to believe (not our beliefs as such, but the first-order propositions we are inclined to believe) and the things we are disposed to do (not our desires or choices as such, but the first-order ends we are inclined to pursue) without reflecting on our own mental states. And secondly, even in cases where we never consider any such question, but simply form a belief unreflectively (or unreflectively draw an inference or set about pursuing an end), it *still* holds true, on the present account, that this first-order cognitive state involves nonpositional consciousness of itself and a non-doxastic taking of its object to warrant such a state. Reflection on these forms of nonpositional awareness actualizes their potential for explicit self-understanding, but this potential is already inherent in the relevant first-order states themselves. In this sense, these states are *never* such as to "dominate" us, if this means to operate on us in a manner impervious to rational reflection. We may in fact fail to exercise our capacity for reflection, but inasmuch as our beliefs, perceptions, desires, etc., are operations of a rational power of cognition, they never force our hand, so to speak.[19]

---

[19] I do not deny, of course, that we may sometimes have mental states that affect us in ways that bypass our very capacity for critical rationality. My point is that those of our cognitive states that *are* actualizations of this capacity do not "dominate us" even if we never reflect on them. For more on these issues, see Boyle 2009 and 2011a.

Korsgaard's better wisdom is expressed, not in formulations like the one just quoted, but in passages like the one that appears as the epigraph of this chapter, in which she writes that

> the human mind *is* self-conscious in the sense that it is essentially reflective. I'm not talking about being *thoughtful*, which of course is an individual property, but about the structure of our minds that makes thoughtfulness possible. (Korsgaard 1996: 92)

This much we should affirm: our perceptions, beliefs, desires, etc.—all the cognitive states that fall within the scope of our power of rational cognition—are essentially such as to be *open* to reflection, including the special kind of self-reflection that ascends to an explicit awareness of these states as such. How exactly self-reflection proceeds is a topic we will examine in the next chapter, and the question of the value of this special kind of reflection—what difference it makes to our lives to be able to reflect, not just on the contents of our attitudes, but on our own attitudes as such—will be taken up in Chapter 10. Even before considering these matters, however, we can recognize here a vindication of the philosophical tradition that links rationality with the capacity to reflect, and the latter with our capacity to know our own minds. The connection is subtler than it is sometimes thought to be, but it is real nonetheless.

7.7. Rational versus Nonrational Minds

Our focus in this chapter has been on the capacity of rational subjects to reflect on their own acts of representation, but what about the kind of animal subjectivity that does not qualify as rational but does undoubtedly qualify as conscious? Do nonrational animals also have some sort of nonpositional consciousness of their own conscious states? How is their consciousness similar to, and how does it differ from, our "rational" consciousness?

This is not the place to present a full theory of the difference between rational and nonrational mentality, nor do I have such a theory to offer.[20] For present purposes, it must suffice to say enough to clarify the scope and the limits of our inquiry. My aim in this book has been to offer an account of how we human beings—who presumably count as rational if any animals do—know our own minds. So my account has focused on our case, and should be judged by how successfully it addresses the problems to which this case gives rise (above all, the Problem of Transparency) and how much light it sheds on the significance of

---

[20] For some first steps, see Boyle 2017.

our human self-awareness. In developing this account, I have drawn on Sartre's notions of nonpositional consciousness and reflection, which he introduces as part of a general theory of what he calls "consciousness." But however Sartre himself may have understood his topic, I have interpreted his account as characterizing human consciousness specifically, and not as directly applicable to the consciousness of those nonhuman animals which lack the capacity for reflection.

In the course of our discussion, I have linked Sartre's account of the relation between nonpositional consciousness and reflection to the traditional distinction between rational and nonrational animals. Sartre does not make use of the latter categories, and I doubt he would endorse their employment in stating his view, so here I am on my own. My thought has been that we rational animals are distinctively capable of reflecting on our own representational states, and thereby of transforming an understanding that we initially possess in a merely applicative form into an explicit, conceptual comprehension. This is, arguably, a capacity that underlies our ability to frame concepts of any kind, but I have argued that it has a special relevance to our capacity to frame concepts of our own representational states and their rational significance: here we transform forms of understanding that are exercised, in the first instance, in the modes in which we represent objects into topics of understanding in their own right. Yet this transformation is possible, I argued, only because the relevant forms of understanding already exist, in an "applicative" form, even before we reflect.

This account invites the question whether nonrational animals too possess the relevant forms of applicative understanding, even if they lack the capacity to reflect on them. Do their modes of presentation of objects express a "nonpositional" consciousness of their own representational states, albeit one they cannot make "positional"? I have no special knowledge of nonhuman animal cognition to draw on here, but as a matter of principle, I think there is room for a distinction between two types of modes of presentation, only one of which implies even a nonpositional awareness of one's own representational states. We might draw this distinction by appeal to the difference between representing in a way that expresses consciousness of a question and representing in a way that does not express such consciousness.

To see the point of this distinction, consider first that it is possible to differentiate attitudes by appeal to the different questions they answer: an intention can be thought of as an answer to the question what to do, a belief that p can be thought of as an answer to the question whether p, a desire for something can be thought of as an answer to the question whether that thing is desirable (in some respect), and so on. In the case of rational animals, however, we can think of their attitudes as answers to questions in an even stronger sense. For it is characteristic of rational animals to *understand* the questions to which their attitudes respond: they can themselves consider such questions in an interrogative mode, can recognize that a range of answers are possible, and can answer these questions in such a way that their responses normally express corresponding attitudes.[21] For this reason, it is attractive to think of the attitudes of rational animals as attitudes *toward* questions: for their attitudes are normally held with an understanding of the relevant questions, and in a manner responsive to the conscious consideration of them, which rational subjects can in principle undertake at any time.[22]

In the case of nonrational animals, by contrast, this conception of attitudes would be a stretch. Although there are in fact questions to which their attitudes correspond, the capacity to *ask* such questions, recognizing that they are open and that a range of answers are possible, need not be a part of their cognitive repertoire. Indeed, we might think of the capacity to consider questions as open as a defining feature of rationality: rational minds are capable of *questioning* what they accept as true, to be done, desirable, and so on, whereas nonrational minds simply hold attitudes that (in fact) bear on questions without having the capacity to consider the relevant questions as such. This would be a way of capturing what is attractive in Korsgaard's idea that only rational animals can "back up" from their own attitudes: stated carefully, the point is not that rational animals must be capable of raising questions about their own attitudes *as such*, but that they must be capable of raising questions about the *topics* that their attitudes concern.

Let me emphasize that I offer this as a proposal about how to *conceptualize* the difference between rational and nonrational minds, not a *test* of whether animals are rational. The proposed link between rationality and the ability to consider a question would be hopeless as a test, since where one sees genuine "consideration of a question" will depend on where one takes the holding of attitudes to have a genuinely rational character. Does a hound chasing a hare, which comes to a fork in the path, hesitates, and then continues down one branch consider the question of which way the hare went? The concept of considering a question does not by itself settle this.

A similar point would apply to any proposed test of rationality. Consider for instance the common idea that only rational animals can speak a language. This proposition may perhaps illuminate the concept of a rational animal, but when considered as a test of rationality, it is hopeless. For what we count as speaking a language will depend on what kinds of communicative behavior we regard as

---

[21] Note that the relevant questions do not concern the subject's own attitudinal state, but the objects toward which attitudes are held. Hence understanding them does not require grasp of concepts of the corresponding attitudes—though it may require grasp of certain concepts (such as desirability or perhaps various more specific counterparts to it) whose application to an object normally *expresses* a corresponding attitude.

[22] For the idea that human attitudes can be conceived of as answers to questions, see especially Hieronymi 2009 and 2014.

genuinely manifesting rationality, and so this supposed test presupposes what it purports to test. Any purported test of rationality would, I believe, be fatally ambiguous in this way. But the conclusion to draw from this, I would suggest, is simply that the assessment of whether a given animal species is rational will need to be holistic rather than experimental in character: it will need to take the form of a global consideration of the form of life of that species, and whether the capacity for reflective thought is essential to it, rather than a piecemeal assessment of its ability to pass particular tests.[23]

The fact that the capacity to consider questions cannot serve as an unambiguous test of rationality does not diminish its usefulness in clarifying the conceptual distinction between rational and nonrational mentality. However we may map it onto the various animal species we encounter, there is a patent distinction of principle between a kind of representer that can merely hold attitudes on (what are in fact) questions and a kind that can pose the relevant questions themselves and consider them in an interrogative spirit. Human beings, at any rate, fall into the latter category, as we can know in our own case by simply reflecting on our own capacity to consider questions. In this sense, although we can know any other animal species to be rational only through a holistic consideration of its form of life, we can know ourselves to be rational animals through mere reflection.

Now my suggestion is that, when we rational animals represent a proposition in the mode characteristic of belief, or an object in the mode characteristic of desire, or a possible action in the mode characteristic of intention, these modes of presentation constitute nonpositional forms of understanding of our own representational states precisely because they are applied in the face of a recognized question. When I represent a proposition as true (where this "as true" expresses, not a distinct concept I apply, but the distinctively doxastic mode in which I represent the relevant proposition), or an object as desirable, or an action as to-be-done, I represent as closed a kind of question that I understand to be applicable and am capable of considering as open. As I will show in more detail in the next chapter, this awareness of closing a question already constitutes an implicit understanding of my own representational state. It is this understanding that warrants me, on reflection, in explicitly ascribing a corresponding representational state to myself.

In the case of nonrational animals, by contrast, attitudes toward (what are in fact) questions do not presuppose a capacity to consider the corresponding questions. (This, to repeat, is simply a stipulation about what we will call "nonrational animals," not a substantive claim about any concrete animal species.) This certainly does not rule out their having beliefs, desires, intentions,

---

[23] For more on this point, see Boyle 2012.

etc., and we can if we like say that they represent the propositions they believe "as true," the objects they desire "as desirable," and the actions they intend "as to-be-done"—nothing hangs on how we use these phrases. But however we describe the modes of presentation of nonrational animals, we should recognize a difference of principle between their significance and the significance of the corresponding rational modes. The rational modes of presentation express consciousness of closing a question; the nonrational ones do not. And since it is this consciousness of closing a question that constitutes the nonpositional self-consciousness that is made explicit in reflective self-ascriptions, we should say that nonrational animals lack such nonpositional self-consciousness, not just the capacity to make it explicit.

I hope it is evident that this distinction marks a real cognitive difference, not an ad hoc line in the sand. The distinction is between those representers whose attitudes express a comprehending stance on a question and those whose attitudes do not express such a stance. My suggestion has been that representers of the former kind possess an implicit understanding of their own representational activities even before they begin to reflect on their own attitudes as such. The foregoing discussion should already have secured some plausibility for this claim, but the case will be strengthened in the next chapter, when we consider how rational subjects can acquire an understanding of their own cognitive capacities through mere "armchair" reflection.

8
Armchair Psychology

8.1. Introduction

Armchair psychology, once a favorite pastime of philosophers, has come to have a bad name. By "armchair psychology," I mean the putative discipline that seeks to understand the nature of our own cognitive capacities on the basis of some kind of introspective or reflective awareness.[1] To suppose there is such a discipline is to suppose it is possible for us to comprehend the nature of our own cognitive capacities without observing human behavior, performing controlled experiments, scanning our brains, etc. It should be possible, in principle, for anyone to achieve such understanding, simply by sitting in an armchair and "reflecting" on what he or she can know about minds of the relevant kind just by having one.

The idea that philosophers can study our minds from an armchair has a distinguished history, but today it is an object of widespread skepticism. A proper science of psychology, it is said, must ground its claims, not in the subjective and unverifiable deliverances of introspection, but in rigorous and objective methods of study; and serious work in the philosophy of mind should take its cues from such science. According to Hilary Kornblith, for instance:

> [I]t has turned out that on issue after issue, we cannot even begin to understand how the mind works without extensive experimental work, and the picture of the mind which armchair methods provide us with is fundamentally flawed from beginning to end. (Kornblith 2014: 198)

In the view of philosophers like Kornblith, to suppose that we can responsibly theorize from an armchair about the nature of perception, cognition, emotion, or action is like supposing that we can responsibly theorize about the most elementary particles of matter from such a position: there may have been a time when this was the best humanity could do, but that time is gone, and to persist in

---

[1] Throughout this chapter, I will use the notion of a "cognitive capacity" broadly, to encompass any capacity that contributes material to our understanding of ourselves and the world we live in. In this broad sense, I count as cognitive capacities, not just capacities to reckon with the world as it is, such as the capacities to perceive, judge, draw inferences, etc., but also capacities, such as imagination and will, which allow us to consider how the world could, should, or shall hereby be.

Transparency and Reflection. Matthew Boyle, Oxford University Press. © Oxford University Press 2024.
DOI: 10.1093/oso/9780199926299.003.0009

such theorizing at this late date is like persisting in churning one's own butter—fine as a quaint re-creation of bygone times, but benighted as a serious response to our contemporary predicament.

Indeed, this comparison may not be damning enough. One *can* make butter with a butter churn, though it is cumbersome to do so. But can we investigate the nature of our minds from an armchair? If we had the sort of awareness of our own minds that Descartes took us to have—an awareness such that "there can be nothing in the mind, in so far as it is a thinking thing, of which it is not aware"[2]—perhaps we could study our minds by mere reflection. But today Cartesianism is widely rejected, and once it is rejected, what more reason can there be for supposing that armchair reflection will reveal the essential nature of our own cognitive capacities than for supposing that it will reveal the essential nature of anything else?

Defenders of armchair psychology sometimes reply that it studies, not the deliverances of introspection, but the content of our *concepts* of perception, reasoning, etc. But again, it is difficult to see how this could yield substantive knowledge of the human mind. For what do we mean by "our concepts"? If we mean the psychological concepts employed by a certain culture at a certain time, or those embedded in a certain natural language, then studying the mind from an armchair looks at best like a way to generate a catalogue of folk *beliefs* about the nature of mental states and processes, and it is not clear why these should receive any greater deference than folk beliefs in any other domain. And in any case, it seems that such beliefs would be better studied, not from an armchair, but by taking surveys of the relevant cultural or linguistic community. (This, indeed, is a central motivation for contemporary "experimental philosophers," who advocate studying philosophically important concepts, not by armchair reflection, but by conducting systematic surveys of diverse populations.)

On the other hand, if defenders of armchair psychology claim to study, not *our* concepts, but *the* concepts of perception, reasoning, etc., we should ask what justifies the definite article here. Philosophers sometimes speak of analyzing "the" concepts of perception, imagination, belief, as if these were objective yet merely conceptual topics. But what anchors these topics so as to ensure that there is (e.g.) a unique, correct concept of perception? If the answer is that *the* concept of perception is the concept that adequately captures what it is to perceive, then it looks like claiming to study "the concept of perception" is tantamount to claiming to study the essential nature of perception itself. But then, again, the question arises why we should suppose that we can investigate the latter topic from an armchair.

---

[2] Descartes, "Fourth Replies" (to Arnauld), *Philosophical Writings*, Vol. II (1984): 171 (AT VII: 246).

Yet in spite of these concerns, there remains something stubbornly attractive about armchair psychological theorizing. The project of investigating the mind in this way is endorsed explicitly, not just in Descartes, but in a range of important figures from Augustine to Kant to Husserl and Sartre. And it seems to be endorsed tacitly in the practice of many other philosophers, past and present, who treat the essential nature of perception, feeling, intention, and so on as topics for *a priori* investigation. What could such philosophers be thinking?

The project of this chapter is to propose an answer to this question. I will not attempt to reconstruct the views of any particular philosopher; my aim will be simply to show how comprehension of our own cognitive capacities *could* be achieved through armchair reflection: what sort of awareness we could draw on in such reflection, and what right we have to take such awareness seriously. If this can be shown, it should help to explain the presumption, shared by many philosophers, that armchair psychological understanding is possible.

8.2. Two Kinds of Armchair Psychology

The term "introspection" is commonly used to name an activity in which we turn our attention to our own mental lives and articulate what we can know about them, and I allowed myself to use it in this way in evoking the project of armchair psychology. When regarded simply as a label for the activity of reflecting on what we can know about our own mental lives, the term is innocuous, for it does not imply any determinate conception of the sort of awareness we draw on or the nature of our reflection on it. Both the etymology of the term "introspection" and the history of its employment suggest a more definite conception of this activity, however, and a crucial first step in defending armchair psychology will be to distinguish this conception from the one I have in mind.

On the more definite conception, to introspect is to focus our attention on a distinct channel of information we receive about our own mental states and processes—a channel to which we mostly do not attend when we are absorbed in worldly affairs, but on which we can concentrate in order to study our own minds. It comes naturally to describe such introspection as a matter of "looking within" ourselves, and this comparison with perception, already implicit in the etymology of the term "introspection," has been reinforced by a long philosophical and psychological tradition of speaking of introspection as involving some sort of "inner sense" that allows us to observe our own mental lives.[3] But we need

---

[3] A classic example is Locke's talk of Reflection as grounded in "the Perception of the Operations of our own Minds within us" (Locke 1979, II.I.4). For influential criticisms of the perceptual model of self-knowledge, see Shoemaker 1994.

not place much weight on the idea that this awareness is analogous to perception. The crucial idea is simply that, when we are in various sorts of mental states, the obtaining of these states themselves contributes to the character of our conscious experience—that there is, as it is said, "something it is like" to be in them, some characteristic "phenomenology" they present. On the more definite conception, introspection consists in attending to the consciously presented aspects of our own mental states and processes. I will henceforth concede the word "introspection" to those who use it in this way, and will call an armchair psychology based on this sort of attention to the phenomenology of our own mental states *introspective armchair psychology*.

Any introspective armchair psychology would face two immediate challenges. First, it would need to explain why the introspective observations of one person should be expected to correlate with those of other persons. As anyone familiar with the fate of introspective psychology in the late nineteenth and early twentieth centuries will know, careful and reasonable scientists have had difficulty achieving consensus, on the basis of introspection, on fundamental questions such as whether consciousness contains elements besides images and affective states, whether thoughts can occur without accompanying imagery, etc.[4] But a concern would arise here even in the absence of actual disagreement: there is no obvious reason—anyway not one discernible from an armchair—why the conscious profile of mental states and processes must be uniform in all persons. But in the absence of such a reason, there seem to be no *a priori* grounds for supposing that any of us can validly investigate the general nature of human cognitive capacities simply by attending to the contents of his or her own conscious awareness. At the very least, we would need to compare the introspective reports of many persons, and this would amount to giving up on the idea that we can investigate such matters simply by introspecting.

A second concern about introspective armchair psychology is that, even setting aside doubts about whether the conscious profile of mental states must be uniform, there is no obvious reason to suppose that introspection will reveal the essential nature of the states and processes it presents. Suppose for the sake of argument that there is some characteristic way in which (e.g.) visual experience presents itself to consciousness: why should we assume that the fundamental *nature* of visual experience—whatever is essential to explaining its specific role in cognition—can be grasped by reflecting on this conscious profile? It is by now a familiar idea that our impressions of our own cognitive states and processes may be misleading. Visual experience seems, for instance, to present what is happening *now*, at the very moment when I am aware of it—but given that the causal processes underlying vision take time, mustn't it really present what *happened*

---

[4] For historical discussion, see Hurlburt and Schwitzgebel 2011: Part I.

a moment ago? Or again, visual experience seems to present things around us as uniformly colored and sharply detailed, but it is well established that, at any given time, our visual experience of color and other detail is quite vague outside of a small foveal region that comprises only a fragment of our visual field. So isn't our conscious visual experience misleading in these respects?

Whether this is the right way to describe things is, of course, disputable; but it suffices for present purposes that it is possible to question the verisimilitude of our conscious experience of vision. If this can be questioned, then we cannot simply assume that an introspective study of visual awareness will reveal the underlying nature of vision. The challenge is to justify this assumption. And this is, of course, just an instance of a broader challenge: Why should we suppose, in general, that the aspect our mental processes present to consciousness is anything more than a "just so" story we are told by our brains, one that conceals rather than reveals how these processes work?[5]

I take these to be serious concerns, but I need not press them further, for my aim here is simply to motivate interest in an alternative conception of armchair psychology, which I will call *reflective armchair psychology*. On this alternative conception, the proper basis for such psychology is, not introspective attention to the conscious profile of our own mental states and processes, but reflection on the psychological understanding implicit in our awareness of the non-mental world.[6] An example will help to clarify this contrast.

8.3. First Illustration: Intentional Action

Consider our capacity for intentional action—i.e., our capacity to think about what to do, settle on a course of action, and do what we have settled on when the time comes. Philosophers have traditionally called this capacity "Will," and have held it to be a capacity possessed only by rational animals. (Nonrational animals are said to be capable of acting in pursuit of what they desire, but only instinctively, not on the basis of thought.) For our purposes, however, it will not matter whether some animals lack a Will; what is clear, at any rate, is that cognitively mature human beings normally have one: they can act on the basis of thinking about what to do.

---

[5] Cf. Carruthers 2011.

[6] The conception of reflective armchair psychology that I develop below owes a significant debt to Rödl 2007, which argues that our human powers of perception, knowledge, and action are "self-conscious powers," which we can comprehend and know ourselves to possess through mere reflection on their acts (Rödl 2007: 158ff.). Although I think Rödl's development of this idea fails to draw the vital distinction between nonpositional self-understanding and explicit, conceptual understanding of our own cognitive capacities, the general structure of Rödl's position has been a crucial inspiration for the view I develop here.

A person who has a Will has the capacity to think about her own future in a special way: she can think about what she will do in a way that expresses her present determination to do so. Consider, for example, the contrast between a person who realizes she has eaten some spoiled food and thinks

(1)   I am going to be sick

and a person who feels tired at a dinner party and thinks

(2)   I am going to go home.

Each person represents her own future as settled in a certain respect. But whereas the person who thinks (1) represents her future as settled by being inevitable, the person who thinks (2) represents her future as settled in a different way: by her intending to make things so, as we theorists may put it.

As we noted in Chapter 3, we could make this distinction explicit by introducing a special form of the future tense to mark this special way of thinking of one's future as settled. Thus we could introduce the practice of saying

(3)   I *will*$_I$ go home

when one regards the matter as settled on the basis of thinking about what to do, and

(4)   I *will*$_{BF}$ go home

when one regards the matter as settled in some other way (to construct a fanciful case: I might think I will$_{BF}$ go home, not voluntarily, but as a result of hypnotic suggestion). But whether we mark this distinction explicitly or not, we are all tacitly familiar with these two different ways of thinking of our own future. For anyone capable of acting intentionally—any possessor of a Will—has the capacity to think about her own future as determinate in the way marked in (3), and to distinguish this sort of determinacy from the kind expressed in (1) and (4).

Nevertheless, a person might possess the capacity to act intentionally without possessing the *concepts* of will, intention, intentional action, etc. This is surely how human cognitive development normally proceeds: well before we come to understand what it is to *intend* to do something or how to determine whether a given action was *intentional*, we learn to answer such questions as "What are you going to do?" and "Why will you do that?," where these questions are heard in a special register—one that calls, not for a well-supported prediction, but for another kind of determination, one made on the basis of reasons *to* do something rather than on the basis of probable evidence that one will *in fact* do something. To learn to answer such questions is a precondition, not of coming to possess the concepts of intention and intentional action, but of coming to *be* an intentional agent, someone whose actions and attitudes exemplify these concepts. For our ability to answer such questions is just the verbal expression of our ability to settle, on the basis of thinking, what we will do, and it is this ability that make us intentional agents at all.

To *be* an intentional agent is one thing; to be able to think *about* intentional agents is another. This point will be crucial to what follows. A person who possesses the *concepts* of intention, intentional action, etc., possesses the capacity to think about intentional agents: she has the ability to think, of an arbitrary agent (herself or another), that she has such-and-such an intention, and of an arbitrary action (hers or another's), that it is intentional. For to grasp a concept just is to possess a piece of general understanding that equips the possessor to comprehend any of an indefinitely wide array of thoughts in which the relevant concept figures.[7] But a person might surely possess the capacity for intentional action without possessing any such general, conceptual understanding. An intentional agent does not need to think *about* what her own intentions are, or whether her own actions are intentional. Her topic is less self-involved: she thinks about *what to do*. She has the ability to think *as* an agent—to consider the question what to do in a distinctively agential mode—but this does not require the ability to think *about* agency as such. The latter is a form of higher-order comprehension that comes into view only when one steps back from the agent's task of considering what to do to consider what one is doing when one acts. If this is right, then a subject can possess the capacity to act intentionally without possessing such concepts.

Still, any subject who possesses the capacity to act intentionally will already possess an *implicit* understanding of the distinction between intentional actions and other events. For, as we have seen, she will already distinguish between future things she $will_I$ do and future things she $will_{BF}$ do, even if she does not mark this distinction in any explicit way. She will express her grasp of this distinction, not by formulating propositions involving the concepts *intention* and *intentional action*, but by treating certain questions about her own future as settled in a distinctive way: not on the basis of probable evidence, but on the basis of reasons that speak to the question what to do. These questions about her future she will treat as matters of intentional action; others she will not treat in this way; and she can do all this without ever thinking of any doing *as* intentional or intended in the way that would require the concepts of intention and intentional action. Her

---

[7] I mean here to invoke something akin to Gareth Evans's well-known "Generality Constraint" on concepts. See Evans 1982: Ch. 4.

understanding of the distinction between intentional actions and other events can thus be implicit in the principles that govern her manner of thinking about her own future, rather than explicit as a distinct element in her repertoire of concepts.

Nevertheless, although a subject capable of acting intentionally need not possess the concepts of intention and intentional action, she will be able to acquire these concepts in a special way: simply by *reflecting* on what she already understands. She could begin this process of reflection by making the following stipulation: my doing A is an *intentional action* just if, in doing it, I make true a corresponding thought that

(5) I shall do A

where "shall" is used to mark the special mode of futurity we noted earlier, the mode that represents a claim about the subject's own future as a response to the deliberative question what to do.[8] This stipulation would need to be generalized, of course, for we can think, not just of our own prospective actions, but also of intentional actions we *could* take, of the actions of other persons, etc. But the relevant generalizations are easily made: an intentional action I could take is an action by performing which I could make true a thought of form (5); where some other person S does A, her doing A is an intentional action just if her so doing makes true a thought of form (5) on her part; etc. In this way, anyone with the capacity for intentional action could, in principle, frame for herself the general concept *intentional action*. She need not rely on anyone to inform her that there are such things as intentional actions, nor need she discover this by observing differences between kinds of events. The category of events marked by the concept *intentional action* will be, for her, not a discovery, but merely an articulation, in the form of a concept applicable to events in the lives of persons, of an understanding she already exercises in her own thinking about what to do.

Contrast this with our relation to ordinary empirical concepts, such as *red*, *horse*, *potato*, etc. To acquire such concepts, we must *learn of* the relevant kinds, whether at first hand through experience, or at second hand, by being informed about these kinds by someone who is already cognizant of them. But we need not learn of intentional actions from experience or testimony, for any person with the capacity for intentional action is necessarily already familiar with them. Of course, we might in fact acquire the concept *intentional action* by learning it

---

[8] It is natural to use "shall" in this way given its association with the question "What shall I do?," which is naturally heard as an invitation to deliberate. Of course, a subject who reflectively introduces the concept of intentional action need not employ a special form of the verb that marks this distinctive mode of futurity, but we have seen that she must treat it as distinctive in her thinking, and this will suffice for her to make the needed stipulation if she reflects upon it.

from our more conceptually sophisticated peers, but we could in principle discern it already latent in the structure of our own thinking. And even if we do learn the concept from others, we understand it only insofar as we grasp the link between its application and the applicability of a certain question that we already understand.

A subject capable of acting intentionally might, indeed, not just frame the concept *intentional action* by making explicit the understanding that structures her thinking about certain aspects of her own future. She might also go on to investigate the *nature* of intentional agency simply by reflecting on this understanding. Here, too, she could in principle proceed simply by reflecting on the connections and distinctions to which her ways of thinking about what to do already commit her. She could first introduce a term for the state she is in when she is presently ready to affirm:

(5) I shall do A.

At any moment when she is ready to affirm a future-tense proposition of form (5), she could stipulate that the following is *now* true of her:

(6) I intend to do A.

In this way, she could frame the concept of a special kind of mental state, an intention for the future. Moreover, she could go on make such observations as these: that intentional actions characteristically fall into nested series such that earlier members of the series are done *in order to* do the things later in the series;[9] that an explanatory inquiry into why an action is worth doing characteristically comes to an end with a characterization that speaks to the desirability of performing the action that is the outermost member of such a series;[10] that an intention to do A explains someone's doing A in a different way from a "mental cause";[11] and so on. In articulating such propositions, our imagined subject would be characterizing, not our *concept* of intentional action, but something more basic than a concept: an understanding exercised, not in thinking about certain events *as* intentional actions, but in thinking efficaciously about what to do.

This point is worth stressing. Philosophers in the analytic tradition have often represented armchair psychology as concerned with clarifying our psychological

---

[9] Anscombe calls this "the A–D order" in her classic study *Intention* (1957: §26).
[10] For more on this, see Anscombe's discussion of "desirability characterizations" (Anscombe 1957: §37).
[11] Cf. Anscombe 1957: §§9–12.

concepts. To cite one classic instance, Gilbert Ryle's *The Concept of Mind* (note the title) begins as follows:

> The philosophical arguments which constitute this book are intended not to increase what we know about minds, but to rectify the logical geography of the knowledge which we already possess.... For certain purposes it is necessary to determine the logical cross-bearings of the concepts which we know quite well how to apply. The attempt to perform this operation upon the concepts of the powers, operations and states of mind has always been a big part of the task of philosophers. (Ryle 1949: 7–8)

Ryle's ambition of "rectify[ing] the logical geography of the knowledge we already possess" places him squarely in the armchair psychological tradition. But if armchair psychology proceeds by reflecting on the kind of understanding exemplified in our ability to think about the question "What shall I do?," then it is at best misleading to describe it as an investigation of "the concepts of the powers, operations and states of mind." It investigates an understanding we exercise, not in applying such concepts, but in exercising the relevant powers themselves.

This orientation exempts reflective armchair psychology from the criticism that it can only be an investigation of the psychological concepts, or the folk psychological beliefs, of some parochial group. For it is not a study of anyone's concept *of* intentional agency, but of an understanding that belongs to *being* an intentional agent. And for related reasons, reflective armchair psychology is also exempt from the other concerns mentioned earlier: that we have no basis for assuming that what introspection presents to one person will hold of others, or that it will reveal the true nature of the phenomena it presents. For this sort of armchair psychology is *not* based on introspection: it is not grounded in a consideration of the conscious profile of our own mental states and processes. It consists, rather, in the reflective articulation of an understanding necessarily implicated in our *exercise* of a certain cognitive capacity (in this case, the capacity to act intentionally). As such, this understanding will necessarily be possessed by any subject who possesses the relevant capacity, and so any such subject will, in principle, have the basis for judging the soundness of a purported articulation of its content.[12]

Moreover, there will be no room for the charge that the understanding articulated in such reflection is merely superficial or illusory. For what such reflection articulates is not a dubitable *conception* of how our own minds work,

---

[12] This does not mean, of course, that it will be easy to articulate such understanding, or that the judgments one makes on the basis of such reflection will be uncontroversial. I say more about this issue in §8.7.

but an understanding we necessarily possess, as intentional agents, of practicable actions and the kinds of reasons we have for performing them. This understanding can indeed be framed in a way that highlights its psychological aspect: it can be characterized as an understanding of what it is to act intentionally and what it is to intend. But it is not merely a conception *of* these topics: it is an understanding that in fact *constitutes* our capacity to think efficaciously about what to do, inasmuch as this capacity itself depends on the relevant understanding. Hence a reflective articulation of this understanding cannot fail to characterize structures that belong essentially to our capacity for intentional action.

8.4. Second Illustration: Perception

Whatever one thinks of this first illustration of reflective armchair psychology, one might doubt whether this method can be extended to a broad range of cognitive capacities. I want to argue, however, that the sorts of points I have made about intentional action can be made wherever a cognitive capacity contributes to our rational standpoint on the world as knowers and agents.

To see how these points generalize, consider our understanding, as perceivers, of what it is to perceive. As in the case of intentional action, so too in the case of perception, it seems clear that the capacity to perceive does not require possession of the *concept* of perception. After all, small children are capable of perceiving the world around them well before it is plausible to attribute to them the concept of perception. To possess the *concept* of perception, one must presumably possess a general understanding of perception as a kind of cognitive activity in which an arbitrary individual—oneself or another—can engage. But the capacity simply to perceive surely does not require such understanding: it enables us simply to *be* perceivers, not to think *about* perceivers in a general way.

Nevertheless, a subject who possesses the capacity to perceive, and in whom this capacity is rationally integrated with her general capacity to think about the world (a qualification about which I will say more soon), will thereby possess an implicit understanding of what it is to perceive. For the objects of which she is perceptually aware will figure in her thoughts in a certain distinctive way, and she will recognize that she is able directly to answer a certain distinctive range of questions about them. Let me say something about each of these points.

First, the objects of which she is perceptually aware will figure in her thoughts in a certain distinctive way. Suppose I am looking at a cat on a mat. As we have repeatedly noted, the fact that I presently perceive the cat puts me in a position to think of it in a special mode, one I could express verbally by speaking of "this cat." A person who has learned to use "this" as a perceptual demonstrative has learned to connect her use of this verbal form with her exercise of a certain cognitive skill: the skill of focusing her perceptual attention on a particular object in her environment, one she is able to keep track of through a period of perceptual awareness in which she is in a position, using her senses, to gather information about it. Her reference to the relevant object, whether she employs a demonstrative joined to a specific common noun (e.g., "this cat") or a bare demonstrative with a placeholder noun ("this thing"), expresses a distinctively perceptual mode of presentation of the object.

Second, this ability to represent perceived objects in a special mode will be connected with an ability to gather specific kinds of information about them. The latter ability will be manifested, in a subject who has mastered the relevant vocabulary, in her treating a certain range of questions about these objects (viz., questions about their perceptible properties, such as color, texture, smell, shape, and movement) as *perceptually decidable*. What I mean by calling these questions "perceptually decidable" is that, other things being equal, a subject will be able to answer them simply on the basis of her perceptual acquaintance with the relevant object, without drawing on information derived from any other source. Thus, for any perceptually decidable concept P, she will recognize that she is able to determine whether *this is P* without needing to rely on independent knowledge about the relevant object. In this respect, her understanding of such concepts will establish a contrast between them and other kinds of concepts (e.g., *is 10 years old*), whose application is not directly decidable on the basis of perception.

If mature human perceptual capacities include all this, however, then a subject with mature human perceptual capacities will possess an implicit understanding of perception. She need not, indeed, have explicitly formulated the *concept* of perception, but she will already distinguish, in her modes of representation of objects, between those that fall within the scope of her present perception and those that do not. She will draw this distinction simply by representing only some objects, at any given time, in the perceptual mode. Hence she will not need to be *informed* of the existence of perception as a human mental process, or to *recognize* it on the basis of empirical investigation of her own cognition. She could, in principle, introduce the concept of perception simply by reflecting on the understanding that is already latent in the structure of her own representing. For she could introduce the concept *perceived object* as a classification for things she is in a position to represent in the distinctive way expressed by a perceptual demonstrative, and she could then define the concept *perception* as the concept of the relation in which she stands to those objects in virtue of which they are presented to her in this way.

She could, moreover, go on to investigate, from an armchair, what her tacit understanding of perception implies about the nature of this activity. She could, for instance, observe that the way she represents *this cat* implies that the cat in question is presently affecting her in a way that makes possible this very representation.[13] She might also reflect on the special singularity that perception introduces into her thinking: the fact that, whereas a definite description of an object leaves open a question about *which* object meets this description, perceptual acquaintance with objects puts us in a position to close such questions.[14] She might go on to reflect on the special kind of object-dependence characteristic of perceptual representations: the fact that, in contrast to definite descriptions of objects, which make a perfectly determinate contribution to the truth-conditions of thoughts even when there is no such object, perceptually based singular representations relate to their object in such a way that, were there no such object, there would in an important sense be no such contentful representation either—no element capable of making a determinate contribution to the truth-conditions of a thought.[15] Such observations might open the way, if she had a sufficiently philosophical bent of mind, to a general investigation of the distinctive way in which perceptual representations depend on their objects, and the special epistemic significance that this gives them, in contrast to other kinds of object-representations. All this might, in principle, emerge simply from reflection on the understanding of her relation to the perceived object implied in her manner of representing it, as *this cat*.[16]

She could also begin to investigate the special range of properties that her senses directly reveal, again simply by reflecting on what she already understands. For she already recognizes certain kinds of questions as directly decidable given certain modes of presentation of objects in her environment. There are, for instance, certain features of objects, namely their colors, that are directly decidable on the basis of a certain kind of *this*-presentation, one whose availability depends on adequate light, etc. These perceptible features are presented as located at a distance from me: I apprehend them without being in contact with them. By contrast, another set of perceptible features, namely tangible properties of perceived objects, are apprehensible only though contact, but can be investigated even in the absence of light. Yet another set of perceptible phenomena, sounds, have a different relation than colors or tactile qualities to objects in our environment: they may *emanate from* objects, but they do not *qualify* them as colors or

---

[13] Cf. Searle 1983: Ch. 2.
[14] Cf. Strawson 1959: Ch. 1.
[15] Suppose it seems to me as if I see a cat, but this is only a hallucination: what, then, does it take for some object to count as the referent of my representation *this cat*? The difficulty we confront in answering such questions suggests that we should think of this putative representation as merely the illusion of a singular representation, rather than a contentful representation that simply fails to net a referent. Cf. Evans 1982: Ch. 6.
[16] Note that I have not appealed to the possibility of illusion and the corresponding distinction between veridical and merely apparent perception. How a recognition of the possibility of illusion or error enters into our reflective understanding of our own cognitive capacities is a further question. It is noteworthy how much can be uncovered even without raising this issue.

tangible features can do. Ontologically, they present themselves as independent processes rather than as properties of space-occupying things.

Now, it is clear that any subject who is capable of sight, hearing, and touch could, in principle, reflectively investigate the natures of these different kinds of perceptible phenomena even before she had concepts of the corresponding sense modalities. And having introduced the general concept of perception in the way outlined above, she could note the specially direct connection of these phenomena with perception, and could begin to draw distinctions between different aspects of her perceptual capacity on the basis of the distinctions between these different categories of perceptibles: she has the ability to perceive things at a distance in respect of their color, to perceive things with which she is in contact in respect of their texture, hardness, etc. In this way, she could begin to form, through mere reflection, concepts of her own sense modalities, and could start to characterize their specific subject matters.[17]

8.5. Modes of Presentation and Implicit Understanding

The foregoing observations make it plausible, I hope, that reflective armchair psychology is possible, not just with respect to our capacity for intentional action, but in the case of other cognitive capacities as well. What are the general preconditions of such reflection? Well, as we have seen, the basic precondition is that an implicit understanding of what it is to exercise a given capacity should be implied in our very possession of that capacity. But when does this hold true? To answer this question, we must consider more carefully what sort of implicit understanding is at issue here.

The notion of implicit understanding that concerns us consists, not in an unconscious cognizance of facts or general principles, but in an ability intelligently to employ various *modes* of presentation that present different types of objects to thought. We introduced this notion of a mode of presentation in §3.4, when we set out the structure of our Sartrean account of transparent self-knowledge. The point I am adding here is that our capacity to employ such modes of presentation expresses an implicit understanding of our own cognitive capacities. The understanding is implicit, inasmuch as the subject need not possess concepts of the relevant capacities, but it is nevertheless a real species of understanding, inasmuch as

---

[17] It is not obvious, admittedly, that this inquiry by itself would lead her to distinguish five senses in the way we standardly do: the extent to which the standard distinctions rest simply on differences recognizable from an armchair is controversial (for a sampling of controversies, see the Introduction to Macpherson 2011). But for our purposes, there is no need to argue that everything we take for granted about the nature of human perception is knowable via armchair reflection. If even some essential features are knowable, this suffices to vindicate armchair psychology as a discipline.

the subject's ability intelligently to employ such modes expresses a nonpositional awareness of the nature of her own cognitive relation to the represented object. This awareness is expressed, not in thoughts *about* her own cognitive activity as such, but in the way she thinks about the object of this activity—the kinds of questions she recognizes as applicable to this object, the kinds of responses she treats as relevant, and the kinds of theoretical and practical implications she is prepared to draw from this consideration. It is this implicit understanding that enables her to frame, on reflection, a concept of the relevant type of cognitive activity, and to formulate principles that characterize this activity. We have seen how such implicit but articulable understanding is implied in our capacities for perception and intentional action, and having seen the point in these cases, it should be possible to envision how it might be extended to others.

Such implicit understanding does not merely facilitate our reflective understanding of our own cognitive capacities; it plays an integral role in making our first-order cognition possible. For only where different cognitive capacities present contents in recognizably different modes are we in a position to take account of the different kinds of support their deliverances lend to our evolving view of the world. For example, it obviously makes a crucial difference to my epistemic situation whether the cat I am now thinking of is perceived, remembered, or merely imagined. Only if I can recognize the difference between these kinds of cat-representations can I think soundly about whether there is such a cat and what is true of it.[18] Yet it is surely possible for me to think soundly about such matters even if I do not yet possess the *concepts* of perception, memory, and imagination. Such concepts are a sophisticated attainment, the first step toward a reflective understanding of my own cognitive capacities. The first-order capacities to perceive, remember, and imagine are preconditions of any such reflection. So although rational subjects must be sensitive to the distinction between perceiving, remembering, and merely imagining a cat, they must be able to distinguish these different modes of representing a cat without needing to think of the relevant representations *as* perceived, remembered, or imagined. They must be able to recognize differences in the modes of the relevant cat-representations themselves.

Drawing on these considerations, we can construct an argument for the thesis that any cognitive capacity whose distinctive contribution to cognition is open to rational consideration must present material in a distinctive mode. Applied to a particular case, the argument would run as follows. To see a cat and to remember seeing a cat are to represent things differently, even if there is no

---

[18] By contrast, whether a given recollection is grounded in short- or long-term memory may in fact make a difference to its trustworthiness, but since the modes of the relevant representations are not differentiated in a way that reflects their different bases, a rational subject who reflects on such representations is not automatically in a position to take account of this difference.

specifiable difference in the appearance of the cat. A subject who is capable of thinking about the reason-giving force of these different modes of representing a cat must be sensitive to the difference between them, even if she does not possess the concepts of seeing and remembering. So there must be some other, more basic distinction in the way these representations present themselves to thought, one that pertains to their general mode of presenting content.

Now, it may be that there are creatures who can perceive, remember, imagine, etc., but in whom the deliverances of these capacities have a more automatic effect on their view of the world, an effect that is not open to rational consideration. If there are such creatures, the foregoing argument does not apply to them. It applies only to creatures in whom these capacities are, as I put it earlier, "rationally integrated with their general capacity to think about the world."[19] As we observed in §7.7, such creatures are capable of taking an interrogative stance toward the world: capable, not just of having attitudes toward propositions, but of considering *whether* some proposition is true, with an awareness of the possibility of different answers. My claim is that, in creatures that are rational in this sense, the differences among basic cognitive capacities must correspond to different modes of presenting objects.

It is our tacit familiarity with such modal differences, I think, that explains why certain commonsense psychological distinctions have an intuitive appeal for us, whereas other well-founded psychological distinctions do not. The relevant commonsense distinctions correspond to recognizably different modes of presentation, whereas other psychological distinctions correspond to no such recognizable difference. It may be true, for instance, that our capacities for short- and long-term memory are functionally and neurologically distinct, but these two capacities do not present remembered facts and events in different modes, and so can be recognized as distinct only by empirical investigation. By contrast, the faculties of, for instance, perception and experiential memory differ in their mode of presenting an object: the former presents its object as something now present, the latter as something formerly presented. This is why it rings false to suggest, as Hume did, that present "impressions" and remembered "ideas" differ only in their "force and vivacity": this amounts to suggesting that these two kinds of mental states present their objects in the same mode, and differ only in their degree of vividness; but in fact we are all tacitly aware that they present their

---

[19] I call the ability to entertain first-order propositional questions, and to consider reasons for and against particular answers to them, the ability to *think*. This is simply a stipulation about how I use "think" and its cognates: I do not mean to deny that animals who cannot deliberate about propositional questions can think in some broader sense. But I believe this usage marks a natural dividing-point, and dovetails with the traditional philosophical practice of reserving the term "thought" for the cognitive activities of a rational animal. A thinker in this sense is capable of taking an interrogative attitude toward the world: capable, not just of having attitudes toward propositions, but of understanding propositional *questions*, and of recognizing the possibility of different answers to them.

contents differently: the one presents the present *as present*; the other, the past *as past*.[20] And for just this reason, our capacities for perception and experiential memory will constitute possible topics of reflective armchair psychology.

I conjecture that all the basic types of cognitive activity recognized in commonsense psychology correspond to such modal differences. An affective response to a person or event, a perception of an object, a judgment on some question: whatever their particular focus, these are generically different modes of having a topic in view for thought. We all tacitly know this, and can, if we reflect, begin to characterize their specific ways of presenting their subject matters. But whether or not this conjecture is true, it should at any rate be clear that the concepts of cognitive activities that present their objects in distinctive modes form a special and interesting class. We might call them *concepts of reflection* to mark their special kind of availability to the subjects who instantiate them. Such concepts define a distinctive branch of human psychology: the branch concerned with those aspects of our psychology that are open to investigation through mere reflection by any subject with a psychology of the relevant type.

8.6. The Nature of Reflection

In armchair reflection, we make modes of presentation, which in the first instance serve as structures through which we represent non-psychological topics, into topics of consideration in their own right. In this way, we are able to transform an understanding implicit in first-order cognition into an explicit comprehension of our own cognitive capacities. So, at any rate, I have argued. But what is the nature of such reflection? How are we able to transform a capacity to represent *in* certain modes into an understanding *of* these modes themselves, and of the cognitive capacities that underlie them? There are, in effect, three stages in the transformation.

8.6.1. The Mode-to-Content Shift

In the first stage, we make modes of presentation, through which we in the first instance think about non-psychological topics, into self-standing topics of conceptual understanding. To do this, we must first abstract from whatever

---

[20] But to repeat: this is to describe the difference as it appears to us in our capacity as theorists. Someone who remembers experiencing something need not represent the episode as formerly presented in a sense that implies application of the concepts *past* or *formerly presented*. When *we* describe her memory as presenting the episode "as past," we are making explicit something about the *mode* in which the episode is presented to her.

particular content is presented in a given mode to a generic consideration of the mode itself, and then frame a general concept of the kind of topic for thought presented in this mode. We have already seen two examples of how this might occur. (i) A subject who is able to deliberate about what to do, and thereby to settle what she will$_I$ do, might introduce the concept *intended action* as a concept applicable to just those actions that figure, for some subject at some time, as things she will$_I$ do in the relevant sense.[21] (ii) A subject who is able to attend to perceived objects and gather information about them might introduce the concept *perceived object* as a concept applicable to just those things she is in a position, at a given time, to think of in a manner expressible with a certain kind of "this."

This kind of step depends on our ability to abstract from differences and recognize what is common to a range of cases, an ability arguably presupposed in all concept formation. But it also depends on a special ability more relevant to our present topic: the power to shift our cognitive focus from *what* we are thinking about—a cat, an upcoming walk to pick up the children, or whatever—to a feature of our *mode* of thinking about it—as *this* cat, as the walk I will$_I$ take. It seems clear enough in particular cases that we can make such a shift, but it is not easy to understand our general warrant for doing so. It is one thing to pass from the perceptual presentation of various cats to the general concept *cat*: this requires the ability to focus on what is common to various *objects* of which we are aware. But it is another thing to pass from the perceptual presentation of various objects to the concept *perceived object*: here the transition is not from diverse objects to a property *they* all have in common, but to a property of *my own* cognitive relation to them. The property of being perceived seems, after all, to be only a "Cambridge property" of objects: it does not affect what they are like in any intrinsic respect. Certainly it is not a property we *perceive* them to have, in the way we might perceive them to be red, or to be cats. So how, by attending to perceived objects, can I come to recognize my own cognitive relation to such objects? How can what I am made aware of by perception—a cat, for instance—alert me to the phenomenon of perception itself?

The puzzle here is obviously related to the Problem of Transparency that occupied us in earlier chapters. The latter problem was prompted by the observation that, in a range of cases, we can answer questions about our own present mental states by referring them to corresponding questions about the non-mental world, but that it is not easy to understand our general warrant for doing this, given

---

[21] I use our special form of the future, "will$_I$," simply for convenience of expression. I am assuming that the subject can recognize the distinctiveness of the relevant mode of thinking about her own future, even if she had no special form of the future tense to mark it. If she can recognize this, she will be able to formulate the necessary stipulation about which doings count as intentional actions.

that the former questions concern our own mental states while the latter concern topics independent of our mental states. In the first part of this book, I argued that a satisfying response to this problem must recognize a nonpositional awareness of our own mental states already implicit in our positional awareness of the non-mental world.

An analogous point applies in the present case: the reason we can transform (e.g.) perceptual awareness of a cat into grasp of the concept of perception is that our perceptual awareness of the cat already draws on a nonpositional *understanding* of the cat as perceived. For such an understanding is, as I argued earlier, already expressed in our comprehension of the perceptual demonstrative mode of presentation itself. Our capacity to perceive such things as cats, and to gather information about their perceptually decidable properties, does not just leave us with beliefs whose source is inscrutable to us: it indicates the basis of these beliefs, precisely by presenting certain cats as *this cat* or *that cat*. Even if we do not possess the concept of perception as such, our capacity to represent things in this mode involves an implicit understanding of the distinctive kind of relation in which we stand to the relevant objects. I understand, for instance, that the object must be in my environment, that it must stand in a particular spatial relationship to me (not by having an explicit conception of this fact, but by possessing the capacity to do such things as reach out for it in an appropriate direction), that it must be available to be perceived (by knowing how to change my vantage point on the object, how to get a better look at it, etc.). All this amounts to an implicit but not unconscious understanding of the kind of relation to an object in which perception consists. It is this understanding that we isolate and articulate in armchair reflection.

8.6.2. Aristotle's Principle

To pass from such reflection to explicit psychological understanding requires, however, a second step: we must grasp how modes of presentation relate to underlying cognitive capacities. In the first instance, what we identify in making the Mode-to-Content Shift are concepts such as *intended action* and *perceived object*: concepts of *objects* considered simply as presented in a given mode. The idea that specific cognitive capacities enable us to engage with such objects is certainly very natural, but if reflection entitles us to this idea, how exactly does it do so?

There is an ancient doctrine about methodology in the philosophy of psychology that seems to me relevant here. In a well-known passage of his *De Anima*, Aristotle suggests that psychological understanding must begin by investigating the *objects* with which our vital powers engage, proceed from these to the *acts* by which we engage with such objects, and arrive finally at the *capacities* exercised in these acts:

> [I]f one is to state . . . what the thinking or perceptual or nutritive capacity is, then one should first say what thinking is and what perceiving is, since activities and actions are prior in account to capacities. But if this is so, and if their proper objects are prior to them, then we should for the same reason first make determinations about these, for instance, about nourishment and the objects of perception and reasoning. (Aristotle 1968: 415a16–22)[22]

Aristotle's methodological principle was much discussed in antiquity and became a cornerstone of scholastic philosophical psychology. In *De Anima*, Aristotle himself proceeds in just this way: he first characterizes the objects of our vital powers (the edible, the perceptible-in-general, the visible, the tangible, the thinkable, etc.), then the psychic activities by which we engage with these objects (nutrition, perceiving seeing, touching, thinking), and finally the capacities underlying these activities. I think reflecting on his reasons for this procedure will help to shed light on the foundations of reflective armchair psychology.

Part of the case for Aristotle's methodological principle turns on a more general principle he affirms in his *Metaphysics*: that acts are prior in the order of understanding to capacities, since capacities must be characterized in terms of what they are capacities *to do* (Aristotle 1942: 1049b10–17). But he goes a step further in *De Anima* when he claims that objects in turn are prior to acts, and the rationale for this further step is not obvious. We might wonder, first, why he thinks that understanding the objects of perception and thought might serve as a basis for understanding perception and thought themselves. After all, I can see horses or think about justice, but a study of horses will not teach me much about vision, nor a study of justice about thinking, however edifying such studies may be. And even if there were some sense in which our cognitive activities might be studied via their characteristic objects, why should we suppose that they *must* be studied in this way?

The point of Aristotle's doctrine comes into focus, however, if we connect it with our observations about the role of reflection in psychological

---

[22] The terms I render as "capacity" (*dunamis* or [term for vital activity]+*etikon*), "act" (*energeia* or [term for vital activity]+*esis*), and "proper object" (*antikeimenon* or [term for vital activity]+*eton*) have been variously translated, and some of my renderings are out of favor. The terms I use are, however, ones standardly used to translate equivalent Latin terms in the writings of scholastic philosophers (though translators of these philosophers often use "power" or "faculty" where I use "capacity"). More cautious contemporary translations of Aristotle's terms (e.g., "potentiality" for *dunamis*, "actuality" for *energeia*, "corresponding object" for *antikeimenon*) may arguably convey a more nuanced sense of Aristotle's meaning, but they obscure the connection between his claims and a long scholastic tradition of commentary and discussion.

understanding. We have seen that, when we reflect on our own cognition, we must begin by abstracting from the particularities of objects to reach an understanding of the several modes in which objects are presented to us. What results from such reflection are concepts of objects *qua* presented in a certain mode, such as *perceived object* or *intended action*. Now, when Aristotle says that our psychic capacities are differentiated by their objects, he surely means "objects" in this sense. His point cannot be that just any difference in the objects of cognition must correspond to a difference in our psychic capacities, for then the difference between horses and cats would require us to distinguish the capacity to perceive horses from the capacity to perceive cats. To draw psychological distinctions in the right places, we must focus on just those differences in objects that correspond to the differences between general capacities such as perception, imagination, thought, etc. But this is precisely what we focus on, in effect, in identifying modal differences between objects of cognition: these are differences that correspond precisely to the different kinds of cognitive relation in which we stand to the relevant objects.[23]

Nevertheless, as we have seen, we can recognize such modal differences prior to framing concepts of our own cognitive capacities. So it is not necessary for us to begin with a concept of perception (e.g.) and frame the concept of a perceived object on its basis. Rather, we can begin by framing the concept of a perceived object, where "perceived object" is initially introduced simply as a stipulative label for a certain kind of *this*. On this basis, we can then frame a concept of the specific type of cognitive act by which a subject represents this sort of object: perceiving. And finally, we can frame a concept of the kind of cognitive power that makes this sort of act possible: the capacity to perceive. Thus we can proceed from object to act to power, just as Aristotle recommends; and indeed we must do so if we are to study our own cognitive powers via armchair reflection. For our starting point in such reflection must, as we have observed, be an awareness of *objects* presented in a certain mode. I believe it is because Aristotle has this kind of investigation primarily in mind that he insists that we must proceed in this way.[24] And this, in fact, is exactly the sort of account that Thomas Aquinas gives in explaining Aristotle's procedure:

---

[23] Medieval philosophers introduced a technical term for this notion of an object: they referred to it as the "proper" or "formal" object of a power, i.e., an object considered just insofar as it is an object of the relevant power (cf. Thomas Aquinas, *Summa Theologiae*, 2012: I.Q1.A3c). Aquinas, who repeatedly endorses Aristotle's methodological principle about investigating powers via their acts and acts via their objects, explicates the principle in terms of this notion of a proper object (ibid., I.Q77.A3).

[24] Aristotle's investigation is clearly influenced by other kinds of information about our vital powers—for instance, by his physiological investigation of the sense organs of human beings and other animals. So it would be implausible to suggest that his investigation of our vital powers proceeds *simply* by armchair reflection. Nevertheless—although this is not the place to defend such an interpretative claim—I believe armchair reflection, as it were, *anchors* Aristotle's understanding of human cognitive powers.

[T]he power of any faculty of the soul is limited to its [proper] object. For this reason its activity is directed first of all and principally to its object. It extends to those things by which it is directed to its object only through a kind of return. Thus, we see that sight is first directed to color, but is directed to the act of seeing only through a kind of return, when, in seeing color, it sees that it sees. (Aquinas 1952: 10.9c; cf. Aquinas 2012: I.Q87.A3)

Armchair reflection can proceed in this regressive way because it begins from a concept of an object-*qua*-presented-in-a-certain-mode, and modes of presentation are liminal things, which straddle the boundary between knower and object known. On the one hand, as modes of presentation of some *object*, they affect the way this object is presented. On the other hand, as modes of *presentation* of an object, they implicate the cognitive capacities of the subject. It is this subject-implicating dimension that we articulate when we introduce, first, the concept of a distinctive kind of cognitive act corresponding to a certain mode of presentation, and second, the concept of the general capacity to perform such acts.

8.6.3. Systematicity

A final question we must consider concerns the potential for systematicity in reflective armchair psychology. I have sketched a way in which we might, through reflection, frame concepts of certain of our own cognitive capacities. But how might we determine whether we have made a *complete* survey of the capacities knowable through reflection, or at least of the most basic such capacities? Moreover, how might we decide which relations of interdependence hold between these capacities? Must a subject who is capable of thinking also be capable of imagining? Must a subject who is capable of wanting to do something also be capable of feeling emotions like fear and anger? Are certain of these capacities essential to any possible mind that is capable of reflective self-knowledge? Do others constitute, as it were, optional additions to such a mind—capacities which might conceivably be absent, but which we know through reflection to be present in our own case?

Such questions are *systematic* in character: they ask whether the concepts and distinctions introduced in reflective armchair psychology form some kind of principled totality, as opposed to a merely adventitious heap of elements. The traditional philosophical view, of course, is that our human cognitive capacities do form a system, and are thus open to systematic investigation—and, as we observed at the beginning of this chapter, it has been widely assumed that this investigation can be conducted from an armchair. This is not to say that there has been general agreement on the list of capacities that an armchair investigation of human psychology should recognize, or on the principles that should govern such recognition. Indeed, there has been surprisingly little discussion of the principles underlying such an investigation. Even thinkers who place great emphasis on the systematicity of their faculty psychology (for instance, Thomas Aquinas and Immanuel Kant) tend to comment on these principles only *en passant*, rather than offering a separate and methodical treatment of the topic.

Nor is this the place where the gap will be filled: these issues are too complex and deeply rooted to address here. It will suffice for present purposes, however, if we can show how systematic questions might be approached within the scope of reflective armchair psychology. For it certainly seems attractive to think that there are *some* systematic interconnections among our cognitive capacities. It is hard to believe, for instance, that there could be a mind that merely had the capacity to form beliefs but not the capacities to perceive or form intentions. It does not seem to be a merely empirical discovery that these capacities co-occur: they seem to form some kind of package. Indeed, the history of philosophy is full of claims about the principled (as opposed to merely empirically discoverable) interdependence of different cognitive capacities—for instance, the dependence of imagination on perception[25] (and perhaps vice versa[26]), the dependence of thought on imagination[27] (and perhaps vice versa[28]), the dependence of will on thought (and perhaps vice versa), etc. Each of these claims needs a separate discussion, of course, and I suspect it would be necessary to draw further distinctions before the relevant claims of interdependence could be stated in a clear and unobjectionable way. But at any rate, if such questions could be addressed *only* by some quite other sort of investigation than the one we have characterized, this would constitute a *prima facie* ground for doubt about the supposed discipline of "reflective armchair psychology." For if this other kind of investigation were sound, and if the faculties it distinguished did not coincide with those recognized in reflective armchair psychology, this would surely raise doubts about the latter. But if the faculties distinguished in the other investigation did coincide with those recognized in reflective armchair psychology, then it would be right to expect an explanation of this coincidence. And if we had such an explanation, we would thereby have an account of the relation of reflective armchair psychology to systematic questions.

A first thought might be that the coincidence could be explained in the following way. There are certain relations of necessary interdependence that hold among our various cognitive capacities, but these relations are, as it were, reflectively inscrutable: it is not possible to see why they hold simply by reflecting on

---

[25] Cf. Aristotle, *De Anima*, III.3.
[26] Cf. Kant KrV A120n, Strawson 1974b.
[27] Cf. Aristotle, *De Anima* III.8; Sartre 2004: Part III and Conclusion.
[28] Cf. Kant KrV §26.

the modes in which these several capacities present their objects. Nevertheless, these relations do hold, and given that they hold, it is no surprise that a subject who reflects on the modes in which these capacities present their objects should come to recognize that she has these various capacities. In short, the results of reflective armchair psychology might *track* relations of interdependence between our cognitive capacities even though reflective armchair psychology could not itself give us *insight* into these relations.

I do not know how to argue that it is impossible for systematic questions to be reflectively inscrutable in this way, but it seems to me that this would be a strange and unsatisfying situation. It would be strange if reflection supplied us with no insight "from within" into the relations between our several cognitive capacities, so that a reflective recognition of our capacity to judge left it open whether (e.g.) this power depends on a capacity for sensible receptivity. I choose this example to evoke a famous claim made by Immanuel Kant: that our power of understanding, whose primary act is judgment, can only perform its function insofar as an object for judgment is given to it by another power, sensibility. How did Kant take himself to know this? He tells us that his first Critique is a project in which our power of cognition seeks to know itself (KrV Axi), and that for just this reason, we should expect it to aspire to systematic completeness:

> [T]hat such a system should not be too great in scope for us to hope to complete it, already admits of being determined from the fact that our object is not the nature of things, which is inexhaustible, but the understanding that judges of the nature of things, and this moreover only in respect of its *a priori* cognition, the supply of which cannot remain hidden from us, since we do not need to search for it externally. (KrV A12–13/B26)

So Kant, at least, appears to have believed that we are entitled to demand systematicity in our investigation of our own cognitive capacities precisely because we can investigate our own power of cognition simply by reflecting on what we necessarily know in having a power of the relevant kind. And Kant's view is attractive: it amounts to the idea that the domain of reflective armchair psychology has a certain autonomy. It is consistent with his position to admit—as we certainly should—that there is a tremendous amount about how our minds work that we cannot know through mere reflection; but if Kant is right, there is a field of topics that reflection can address systematically without relying on any other source of knowledge of how our minds work. We might call this the claim of *the autonomy of reflection*.

I am all too conscious of how far I am from being able to state this claim with adequate clarity, much less to defend it as true; but I believe I have some notion of how a reflective investigation of the systematic interrelations of our cognitive capacities might proceed. Consider Kant's claim that our cognition depends on two distinguishable but interdependent powers, sensibility and understanding, the former being a power of representing objects in virtue of being sensibly affected by them, the latter a power to "think" such objects by applying concepts to them in spontaneous acts of judgment. On what basis did Kant take himself to know these facts about the structure of the human power of cognition? And on what basis, for that matter, do undergraduates find these claims plausible when one informs them of Kant's views in an introductory course? For I can attest from personal experience that they do find these claims plausible, although they are ready to protest at much else in Kant's system. Do they, then, assess the question by reference to general views about human psychology that they have absorbed in their education or upbringing? Do they confirm it by observing themselves or their peers? Do they test it employing some power of "introspection"?

I can imagine such accounts, but it seems to me that a more straightforward story can be told by appealing to the kind of armchair reflection that we have been considering. The undergraduates (or Kant himself) might begin, I suppose, by reflecting on a contrast between the individual things about which they think—*this* or *that*—and what they think concerning these things—that this one is *a cat*, or is *gray*, or whatever. They might also reflect on the way in which these elements join together to constitute a topic of possible knowledge, something which can be true or false—in the simplest case, a singular proposition such as *This is a cat* or *This cat is gray*. Now, in describing this process, I have made free use of commonsense psychological vocabulary—thinking, knowledge, etc.—but it should be clear that the real topic of reflection here is a set of distinction in the *objects* of thought and knowledge, and I hope that the foregoing discussion has made it plausible that the psychological vocabulary to which I have appealed could, in principle, be introduced on the basis of reflection. So all of the reflection I have so far described is on what we think *about*.

Kant's own term for this kind of reflective differentiation of types of representational contents is "logical reflection," which he characterizes as the "mere comparison" of representations (i.e., of the contents of representations) without reference to "the cognitive power to which the given representations belong" (KrV A262–263/B318–319). Elsewhere he writes:

> If we reflect on our cognitions in regard to the two essentially different basic faculties, sensibility and the understanding, from which they arise, then here we come upon the distinction between intuitions and concepts.... The former have their source in *sensibility*, the faculty of intuitions, the latter in the *understanding*, the faculty of concepts. This is the *logical* distinction between understanding and sensibility, according to which the latter provides nothing but intuitions, the former on the other hand nothing but concepts. The two basic

faculties may of course be considered from another side and defined in another way: sensibility, namely, as a faculty of *receptivity*, the understanding as a faculty of *spontaneity*. But this mode of explanation is not logical but rather *metaphysical*. (JL 8:36)

This passage suggests an account of how Kant might have arrived at the distinction between sensibility and understanding. He might have begun by drawing the "logical" distinction between intuitions and concepts: the former are *singular* representations through which an individual object is presented, whereas the latter are *general* representations that relate "mediately" to an object by applying to a singular, intuitive representation of one (cf. KrV A320/B377, JL 9:91). That is the distinction we already have noticed between *this* and *that*, on the one hand, and *gray* and *cat*, on the other: Kant simply introduces some theoretical vocabulary (singular intuition, general concept) to assist in making these differences reflectively explicit. He then applies (what is in effect) Aristotle's Principle: that where there is a formal difference in the *objects* of cognition, there must be a corresponding difference in our *acts* of cognition, and hence a difference in cognitive *capacities*. This yields the "logical" distinction between sensibility, the faculty of intuitions, and understanding, the faculty of concepts. He then goes on—through, I would argue, further reflection on the modes in which these different types of objects are presented—to recognize that the singular element is presented as given through affection, whereas the general element is presented not as something given, but as something framed, so to speak. This, together with another application of Aristotle's Principle, yields what he calls the "metaphysical" distinction between sensibility, the faculty of receptivity, and understanding, the faculty of spontaneity.

Kant's term for the process by which we move from a logical distinction in the contents of our representations to a metaphysical distinction in the cognitive faculties that ground them is "transcendental reflection," which he defines as "[t]he action through which I make the comparison of representations in general with the cognitive power in which they are situated" (KrV A261/B317). My point is that this Kantian terminology, abstruse though it may seem, is in fact just an articulation of distinctions to which any of us might be led in armchair reflection on our own cognition. This point holds true both of Kant's specific cognitive distinctions (e.g., intuition vs. concept, sensibility vs. understanding) and of his general methodological notions (e.g., logical vs. transcendental reflection). And what is crucial for present purposes is that this point holds also of his claim that sensibility and understanding are functionally distinct but interdependent, so that "neither concepts without an intuition in some way corresponding to them, nor intuition without concepts, can yield a cognition" (KrV A50/B74). Before we recognize this as a true proposition of "transcendental psychology," we have an implicit understanding of it in our nonpositional understanding of how a singular element and a general element must join together to constitute a minimal thing to know.[29] This, I believe, is why undergraduates do not tend to balk at this claim, though of course it is hardly immune to philosophical dispute.

The idea that the interdependence of these elements reflects an interdependence in our cognitive faculties arises in the way I have sketched, by logical reflection on different types of thinkables supplemented by transcendental reflection on the cognitive powers that ground these diverse elements. And this case shows how, in principle, reflective armchair psychology might approach systematic questions: namely, by beginning from recognition of interdependencies in the *objects* of thinking, and reflecting on the nonpositional understanding of their basis that is embodied in the modes of presentation of their respective objects. This kind of investigation could aspire to completeness insofar as it could identify some single most embracing object of our thinking in general—an object we might simply call "the world"—and could trace the distinguishable types of objects of representation that contribute to the representation of this most embracing object. The sketchiness of this description reflects the limits of my own understanding, but I hope this discussion makes it plausible that a reflective armchair psychology could address systematic questions without betraying its own principles.

8.7. Implications

The preceding section emphasized the deep historical roots of our topic, but I want to conclude by noting some implications for contemporary debates.

The main point of this chapter has been to argue that there is an aspect of our psychology that we can study from an armchair—a point about which many contemporary philosophers harbor doubts. Recall Kornblith's remark:

> [I]t has turned out that on issue after issue, we cannot even begin to understand how the mind works without extensive experimental work, and the picture of

---

[29] The term "transcendental psychology" is, so far as I know, never used by Kant, but it has come to be widely used by interpreters as a label for his Critical investigation of our cognitive powers. The popularity of the label is primarily due to its use in P. F. Strawson's seminal study of the first Critique, which famously dismisses transcendental psychology as an "imaginary subject" (Strawson 1966: 97). Whatever one thinks of the details of Kant's delineation of our cognitive faculties, I hope that the present chapter brings out that this subject matter is not imaginary. (My thinking about this topic owes debts to Henrich 1989 and Smit 1999, though I differ from them in my emphasis on the crucial role of pre-reflective consciousness in providing a basis for reflective self-understanding of our own cognitive faculties. I treat interpretative questions about Kant's conception of reflection in greater depth in Boyle forthcoming.)

the mind which armchair methods provide us with is fundamentally flawed from beginning to end. (Kornblith 2014: 198)

I would certainly grant that there are many things about how our minds work that we cannot understand without extensive experimental work; but Kornblith appears to mean something stronger: that there is *no* legitimate armchair inquiry into the nature of our own mentality. As he elsewhere puts it:

At this late date, how things seem from the first-person point of view or how they seem from the armchair are no more relevant to these inquiries than they are for an investigation of the mechanisms involved in digestion. (Kornblith 2014: 201)

If there is merit in the conception of armchair psychology developed here, then this suggestion is unfounded. I have not sought to explain how armchair reflection might supply us with the basic analytical framework of capacities, acts, and objects: I have simply taken these fundamental notions for granted.[30] But provided these materials are available, I believe I have shown how concepts of specific cognitive capacities might be acquired via armchair reflection, and also how such reflection might supply us, not just with concepts of these capacities, but with an understanding of essential aspects of their nature. If this is right, then substantive psychological knowledge can be acquired from an armchair.

Our discussion also puts us in a position to offer responses of some prominent contemporary criticisms of armchair psychology. Consider, for instance, a kind of doubt about the cognitive value of introspection raised by Eric Schwitzgebel in a series of influential papers:

Close your eyes and form a visual image. . . . Imagine, for example, the front of your house as viewed from the street. Assuming that you can in fact form such imagery, consider this: How well do you know, right now, that imagery experience? . . . How much of the scene can you vividly visualize at once? Can you keep the image of the chimney vividly in mind at the same time you vividly imagine the front door? Or does the image of the chimney fade as you start to think about the door? How much detail does your image have? How stable is it? . . . Now these are pretty substantial questions about your imagery experience. . . . If I asked you questions at that level of detail about an ordinary external object near to hand, you would have no trouble at all—about a book,

---

[30] This is not, however, to suggest that such notions *could not* be acquired by armchair reflection. I suspect they could, but an investigation of how this might occur lies outside the scope of the present chapter.

say. How stable is it? Does it flash in and out of existence? Does its cover have a durable color? (Schwitzgebel 2012: 186)

I quote Schwitgebel's discussion at length because I think it is forceful. Prior to his intervention, I would have said that I know what it is to imagine the façade of my own house, yet I find it surprisingly difficult to answer his questions. Moreover, I accept his claim that parallel problems arise, not just for an introspective account of visual imagery, but for many other kinds of conscious mental states and activities: although we might expect that our conscious acquaintance with these states and activities would give us a detailed familiarity with their natures, we in fact prove incapable of answering basic questions about them.

Schwitzgebel has produced such bafflement in us, however, only by first pointing us in the wrong direction. He assumes that the basis of armchair psychological understanding must be, if anything, our familiarity with what various kinds of mental states and activities "are like"—i.e., with what he, in the company of many other contemporary philosophers, calls their "phenomenology." But as we have seen, armchair psychology can draw from a different source: not from *introspective* attention to our conscious "imagery experience" (whatever that might be), but from a *reflective* articulation of the mode of presentation of imagined objects.[31] The idea that anyone capable of imagining the front façade of a house must be implicitly familiar with what it is to imagine something in no way implies that anyone capable of such acts of imagination must have a definite view about how much of a façade they can "vividly visualize" or how stable their "image" is. It implies only that they understand, without needing to make observations or be informed by others, the general mode of presentation characteristic of imagining something.

The fact that we are implicitly familiar with such modes of presentation also does not ensure that it will be easy for us to achieve a reflective understanding of the corresponding cognitive capacities. Part of Schwitzgebel's critique of introspection turns on the thought that we should be surprised to find it difficult to describe what we supposedly know so well. But this conflates two different issues. It is one thing to claim that each of us necessarily possesses the *basis* for understanding our fundamental cognitive capacities, another to suggest that we should find it easy to answer questions about how rightly to *conceive* of these capacities. As we have seen, answering such questions requires transforming an implicit understanding drawn on in exercising the relevant capacities into an explicit, conceptual understanding of these capacities themselves, and there is no reason to expect this task to be straightforward. Learning to articulate the content of one's implicit understanding, without addition or distortion, requires

---

[31] Sartre 2004 is a classic work on this topic.

insight and discipline. One's ability to perform such reflection can doubtless be improved by practice, and by the study of successful examples of the form. In these respects, skill in reflection is analogous to skill in realistic painting: what makes a skilled painter capable of rendering a scene more satisfactorily than an untrained person is not that more is *visible* to the painter, but that she has become more adept at noticing and depicting what is visible to anyone.

Even this comparison, however, does not fully capture what makes reflective armchair psychology difficult. It is hard to paint a bowl of pears realistically, but we can at least generally agree about when this has been achieved. Efforts at armchair psychology, by contrast, do not so readily produce consensus. No doubt there are many reasons why consensus is not the norm in philosophy, and some probably trace to factors unrelated to the activity of reflection per se. But even leaving these other factors out of account, it is not surprising that the results of armchair reflection should prove contentious. For the assessment of these results depends on judgments about how best to bring conceptual order and systematicity to matters that are not in the first instance apprehended conceptually and systematically. Hence we should not expect easy consensus in armchair psychology; but by the same token, we should not take the persistence of dispute to show that no such discipline is possible. At any rate, my point in defending armchair psychology is not to propose a method that would simplify the task of philosophers, or remove the causes of illusion and dispute, but simply to indicate the standard by which such claims and disputes might be adjudicated.

A final, broader implication concerns the role of self-consciousness in cognition. There is a familiar kind of debate in philosophy, which my friend Doug Lavin refers to as "the Battle between the Zombies and the Narcissists." The Narcissists claim that, in order to know the world, we must understand the nature of our own knowing—for instance, that in order to represent mind-independent objects, we must understand the distinction between how things are and how we represent them to be; that in order to perceive mind-independent objects, we must possess some basic understanding of what it is to perceive; etc. The Zombies reply that this yields a radically over-intellectualized account of the relevant capacities: the capacities to perceive and learn about (what are in fact) mind-independent objects are widespread in the animal kingdom, whereas a conceptual understanding of these capacities is rare even among humans. In first-order perception and knowing, the Zombies say, we may be fundamentally oblivious to ourselves.

The Narcissists had a heyday in the mid-twentieth century, with the rise of a certain neo-Kantian program in the philosophy of mind. More recently, as philosophical attention to empirical psychology has grown, it seems to me that the Zombies have gained the upper hand. A lesson of our discussion, however, is that we need not choose sides in this dispute. We may concede to the Zombies that

226 REFLECTION AND SELF-UNDERSTANDING

it is possible to perceive and acquire knowledge of a mind-independent world without possessing concepts such as *perception, perceptual appearance, representation*, etc. But we may concede to the Narcissists that, at least in mature human beings, the ability to perceive objects implies an understanding of what it is to perceive. For the fundamental form of such understanding is not conceptualization as such.

9
Self-Understanding

> History consists of the thoughts and actions of minds, which are not only intelligible but intelligent, intelligible to themselves, not merely to something other than themselves.
> —R. G. Collingwood, *The Idea of History* (1946): 112

9.1. Introduction

Although much in our lives is opaque to us, it is nevertheless true that a central strand of our thought and action has a certain seeming intelligibility. Suppose you and I have an argument about whether a certain philosophical theory is sound. I vigorously maintain that it is, but your objections linger with me, and gradually I become persuaded that you are right. I become convinced that the theory won't do, and I seem to know why: I know what considerations persuaded me. Or, to take a more mundane example, suppose you ask me whether I want to come along to the beach. I am at a phase in life where this involves daunting preparations: wrestling uncooperative children into swimsuits, applying oily sunscreen while they struggle to escape, finding lost shoes, etc. The prospect of all this is almost too much to contemplate. But then I think of the strange bravery that comes over my children when they finally are in the water, the yell of triumph my daughter lets out when she is hit by a wave, and I decide to come along after all. Again, I seem to know why I decided as I did, what persuaded me. I could talk about it at some length, if anyone were interested.

In these and similar ways, we normally stand ready to answer questions about why we believe what we believe and do what we do.[1] It is true that we sometimes find our own thoughts and choices mystifying. Still, we are, to a striking degree, prepared to offer, without self-observation or inference from other evidence, explanations of our own beliefs and choices. We appear to presume that

---

[1] I will consider both our understanding of mental *events* such as judgment and choice and of mental *states* such as belief, desire, and intention. Obviously, there are important differences between these two kinds of mental phenomena, but both raise the question of self-understanding, and the differences between them will not matter to my argument. When I need a generic term for the objects of self-understanding, I will speak sometimes of "thoughts," sometimes of "attitudes," but I intend what I say to apply, *mutatis mutandis*, to both attitudinal states and attitude-expressive events.

we normally know our own grounds for belief and action, and indeed, that we do not merely know them, but are—in a sense that is not easy to clarify—in charge of their influence. This is why we count these judgments and decisions as, in Collingwood's elegant phrase, "not only intelligible but intelligent": they do not just strike us as comprehensible; we take them to proceed *from* our conscious acceptance of the adequacy of certain reasons. I do not merely suppose that I *know* what caused me to hold a given philosophical view, or what caused me to come along to the beach; I suppose that I myself was *responsible* for the action of the relevant causes, which would not have operated without my assent. We could express this point by saying that our normal understanding of our own judgments and decisions purports to be *directive* rather than *post hoc*: it purports to be the kind of understanding possessed by someone who knowingly *makes* something so for certain reasons, rather than the kind of understanding possessed by someone who merely *takes* something to be so for certain reasons, without supposing his so taking things has a decisive influence on the matter.

We might call this complex of ideas about our normal understanding of our own judgments and choices our *everyday assumption of self-understanding*. It is an assumption we seem to take for granted in our practices of making and explaining our own judgments and choices, even if we never articulate the content of this assumption in a reflective form. As I have mentioned in the Introduction, however, important results in social and behavioral psychology have given rise to a widespread skepticism about this everyday attitude. Psychologists have devised a variety of ways of showing that our professed reasons for judging and choosing are often not our true reasons, and that we are ready to offer confabulated rationales with no more self-examination, and no less assurance, than we exhibit in more straightforward cases. These observations have led a number of philosophers and psychologists to suggest that our sense of immediate self-understanding is an illusion, not just in certain cases, but in general. According to Hilary Kornblith, for instance:

> What appears in introspection to be the direct apprehension of causal relations among our mental states is really, at bottom, the result of a process of rational reconstruction: we are actually engaged in a subconscious process of theorizing about what the source of our beliefs must have been. (Kornblith 2014: 198–199)[2]

Skeptics about self-understanding like Kornblith maintain that, in many cases, we are mistaken about what explains our own beliefs and actions. But even when our explanations are correct, they argue, the process by which we arrive

---

[2] Kornblith makes a more detailed case for this outlook in his 2012 and 2018.

at our account is essentially the same as the one operative in cases of confabulation: we *reconstruct* our grounds, on the basis of general assumptions about what the causes of our beliefs and actions are likely to be. This activity of self-interpretation may not occur consciously: it may be performed subconsciously by a dedicated "mind-reading faculty." But however evident our explanations may seem, they are at bottom interpretations resting on a kind of speculation about the causal determinants of our thoughts and actions, rather than on any immediate awareness of these determinants. In this way, such skeptics call into question, not merely the reliability of our self-understanding, but whether it can ever be what it purports to be: an immediate apprehension of what explains our own beliefs and actions.

My aim in the present chapter will be to consider how serious a threat these kinds of results pose to our everyday assumption of self-understanding, and what can be said on behalf of this assumption. I will argue that the case for skepticism is overstated, and that the everyday view has a deeper basis than its critics recognize, one that has important links to the reflectivist approach to self-knowledge that we have developed in the preceding chapters.

9.2. Skepticism about Self-Understanding

Skeptics about self-understanding,[3] as I will use the term, are philosophers and psychologists who hold that we do not have any immediate awareness of our own grounds for belief and action. The case for such skepticism often begins with the claim that we are sometimes mistaken about our own grounds for belief and action, but the skeptic's ultimate target is not just a claim about how often we are correct, but a certain intuitive conception of how these matters are known to us—namely, that they are somehow immediately or transparently available. I will have more to say later about how we might understand such transparency. Skeptics generally do not spend much time trying to characterize it, since they doubt that there really is any such mode of availability. Their focus is on arguing that we have no reason to believe in such transparency, whatever it might amount to.

To make matters concrete, I will focus on the version of skepticism presented by Peter Carruthers in his *The Opacity of Mind* (2011), which gives an unusually detailed and sophisticated presentation of the case for skepticism. Carruthers offers many kinds of evidence for his position, but I will focus on one main strand

---

[3] For brevity, I'll sometimes just call them "skeptics." Besides Kornblith and Carruthers, other recent authors writing from a broadly similar standpoint include Cassam 2014, Doris 2015, and Rosenberg 2016.

in his argumentation, a strand that also figures prominently in the work of other prominent skeptics.[4] The points I make in response could, I believe, be adapted to apply to other common skeptical arguments.

The argument on which I want to focus begins from the observation that, in various kinds of circumstances, people can be induced to *confabulate* about their grounds for belief or action—that is, to produce, with apparent assurance and sincerity, demonstrably false accounts of their own grounds for belief and action. Thus—to begin with an extreme case—"split brain" patients who have undergone a cerebral commissurotomy, in which the connection between the two hemispheres of the brain is severed by bisecting the corpus callosum, can be brought to offer confabulated accounts of their own actions. Carruthers describes a case in which a commissurotomized subject was shown a card with the word "Walk!" on it, presented in such a way that the card could be seen only by his left eye (which transmits signals exclusively to the right brain hemisphere). The subject then stood up and began to leave the testing space, and when asked where he was going (a verbal inquiry processed by the speech centers in his left brain hemisphere), replied, "I'm going to the house to get a Coke." In this and many similar cases, it is natural to conclude that what such subjects offer as their grounds for action are not their true motives, but *post hoc* rationalizations invented in response to a demand for an account where the true account is unavailable. What is striking about such cases, however, is that the confabulating subjects are in many instances conscious neither of any uncertainty about their motives nor of any effort of self-interpretation. Their awareness of their own grounds for action seems to them just as direct as it is in ordinary, unproblematic cases.

What leads commissurotomized subjects to confabulate is, of course, a rare and pathological brain condition, but Carruthers argues that such confabulation can also be induced in subjects whose brains are perfectly normal. This seems to be the lesson of a vast body of experimental evidence accumulated over the last several decades by social psychologists. The experiments take a variety of forms, but their general structure can be stated as follows: the experimenters produce a situation in which the judgments or choices of experimental subjects are significantly affected by some surprising factor, and then interrogate the subjects about why they judged or chose as they did. The subjects prove to be strikingly unaware of the role that the surprising factor played in affecting their choice—indeed, in many cases, they are incredulous at the suggestion that this factor played a role. Instead, they cite, with apparent assurance, factors that cannot plausibly have played a decisive role. Hence their accounts of why they judged or chose as they did are regarded as cases of confabulation.

---

[4] This strand is the main focus of the briefer case for skepticism in Carruthers 2010.

As an illustration, Carruthers describes a widely cited experiment reported by Richard Nisbett and Timothy Wilson in their influential paper "Telling More than We Can Know" (1977). In a mall in suburban Michigan, Nisbett and Wilson conducted what purported to be a consumer survey in which they asked shoppers to inspect four identical pairs of nylon stockings arrayed on a table and to determine which was "the best quality." After the subjects had made a choice, they were asked why they chose as they did. A pronounced "position effect" was observed, such that the farther right the stockings were in the array, the more frequently they were chosen as of highest quality, and the right-most pair was preferred to the left-most pair by a factor of nearly four to one. This was, in fact, predicted by the experimenters, since "position effects" on choice constitute a well-established phenomenon in the psychology of decision. Yet when the subjects were asked why they chose as they did, none mentioned position, and when asked whether position had played a role in their judgment, nearly all of them confidently denied it (with the exception of one subject who was taking a psychology course that had recently discussed position effects). Instead, they pointed to attributes of the preferred pair, such as its superior knit, sheerness, or elasticity. But given that the stockings were in fact identical, it is not credible that such attributes played a decisive role. Nisbett and Wilson take this and numerous similar results to show that "the accuracy of subject reports about higher order mental processes may be very low" since "such introspective access as may exist is not sufficient to produce accurate reports about the role of critical stimuli in response to questions asked a few minutes or seconds after the stimuli have been processed and the response produced" (Nisbett and Wilson 1977: 246). And since the proffered reasons were not in fact decisive factors, such results are also commonly taken to show that we readily confabulate about our reasons for judgment and choice (cf. Wilson 2002: Ch. 5; Carruthers 2011: Ch. 11).

Carruthers draws two conclusions from these sorts of results. First, he concludes that our subjective impression of having immediate awareness of our own grounds for judgment and decision must be taken with a grain of salt. As he puts it:

> [W]e don't have any subjectively accessible warrant for believing that we ever have transparent access to our own attitudes. This is because patients can report plainly-confabulated explanations with all of the same sense of obviousness and immediacy as normal people. (Carruthers 2011: 43)[5]

---

[5] Carruthers's focus is not on our awareness of *why* we think and act as we do, but on our awareness of our own attitudes and choices themselves. But he clearly takes the point to apply also to our subjective impression of having immediate knowledge of our own grounds for belief and action.

Secondly, he takes the results to show that, in general, people have the ability rapidly and subconsciously to construct interpretations of their own behavior. The confabulated explanations offered by brain-damaged subjects clearly draw on such an ability, and the kinds of results described by Nisbett and Wilson seem to show that subjects whose brains are normal can also be induced to construct confabulated self-interpretations in quite ordinary sorts of circumstances.[6]

Once we have admitted that we have such a self-interpretative faculty, however, it is natural to ask whether it might be operative, not just in cases where confabulation is conspicuous, but also in cases where everything seems normal. Carruthers calls this the "universal mind-reading hypothesis" (UMRH). In general, according to UMRH, we acquire beliefs about our own attitudes and their causes by subconsciously framing interpretations of the available data—data which may include facts about our history and circumstances, observation of our own words and deeds, and awareness of our own "phenomenally conscious" states. Sometimes our self-interpretations are inaccurate, but even when they are accurate, the explanations we offer do not reflect any immediate insight into our own reasons for judgment and action. We have no such insight: the only advantage we have over others, in interpreting ourselves, is access to some data to which others are not privy.

Carruthers argues that UMRH is not ruled out by our intuitive sense that our awareness of our grounds for judgment and decision is sometimes immediate, since subjects who undoubtedly confabulate, such as split-brain patients and people duped by social psychology experiments, also characteristically take themselves to have immediate awareness of their own grounds. Moreover, UMRH provides an attractively simple and unified explanation of how we arrive at an understanding of our own beliefs and choices. The only alternative, seemingly, is to accept a "dual method" hypothesis (DMH), according to which we *sometimes* form views about our own reasons for belief and action by relying on a self-interpretative faculty, but on other occasions become aware of them in some more immediate way.[7] But once our subjective impression of having immediate knowledge of our own reasons has been discounted, there seems to be no strong reason to prefer DMH, and considerations of theoretical simplicity as well as a great deal of experimental evidence appear to favor UMRH. Thus, Carruthers concludes, UMRH is probably true, and so our sense of immediate self-understanding is probably an illusion.

---

[6] Carruthers holds that this capacity is grounded in the very same "mind-reading faculty" we bring to bear in interpreting the words and actions of other people, but this additional claim won't be crucial here.

[7] Cf. Carruthers 2011: 45.

9.3. Processualism about Self-Understanding

Carruthers's case for skepticism might be questioned at various points, but here I want to focus on a general background assumption that he and other skeptics make about the nature of self-understanding.

The assumption that interests me is expressed in the opening lines of Nisbett and Wilson's "Telling More than We Can Know," a paper that is a touchstone for skeptics:

> "Why do you like him?" "How did you solve this problem?" "Why did you take that job?" In our daily lives we answer many such questions about the cognitive processes underlying our choices, evaluations, judgments, and behavior. (Nisbett and Wilson 1977: 231)

The questions with which Nisbett and Wilson begin evoke a familiar kind of situation: one in which people are asked about what *persuades* them to do something, think something, or feel a certain way—that is, why this way of acting, thinking, or feeling seems to them reasonable, or at any rate seems to have some reason that speaks in favor of it.[8] Nisbett and Wilson immediately go on, however, to characterize these questions as concerned with "the cognitive processes underlying our choices, evaluations, judgments, and behavior," and they set about assembling evidence that we are often mistaken about the factors that influence these processes. That is, they represent subjects who answer these questions as claiming insight into what *precipitated* or *brought about* a given thought, attitude, or action. They assume that, when we answer questions such as "Why do you like him?" or "Why did you take the job?," we are offering an account of some *process*—some connected sequence of events unfolding over time that caused the relevant attitude or act. I will refer to this assumption as *processualism* about self-understanding.

Processualism can seem like an inevitable consequence of the thought—which I do not dispute—that self-understanding is a form of causal understanding, an understanding in which we trace judgments and decisions to the factors that explain their existence. It is this seeming inevitability, presumably, that accounts for Nisbett and Wilson's unargued transition from speaking of

---

[8] Looked at from this standpoint, the question "How did you solve this problem?" is an outlier, since (on one reading) it asks the subject to reconstruct the mental process by which she arrived at her solution, which is a question about her actual psychological history rather than about her current reasons. But there is another reading of the question that tends to predominate when it is placed in the context of the other questions: one on which it asks the subject to explain what she has grasped about how *to* solve the problem. And this, again, is a question that invites an explanation of how, according to the subject, the problem can be solved, not a narrative of the thoughts and images that passed through the subject's mind as she considered how to solve it.

answers to explanatory questions to speaking of cognitive processes. I want to suggest, however, that this is a substantive and dubious transition, and that once we query it, the case for skepticism about self-understanding loses much of its force. For only if processualism is true does evidence that we are often ignorant of important factors in the causal history of our attitudes support skepticism about self-understanding.

Suppose you have a somewhat abrasive friend, and some other friend asks, "Why do you like him?" Perhaps you might answer that you know he can be abrasive, but you think this just reflects his discomfort in social situations, and over the years he has proved to be loyal and kind when it counts. The details here don't matter; the thing to notice is simply that, to the extent that it is right to represent your answer as citing psychological causes of your present affection, these causes are not past but present mental states. You like this friend because you *think* his abrasiveness is superficial and you *take* him to have been loyal and kind when it counts. It is your *present* conviction on these points, and your *presently* taking them to speak in favor of your affection, that you put forward as explaining your liking him. Of course, the present you describe is not an "instantaneous present": you aim to characterize a standing relationship between an attitude you hold and other things you take to be true, a complex cognitive state which has existed for some time and persists into the present. In this sense, your explanation may have implications, not just for the present moment, but for your reasons for *having liked* this friend for some time. Your explanation does not, however, commit you to any claims about the cognitive *processes* by which your affection arose: it describes what (presently) *sustains* your affection, not the causal processes that *brought it about*.

One feature of such explanations that may lead us to overlook their nonprocessive character is that they often cite facts about the past as grounds for present attitudes. The foregoing explanation, for instance, cites the fact that your friend *has been* loyal and kind when it counts. But here it is important to distinguish between the rational *ground* of an attitude and its proximate psychological *cause*. What makes it reasonable to feel affection for this person is a fact about the past: that on earlier occasions, your friend showed himself to be loyal and kind. But this fact forms the content of a *present* mental state: you *take* your friend to have been loyal and kind in the past. And it is your presently taking this to be so, not the sheer past fact, that explains your attitude. It is true that ordinary explanations of attitudes often leave such present mental states implicit: they simply cite facts about past, allowing the subject's present awareness of these facts to be implied by general presuppositions of explanatory relevance. But it should be clear, on reflection, that a fact about the past that rationally supports a certain attitude can figure in a reason-giving explanation of the attitude's presently being held only if this fact is presently known to the attitude-holder.

To bring out the importance of this requirement of present awareness, it will help to consider a case in which the requirement is not met. Suppose it is true that

(E)   You like NN because he has been loyal and kind to you

but the relevance of his loyalty and kindness to your present affection is not accessible to you when you consider the question why you like him. What sort of explanation of your affection could (E) be in that case? It could not be an explanation of what you now find *likable* about him, what *speaks in favor* of liking him from your perspective, for what you do not know cannot persuade you of something. (E) must, then, be a different kind of explanation, one that asserts your present affection for NN to *result* from certain experiences you had in the past. But if this is what (E) means, it is surely not the kind of explanation we normally presume ourselves to be able to give, without self-observation or inference from other evidence, of our present attitudes. For there is no reason to presume that I will remember psychological factors that figure in the causal history of my attitudes; and even if I do remember them, the claim that their occurrence is causally relevant to my present attitude is hardly one on which I would be able to comment without further investigation, were it not for the fact that they operate through my regarding them as reasons *to* feel affection for my friend. But if these experiences affect my attitude through my presently taking them to support my attitude, then they operate by being the content of contemporaneous awareness, and this awareness explains my attitude non-processively.

It might be objected that this analysis cannot apply to other questions on Nisbett and Wilson's list, such as "Why did you take that job?" and "How did you solve this problem?" These questions invite the addressee to explain an event that is itself in the past: How can this be explained by a present appreciation of a case for holding an attitude?—Well, it is true that these questions invite the subject to explain, not why she is presently persuaded to do something, or how she thinks something can be done, but why she was persuaded, or how she did it. But although the *explanadum* here is in the past, this does not imply that the *explanation* must appeal to a process. When I explain why I took a certain job, I appeal, presumably, to my memory of what *persuaded* me to take the job. But though this decision is now in the past, it was once made in the present, and I would then have been able to explain it by citing things I *presently* believed, wanted, thought, etc. My ability to speak, now, about my reasons for past decisions surely depends on my ability to remember how the world looked to me then: I am able to speak for my reasons to the extent that I am able to project myself back into my earlier point of view, the one from which I made the decision. But to the extent that I can do this, I can explain the decision as if I were making it now—by speaking, from the point of view I remember, to the question of what grounds I see *for* making the decision. So although what I explain is a past attitude, my explanation of why I held that attitude remains non-processive.

Something broadly similar applies in the case of my ability to answer the question "How did you solve this problem?" If the question is understood simply as a request for an account of the sequence of thoughts, images, etc., that led up to my discovery of the solution, then there is little reason indeed to expect that I will remember everything relevant, or that I will be competent to judge what caused what. But there is another reading of the question, one that naturally occurs to us when it is listed together with "Why do you like him?," "Why did you take that job?," etc. On this other reading, the question is understood as a request to explain what I grasped about how *to* solve the problem. My answer to this question may take the form of a narrative ("Well, I saw that if you multiply through by the denominator then you eliminate the fraction, and then I noticed . . ."), but what I am really recalling is what I understood about how the problem can be solved, and narrating this understanding in a sequence of steps. This is not primarily an account of the *process by which I came to discover* my solution, but of my *solution* itself.

These considerations suggest a principled reason why our ability to answer questions about the grounds for our own attitudes must appeal to present mental states and events. It is only in virtue of the fact that I can treat the question why I hold a given attitude as "transparent" to the question whether *to* hold this attitude that I am in a position to answer it without self-observation or inference. But the latter question is not a question about whatever events may have brought about my attitude, considered as a psychological reality, but about the *case* for holding the attitude, considered as a possible response to some question of attitude-transcendent fact. This case can indeed be transposed into a psychological register: instead of answering "Why do you like him?" by saying, "Well, *p* and *q*," I might equally answer, "Well, I know that *p*, and I think that *q*." And I see no reason to deny that, if true, this psychological rendering of the explanation gives a causal account of my affection for my friend, by citing other attitudes that sustain it. But if my appreciation of a case for holding a certain attitude is to explain my holding the attitude, the relevant explanation must travel through my capacity to appreciate the reason-giving force of a case for an attitude, and this requires that I grasp the case as a whole and appreciate its import at one time.[9] Thus the transparency of first-person attitude explanations implies their non-processuality.

---

[9] This is, indeed, implied in the very idea that my *appreciation* of the case explains my attitude: to appreciate a case is not merely to hold a manifold of attitudes toward the several propositions that comprise the case, but to hold some sort of attitude toward the case as a whole, and thus to comprehend the several elements of the case and their import at one time. I say more about this topic is Boyle 2011a.

9.4. Processualism and Skepticism

I will say more about such transparency below in §9.5. In the meantime, let us consider the bearing of these observations on skepticism about self-understanding.

Skeptics commonly take evidence that people are ignorant of factors that played an important role in bringing about their judgments and decisions as evidence that they lack insight into why they make the relevant judgments and decisions. In one sense, this is surely correct: the experimental results, if valid,[10] show that factors to which we are oblivious may influence our judgments and decisions; and it is plausible that such factors operate, not just in artificial experimental conditions, but in many ordinary situations in which we judge and decide. That factors such as the ordering of objects in an array can influence our preferences is disconcerting enough, and it is all the more unnerving to know that we are ready to offer quite unrelated rationales for such preferences. But do such observations show that the explanations we then offer are false and confabulated?

The skeptical conclusion that they are must rest, it seems to me, on something like the following line of thought:

> The fact that a certain pair of stockings was on the right in the presented array was crucial to producing the subjects' preference for this pair. But the explanations subjects offer of their preference makes no mention of its position; and furthermore, their belief that the stockings have the attributes appealed to in their explanation (superior knit, sheerness, elasticity, etc.) can itself be plausibly explained only by a preexisting disposition to prefer stockings on the right-hand side of the array. So the explanations these subjects offer must not be the true explanations of their preferences; they must rather be confabulated.

Our discussion of processualism equips us to notice an equivocation in this line of thought. There is compelling evidence that subjects may be unaware of a factor that plays a decisive role in *bringing about* their preference, and it is implausible that the factors they do cite are the real determinants of this process. Does it follow that they do not know why they have the relevant preference? Only if the relevant "why?"-question is understood as an inquiry into the process by which their preference came to exist; for only then does their ignorance of what was decisive in this process imply that they are ignorant of what explains their preference. But in fact, as we have seen, the relevant sort of "why?"-question inquires

---

[10] There is an ongoing controversy about the replicability of many widely cited findings in social psychology, but I am not in a position to evaluate this controversy. For the sake of argument, I will take it for granted that the relevant results are valid.

into a different topic: what considerations *sustain* the subject's attitude in the present. This is not an inquiry into the causal history of her attitude, but into the broader outlook that supports her holding it.[11]

For all these experimental results show, then, the belief that (e.g.) this pair of stockings is of superior knit might indeed be the basis on which a certain subject prefers it—though it might also be true that the pair's being on the right-hand side of the array brought it about that he had this belief (perhaps by leading him to attend to its knitting with a more favorable eye). So the experimental results do not prove that subjects do not know the "real reasons" for their preferences, though they may show that our perceptions and judgments can be influenced by factors of which we are ignorant and whose influence we would not countenance if we were aware of it. But our ignorance of the factors that played a decisive role in the *process* by which our preferences arise does not show that we are ignorant of what *persuades* us to prefer a given pair of stockings, for this is not a question about a mental process. To draw this distinction is not, of course, to offer any positive proof that the accounts subjects give of their preferences do capture what really persuades them; but as far as I can see, the kinds of experiments standardly cited by skeptics fail to show that they do not.

Even this modest anti-skeptical conclusion may seem too quick. Recall the case of the commisurotomized subject who was shown a card that said "Walk!" and explained his getting up and walking by saying that he was "going to the house to get a Coke." Surely his decision to get up and walk (or his voluntarily beginning to walk, if there was no decision) preceded his inventing this rationale. It seems obvious here that the rationale was concocted under pressure to explain already extant facts, and was thus a textbook case of confabulation. But if it was a confabulated account of extant facts, how can it be any kind of genuine explanation, processive or otherwise, of those facts? If the decision to walk preexisted any thought of going to the house to get a Coke, then this thought can't explain the decision—not even in the sense of being what non-processively persuaded the subject to walk. And if we grant this point, it seems that a similar argument will apply to the preferences in the Nisbett and Wilson experiment: the subjects find themselves preferring the stockings on the right-hand side of the array, and under pressure to find a reason for their preference, they seek a feature that would justify it. That they come to believe the stockings possess this feature—superior knit, or whatever—surely reflects an already existing tendency to find stockings on the right-hand side preferable. But then their judgment that the stockings

---

[11] Closely related points are made in Malle 2006, though Malle frames his objection in terms of a distinction, which I do not accept, between "reasons" and "causes." Nevertheless, I am indebted to his discussion.

have this feature can't genuinely explain their finding these stockings preferable, for their preference preexisted any such judgment.

I think this criticism still depends on processualist assumptions. Let us grant for the sake of argument that the commisurotomized subject begins to walk before thinking of going to get a Coke, and that the subject who prefers stockings on the right-hand side does so before becoming convinced of their superior knit. On these assumptions, it is certainly true that the thought of going to get a Coke does not *bring about* the subject's walking, and that the judgment that the knit of these stockings is superior does not *bring about* the subject's preference for them. But again, this is not the sort of explanation we are seeking when we ask a subject why he *holds* a certain preference or *is performing* a certain action. We are asking for an explanation, not of what brought about a judgment or choice, but of what *sustains* it here and now—why the subject presently holds the relevant view or is willing to carry on with the relevant action. For all these experiments show, it might be that the pressure of a "why?"-question from the experimenter brings about a crystallization in the subject's outlook, such that she is *now* walking to the house with the aim of getting a Coke, or *now* prefers these stockings on the basis of their knit. Whether the preference or choice *preexisted* what presently guides or sustains it is neither here nor there.

This might seem like a pyrrhic victory over the skeptic.[12] If we deny that rationalizing explanations make claims about the processes by which judgments and decisions come to exist, are we not insulating such explanations from criticism by depriving them of any real significance? Are we not, indeed, conceding the skeptic's point in all but name? Skeptics maintain that our judgments and choices are often influenced by factors of which we are unaware, and that the rationales we offer for them are *post hoc* rationalizations rather than accounts of the grounds on which we *consciously make* the relevant judgments and choices. If we reply that these rationalizations may nevertheless come to *sustain* the relevant judgments and choices, isn't this just grist for the skeptic's mill? Doesn't it amount to conceding that our capacity to reflect on our reasons for judgment and choice operates, not as a power consciously to determine what we judge and choose, but merely as a factor that tends rationalize and reinforce determinations that arise from other, non-conscious factors?

Again, I think this response seems compelling only if we are still in the grip of processualist assumptions. Let me make two points in response. First, the fact that rationalizing explanations speak to what sustains judgments and choices, rather than to what brought them about, does not trivialize these explanations. To represent an attitude as non-processively explained by other attitudes is to

---

[12] This paragraph attempts to capture a concern put to me in conversation by Sebastian Watzl. For a similar objection, see Kornblith 2018, §5.3.

assert that a subject's being in one *state* depends on her being in other *states* she is in, and this mode of understanding can only get a grip where there is a certain stable relation of dependence between aspects of the subject's outlook. There is a real and significant form of explanatory dependence here, one that may persist *through* time, though it does not consist in a causal process unfolding *over* time. To assess whether such a relation holds, we need to consider, not how the relevant attitudes originated, but how the continued existence of one is related to the continued existence of the other. *Does* the subject who says she is "going to the house to get a Coke" actually follow through on this project? *Is* the judgment of the subject who says she prefers these stockings because of their knit responsive to changes in her assessment of their knit? It is characteristic of these experimental situations that nothing of significance hangs on the relevant attitudes and projects, so their robustness in counterfactual conditions is likely to be weak. But in principle, these sorts of counterfactuals are what must be tested to assess a claim about what *sustains* a preference or *guides* an action.

Secondly, the impression that results like those reported by Nisbett and Wilson show that our rationales for our own judgments and choices must in general be *post hoc* rationalizations, rather than expressions of directive awareness of what determines our attitudes, presupposes what we might call a "ballistic" picture of the causation of judgment and choice. In the normal course of things—though not, typically, in the kinds of situations produced in these experiments—we make judgments and choices about topics that *matter* to us, topics concerning which our being wrong or unreasonable has a cost. Moreover, we must *persist* in these attitudes through some period of time—the time it takes to carry out a complex project, or the period during which we persist in accepting a certain judgment. The *sustainability* of our views and projects requires that our overall view of things—of what is true and what is worthwhile—has a certain order and coherence.[13] Only if we thought that, once "launched," particular judgments, preferences, etc., were carried forward by their own momentum, without need for support from the rest of our outlook on the world—only if our picture of the explanation of judgments and choices were in this sense ballistic—could we suppose that our views about why the relevant judgments and choices are sound are mere rationalizations of no real explanatory significance. But the kinds of experimental results we have been considering establish no such thing.

The kinds of results reported by Nisbett and Wilson are certainly unsettling: they show how easily our judgments and choices can be influenced

---

[13] Not, to be sure, total order and coherence: it is a familiar fact that our judgments may be inconsistent, and that our projects may embody incompatible values. Nevertheless, I assume that a tendency toward order and coherence holds broadly and on the whole, and the idea of a judgment or choice that is wholly isolated from other supporting views about what is true or valuable is at best a pathological, limiting case. I say more about these issues below in §§9.5–9.6.

by factors of which we are unaware. But I do not see how they could show that our judgments and choices are in general independent of our (relatively stable, relatively coherent) overall view of what is true and what is important. If they are thus dependent, however, then any given idea or preference, whatever its origin, will normally be able to persist only insofar as it can find a place in our general view of what is (knowably) the case and what is (intelligibly) worthwhile. In this way, our conscious reasons for accepting given judgments and choices *matter* to the existence of these judgments and choices. Indeed, when seen from this perspective, our tendency to "rationalize" our own judgments and choices takes on a different aspect: it appears as the operation of our power to consider the relation between given judgments and choices and the background of attitudes that sustains them. The fact that this power can, in certain kinds of cases, be induced to rationalize attitudes for which there is no preexisting rationale does not show that, in general, it is irrelevant to our holding the attitudes in question.

9.5. Transparency and Self-Understanding

So far, I have simply argued that the kinds of observations cited by skeptics fail to show that our naïve assumption of self-understanding is false. But what can be said in support of this assumption? I'll conclude with some remarks about this, drawing on the reflectivist approach to transparent self-knowledge developed in previous chapters.

We have already noted a close connection between our ability to offer explanations of our own attitudes and our ability to treat the question why we hold a given attitude as "transparent" to the question whether *to* hold such an attitude—a question whose focus is, not the *explanation* of an extant attitude, but what *speaks in favor of holding* a possible view about some non-psychological topic. For instance, in answering the explanatory question why I reject a certain philosophical theory, I can normally treat this as equivalent to the justificatory question why the theory is to be rejected, and convert my answer to the latter question into an answer to the former by transposing the justifying reasons I would offer into claims about the beliefs that contribute to explaining my judgment. And similarly, if I am asked why I chose to come along to the beach, I can normally treat this as equivalent to the justificatory question what made it attractive to come, and transpose my answer into an explanatory register by rephrasing my rationale for coming as an account of the background of attitudes that explains my choice to come.[14]

---

[14] In some cases, of course, I will have no elaborate rationale to offer for an attitude. For some judgments, I will only be able to say, "It just seems obvious"; for some choices, I will only be able to say, "It just seemed attractive"; etc. But even when I offer only such minimal explanations, I presuppose

Like the other forms of transparency we have considered, this kind of transparency of an explanatory question about an attitude to a justificatory question about how to view the world (henceforth, "explanatory transparency") is not trivial, for the two questions are distinct on their face: the one concerns the causes of my own psychological states; the other, the right or appropriate attitude toward some non-psychological topic.[15] Moreover, explanatory transparency does not always hold: it is a familiar aspect of the frailty of human rationality that we sometimes cannot bring ourselves to hold an attitude that we judge to be warranted, or cannot bring ourselves to give up an attitude that we recognize to be poorly supported. But to the extent that I cannot see a justification for a given attitude, I will also not take myself to be able to explain my own attitude in the characteristically immediate, non-speculative way on which skeptics seek to cast doubt. So the case where explanatory transparency holds is the one that should interest us: Why does this relationship hold when it does?

Just as, in earlier chapters, I argued that our capacity for transparent knowledge of our own mental states rests on a nonpositional self-consciousness that belongs to the very nature of these states, so I want to suggest here that our capacity to give transparent *explanations* of our own mental states is grounded in a nonpositional self-understanding that belongs to the very nature of these states. To see this, consider the now-familiar idea that we can think of intentional acts and attitudes—judgments and beliefs, choices and intentions, preferences, desires, hopes, fears, etc.—as stances on characteristic questions. Thus a belief that p is an affirmative stance on the question whether p; an intention to φ is an affirmative stance on the question whether to φ; a preference for A over B is an affirmative stance on the question whether A is preferable to B; a desire for O is an affirmative stance on the question whether O is desirable; a hope that p is an affirmative stance on the question whether p is to be hoped for; a fear of X is an affirmative stance on the question whether X is to be feared; and so on. If we define a rational animal as one that can *think* about such questions—one that can consider them in an interrogative mode, and deliberate about what speaks for a given answer to them, rather than simply coming unthinkingly to accept some answer—then we may say that, for rational animals, holding an attitude will in general involve being *disposed* to resolve the relevant question in a certain way.[16]

my ability to speak to the explanation of my attitudes by speaking to the question of why, from my perspective, they appear justified. In this case, I claim that the relevant appearance is primitive and not further explicable. I say more about this point shortly.

[15] In special cases, of course, I may hold an attitude that is *about* some psychological topic, and in this case my answer to the justificatory question will itself concern psychology. The important point, however, is that the justificatory question concerns the *topic* of one of my attitudes, not my *attitude* toward that topic. Having noted this point, I will continue, for simplicity, to refer to the first-order topic as "non-psychological."

[16] Compare our earlier discussion of the rational/nonrational distinction in §7.7.

This will be true even if they do not actually deliberate about the corresponding question: even if they never consider this question as such, their attitude will involve some standing conception of why the question is rightly so answered, which will connect their answer to this question with other things they hold true, desirable, choiceworthy, etc.

If the attitudes of rational animals are states of this sort, then such animals will in general have a special kind of understanding of their own attitudes: an understanding "from the inside," so to speak. For their holding a given attitude will itself involve their being disposed to answer some corresponding world-directed question in a certain way on a certain basis, and they will be capable, on reflection, of reformulating this view of how *to* answer the relevant question as an explanation of why they *do* hold a certain attitude on that question. This, I believe, is what accounts for the phenomenon of explanatory transparency. What accounts for such transparency is not that we "make up our minds" at the moment when a question about our own attitude arises, and know the grounds on which we have reached this new assessment.[17] This may occur in certain cases, but the phenomenon of explanatory transparency is more general: in many cases in which we already hold a settled attitude on some topic, including cases in which we have never reflected on the attitude in question, we take ourselves to be able to explain why we hold the attitude by speaking to the question what speaks in favor of holding this attitude. What accounts for this phenomenon in its full generality, I suggest, is that, for rational animals like ourselves, holding an attitude just *is* being disposed to find a certain answer to a question compelling on a certain basis (or, in the limiting case, primitively). There are many different ways of finding an answer to a question compelling, of course, and in many instances what makes a given answer seem compelling will be only a very vague conception of how this answer fits into our overall understanding of the world and our own bases for making determinations about it. But this is no objection to our account of explanatory transparency: it represents our ability to explain our own attitudes as no stronger, but also no weaker, than it in fact tends to be.

This might seem like an excessively rationalistic conception of human thought and action. Don't we often think and do things for which we can offer no justification, or indeed which we take to be unjustified? Of course we do, but this is not in tension with the conception of self-understanding defended here. I have admitted that the limiting case of self-understanding—a case which may in fact be common—is one in which we have no particular reason for an attitude or action, or none beyond our general sense that it seems primitively true or attractive. Even when we admit to having no particular reason for a given attitude or action, we lay claim to self-understanding, inasmuch as we claim to know what

---

[17] Moran 2001 is often read—mistakenly, I think—as proposing an account of this sort.

our own reasons are. To claim that one has no specifiable reason for a given attitude or action is to assert that one *does* have a perspective "from the inside" on the relevant attitude or action, and that what this perspective reveals is precisely that the relevant attitude or action is primitively compelling.

A defender of the position I have outlined can admit, moreover, that a person's attitude on a question is not always identical with her all-things-considered judgment on that question.[18] A person may, for instance, judge that, all things considered, it is not desirable for him to have another beer—perhaps because he anticipates that he will say things he shouldn't, that he will regret it tomorrow, etc.—yet he may still very much want another beer. But this is perfectly compatible with my claims about the connection between holding an attitude and possessing self-understanding. A person who, despite his better judgment, wants another beer normally *does* have an understanding "from within" of his own desire. He does not find himself calling for another beer as if driven by an alien compulsion. On the contrary: he can speak, in whatever minimal way, to what seems desirable about having another beer, and his finding the prospect desirable on this basis just *is* his desiring it. He may not understand why the attractions of this prospect triumph over his all-things-considered judgment, but he understands why he desires what he does, because he understands the perspective from which he finds having another beer desirable. In this way, even recalcitrant attitudes, which resist our better judgment, can, and normally do, constitutively involve self-understanding.

Perhaps there are also attitudes and actions from which we are alienated in a more radical sense, ones that really do present themselves as alien compulsions whose grounds are inscrutable to us. I do not find it easy to think of such examples in my own life, but this does not convince me that such alienation is impossible. What is impossible, if my argument is sound, is that this sort of alienation should be the rule, rather than the exception, in the life of a rational animal. For a rational animal is one that can think about the questions that are the topics of its attitudes, and such thinking is possible only where, as a rule at least, the views such thinking expresses are the ones the animal in fact holds. In this sense, although our self-understanding may be fallible and corruptible in all kinds of ways, its foundations are secure insofar as we are as rational, thinking beings at all. And that we are such beings is, as Descartes famously observed, not something any of us can easily place in doubt, since even in attempting to doubt this, we exercise our capacity to think, and can recognize this on reflection.[19]

---

[18] This paragraph responds to a question put to me in conversation by David Owens.
[19] This point bears on a claim made by Rosenberg in his *New York Times* Op-Ed summarizing the case for skepticism about self-understanding. Having surveyed the kinds of considerations we noted above in §2, Rosenberg draws the following bold conclusion:

> There is no first-person point of view. Our access to our own thoughts is just as indirect and fallible as our access to the thoughts of other people. We have no privileged access to our

If this account of explanatory transparency is sound, then there can be no basis for a *general* skepticism about the self-understanding of rational animals. It may be that we are easily misled about the explanation of our own attitudes, and that our attitudes can be influenced by factors of which we are unaware and whose effects we would not endorse. Still, insofar as we are capable of holding attitudes toward questions at all, this will in general involve our finding answers to corresponding questions compelling on certain grounds (or primitively), and this stance will enable us, on reflection, to offer real explanations of the relevant attitudes, by converting the case we see for a given answer into an account of the background that sustains the corresponding attitude. A subject who offers this sort of explanation will be speaking *from the perspective* of her own attitude, articulating the wider worldview that makes a certain answer to an attitude-defining question seem compelling. What she then offers will indeed be an explanation of her attitude, but it will be an explanation that is integral to the first-order outlook she describes, rather than a mere hypothesis about what brought her attitude into being.

There can be no basis for a general skepticism about such self-understanding, in short, because the relevant understanding simply makes explicit commitments involved in the subject's holding the relevant first-order attitudes themselves. Consider again our subject whose affection for her abrasive friend rests on his record of loyalty and kindness at moments that matter. On our analysis, her attitude toward her friend *consists* of her taking him to be likable—worthy of affection—on these grounds. Hence, when she makes these grounds explicit in an explanation of her affection, she will not merely be offering a hypothesis about what brought her attitude into being, but characterizing the particular way of answering the question of his likability in which her attitude consists. There may be countless other ways of finding a person likable, but this is hers. Hence the explanation she offers of her affection characterizes her holding of this attitude intrinsically, rather than merely identifying certain extrinsic causes of her holding this attitude. Of course, any number of confounding factors may lead her to mischaracterize the explanation of her own attitude, but such mischaracterizations, however frequent they may be in practice, are secondary in principle. For insofar as she holds the relevant attitude at all, the primary

---

own minds. If our thoughts give the real meaning of our actions, our words, our lives, then we can't ever be sure what we say or do, or for that matter, what we think or why we think it. (Rosenberg 2016: 5)

Rosenberg does not conclude that we have no thoughts or that our words and actions have no meaning at all. But if I am right, the question of the existence of these *explananda* and the question of the possibility of the relevant kind of explanation are not separable in the way Rosenberg assumes.

explanation of her holding it will necessarily be available to her reflection, provided that she is not distracted, deluded, or otherwise misled.

9.6. Conclusion: Intelligibility and Intelligence

It is not a new idea that human beings, as rational animals, are distinguished from nonrational animals by the fact that we lead our lives with a certain implicit self-understanding. One classic expression of this thought is the claim that the "human" sciences (*Geisteswissenchaften*: the sciences concerned with the lives of thinking beings) are set apart from the natural sciences (*Naturwissenschaften*) by the fact that they seek a different kind of understanding of phenomena, not "lawlike explanation" (*Erklären*) but "interpretative understanding" (*Verstehen*). The nature and defensibility of any such distinction is, of course, controversial, but a recurring theme in the writings of Dilthey, Collingwood, and other defenders of such a distinction is that humanistic understanding seeks to capture the *internal standpoint of a participant* on the events, institutions, and practices under consideration. Thus Collingwood writes (commenting approvingly on a theme he finds in Hegel):

> [H]istory consists of actions, and actions have an inside and an outside; on the outside they are mere events, related in space and time but not otherwise; on the inside they are thoughts, bound to each other by logical connexions.... [T]he historian must first work empirically by studying documents and other evidence; it is only in this way that he can establish what the facts are. But he must then look at the facts from the inside, and tell us what they look like from that point of view. (Collingwood 1946: 118; cf. Dilthey 1989: 58–59)

Collingwood's thought is that the kind of understanding sought in what he calls the "historical sciences" is one that takes account of the *self-understanding* of the parties involved. He holds that an adequate understanding of human affairs must comprehend this "internal" perspective because he assumes that human events are shaped, in the main and on the whole, by our own self-understanding. This is what he means when he says, in the passage quoted as an epigraph to this chapter, that human thoughts and actions are "not merely intelligible, but intelligent": they are not merely comprehensible by others *post hoc*, but are guided *ab initio* by the subject's own understanding. Hence any adequate understanding of these phenomena must take account of this perspective.

Our discussion enables us to see a valuable point in this way of thinking. The point is not merely that we human beings characteristically have views about our own grounds for thinking and acting, but that, in the fundamental case, these views merely bring to reflective articulacy a standpoint that constitutively informs the relevant thoughts and actions themselves: a standpoint whose primary focus is not the explanation of our own thoughts and actions, but questions about the world in which we think and act. Such understanding is directive rather than merely *post hoc*, inasmuch as it is a condition of the existence of the relevant attitudes and actions: not an extrinsic, productive cause of their coming into being, but an intrinsic, sustaining cause of the stance in which they consist. It is the fact that our attitudes and actions consist in ways of answering such questions that ensures that human beings have a perspective "from the inside" on their own thoughts and actions, and that this perspective is, not just a well-informed piece of speculation, but a standpoint comprehension of which is essential for understanding the relevant thoughts and actions themselves.

This certainly does not imply, and Collingwood did not take it to imply, that the understanding people have of their own thoughts and actions must always be taken at face value, or must exhaust what there is to understand about human events. It implies only that, for any such thought or action, there will be some standpoint on a question which belongs to it constitutively, and which can, in favorable conditions, be transformed through reflection into an explicit self-understanding. Comprehending this standpoint is not the end, but at most the beginning, of understanding why people think and act as they do. Nevertheless, it is a crucial beginning, inasmuch as it is essential to a full understanding of why the relevant thought or action exists and what it means. Any serious defense of the value of the humanities or "human sciences" against the various challenges they face in contemporary culture must, I think, begin with a defense of this basic proposition. For if this point is accepted, it follows that these disciplines can make genuine contributions to our comprehension of a distinctive subject matter; whereas if it is rejected, they will at best appear to offer a pleasant consolation for idle moments, not an essential requisite for a genuine understanding of our own lives.

10
The Examined Life

> SOCRATES: I am still unable, as the Delphic inscription orders, to know myself; and it really seems to me ridiculous to look into other things before I have understood that. This is why I do not concern myself with them.... I look not into them but into my own self: Am I a beast more complicated and savage than Typhon, or am I a tamer, simpler animal with a share in a divine and gentle nature?
>
> —Plato, *Phaedrus*, 229e–230a

10.1. Introduction

The Western philosophical tradition has long stressed the importance of knowing oneself. But what is the point of self-knowledge, at the end of the day? Why *should* we examine our lives, as Socrates famously urged us to do, and why, in particular, should we examine our "inner" lives of thoughts, impressions, and feelings?

Obviously, there is room for more than one answer to this question. We need only think of the radically different forms that self-reflection takes in, for instance, Augustine's *Confessions*, Michel de Montaigne's *Essays*, and Sigmund Freud's *Interpretation of Dreams*, in order to see that the benefits of paying heed to one's inner life may be enormously various. It is clear, at any rate, that in cases like these, one person's self-reflection may be of value to all humanity. What, then, can we be asking when we ask about the point of knowing ourselves?

Well, if self-reflection can produce such profound meditations on the human condition, it can also, as we are all aware, produce forms of self-absorption that benefit no one. It has, indeed, its own characteristic vices, notably a kind of narcissistic concern with oneself that depletes one's appreciation for the wider world, and a form of excessive self-attention that impairs one's ability to act skillfully and resolutely. These twin pathologies of self-reflection are well-attested human phenomena, and they have been long-standing concerns of philosophers.[1] The capacity for self-reflection thus seems to be one of the proverbial "double-edged

---

[1] And also recent concerns, notably in Williams 1981 (on the narcissistic vices) and in Dreyfus 2007 (on the self-undermining effects of excessive self-attention).

swords" given to humanity, and it is hardly obvious that its benefits outweigh its burdens. It is worth remembering that the very culture that gave us the maxim "Know thyself" also produced, in *Oedipus Rex*, one of the most famous meditations on the dubious value of the human capacity for self-knowledge.

In any case, it is not clear that the sort of self-knowledge that has been our focus in this book is the sort that philosophical tradition singles out for praise. In Xenophon's *Memorabilia*, Socrates explains the meaning of the Delphic maxim "Know thyself" in these terms:

> Do you think a man knows himself who knows only his name? Or is the case like that of the men who buy horses, who do not think that they know the horse they want to buy until they have examined whether it is tame or wild, strong or weak, swift or slow, and how it is in all the other respects which make a horse useful or useless. Does not a man make this kind of examination as to what is his human use, and in this way come to know his own powers?[2]

If Xenophon's report is to be trusted, what Socrates meant by "knowing oneself" was knowing one's fundamental capacities and traits of character—the analogues of such equine traits as spiritedness, tractability, speed, and strength. In the ensuing discussion, it becomes clear that Socrates also has in mind knowing what is truly good for human beings, what genuinely benefits us.[3] This explains how Socrates can speak, in the *Apology*, of "the examined life" as requiring philosophical discussion of human virtue: to reflect on this counts, for him, as a way of examining our own lives because it belongs to understanding the human good.[4] But although knowledge of our fundamental character traits and of what is genuinely good for us as human beings should certainly count as varieties of self-knowledge, they are not the varieties on which our inquiry has focused.

We have been concerned with the ability of rational subjects to ascend from conscious engagement with the world to reflective knowledge of their own present mental states.[5] We have argued that this sort of reflection does *not* demand careful study of ourselves, but merely the reflective articulation of an awareness we already possess in representing the world. In this domain, the representing subject seems to have a kind of inalienable privilege: just in virtue of being in various first-order mental states, she is in a position—provided nothing interferes—to know herself to be in these states. In this sense, she has the

---

[2] Xenophon, *Memorabilia* (2001), IV.2.25.
[3] Ibid., IV.2.30f.
[4] Plato, *Apology of Socrates* (in Plato 2011), 38a3–4.
[5] In Chapter 7, I introduced the term "self-reflection" for this special way of becoming aware of our own mental states, and I will use the term in the same way here. It should be clear that not every case of coming to know my own mental states counts as self-reflection in this sense.

capacity for *immediate* knowledge of these aspects of her own mind. By contrast, the questions of concern to Socrates are ones that require careful consideration to answer. They are not—at least not obviously—ones we can answer simply by reflecting on what we already know. I cannot tell whether I am kind, generous, or brave by mere reflection; I must examine how I actually conduct myself in cases where something real is at stake. Moreover, another person is often a better judge of such matters than I am, for I am liable to be biased in assessing my own case. And Socrates's questions about what is genuinely good for human beings seem, if anything, even more difficult to answer. For, as Socrates emphasizes, people lacking in virtue will tend to judge such matters poorly, taking things to be good which are not genuinely so. Hence, since most of us presumably do not begin from a state of perfect virtue, it is far from clear how we might get ourselves into a position even to make well-grounded judgments about the aspects of life whose examination Socrates recommends.

The striking contrasts between the difficult-to-attain self-knowledge that was praised by Socrates and the easily available self-knowledge that has preoccupied post-Cartesian philosophers have led several recent writers to distinguish two kinds of self-knowledge, "Socratic" or "substantial" self-knowledge, on the one hand, and "Cartesian" or "immediate" self-knowledge, on the other.[6] We will have more to say about this distinction in due course, but for the moment we may grant it in order to formulate our problem more sharply. Supposing this distinction is sound, there seems to be a special difficulty about the importance of immediate, Cartesian self-knowledge. Perhaps the point of seeking Socratic self-knowledge is clear enough: if it were possible to know our own fundamental character traits and what is really good for us, doubtless this would be useful information for us to have in seeking to lead good lives. But what is the point of bringing our immediate awareness of our own minds to reflective articulacy? Isn't such knowledge *trivial*—as several recent authors have alleged[7]—in direct proportion to its ready availability?

The account we have given of the basis of reflective self-knowledge makes this difficulty, if anything, even more acute. For it has been a crucial theme of our discussion that, even before a person reflects on her own mental states, she already possesses a kind of implicit awareness of these states. Moreover, we have rejected the idea that only a subject who reflects on her own mental states can bring her capacity for rational deliberation to bear on them. On the contrary, we have maintained that a subject can think rationally about the *contents* of her mental states without needing to reflect on her own mental states *as such*. To

---

[6] For the Socratic/Cartesian contrast, see Renz's Introduction to Renz 2017. For the substantial/immediate contrast, see Cassam 2014: Ch. 1.

[7] Schwitzgebel 2011, Cassam 2014.

be sure, we have affirmed that rationality implies the capacity for self-reflection, inasmuch as any rational subject could, through reflection, frame relevant psychological concepts and employ them in making explicit self-ascriptions of her present mental states. But to say that rationality implies the *capacity* for such self-reflection is not yet to explain the point of *exercising* this capacity. This is our problem: What is the point of *actually* reflecting on our own mental states as such? This is undoubtedly a topic that human beings can consider, and if Aristotle is right that all human beings by nature desire to know, then perhaps some of us will take a special interest in knowing ourselves, as others take an interest in botany or Roman history. But would someone who did not take an interest in this particular kind of knowledge—someone who led a life replete in knowledge and experience of other kinds, but who never brought her own thoughts and feelings into focus in this way—miss out on anything of vital importance? If so, why? We may call this the problem of *the point of self-reflection*.

A major advantage of our "reflectivist" approach to self-knowledge, I will suggest, is that it can offer a satisfying response to this problem—an account of the sort of difference that self-reflection makes to our lives, and also of the kinds of pathologies to which it is characteristically subject. The aim of this final chapter will be to bring out the bearing of our reflectivism on these topics, and in the process to shed some light on a Sartrean thought mentioned long ago in the Introduction: that "for human reality, to exist is always to *assume* its being" in such a way that self-understanding is "not a quality that comes to human reality from without, but its own mode of existence" (Sartre 1994: 9). Our first task will be to clarify our topic by thinking more carefully about what it could mean to speak of the "point" of reflective self-knowledge (§10.2). Having done this, we will be in a position to analyze the kind of difference that reflection can make to our lives (§10.3), and in the light of this, to return to our question about the point of such reflection (§10.4) and to the supposed distinction between "Socratic" and "Cartesian" self-knowledge (§10.5). I will close with some remarks about the relevance of our conclusions to the Sartrean idea that human beings "assume their being" (§10.6). What I have to say about the latter idea will constitute only a very preliminary approach to a profound topic, but I hope it will convince the reader that there is a profound topic here, one that connects our study of reflective self-knowledge with the venerable idea that human beings need self-knowledge in order to live well.

10.2. Refining the Claim

We have framed our problem as one about the point of self-reflection, but in what sense might such reflection be said to have a point?

Philosophers commonly distinguish between pursuits that are intrinsically valuable and those that are merely instrumentally valuable, and it is sometimes suggested that if our capacity for self-reflection has a point, it must be valuable to us in one of these two ways.[8] To assert that our capacity for self-reflection has *instrumental value* would be to claim that this capacity is valuable because its exercise tends to promote valuable ends other than the end of self-knowledge itself (whether because knowing our own minds facilitates our pursuit of whatever ends we happen to have, or because it leads us to pursue ends we ought to have). To assert that our capacity for self-reflection has *intrinsic value*, on the other hand, would be to claim that it is valuable because achieving the relevant sort of self-knowledge is worthwhile just as such, even if we exclude any tendency it has to promote our attainment of other valuable ends. These two forms of value are not mutually exclusive, of course: our capacity for self-reflection might have both forms of value. In spite of the long philosophical tradition of praising self-reflection, however, it is difficult to see how a case for the essential importance of self-reflection could be made on either of these two bases.

A defense of the claim that our capacity for self-reflection is instrumentally valuable would need to show that exercising this capacity tends to improve the quality of our thought and action; but this is hardly obvious. As we saw in the previous chapter, important results in the psychology of judgment and decision suggest that self-reflection often worsens the quality of our judging and deciding, rather than improving it. Moreover, a defense of the instrumental value of our capacity for self-reflection would need to demonstrate that its benefits outweigh the drawbacks mentioned earlier—its links to narcissism, to crippling self-attention, etc. Finally, such a defense would need to show that whatever benefits we gain from self-reflection could not be achieved in some other, more straightforward way. If these benefits are, for instance, supposed to derive from our giving critical consideration to the reasons for our own beliefs and choices, we must explain why these benefits could not be obtained by a subject who merely considered the truth of the *propositions* she (in fact) believes and the value of the *ends* she (in fact) intends to pursue, rather than considering the reasonableness of her own beliefs and choices *as such*.

In any case, the very idea of reckoning up the "benefits" and "burdens" of our capacity for self-reflection surely has something fatuous about it. It is clear that this capacity not only influences our pursuit of ends we already possess, but introduces into the field of human possibility countless purposes and projects that would be inconceivable without it (think of the idea of earning someone's approval, or of becoming an online "influencer"). Who can say whether such

---

[8] Cf. Cassam 2014: Ch. 15.

a transformation in our mode of existence is beneficial, or by what standard we might measure its advantages and disadvantages? The changes in our lives brought about by our capacity for self-reflection seem incalculable.

For all these reasons, the idea that we might explain the point of self-reflection by appeal to its instrumental value seems unpromising. Yet the idea that such reflection is *intrinsically* valuable also seems rather dark when one considers it. Perhaps there are some things whose value is self-evident and not further explicable—the feeling of being alive on a spring day, the sight of a child's delight, or what you will—but reflective knowledge of our own mental states does not seem to fall into this category. Most people would admit that there are good lives that do not involve much self-reflection: lives of courage in the service of worthwhile ends, of selfless concern for others, of the kind of absorption in scientific questions that leads one to pay little heed to oneself, and so on. It would seem petty to say, of a person who devoted her life to one of these pursuits, "Ah, but she did not examine herself!"; and it would seem not just petty but daft to say this if the kind of self-examination in question were, not the kind that aims at Socratic self-knowledge, but merely the kind that brings the subject's own mental states to reflective articulacy. If we call such reflection good, we surely owe some account of wherein its goodness consists. Why should *that* be so important?

These difficulties suggest that we have taken a wrong turn somewhere. Intuitively, our capacity for reflective self-knowledge is not pointless: although some of the mental states on which we reflect may be mundane, our general capacity to reflect on our own mental lives seems to enable us to bring our lives into focus in some important way. Yet seeking to locate the point of this capacity with respect to the instrumental/intrinsic distinction seems to render its importance invisible. Where did we go wrong?

I want to suggest that we went wrong in assuming that the value of our capacity for self-reflection is to be judged by the value of the *information* it provides us about our own mental states. If we assume this, we are left with the task of explaining the value of having such information, and the question whether this value is intrinsic or merely instrumental will look inevitable. But this overlooks a different way in which self-reflection might matter: not in informing us *about* our own mental lives, but in altering the character of the lives on which we reflect. This idea should by now be familiar: that our capacity for self-reflection does not merely supply us with knowledge *of* our first-order representational states, but can transform our first-order representing itself, so that what we formerly represented without explicit self-awareness, we now represent *reflectively*. This observation does not yet explain the point of self-reflection, but it opens a different perspective on this question, one that focuses, not on why it might be valuable to *know about* one's own mental states, but on why it might be valuable to *inhabit* those very states in a reflective way.

The distinction between a kind of self-knowledge that is merely informative and a kind that is transformative is a recurring theme in Freud's remarks of the role of self-knowledge in psychoanalysis. In a well-known passage of his *Introductory Lectures on Psychoanalysis*, he remarks:

> From what I have so far said a neurosis would seem to be the result of a kind of ignorance—a not knowing about mental events that one ought to know of.... Now it would as a rule be very easy for a doctor experienced in analysis to guess what mental impulses had remained unconscious in a particular patient. So it ought not to be very difficult, either, for him to restore the patient by communicating his knowledge to him and so remedying his ignorance....
>
> If only that was how things happened! We came upon discoveries in this connection for which we were at first unprepared. Knowledge is not always the same as knowledge: there are different sorts of knowledge, which are far from equivalent psychologically.... The doctor's knowledge is not the same as the patient's and cannot produce the same effects. If the doctor transfers his knowledge to the patient as a piece of information, it has no result.... But our thesis that the symptoms vanish when their sense is known remains true in spite of this. All we have to add is that the knowledge must rest on an internal change in the patient such as can only be brought about by a piece of psychical work with a particular aim. (Freud 1989: Lecture XVIII, 347–349)

I believe Freud's distinction between a kind of self-knowledge that is merely possessed "as a piece of information" and a kind that "rests on an internal change" is separable from the details of his psychoanalytic theory. The general point, which any theory of self-knowledge should acknowledge, is that there is a crucial difference between merely *knowing of* one's own mental states and inhabiting the relevant states *reflectively*—where the latter, adverbial formulation implies that subject's awareness of her first-order state somehow informs her first-order state itself. We have seen in earlier chapters that there is such distinction. We may take Freud's suggestion to be that the kind of self-knowledge that genuinely matters to our lives—the kind whose achievement itself constitutes a step toward greater psychic well-being, rather than merely providing us with information that we might draw on in pursuit of such well-being—is knowledge of the latter sort: knowledge that informs our first-order states themselves.

To state this claim is not yet to explain why it should hold true, but it at least points us toward a more fruitful line of inquiry. Rather than asking why it is good to have information about our own mental states, we should inquire into the kind of difference it makes to our mental states that they be inhabited knowingly. To make progress on the latter question, we will need to consider, first, what it is to come to inhabit a mental state knowingly, and, second, how this transformation might make a difference to our lives. These will be the topics, respectively, of the next two sections.

10.3. Reflection in Good and Bad Faith

When we first introduced the notion of reflection, we characterized it as the activity by which we transform nonpositional consciousness-as-subject into positional self-knowledge. We noted, however, that such reflection need not give rise to a distinct, second-order awareness of one of our own first-order mental states. Rather, we said, it can give articulate expression to our first-order state itself, and indeed can transform it, in such a way that this first-order state can now be said to be held *reflectively*, where the adverbial modifier indicates a change in the manner of existence of this state. Thus I can come, not just to find something you have done immediately infuriating, but to feel a reflective form of anger toward you, one whose existence essentially involves a conception of itself as justified (or not). Or again, I can come, not just to find things you say immediately credible, but to have a reflective form of faith in your word, one whose existence essentially involves a conception of itself as my confirmed and unwavering attitude. In such cases, reflection does not merely allow me to make my preexisting attitude explicit, but infuses my response to the object of my attitude (your action, your word) with reflective thought. It thus transforms my first-order attitude itself, rather than merely supplying me with explicit knowledge of this attitude.

We noted this possibility in Chapter 7, but our purposes there permitted us to leave it relatively abstract and undeveloped. Since our interest here is in the point of self-reflection, it will be useful to consider this topic in greater depth. The matter intersects, as we shall see, with Sartre's famous distinction between good and bad faith.

Suppose I become angry at something you have done and then reflect on my anger. In the first instance, I represent your action in a certain manner, one specifically characteristic of anger. We might say that I represent your action *as infuriating*—though, for reasons that are by now familiar, we must take care in interpreting this characterization. I need not take your action to be infuriating in the sense that requires my thinking of it as falling under this concept. Indeed, I need not possess the concept *infuriating* at all to represent your action in this manner. The phrase "as infuriating" functions here simply as a label for a certain characteristic mode of presentation of an object (in this case, your action): it provides a convenient way for theorists to refer to the mode in question, but need not correspond to any distinct concept applied or even possessed by the subject who feels angry. If I am the subject in question, I may simply experience a certain characteristic kind of preoccupation with your action, one that involves finding it un-called-for, regarding it as some kind of slight to me, finding it unignorable in certain characteristic ways, etc.[9] I need not conceptualize my own state of anger as such: these modes of concern with your action will *constitute* my anger, which does not yet know itself.

But of course, as a mature human knower, I do possess the concept *anger*, along with a battery of other concepts of this mode of consciousness, its proper objects, and its characteristic forms of expression. I possess these notions as part of the repertoire of concepts of human subjectivity that I acquired in learning my first language, though—as we observed in Chapter 8—I might in principle have framed at least the most basic of these concepts for myself through mere reflection. At any rate, given that I do possess such concepts, I can, if the occasion arises, reflectively self-ascribe my own state of anger. When I do this, I (1) represent *myself* as in a certain mental state (being angry at what you did), while also continuing (2) to represent *your action* in modes that express anger. Let us consider what sorts of relations might hold between these two representations.

One possibility is that these representations might constitute wholly distinct representational states: my first-order anger at your action on the one hand, and my second-order awareness of my own anger on the other. If this is the situation, then when I express my awareness that I am angry, I will not thereby express my anger itself. For this reason, it is hard to see how I could have this sort of awareness of my anger through mere reflection on the object of my anger. An awareness I could have through mere reflection would simply give articulate expression to my experience of your action as infuriating, whereas the awareness we are imagining does not, by hypothesis, involve an experience of *your action*, but merely an apprehension of my own mental state. Hence it seems that this kind of awareness of anger must involve a certain distance from my own state of anger: I will be aware *that* I am angry, but this second-order awareness will not itself involve a conscious experience of your action as infuriating. When we seek to illustrate such awareness, it is natural to think of cases in which I become aware of my own anger by observing signs in my own behavior—a certain harshness in my voice, a flush coming over my face, etc.—rather than via a "transparent" consideration of the infuriating features of your action.

It is important to see, however, that this sort of total alienation from my own anger is merely the extreme case on a continuum of possibilities. In another kind of case, I might know that I am angry simply by reflecting on the (seemingly) infuriating features of your action, and yet I might also judge that your action should not strike me as infuriating, since it was unintended, or reasonable in

---

[9] Or whatever. I will not attempt a serious analysis of how anger represents its object, nor do I assume that all forms of anger must represent their objects in the same way. It will suffice for present purposes if what I say is a plausible first stab at a characterization of one type of anger.

context, or not a genuine slight to me at all. I might judge this even though my experience of your action as infuriating persists, in something like the way I can judge a perceptual experience to be illusory even as the illusion persists. This, indeed, is a familiar kind of experience one can have in a quarrel (familiar to me, at least): one finds oneself doubting whether things really are as one feels them to be, and yet one cannot overcome one's anger and the way of experiencing the world that it involves. Here one's reflective alienation from one's own anger is not total: one does, or can, experience the world from the standpoint of the anger, and so does not need to know that one is angry by self-observation. Nevertheless, one's awareness that one is angry involves at least a partial alienation from this feeling: since one does not unequivocally accept the standpoint that one's anger presents as valid, one has a measure of distance from one's own feeling. *Its* point of view is not experienced as wholly *one's own* point of view, and so the anger presents itself as a condition with which one has to cope, rather than simply as a transparent apprehension of how things stand.

The possibility of this kind of case shows that the standard philosophical contrast between non-alienated, "first-personal" awareness of one's own mental states and alienated, "third-personal" awareness of them is too crude: one can have immediate, "first-personal" awareness of a mental state and still be alienated from this state in a significant way.[10] What is true is that, if we call self-awareness "alienated" to the extent that the point of view of the reflecting subject does not coincide with point of view embodied in the mental state on which she reflects, then cases of alienation fall on a continuum, at one end of which lies the sort of total alienation in which one can only have observational, "third-personal" knowledge of one's first-order mental state.

At the other end of this continuum lie cases of what Sartre calls "pure reflection," in which the subject simply articulates her first-order point of view reflectively, without taking up some critical stance on this point of view.[11] In this kind

---

[10] Moran 2001 is sometimes read as drawing the crude contrast I criticize here, and some of his language does invite this reading, though I think this is not his considered view. See Lear 2011: Ch. 2, and Moran 2011 for valuable reflections on this issue.

[11] Sartre draws a distinction between two species of reflection: pure and impure. Pure reflection he characterizes as "the simple presence of the reflective for-itself to the for-itself it reflects on," and he calls this the "original form" of reflection (BN 223/190). Impure reflection, he says, "appears on the foundation" of pure reflection; it "includes pure reflection but goes beyond it" by "press[ing] its claims further [*étend(ant) ses prétentions plus loin*]" (ibid.). I take his point to be that, although it is possible simply to be in a first-order mental state *reflectively* (the pure case), actual reflection commonly involves further self-directed thoughts spawned by this pure reflective awareness, thoughts which go beyond sheer reflective awareness of one's first-order state to make some judgment about it. Insofar as reflection involves such further thoughts, it is "impure." This distinction enables Sartre to acknowledge the continuum of different cases of reflective awareness that we have noted, while still maintaining that, in the fundamental case, reflection . . . is not the appearance of a new consciousness directed on the for-itself, but a modification in its internal structure, actualized in itself

of case, although the subject may be said both to be in a certain first-order mental state and to be aware of this state, this does *not* consist in her being in two distinct representational states. Rather, her awareness of her first-order state is merely the reflective aspect of the obtaining of her first-order state itself. She does not find her friend's action infuriating, and, as a distinct matter, know that she feels angry; she *knowingly* finds her friend's action infuriating, in such a way that her representation of her friend's action and her representation of her own state constitute two aspects of a single psychic condition focused on her friend's action. Hence, when she expresses this sort of awareness of her own anger, she will at the same time express her anger itself.

Like total alienation from one's first-order state, such total reflective identification with one's first-order state is a limiting case. In general, the mere distinction between object-representation and self-representation—in the case we have been considering, the distinction between representing *your action* as infuriating and representing *myself* as angry at your action—will induce some measure of discrepancy between the point of view of the reflecting subject and the point of view embodied in the state on which she reflects. Even if the reflecting subject wholly accepts the view of the object embodied in her first-order attitude, her awareness of this *as* her own attitude will complicate her condition, giving rise to a subtle interplay between her conception of the object and her conception of herself. This interplay is the theme of Sartre's famous reflections on bad faith (BN Part I, Chapter 2).

Sartre says that bad faith exploits "the twofold property of human beings, of being a *facticity* and a *transcendence*," aspects of our being which "ought to be capable of a valid coordination" but which, in bad faith, we seek not to coordinate but to treat as independent (BN 99/91). Our "transcendence" consists (to a first approximation, at least) in the fact that our consciousness takes on a determinate state only by positing an object external to itself. As we have seen, Sartre maintains that all consciousness is consciousness of some object, and it is precisely by "transcending" itself toward its particular object, and allowing itself to be determined by this object (as my anger understands itself to be determined by the infuriating qualities of your action), that it is the specific state of consciousness that it is. Nevertheless, the state of consciousness thereby constituted can, from another perspective, be regarded as a "facticity": a contingent state of the subject which can obtain whether or not the relevant object really is as

---

by the for-itself (BN 220/188). In such pure reflection, Sartre says, "the for-itself" (i.e., the conscious subject) does not merely become conscious of its own first-order conscious state; it transforms its manner of being conscious of some transcendent object. This possibility of what Sartre calls "modification in the internal structure" of consciousness through reflection will turn out to be of crucial importance to our inquiry in this chapter.

she represents it to be.[12] These two perspectives on consciousness—the implicit self-understanding that it has in apprehending its object, and the explicit self-conception that it achieves in reflecting on its own existence—ought to be "capable of a valid coordination," since both are essential to the very possibility of human consciousness. Nevertheless, the distinction between them opens the possibility of forms of bad faith in which we seek, as Sartre puts it, to "affirm the identity [of facticity and transcendence], even while preserving their differences" (BN 99/91).

Thus, to take one of Sartre's examples (BN 70–71/67–68), a gambler in the midst of a run of bad luck might resolve never to gamble again, but then, observing that he has often failed to keep such resolutions in the past, he might conclude that it is futile to attempt to quit.[13] The latter thought might indeed present itself as a counsel of mere realism; yet there would clearly be something problematic in a person's seeking to assess the likely efficacy of his own resolution in this way. For his resolution cannot be *for him* a sheer fact whose probable effects are open to empirical investigation, since it exists only insofar as he thinks of a question about his own future—whether he will gamble—as settled by his now resolving not to go on gambling. Insofar as he regards the question whether he will go on gambling as depending on the empirical relationship between a certain kind of psychological fact about himself (his having made a resolution) and his subsequent behavior, he has already abandoned the perspective on his future that is essential to his capacity to make resolutions. It involves bad faith, then, for him to think of the question whether he will continue to gamble as simply a question of what a certain psychological fact about himself makes probable: in posing the question in this way, he attempts to treat as mere "facticity" what can exist for him only as "transcendence." In so doing, he already deprives his resolution of its power to shape his future, in such a way that there can be no further question of whether it is likely to be effective. Thus, imagining the standpoint of such a gambler, Sartre describes the situation as follows:

> It seemed to me that I had thereby constituted a *real barrier* between myself and the game [when I resolved yesterday to stop gambling], and suddenly now I realize that this synthetic apprehension is only the memory of an idea, the memory of a feeling. For it to help me again, *I must reproduce it ex nihilo*, and

---

[12] More generally, Sartre uses the term "facticity" to designate the aspect of a person's being which is presented as a matter of settled fact, not a question whose answer I hereby determine in an act of transcendence. Hence the "factical" aspect of our existence includes much that is not psychological in character—e.g., the fact that I was born at a certain time and place, the fact that my body has certain (largely) inalterable physical features, etc. My focus here is on the possibility of regarding our own states of consciousness as factical in this sense, but for Sartre this is only a special case of a more general pathology.

[13] Here I follow the insightful discussion of this example in Moran 2001: Ch. 3.

freely; it is only one of my possibilities, just as the fact of gambling is another, neither more nor less. This fear of destroying my family needs me to *rediscover* it, to recreate it as a lived fear; it stands behind me like a boneless ghost, and depends on me alone to lend it flesh. I am alone and naked before temptation as I was yesterday. (BN 71–72/68)

Sartre describes a range of other forms of bad faith, but a full exploration of this topic would take us too far afield. For present purposes, the important point concerns what a "valid coordination" between the "factical" and "self-transcending" aspects of our consciousness would need to involve. In reflection, I represent *myself* as (factically) in a certain first-order state, yet the relevant first-order state can obtain only insofar as I represent its *object* (transcendently) in the specific manner that constitutes this state. As we have seen in the case of the self-doubting gambler, the distinction between these two topics can induce a tension between the standpoint I take up in reflection and the standpoint on which I reflect. In order for reflection on my own first-order state *not* to induce such a tension in me, however, my reflective representation must not distance me from the standpoint expressed in my first-order attitude. In recognizing that (e.g.) I am resolved never to gamble again, I must, in the very same act of mind, settle in the negative the first-order question whether I will continue to gamble.

This in turn requires that the two aspects of my representational act—answering the first-order question of whether to stop gambling and representing myself as resolved to stop gambling—should exhibit a certain interdependence. One aspect of this interdependence—the aspect that has been our primary focus in this book—is the *transparency* of the second-order question whether I am resolved to stop gambling to the first-order question whether to stop gambling: I must be able to treat the answer to the latter question as settling the answer to the former. But where my representation of myself as resolved to stop is not merely a transient expression *of* my resolution but a reflection that transforms my resolution itself, there is also a converse aspect of this interdependence: I must be able to answer the first-order question of whether to stop gambling *in* representing myself as resolved to stop.[14] That is, my thought of myself *as* resolved to stop gambling must come to play an essential role in my *being* resolved to stop: it must become integral to my first-order resolution itself. It follows that a genuinely reflective resolution to stop gambling (as opposed to a resolution on which I transiently reflect) will have a different character from an unreflective resolution: it will be a resolution governed by an understanding of itself *as* my settled resolution, and in this way will be a different, more sophisticated kind of resolution. At

---

[14] For the distinction between transient and transformative kinds of reflection, see our earlier discussion in §7.6.

any rate, this will hold true in the limiting case in which my first-order resolution and my reflective awareness of this resolution form two aspects of a single psychic condition. In this limiting case, we might say—using another visual metaphor to complement the metaphor of transparency—that reflection *illuminates* the state it understands, transforming its nature rather than increasing the complexity of its psychic surroundings.

In addressing our question about the point of self-reflection, this is the observation to which we must hold fast. Self-knowledge can be, not just informative about, but transformative of, our first-order attitudes toward the world. Our next task will be to consider what difference it might make to our lives for our attitudes to be transformed in this way.

10.4. The Point of Self-Reflection

With these observations in hand, we can return to our initial question. What sort of difference does reflecting on our own mental states make to the character of these states, and why might this difference matter to our lives? What, in short, is the point of self-reflection?

To sharpen our sense of the difficulty here, it will be useful to consider an exchange between Jonathan Lear and Richard Moran that is recorded in Lear's *A Case for Irony* (2011), which collects Lear's Tanner Lectures on Human Values. In his lectures, Lear argues that, when things go well, a patient in psychoanalysis can develop the ability verbally to express aspects of her identity that had formerly existed only as unconscious fantasies and were expressed only in uncomprehending forms. When a patient's words come genuinely to express such fantasies, Lear suggests, this step toward articulacy is at the same time a step toward greater psychic autonomy:

> I want to claim that as I acquire the ability to *express* this organizing fantasy verbally I also gain first-person authority with respect to it. I am *putting myself into words*. I am right there in the words that are expressing (as well as perhaps describing) who I am. Thus the verbal expression of what had hitherto functioned as an unconscious practical identity facilitates my ability to shape my practical identity. (Lear 2011: 59)

In his response to Lear's lecture, Moran raises an interesting question about this:

> The idea of 'replacing' one mode of expression for another is not perfectly clear to me, particularly in the therapeutic context into which Lear is importing the idea. On a basic level, we might ask: If the two modes of expression are really

doing the same work, then what is the *point* of 'replacing' one with the other. If we take the notion of replacement literally, then what is gained, for instance, by substituting some words for some tears? (Moran 2011: 113)

I take it Moran does not genuinely doubt that what Lear calls "putting oneself into words" can constitute a step toward greater autonomy. His point is rather to raise a question about how it can do so if what takes place is simply the substitution of a verbal expression of a mental state for a nonverbal one. If the words I now utter play the very same expressive role that was formerly played by my shedding some tears, why should this substitution give me a more autonomous relation to my own condition? Yet if verbalizing my condition does not merely give me an alternative way of expressing it, but a changed relation to the condition itself, how does it do so? What sort of difference does verbalization make, and why is it connected with increased autonomy?

This seems to me a good question, and one that becomes especially pressing once we set aside whatever instrumental value there may be in being informed *about* one's own mental states. The crucial question is what difference it makes to these states themselves to come to self-articulacy (as we may put it), not how we might benefit from being informed of their existence.[15] Being informed of the existence of our own mental states might enable us to cope with them more effectively, but that is clearly not the sort of difference Lear has in mind, and for reasons already given, it is not the sort of difference that should interest us here.

In responding to Moran's question, the first point to notice is that the issue is not fundamentally one of verbalization, though in real cases the transformation will very likely be verbalized. The crucial step, however, is not the *expression* of a mental state in words, but the transformation in what is *expressed*: the mental state itself, which formerly existed in an uncomprehended form and now exists in a manner informed by self-understanding. We saw in the previous section that a reflective understanding of my own mental state can transform my first-order state, and it is surely this sort of transformation in my psychic condition itself, rather than any mere transformation in how I express this condition, that would constitute a step toward greater autonomy. Nevertheless, the claim that it does constitute such a step is not a truism. A wish or desire (e.g.) that is not informed by *self*-understanding may draw on considerable understanding of other sorts: the focus of this understanding will simply be the object of the wish, rather than on me, the subject who wishes for something. Our question is why coming

---

[15] I do not mean to suggest that Lear lacks an answer to this question, just that it is a crucial question that any such proposal must face. In what follows, I will not pursue Lear's own answer further, but will simply sketch the kind of answer that is suggested by our reflectivist approach to self-knowledge.

to represent the world in a way informed specifically by *self*-understanding is significant, and our problem is that it is not clear what the deployment of this particular form of understanding accomplishes.

To make progress here, it will help to return to our idea that reflection makes what was formerly an aspect of the mode of presentation of some object into a topic of representation in its own right. What is accomplished by such a transformation? Well, consider again the familiar transition from (1) to (2):

(1) This cat is gray.
(2) I see a gray cat.

If our reflectivist account of this transition is sound, there is a sense in which (2) does not add anything substantive to (1). Both (1) and (2) posit the existence of a particular gray cat, and although (2) adds that this cat is seen by the representing subject, our reflectivist account holds that this was already implicit in the mode of presentation expressed by "this" in (1). There is thus no possible state of affairs that (1) leaves open but (2) excludes: the latter only makes explicit something that was presupposed in the former. Moreover, our account holds that this presupposition was already within the scope of the subject's awareness, albeit "nonpositionally," when she merely represented (1). So what kind of intellectual advance can there be in moving from (1) to (2), given that (2) seems to affirm nothing more than what was already implicit in the subject's awareness of (1)?

The natural reply here is that the transition from (1) to (2) involves a change, not in what I am aware of, but in the type of understanding I bring to bear on this awareness. Formerly I represented a cat in a distinctively visual manner; now I bring to bear a first-person representation and a psychological concept in a way that allows me to comprehend this distinctive mode of awareness. In (1), the nature of my awareness was registered only in the mode of presentation of the cat. Now I conceptualize it, which enables me to grasp a similarity between this episode of awareness and other episodes whose objects are *toto caelo* different: a similarity in my mode of awareness itself. Conceptualizing this similarity enables me to think about *seeing* in general: for instance, about the conditions in which I am able to see, the types of facts of which seeing can make me aware, the kinds of frailty to which my capacity to see is subject, etc. In this way, self-reflection links my awareness of this cat to my general understanding of my capacity to see, and thus introduces the possibility of a distinctive kind of circumspection in my attitude toward the cat: understanding that my awareness of this cat is grounded in a (purported) exercise of a specific kind of capacity enables me to consider the conditions for the exercise of this capacity and whether they are met in this case, on the limits within which this capacity is reliable and how this case relates to them, and so on. This, I take it, is part of what is at stake when authors like Korsgaard say that our capacity for self-reflection enables us to "back up" from our own representations and call their purport into question.[16]

As we have so far described the transition from (1) to (2), however, it need not involve any transformation in the subject's first-order state of seeing the cat. All the points we have made would hold true even if, in thinking (2), she merely had a transient reflective thought about her own state of seeing, a thought that left her first-order state unchanged. Indeed, it is not clear that seeing *could* be transformed by an act of reflection. For seeing seems to be a passive experiential state, not an *activity* that the subject could perform reflectively or unreflectively.[17] But in the kind of case that is of relevance to our question about the point of self-reflection, we said, the reflection *transforms* our first-order representational states themselves. In such cases, reflection allows us, not merely to "back up" from these representations and query what they purport to present, but to engage in the relevant first-order acts of representing in a manner that is informed by reflective understanding. "Substituting some words for some tears" matters, we might say, just inasmuch as it expresses this sort of transformation in our first-order mental state. So let us turn to a case of this sort and consider what this transformation accomplishes.

The idea that our first-order representational state could be transformed by reflection has clearest application to attitudinal and emotional states, which can themselves be thought of as acts of taking-to-be or regarding-as. I have defended a conception of attitudinal states as ongoing "acts" of the representing subject elsewhere (cf. Boyle 2011a, 2011b), and I will not repeat my arguments here. Suffice it to say that, inasmuch as attitudes can in general be conceived as consisting in the subject's holding some view on some question, it should be clear that such holding can have a reflective or an unreflective character. Consider again the two examples I gave at the start of §10.3. (1) I can find something you have done immediately infuriating, but I can also come to feel a reflective form of anger toward you, one whose existence essentially involves a conception of itself as justified anger. (2) I can find things you say immediately credible, but I can also come to have a reflective form of faith in your word, one whose existence essentially involves a conception of itself as my confirmed and unwavering attitude. In each of these cases, we see a contrast between an unreflective and a reflective attitude, where calling the relevant attitude "reflective" does not mean merely that I hold it and am reflectively cognizant of its existence, but that my reflection infuses my response to the object of my attitude (your action, your word)

---

[16] See Korsgaard 1996: 93, discussed above in the Introduction and Chapter 7.
[17] There may, however, be forms of intelligent activity that are closely related to seeing, such as watching and looking. For illuminating discussion, see Crowther 2009.

with self-understanding. Any serious inquiry into the point of self-reflection must consider its effect when it plays this sort of transformative role.

There is an evocative passage in John Berger's essay *A Fortunate Man* (1967) that helps to bring out the kind of difference that such a transformation can make. The essay describes the work of a country doctor tending to an impoverished rural community in southwest England in the 1960s. Commenting on the taciturn character of many residents of this region, Berger remarks:

> The inarticulateness of the English is the subject of many jokes and is often explained in terms of puritanism, shyness as a national characteristic, etc. This tends to obscure a more serious development. There are large sections of the English working and middle class who are inarticulate as the result of wholesale cultural deprivation. They are deprived of the means of translating what they know into thoughts which they can think. They have no examples to follow in which words clarify experience. Their spoken proverbial traditions have long been destroyed: and, although they are literate in the strictly technical sense, they have not had the opportunity of discovering the existence of a written cultural heritage.
>
> Yet it is more than a question of literature. Any general culture acts as a mirror which enables the individual to recognize himself—or at least to recognize those parts of himself which are socially permissible. The culturally deprived have far fewer ways of recognizing themselves. A great deal of their experience—especially emotional and introspective experience—has to remain *unnamed* for them. Their chief means of self-expression is consequently through action: this is one of the reasons why the English have so many 'do-it-yourself' hobbies. The garden or the work bench becomes the nearest they have to a means of satisfactory introspection. (Berger and Mohr 1967: 98–99)[18]

I do not endorse everything in this passage: there are moments that strike me as condescending to the people under consideration. Nevertheless, I think Berger's main idea is insightful and relevant to our problem about the point of self-reflection. In effect, Berger sees any "general culture" as (among other things) a repository of what we have called "concepts of reflection": concepts that enable the articulation of aspect of our lives of which we are in the first instance only "nonpositionally" conscious. When "cultural deprivation" leaves people without a rich repertoire of such concepts, Berger suggests, they are thereby "deprived of the means of translating what they know into thoughts which they can think." In light of our discussion, we can see that this superficially paradoxical formulation captures a real distinction: the difference between having merely nonpositional

---

[18] I learned of this passage from Cora Diamond's essay "Losing Your Concepts" (1988).

consciousness-as-subject of a certain aspect of our lives and having the developed capacity for positional knowledge of this *as* an aspect of our lives.

Berger adds that such deprivation leaves people without a means for "recognizing" themselves, and this seems true enough, but his more illuminating remark, I think, is that it leaves them without a means of articulate *self-expression*. This latter formulation places emphasis, not on how a repertoire of reflective concepts gives us tools to *identify* aspects of ourselves that are already extant, but on how such a repertoire can enrich the activities through which we express ourselves and how we see the world. This is not merely a matter of coming to recognize our own activity for what it is, but of coming to act in ways that are informed by an understanding of what we are doing. If Berger is right, the "do-it-yourself" hobbies of the English working and middle classes give unreflective expression to (I suppose) such things as a sense of beauty and a conception of value, and these senses might, in happier circumstances, be not just recognized but informed and refined by thought. Moreover, although Berger focuses on activities rather than the mental states that underlie them, I take it that an analogous point would apply to these states themselves. Underlying the forms of activity that *express* a sense of beauty or a conception of value, for instance, are states of finding certain sorts of things beautiful or valuable. Such attitudinal states can themselves be conceived as stances toward the world: they regard things in some characteristic way. Insofar as the relevant attitudes remain unreflective, a subject's holding of these stances will remain uninformed by thought, however subtle her thinking about the *objects* of her attitudes may be. Insofar as her attitudes become reflective, by contrast, she will become capable, not just of *recognizing* her own attitudes toward beauty and value, but of finding things beautiful or valuable in a thoughtful and comprehending way.

To bring out the stakes in such a shift, it will help to focus on a simpler case. Consider a person whose choices express an unreflective preference for her own pleasure over other kinds of goods. Although it is somewhat old-fashioned to speak this way, we might say that she takes pleasure to be the good. (In characterizing her in this way, we would be using "the good" as the label for the formal object of her power of choice: whatever value operates as the preeminent standard on the basis of which she makes choices. Our imagined person identifies her own pleasure as this preeminent object.) As we have described the case, however, this fundamental practical commitment remains unreflective: it manifests itself in the way our imagined subject chooses, but it does not rise to the level of articulate thought. Now suppose some Socrates comes along who forces her to reflect on the importance she assigns to pleasure. (Or to mark the importance of "general culture," suppose that she is given a copy of Plato's Dialogues and encounters Socrates through Plato's depiction of him.) This will involve her acquiring various concepts: at a minimum, *pleasure*, as the concept of a distinctive kind of experience of an achieved object, and *the good*, as the concept of the formal object of her power of choice. Her encounter with Socrates might draw these concepts to her attention, but they are concepts that she could in principle frame simply by reflecting on modal distinctions in her own awareness: they are what we have called "concepts of reflection." Moreover, her knowledge that she takes pleasure to be the good need not be based merely on self-observation or testimony: it will be available to her simply by reflecting on what she herself finds choice-worthy. Her acknowledgment that she takes pleasure to be the good will thus articulate something of which she was already nonpositionally conscious, but which she now makes into a topic of consideration in its own right.

We can imagine different outcomes of this consideration. Perhaps she becomes convinced that pleasure is not fit to play the role her unreflective choosing assigns to it; or again, perhaps she becomes an articulate defender of her preference, a kind of modern-day Epicurus. For our purposes, the substance of her view is immaterial: what matters is that this view can become, not merely a set of higher-order thoughts she has *about* her own sense of what is choiceworthy, but an enrichment of this sense itself (where by "her sense of what is choiceworthy," I mean the sense expressed in her first-order choosing).

Now does it benefit our imagined subject to hold her attitude toward pleasure in a reflective manner, rather than unreflectively? Is she better off for having examined her life in this respect? This question is plainly ill-posed. Reflectiveness is a merely formal attribute: whether it is better to do something reflectively will depend on what this "something" is. We can, however, say this: if our reflectivist account is correct, *any* attitude will involve some at-least-implicit self-understanding. Even an unreflective identification of pleasure as the good will involve a nonpositional sense of pleasure as the fit and proper object of one's own choosing. Similarly, even unreflective anger will involve a nonpositional sense of one's own anger as warranted by some perceived slight or mistreatment, and even unreflective belief will involve a nonpositional sense of one's rightly holding a propositional question to be closed. If this is right, then the proper way to pose a question about the value of self-reflection is not to ask whether it is better to live with or without self-understanding; for in an important sense, living without self-understanding is simply not an option for creatures like us. Our only choice is between accepting a certain self-understanding unreflectively and accepting it in a manner that is informed by reflection.

These considerations do not show that reflection benefits us in any independently specifiable sense, and I will not attempt to argue that it does. A friend once gave me a t-shirt across the chest of which was written "Denken hilft"—thinking helps—and I wore it with gratitude, but I take it that what makes this an amusing thing to put on a t-shirt is that the proposition is not, as such, a candidate for serious affirmation or denial. Either it is a truism (if we presuppose that the only alternative is to make choices without thinking) or it is a dubious claim about the superiority of living by thought to living "by instinct." To the extent that we live by instinct, we do not choose, and whether this produces good or bad outcomes depends on our instincts and the environment we face. To the extent that we do choose, we do what we *think* would be good, and in this context it does not need arguing that it is worth thinking as well as we can, which presumably requires thinking carefully.

So too, *mutatis mutandis*, for the value of "knowing ourselves." If the question is whether it is better to be a self-knowing creature than to be one that lives by instinct, then the matter is at least undecidable without further information, and probably ill-posed: for by whose standard should we judge? But if the question is whether, as a creature who necessarily possesses *some* self-understanding, it is better to frame the relevant understanding thoughtfully or thoughtlessly, the answer does not really need argument. Whether living in a way that is informed by reflection will produce "better outcomes" in any independently specifiable sense is not decidable *a priori*, but insofar as one's way of living expresses some self-understanding or other, the claim that this understanding should be well-considered rather than ill-considered is a truism. Against this background, it is possible to sympathize with Socrates's claim that the unexamined life is not worth living: not because self-examination is what makes a life worthwhile, but because examining one's life is simply the attempt to perform well the activity in which, for a certain type of creature, living consists.

Socrates is remembered for saying that the unexamined life is not worth living, but what he said in full is that the unexamined life is not worth living "for a human being [ἀνθρώπῳ]" (*Apology* 38a4). It obviously would not make sense to say such a thing about the life of an elephant, or to chisel "Know thyself" into the lintel of an elephant temple, if there were such a thing. These are injunctions appropriate to creatures with a certain nature, one that makes self-knowledge needful. We have now reached a point from which we can see why we human beings might be such creatures: we are creatures to whose lives a certain implicit self-understanding is essential, even before we reflectively know ourselves. This is not to claim that we necessarily understand ourselves soundly, but merely that we necessarily operate with some self-understanding (be it sound or distorted) in crucial aspects of our own lives, and that this is an understanding we can either improve through reflection or leave undeveloped. It is to such creatures that the Delphic injunction sensibly applies.

10.5. Socratic and Cartesian Self-Knowledge

In the light of these observations, we can return to the contrast that some recent philosophers have drawn between the "substantial" self-knowledge that Socrates praised and the "immediate" self-knowledge to which Descartes drew attention. According to Quassim Cassam, for instance:

> To know that you have a particular character trait, say fastidiousness, you need behavioural evidence from which you can infer that you are fastidious. In contrast, you don't normally infer your own beliefs from behavioural or, for that matter, any other evidence. But if knowledge of your own mundane beliefs and desires is, in this sense, immediate, then it would be natural to ask how such epistemologically immediate self-knowledge is possible. This is the question which many philosophers of self-knowledge are trying to answer. They don't worry about how substantial self-knowledge is possible, because it isn't [epistemologically] special. (Cassam 2014: viii)

I have already long since objected to the idea that the philosophical interest of "immediate" self-knowledge lies primarily in its special epistemology. As we observed in the Introduction, its primary interest lies rather in its connection with questions about the general soundness of our first-person perspective on our own lives, and thereby, in the complex ways we have studied in foregoing chapters, with the idea that we are rational animals. We are now in a position to add a further point, however, about the supposed contrast between "immediate" and "substantial" self-knowledge.

Undoubtedly there is a contrast between the sorts of things we can know about ourselves immediately and the sorts of things we can recognize only with effort and consideration; and undoubtedly, too, there is a contrast between philosophical work that focuses on the former type of self-knowledge and work that focuses on the latter. For reasons we can now appreciate, however, it is misleading to represent these two varieties of self-knowledge as fundamentally different in principle. While it is true that there are some aspects of our lives that are immediately available to our reflection and others that we can come to recognize only after careful consideration, these are not two fundamentally different types of self-knowledge, but two cases that lie at different ends of what is in fact a continuum. The reason for this is not—as authors like Cassam and Carruthers maintain—that even the supposedly immediate self-knowledge depends on the operation of unconscious processes that generate hypotheses about our own mental states. It is rather that even the less-immediately available forms of self-knowledge are forms of knowledge of a being whose life, even before reflection supervenes, involves an at-least-implicit self-understanding. Even when we seek the more substantial kind of self-knowledge that Socrates praised, it is *this* sort of being whom we seek to know, and this implies that the relevant self-knowledge cannot be simply a discovery of hitherto unknown facts.

I can illustrate the point I have in mind by considering a case vividly described by Krista Lawlor (2009), in which a woman considers whether she wants to have another child. Lawlor describes the case as follows:

> Katherine, a young woman, stands by her son's crib, watching him sleep. 'Have another'—she hears the words in her head. She is startled.... When Katherine hears these words, have another, she realizes that she has been thinking on and off about the possibility. So, on hearing the words, she thinks perhaps she has already been deliberating, and here is the answer: have another. But then, if this is an answer, it does not feel decisive. And so she thinks perhaps she has not been deliberating, but merely entertaining a possibility without thinking squarely and focusedly about it.... The question Katherine faces is not just the question of what her ends are to be, or of what she should all-things-considered pursue. She also faces the question, a distinct question, of what it is that she wants....
>
> Now that the question has been called, Katherine starts noticing her experiences and thoughts.... Putting away her son's now-too-small clothes, she finds herself lingering over the memory of how a newborn feels in one's arms. She notes an emotion that could be envy when an acquaintance reveals her pregnancy. Such experiences may be enough to prompt Katherine to make a self-attribution that sticks. Saying 'I want another child', she may feel a sense of ease or settledness. More likely, however, her experiences do not prove decisive. Since she has for months felt wistfulness and wonder at her son's growing up, the aforementioned emotions and rememberings are routine, and haven't settled the question for her. More likely, then, if she makes a self-attribution at this point at all, it will have a provisional quality. She'll say to herself, 'I think I want another', and see if it sticks—does she resist the self-attribution or not? And she might resist. (Lawlor 2009: 47, 57)

Lawlor argues that, for such a person, knowing what she wants is a "cognitive accomplishment," not a matter of immediate awareness or a mere decision about what it would be best for her to want. She goes on to suggest that someone like Katherine would determine whether she really wants another child by making an "inference" from "internal promptings" to "their likely causes" (Lawlor 2009: 48–49). Lawlor's idea, in other words, is that Katherine works out what she wants by trying to ascertain whether an underlying state of wanting another child causes the various occurrent thoughts and feelings that she notices, including the ones she has when she tries the experiment of saying to herself, "I want another child."

These characterizations seem to me to hover on the border between something true and something fundamentally mistaken. It is very plausible that, in cases like the one Lawlor describes, one may need to pay careful attention to one's own thoughts and feelings to determine whether one really has a stable and sustainable desire to undertake something so momentous. But the idea that what Katherine needs to do is *discover* whether a certain state figures in the causal background of her thoughts and feelings seems to me to involve a fundamentally alienated conception of how one works out what one "really wants." Katherine's feelings when she boxes up outgrown clothes and receives news of her friend's pregnancy may certainly be indications of an incipient desire, but "incipient" is important here. It is natural to imagine her also thinking of ways in which having another child would make it difficult to pursue other things she cares about. What she wants to know, presumably, is whether the decision to have another child is one she can genuinely embrace, and though her thoughts and feelings may serve as trial expressions of such readiness, assessing their significance is not a question of simply discovering some standing fact of the matter, but of reaching a settled attitude. To put it in a way that emphasizes the aspect of transparency: Katherine needs to come consciously to experience her *world*—not merely in flashes or in the mode of fantasy, but as a stable impression of how things actually are—as one in which it is *desirable* to have another child. To investigate whether she wants another child as if it were a matter of inferring a cause from its effects involves a form of alienation from her own desire, or indeed a form of bad faith. Even if she became convinced that her feelings when she boxes up clothes or hears of a friend's pregnancy are caused by a desire for another child, if this did not involve her having a stable conscious impression of her world as one in which having another child is desirable, this (presumably unconscious) desire would hardly give her the normal sort of reason to have another child. Why should *she*, as a conscious agent, act on *that*?

This case illustrates my more general point. The self-knowledge that Katherine seeks is *not* immediately available. It is knowledge she achieves only through reflective attention to her own thoughts and feelings, and it is certainly knowledge that matters to her life (not to mention to the life of any child she might have). To this extent, it should presumably count as a case of "substantial" self-knowledge. Nevertheless, as we have seen, her problem is not simply to discover a fact about herself, but to settle an aspect of her conscious view of the world. To the extent that she cannot achieve this, any self-knowledge she acquires will have an alienated character: it will be knowledge of a fact about her inner workings, rather than recognition of an aspect of her conscious view of the world. Where no better prospect is available, such alienated self-knowledge doubtless has its uses—it might enable Katherine to cope better with herself—but it will necessarily have a problematic character, for there will remain a sense in which she does *not* see the world in the relevant way. Moreover, it will not be the kind of self-knowledge that bears on a crucial life-decision in the way that Lawlor has in mind: not the kind that speaks directly to the question of the desirability, from Katherine's point of view, of having another child. In this way, even when we seek "substantial" self-knowledge, it is vitally important that the mind we seek to know is one whose relation to its own states is characterized by a certain immediacy, one that problematizes the idea of a mere *discovery* of these states.

If this is right, why do theorists of self-knowledge so often overlook it? What disposes us to conceive of self-knowledge as a matter of merely possessing information about our first-order mental states, rather than as a reflective but immanent awareness of these states? Well, a long-standing theme in philosophical discussions of self-awareness is that we are disposed to attribute to the knowing subject properties that could only belong to an object. Kant famously offers this as his diagnosis of the fallacy in "Rational Psychology," the spurious science that seeks to draw metaphysical conclusions about the nature of the soul from our apperceptive awareness of our own thinking:

> One can place all [such] *illusion* in the taking of a *subjective* condition of thinking for the cognition of an *object*. (KrV A396)

And a similar idea is expressed, in more colorful language, in the tenth book of Augustine's *On the Trinity*:

> [T]he force of love is so great that the mind draws in with itself those things upon which it has long reflected with love, and to which it has become attached by its devoted care, even when it returns in some way to think of itself. And because they are bodies which it has loved outside of itself through the senses of the body, and with which it has become entangled by a kind of daily familiarity, . . . it fastens together their images, which it has made out of itself, and forces them into itself. . . .
>
> From this arises [the mind's] shameful error, that it can no longer distinguish the images of sensible things from itself, so as to see itself alone. (Augustine 2002: 10.5, 50, and 10.8, 53)

These remarks from Kant and Augustine suggest a general account of our temptation to conceive of self-knowledge as fundamentally a matter of having information about ourselves. The proposal is that, because the primary topic of our cognition is sensible bodies, whose condition is in general independent of what we think about them, we are disposed to import the structure of thought about such bodies to a context to which it is fundamentally alien: the case of knowing our own minds. The result is a series of predictable distortions in our conception of this topic: the idea that our awareness of our own mental states is grounded in some kind of inwardly directed perception,[19] the idea that we exercise control over our own attitudes by somehow acting upon them,[20] and the idea that self-knowledge is primarily of instrumental value, inasmuch as it gives us the information we need to cope with our own psychic condition.[21]

At the root of all these errors lies a false separation of the standpoint we take up in reflection from the standpoint on which we reflect: a conception of self-awareness as one more case of awareness of an independently existing state of affairs, exemplifying the various structures that characterize our cognitive and practical relations to such states of affairs. On Augustine's view, indeed, this separation is not a mere error but the expression of a kind of obsession: an excessive love of sensible things, which hobbles our thinking when we turn to a certain dimension of our own lives. This Augustinian claim might seem to express merely a familiar form of early Christian hostility to our sensible nature; but I think it is more interesting than that. Augustine's idea is that our capacity to know is guided by a certain pre-reflective understanding of what a knowable object must be, and consequently that, insofar as we human beings by nature desire to know, we are disposed to treat this sort of object as the measure of what is worth knowing. It is this conception of what is worth knowing, together with our very sense that self-knowledge is worthwhile, that Augustine takes to produce the kinds of distortions we have been considering.

This idea is also to be found, oddly enough, in Sartre, who stresses the unfulfillable desire of the human "for itself" to make itself into an "in itself," something that simply is what it is, not something perpetually in the process of becoming what it takes itself to be. A major aim of this book has been to bring out why this reifying conception of the knowable distorts our understanding of self-knowledge; but our reflections should also enable us to see why this conception is tempting: its attractions are rooted in the understanding of an object involved in the act of "positing" itself.

10.6. Human Beings as "Beings for Themselves"

With these thoughts in mind, I want to return, in closing, to the Sartrean claim that I quoted in the Introduction:

---

[19] For a classic critique of this idea, see Shoemaker 1994.
[20] For criticisms, see Hieronymi 2009 and also Boyle 2009b and 2011a.
[21] For critical but ultimately sympathetic discussion of this idea, see Cassam 2014: Ch. 15.

> [F]or human reality, to exist is always to assume its being; that is, to be responsible for it instead of receiving it from outside, as a pebble does. . . . This 'assumption' of itself . . . implies an understanding of human reality by itself, however obscure this understanding may be. . . . For this understanding is not a quality that comes to human reality from without, but its own mode of existence. (Sartre 1956: 23–24)

This remark reflects an idea that Sartre takes from Heidegger: that a human being is a kind of being "whose being is at issue for it in its being."[22] (Sartre's phrase "human reality" [*réalité humaine*] was at the time the standard French translation of Heidegger's "*Dasein*.") As Sartre understands it, Heidegger's suggestion is that human beings are beings for whom the question of what to be does not merely arise at a reflective level, when we "back up" to consider our present state of existence and ask whether it is as it should be; it is rather a question to which our very existence always already constitutes a response.[23] Moreover, inasmuch as, for each of us, our being what we are constitutes our specific response to the question of what to be, it is supposed to follow that each of us possesses an understanding of the general question of being that defines "human reality" and of our own particular way of being as a specific response to this question.

Such propositions belong to a more grandiose era of philosophy. It is easy to report that Heidegger and Sartre thought such things, but harder to affirm them ourselves with any conviction that we know what we are saying or what grounds we could have for holding such claims to be true. Nevertheless, I hope that the preceding chapters have suggested a path of approach to these large themes. The path runs via a thought about the nature of human *consciousness*, understood in the broad Sartrean sense: any awareness, whether occurrent or stative, that "posits" some intentional object. The thought, which we have developed in the preceding chapters, is that the very existence of such consciousness involves at least a "nonpositional" consciousness of itself. I have argued that this implies that any state of consciousness will be what it is in virtue of a certain nonpositional self-understanding. If we were entitled to the further claim that what a human being is, in some fundamental sense, is defined by her own consciousness, then we could extend this point from a claim about the nature of human consciousness

---

[22] See Heidegger, *Being and Time* (1962) §4: 32. Sartre accepts this formula as characterizing human consciousness, but adds that we might better say that consciousness has a type of being "such that in its being, its being is in question in so far as this being implies a being other than itself" (*Being and Nothingness*, 1956, Introduction §V: lxii/28–29). He has his reasons for this, but his reformulation certainly loses the pithiness of the Heideggerian original.

[23] Whether what Heidegger meant by his formula is really what Sartre understood him to mean is a contentious question that I cannot take up here. My understanding of Sartre's views on these topics is much indebted to conversations with Raoul Moati, and to his important book on Sartre's conception of "human reality" (Moati 2019).

to a claim about the nature of "human reality" in general. And perhaps we can find the basis for such an extension in the thought, developed in Chapter 5, that what "I" fundamentally signifies is the *subject* of consciousness. If the question of what "human reality" is must be approached by asking what sort of being *I* am, and if what I am is fundamentally a subject of consciousness, then whatever else we may say about the nature of human beings, our first principle must be that they are subjects of consciousness in the sense of which the Heideggerian formula holds true.

The path I have just sketched is in fact the path that Sartre follows: he introduces the Heideggerian formula, in the first instance, as a characterization of the being of human consciousness, and then argues that

> we can now begin an ontological study of consciousness, not as the totality of human being, but as its instantaneous kernel. (BN 117/106)[24]

Sartre's characterization of consciousness as the "instantaneous kernel" of the human being points toward his investigation of the temporality of human existence and how this temporality is shaped by our conscious perspective on our lives—topics that lie beyond the scope of the present study. Suffice it to say that Sartre's investigation arrives at a conception of human beings on which their fundamental mode of being is what he calls "being-for-itself," and that he takes it to follow that each of our lives embodies a unique solution to the problem of being such a being.

For us beings-for-ourselves, Sartre holds, self-awareness is not a mere cognizance of our condition that occasionally supervenes on this condition; it is, in a more fundamental sense, the very medium in which our lives take shape. Each of our lives embodies what he calls a "fundamental project," an individual solution to the problem of being a human being, and although most of us have only a relatively superficial reflective understanding of our own project, and none of us comprehends ourselves completely, nevertheless Sartre holds that the projects that our lives embody are in an important sense entirely within the scope of our own awareness. For in order to comprehend my own project, I do not need to *discover* anything of which I was formerly unaware, but only to reflect on an already extant nonpositional awareness in a way that brings it to conceptual clarity. This is the task of Sartre's proposed discipline of "existential psychoanalysis":

> Existential psychoanalysis rejects the postulate of the unconscious: for it, the psychological fact is coextensive with consciousness. But if the fundamental

---

[24] Heidegger would, I believe, repudiate this path to the concept of *Dasein* as too subjectivistic in its orientation. But I must leave that issue for another day: I can only begin from where I find myself.

project is fully *lived* by the subject and as such, fully conscious, that does not at all mean that it must by the same token be *known* by him. . . . This [consciousness] is, certainly, entirely constituted by a pre-ontological understanding of the fundamental project; better still, in so far as reflection is also a non-thetic consciousness of itself as reflection, it *is* this very project. . . . But it does not follow from this that it commands the instruments and techniques necessary to isolate the symbolized choice, to determine it in concepts, and to bring it forth into the full light of day. (BN 740/616)

My aim here is not to pursue these thoughts, but simply to draw attention to their interest. If Sartre is right, then the contrast between "Socratic" and "Cartesian" self-knowledge is fundamentally misleading. While it is true that there are aspects of our lives which are immediately available to our own reflection and other aspects which we can recognize only after careful consideration, these are not two fundamentally different types of self-knowledge, but two different ends of what is in fact a continuum. For "Socratic" self-knowledge simply requires a fuller and deeper comprehension, via better reflective concepts, of the life of a kind of being whose existence has a fundamentally "Cartesian" character: one whose very being, in fundamental respects, involves a nonpositional consciousness of so being. Moreover, Sartre takes this to imply that each of our lives embodies a set of pre-reflective answers to various fundamental human questions—such questions as what it is for me to be what I am, what the good could be for me, what other people are and what they are to me, and so on.[25] In this way, each of our lives embodies a kind of pre-reflective philosophy of our own existence and of our place in the world, and so the kinds of reflective

---

[25] In thinking about this theme in Sartre, I have been greatly helped by parallel ideas developed in Jonathan Lear's writings on Freudian psychoanalysis, ideas expressed in remarks such as the following:

> What I have found over and over again is that if one allows a person—who, for all the world, looks like a healthy human being with some problems to discuss—to lie down on a couch and say whatever comes into his or her mind, one will find not only that the person does not quite fit into his or her skin, but that what lies 'outside' is a basic organizing principle, working around primordial human challenges: for example, what it means to be the firstborn or second-born, what it means to lose a parent early in life, what it is to be the child of divorced parents; how one could trust or be faithful to another person or, to take the classic case, what it is to be a person who is, for a while, a child, but who then must grow into adulthood, old age, and die. Unconscious motivations are not simply this or that temptation to break a socially accepted norm they are also organized attempts to form an identity around the solution to a primordial human problem. At the same time, and in uncanny ways, the unconscious uses received social pretenses to both express and attempt solutions to these problems (Lear 2011: 50).

Although Sartre rejects the Freudian idea of "the unconscious," I believe he recognizes and appreciates this theme in Freudian psychoanalysis: his criticism is less of Freud's theory of the organization of the human psyche than of the ontological ideas about what a human mind is on which this theory is founded.

questions pursued by philosophers are not as discontinuous with the problems of ordinary life as they might first appear.

Not everyone will have patience for this conception of human existence, but I will say that it speaks to my condition. At any rate, if the preceding chapters have brought us to a place from which we can begin to see a point in such ideas, I will be content to pause here for a while and look out upon this bright vista.

Bibliography

Works by Kant and Sartre

References to works by Kant are to volume and page number in the Academy edition of his works (1900–), except in the case of the *Critique of Pure Reason*, where I give citations in the usual "A/B" form. I generally follow the translations given in the Cambridge Edition of Kant's works, though I have occasionally modified these translations without comment. Where possible, I cite works by Sartre with two page references: first a standard English translation and then (after a slash) in a corresponding French edition (details below). Again, I have occasionally modified translations without comment. Commonly cited works by these authors are identified by the abbreviations given in brackets.

Kant, I. 1900–. *Gesammelte Schriften*. 29 vols. Ed. German (formerly Royal Prussian) Academy of Sciences. Berlin: de Gruyter (and predecessors).
Kant, I. 1998. *Critique of Pure Reason* [KrV]. Trans. P. Guyer and A. W. Wood. New York: Cambridge University Press.
Kant, I. 2004. *Jäsche Logic* [JL]. In *Lectures on Logic*. Trans. J. M. Young. New York: Cambridge University Press, 519–640.
Kant, I. 2006. *Anthropology from a Pragmatic Point of View* [An]. Trans. R. B. Louden. Cambridge: Cambridge University Press.
Sartre, J. P. 1943. *L'Être et le néant*. Paris: Éditions Gallimard.
Sartre, J. P. 1962. *The Transcendence of the Ego* [TE]. Trans. F. Williams and R. Kirkpatrick. New York: Farrar, Straus and Giroux.
Sartre, J. P. 1966. *La Transcendence de l'ego*. Paris: Librairie Philosophique J. Vrin.
Sartre, J. P. 1948 (1967). "Consciousness of Self and Knowledge of Self." Originally published as "Conscience de Soi et Connaissance de Soi" in *Bulletin de la Société française* XLII (3). Translated in *Readings in Existential Phenomenology*, ed. N. Lawrence and D. O'Connor. Englewood Cliffs, NJ: Prentice Hall, 113–142.
Sartre, J. P. 1963. *Search for a Method*. Trans. H. Barnes. New York: Vintage.
Sartre, J. P. 1994. *Sketch for a Theory of Emotions*. Trans. P. Mairet. New York: Routledge.
Sartre, J. P. 2004. *The Imaginary*. Trans. J. Webber. New York: Routledge.
Sartre, J. P. 2018. *Being and Nothingness* [BN]. Trans. S. Richmond. New York: Routledge.

Works by Other Authors

Allison, H. E. 1996. "Kant's Refutation of Materialism." In his *Idealism and Freedom: Essays on Kant's Theoretical and Practical Philosophy*. Cambridge: Cambridge University Press, 92–108.
Alshanetsky, E. 2019. *Articulating a Thought*. Oxford: Oxford University Press.
Anscombe, G. E. M. 1957. *Intention*. Oxford: Basil Blackwell.
Anscombe, G. E. M. 1962. "On Sensations of Position." *Analysis* 22 (3): 55–58.
Anscombe, G. E. M. 1975. "The First Person." In S. Guttenplan, ed., *Mind and Language*. Oxford: Oxford University Press, 45–65.

Aquinas, Thomas. 1952. *Truth: A Translation of Questiones Disputatae De Veritate*. 3 Volumes. Trans. R. W. Mulligan. Washington, DC: Regnery Publishing.
Aquinas, Thomas. 2012. *Summa Theologiae*. Trans. Fathers of the English Dominican Province. Steubenville, OH: Emmaus Academic Publishers.
Ariely, D. 2009. *Predictably Irrational*. Revised edition. New York: HarperCollins.
Aristotle. 1942. *Metaphysics*. Trans. W. D. Ross. Oxford: Oxford University Press.
Aristotle. 1968. *De Anima*. Trans. D. W. Hamlyn. Oxford: Clarendon Press.
Armstrong, D. M. 1962. *Bodily Sensations*. London: Routledge & Kegan Paul.
Armstrong, D. M. 1968. *A Materialist Theory of the Mind*. London: Routledge & Kegan Paul.
Augustine. 1984. *City of God*. Trans. H. Bettenson. New York: Penguin Books.
Augustine. 2002. *On the Trinity*. Trans. S. McKenna. Ed. G. B. Matthews. Cambridge: Cambridge University Press.
Baker, L. R. 2013. *Naturalism and the First Person Perspective*. Oxford: Oxford University Press.
Bar-On, D. 2004. *Speaking My Mind*. Oxford: Oxford University Press.
Bar-On, D. 2015. "Transparency, Expression, and Self-Knowledge." *Philosophical Explorations* 18 (2): 134–152.
Berger, J., and J. Mohr. 1967. *A Fortunate Man*. New York: Holt, Rinehart, and Winston.
Bermúdez, J. L. 1998. *The Paradox of Self-Consciousness*. Cambridge, MA: MIT Press.
Bermúdez, J. L. 2005. "The Phenomenology of Bodily Awareness." In *Phenomenology and the Philosophy of Mind*, ed. D. W. Smith & A. L. Thomasson. Oxford: Clarendon Press, 295–316.
Bermúdez, J. L., A. Marcel, and N. Eilan, eds. 1995. *The Body and the Self*. Cambridge, MA: MIT Press.
Bilgrami, A. 2006. *Self-Knowledge and Resentment*. Cambridge, MA: Harvard University Press.
Boghossian, P. 2014. "What Is Inference?" *Philosophical Studies* 169: 1–18.
Boyle, M. 2009. "Two Kinds of Self-Knowledge." *Philosophy and Phenomenological Research* LXXVIII (1): 133–164.
Boyle, M. 2009b. "Active Belief." *Canadian Journal of Philosophy* 39 (S1): 119–147.
Boyle, M. 2010. "Bar-On on Self-Knowledge and Expression." *Acta Analytica* 25 (1): 9–20.
Boyle, M. 2011a. "'Making up Your Mind' and the Activity of Reason." *Philosophers' Imprint* 11 (17): 1–24.
Boyle, M. 2011b. "Transparent Self-Knowledge." *Proceedings of the Aristotelian Society*, Supp. Vol. 85 (1): 223–241.
Boyle, M. 2012. "Essentially Rational Animals." In *Rethinking Epistemology*, ed. G. Abel and J. Conant. Berlin: Walter de Grutyer Verlag, 395–427.
Boyle, M. 2015. "Critical Study: Cassam on Self-Knowledge for Humans." *European Journal of Philosophy* 23 (2): 337–348.
Boyle, M. 2017. "A Different Kind of Mind?" In *The Routledge Companion to the Philosophy of Animal Minds*, ed. K. Andrews and J. Back. New York: Routledge, 109–118.
Boyle, M. Forthcoming. "Kant on Categories and the Activity of Reflection." In *The Palgrave Handbook of German Idealism and Analytic Philosophy*, ed. J. Conant and J. Held. London: Palgrave Macmillan.
Brewer, B. 1995. "Bodily Awareness and the Self." In Bermúdez, Marcel, and Eilan 1995, 291–309.
Burge, T. 1998. "Reason and the First Person." In Wright, Smith, and Macdonald 1998, 243–270.

Burge, T. 2009. "Perceptual Objectivity." *Philosophical Review* 118 (3): 285–324.
Byrne, A. 2005. "Introspection." *Philosophical Topics* 33 (1): 79–104.
Byrne, A. 2011. "Transparency, Belief, Intention." *Proceedings of the Aristotelian Society Supplementary Volume* LXXXV: 201–221.
Byrne, A. 2012. "Knowing What I See." In Smithies and Stoljar 2012, 183–210.
Byrne, A. 2018. *Transparency and Self-Knowledge*. Oxford: Oxford University Press.
Campbell, J. 2002. *Reference and Consciousness*. Oxford: Oxford University Press.
Cappelen, H., and J. Dever. 2013. *The Inessential Indexical*. Oxford: Oxford University Press.
Carroll, L. 1895. "What the Tortoise Said to Achilles." *Mind* IV (14): 278–280.
Carruthers, P. 2010. "Introspection: Divided and Partly Eliminated." *Philosophy and Phenomenological Research* 80 (1): 76–111.
Carruthers, P. 2011. *The Opacity of Mind*. Oxford: Oxford University Press.
Cassam, Q., ed. 1996. *Self-Knowledge*. Oxford: Oxford University Press.
Cassam, Q. 1997. *Self and World*. Oxford: Oxford University Press.
Cassam, Q. 2014. *Self-Knowledge for Humans*. Oxford: Oxford University Press.
Chierchia, G. 1989. "Anaphora and Attitudes De Se." In *Semantics and Contextual Expressions*, ed. R. Bartsch, J. van Benthem, and P. van Emde Boas. Berlin: de Gruyter, 1–32.
Cole, J., and J. Paillard. 1995. "Living without Touch and Peripheral Information about Bodily Position and Movement: Studies with Deafferented Subjects." In Bermúdez, Marcel, and Eilan 1995, 245–266.
Coliva, A. 2016. *The Varieties of Self-Knowledge*. London: Palgrave Macmillan.
Collingwood, R. G. 1946. *The Idea of History*. New York: Oxford University Press.
Crowther, T. 2009. "Watching, Sight, and the Temporal Shape of Perceptual Activity." *Philosophical Review* 118 (1): 1–27.
de Vignemont, F. 2007. "Habeas Corpus: The Sense of Ownership of One's Own Body." *Mind and Language* 22 (4): 427–449.
de Vignemont, F. 2013. "The Mark of Ownership." *Analysis* 73 (4): 643–651.
Descartes, R. 1984. *The Philosophical Writings of Descartes*. Vol. II. Trans. J. Cottingham, R. Stoothoff, and D. Murdoch. Cambridge: Cambridge University Press.
Descartes, R. 1986. *Meditations on First Philosophy*. Trans. John Cottingham. Cambridge: Cambridge University Press.
Diamond, C. 1988. "Losing Your Concepts." *Ethics* 98: 255–277.
Dilthey, W. 1989. *Introduction to the Human Sciences*. Ed. R. A. Makkreel and F. Rodi. Princeton, NJ: Princeton University Press.
Doris, J. M. 2015. *Talking to Our Selves*. New York: Oxford University Press.
Dretske, F. 2003. "How Do You Know You Are Not a Zombie?" In *Privileged Access: Philosophical Accounts of Self-Knowledge*, ed. B. Gertler. Aldershot, UK: Ashgate, 1–13.
Dretske, F. 2012. "Awareness and Authority: Skeptical Doubts about Self-Knowledge." In Smithies and Stoljar 2012, 49–64.
Dreyfus, H. 2007. "The Return of the Myth of the Mental." *Inquiry* 50 (4): 352–365.
Evans, G. 1982. *The Varieties of Reference*. Oxford: Oxford University Press.
Fernandez, J. 2013. *Transparent Minds: A Study of Self-Knowledge*. Oxford: Oxford University Press.
Finkelstein, D. 2003. *Expression and the Inner*. Cambridge, MA: Harvard University Press.
Finkelstein, D. 2012. "From Transparency to Expressivism." In *Rethinking Epistemology*, ed. J. Conant and G. Abel, vol. 2. Berlin: De Grutyer, 101–118.

BIBLIOGRAPHY

Foot, P. 2001. *Natural Goodness*. Oxford: Oxford University Press.
Ford, Anton, Jennifer Hornsby, and Frederick Stoutland, eds. 2012. *Essays on Anscombe's Intention*. Cambridge, MA: Harvard University Press.
Freud, S. 1989. *Introductory Lectures on Psychoanalysis*. Trans. J. Strachey. New York: Liveright Publishing.
Fricker, E. 1998. "Self-Knowledge: Special Access versus Artefact of Grammar—A Dichotomy Rejected." In Wright, Smith, and MacDonald 1998, 155–206.
Gallagher, S. 2003. "Bodily Self-Awareness and Object Perception." *Theoria et Historia Scientiarum*, 7 (1): 53–68.
Gallois, A. 1996. *The World Without, the Mind Within*. Cambridge: Cambridge University Press.
Gallup, G. G., J. R. Anderson, and D. J. Shilito. 2002. "The Mirror Test." In *The Cognitive Animal*, ed. M. Bekoff, C. Allen, and G. M. Burghardt. Cambridge, MA: MIT Press, 325–334.
Gardner, S. 2009. *Sartre's 'Being and Nothingness': A Reader's Guide*. New York: Continuum.
Gertler, B. 2011. *Self-Knowledge*. New York: Routledge.
Gladwell, M. 2005. *Blink*. New York: Little, Brown.
Hatzimoysis, A., ed. 2011. *Self-Knowledge*. Oxford: Oxford University Press.
Hawthorne, J., and M. Scala. 2000. "Seeing and Demonstration." *Philosophy and Phenomenological Research* LXI (1): 199–206.
Heidegger, M. 1962. *Being and Time*. Trans. J. Macquarrie and E. Robinson. Oxford: Blackwell.
Henrich, D. 1989. "Kant's Notion of a Deduction and the Methodological Background of the First *Critique*." In E. Förster, ed. *Kant's Transcendental Deductions*. Stanford, CA: Stanford University Press, 27–46.
Hieronymi, P. 2009. "Two Kinds of Agency." In *Mental Action*, ed. L. O'Brien and M. Soteriou. New York: Oxford University Press, 138–162.
Hieronymi, P. 2014. "Reflection and Responsibility." *Philosophy and Public Affairs* 42 (1): 3–41.
Hume, D. 2000. *Treatise of Human Nature*. Ed. D. F. Norton and M. J. Norton. Oxford: Oxford University Press.
Hurlburt, R., and E. Schwitzgebel. 2011. *Describing Inner Experience: Proponent Meets Skeptic*. Cambridge, MA: MIT Press.
Kahneman, D. 2011. *Thinking, Fast and Slow*. London: Allen Lane.
Kornblith, H. 2012. *On Reflection*. New York: Oxford University Press.
Kornblith, H. 2014. "Is There Room for Armchair Theorizing in Epistemology?" In *Philosophical Methodology: The Armchair or the Laboratory*, ed. M. C. Haug. New York: Routledge, 195–216.
Kornblith, H. 2018. "Philosophy, Science, and Common Sense." In *Scientism: Problems and Prospects*, ed. J. de Ridder, R. Peels, and R. van Woudenberg. New York: Oxford University Press, 127–148.
Korsgaard, C. M. 1996. *The Sources of Normativity*. New York: Cambridge University Press.
Korsgaard, C. M. 2018. "Rationality." In *Critical Terms for Animal Studies*, ed. L. Gruen. Chicago: University of Chicago Press, 294–306.
Lavin, D. 2011. "Problems of Intellectualism: Raz on Reason and Its Objects." *Jurisprudence* 2 (2): 367–378.
Lawlor, K. 2009. "Knowing What One Wants." *Philosophy and Phenomenological Research* 79: 47–75.

Lear, J. 2011. *A Case for Irony*. Cambridge, MA: Harvard University Press.
Lehrer, J. 2010. *How We Decide*. New York: Houghton Mifflin Harcourt.
Lewis, D. 1979. "Attitudes *De Dicto* and *De Se*." *Philosophical Review* 88 (4): 513–543.
Lichtenberg, G. W. 2000. *Waste Books*. Trans. R. J. Hollingdale. New York: New York Review of Books Classics.
Locke, J. 1979. *An Essay concerning Human Understanding*. Ed. P. H. Nidditch. Oxford: Clarendon Press.
Longuenesse, B. 2017. *I, Me, Mine*. Oxford: Oxford University Press.
Mach, E. 1886. *Beiträge zur Analyse der Empfindungen*. Jena: Verlag von Gustav Fischer.
Macpherson, F., ed. 2011. *The Senses: Classical and Contemporary Philosophical Perspectives*. Oxford: Oxford University Press.
Magidor, O. 2015. "The Myth of the *De Se*." *Philosophical Perspectives* 29 (1): 249–283.
Malle, B. 2006. "Of Windmills and Straw Men: Folk Assumptions of Mind and Action." In *Does Consciousness Cause Behavior?*, ed. S. Pockett, W. P. Banks, and S. Gallagher. Cambridge, MA: MIT Press, 207–231.
Martin, M. G. F. 1995. "Bodily Awareness: A Sense of Ownership." In Bermúdez, Marcel, and Eilan 1995, 267–290.
McDowell, J. H. 1994. *Mind and World*. Cambridge, MA: Harvard University Press.
McDowell, J. H. 1998. "Referring to Oneself." In *The Philosophy of P. F. Strawson*, ed. L. E. Hahn. Chicago: Open Court, 129–150.
McDowell, J. H. 2011. "Anscombe on Bodily Self-Knowledge." In Ford, Hornsby, and Stoutland 2012, 128–146.
McGinn, C. 1996. *The Character of Mind*. Second edition. Oxford: Oxford University Press.
Millikan, R. G. 1990. "The Myth of the Essential Indexical." *Noûs* 24 (5): 723–734.
Mlodinow, L. 2013. *Subliminal: How Your Unconscious Mind Rules Your Behavior*. New York: Penguin Random House.
Moati, R. 2019. *Sartre et le mystère en pleine lumière*. Paris: Cerf.
Moore, G. E. 1903. "The Refutation of Idealism." *Mind* 12 (48): 433–453.
Moore, G. E. 1959. "Wittgenstein's Lectures in 1930–33." In his *Philosophical Papers*. London: George Allen & Unwin, Ltd, 252–324.
Moore, G. E. 2013. "Moore's Paradox." In *G. E. Moore: Selected Writings*, ed. T. Baldwin. New York: Routledge, 207–212.
Moran, R. 1999. "The Authority of Self-Consciousness." *Philosophical Topics* 26 (1–2): 179–200.
Moran, R. 2001. *Authority and Estrangement*. Princeton, NJ: Princeton University Press.
Moran, R. 2003. "Responses to O'Brien and Shoemaker." *European Journal of Philosophy* 11: 402–419.
Moran, R. 2011. "Psychoanalysis and the Limits of Reflection." In Lear 2011, 103–114.
Moran, R. 2012. "Self-Knowledge, 'Transparency', and the Forms of Activity." In Smithies and Stoljar 2012, 211–238.
Moran, R. 2018. *The Exchange of Words: Speech, Testimony, and Intersubjectivity*. Oxford: Oxford University Press.
Musholt, K. 2015. *Thinking about Oneself*. Cambridge, MA: MIT Press.
Nagel, T. 1986. *The View from Nowhere*. Oxford: Oxford University Press.
Nichols, S., and S. P. Stich. 2003. *Mindreading: An Integrated Account of Pretence, Self-Awareness, and Understanding Other Minds*. Oxford: Oxford University Press.
Nisbett, R. E., and T. D. Wilson. 1977. "Telling More than We Can Know." *Psychological Review* 84 (3): 231–259.

O'Brien, L. 2003. "Moran on Agency and Self-Knowledge." *European Journal of Philosophy* 11 (3): 391–401.

O'Brien, L. 2007. *Self-Knowing Agents*. New York: Oxford University Press.

O'Shaughnessy, B. 1995. "Proprioception and the Body Image." In Bermúdez, Marcel, and Eilan 1995, 175–204.

O'Shaughnessy, B. 2003. *Consciousness and the World*. Oxford: Oxford University Press.

Peacocke, C. 1992. *A Study of Concepts*. Cambridge, MA: MIT Press.

Peacocke, C. 1998. "Conscious Attitudes, Attention, and Self-Knowledge." In Wright, Smith, and Macdonald 1998, 63–98.

Peacocke, C. 2008. *Truly Understood*. Oxford: Oxford University Press.

Peacocke, C. 2014. *The Mirror of the World: Subjects, Consciousness, and Self-Consciousness*. Oxford: Oxford University Press.

Perry, J. 1979. "The Problem of the Essential Indexical." *Noûs* 13 (1): 3–21.

Perry, J. 1986. "Thought without Representation." *Proceedings of the Aristotelian Society*, Supplementary Vol. 60: 137–151.

Perry, J. 2000. "Myself and I." In *The Problem of the Essential Indexical and Other Essays*. Expanded edition. Stanford, CA: CSLI Publications, 325–340.

Perry, J. 2002. "The Self, Self-Knowledge, and Self-Notions." In his *Identity, Personal Identity, and the Self*. Indianapolis: Hackett Publishing, 189–213.

Pippin, R. B. 1987. "Kant on the Spontaneity of Mind." *Canadian Journal of Philosophy* 17 (2): 449–476.

Recanati, F. 2007. *Perspectival Thought*. Oxford: Oxford University Press.

Recanati, F. 2012. "Immunity to Error through Misidentification: What It Is and Where It Comes from." In *Immunity to Error through Misidentification: New Essays*, ed. S. Prosser and F. Recanati. Cambridge: Cambridge University Press, 180–201.

Renz, U., ed. 2017. *Self-Knowledge: A History*. Oxford: Oxford University Press.

Rödl, S. 2007. *Self-Consciousness*. Cambridge, MA: Harvard University Press.

Rosenberg, A. 2016. "Why You Don't Know Your Own Mind." The Stone Blog, *New York Times*, July 18, 2016. Available at: https://www.nytimes.com/2016/07/18/opinion/why-you-dont-know-your-own-mind.html.

Ryle, G. 1949. *The Concept of Mind*. New York: Hutchison.

Sacks, O. 1970. "The Disembodied Lady." In his *The Man Who Mistook His Wife for a Hat*. New York: Simon & Schuster, 43–54.

Schwitzgebel, E. 2011. "The Unreliability of Naïve Introspection." In his *Perplexities of Consciousness*. Cambridge, MA: MIT Press, 117–138.

Schwitzgebel, E. 2012. "Self-Ignorance." In *Consciousness and the Self*, ed. J. Liu and J. Perry. Cambridge: Cambridge University Press, 184–197.

Searle, J. 1983. *Intentionality*. Cambridge: Cambridge University Press.

Setiya, K. 2012. "Knowledge of Intention." In Ford, Hornsby, and Stoutland 2012, 170–197.

Shah, N., and J. D. Velleman. 2005. "Doxastic Deliberation." *Philosophical Review* 114 (4): 497–534.

Shoemaker, S. 1968. "Self-Reference and Self-Awareness." *Journal of Philosophy* 65 (19): 555–567.

Shoemaker, S. 1988. "On Knowing One's Own Mind." *Philosophical Perspectives* 2: 183–209. Reprinted in Shoemaker 1996.

Shoemaker, S. 1991. "Rationality and Self-Consciousness." In *The Opened Curtain: A U.S.-Soviet Philosophy Summit*, ed. K. Lehrer and E. Sosa. Boulder, CO: Westview Press, 127–149.

Shoemaker, S. 1994. "Self-Knowledge and 'Inner Sense': The Royce Lectures." *Philosophy and Phenomenological Research* LIV: 239–314. Reprinted in Shoemaker 1996.
Shoemaker, S. 1996. *The First Person Perspective and Other Essays*. Cambridge: Cambridge University Press.
Silins, N. 2012. "Judgment as a Guide to Belief." In Smithies and Stoljar 2012, 295–328.
Slater, M., D. Perez-Marcos, H. Henrik Ehrsson, and M. V. Sanchez-Vives. 2009. "Inducing Illusory Ownership of a Virtual Body." *Frontiers in Neuroscience* 3 (2): 214–220.
Smit, H. 1999. "The Role of Reflection in Kant's *Critique of Pure Reason*." *Pacific Philosophical Quarterly* 80: 203–223.
Smithies, D., and D. Stoljar, eds. 2012. *Introspection and Consciousness*. Oxford: Oxford University Press.
Stanley, J. 2013. *Know How*. Oxford: Oxford University Press.
Strawson, P. F. 1959. *Individuals*. New York: Routledge.
Strawson, P. F. 1966. *The Bounds of Sense*. New York: Routledge
Strawson, P. F. 1974a. *Freedom and Resentment and Other Essays*. New York: Routledge.
Strawson, P. F. 1974b. "Imagination and Perception." In Strawson 1974a, 50–72.
Strawson, P. F. 1974c. "Self, Mind, and Body." In Strawson 1974a, 86–95.
Taylor, C. 1979. "The Validity of Transcendental Arguments." *Proceedings of the Aristotelian Society* 79 (1): 151–165.
Thaler, R. H. and Sunstein, C. R. 2008. *Nudge*. New Haven, CT: Yale University Press.
Thompson, M. 2013. "Propositional Attitudes and Propositional Nexuses." In *Sinnkritisches Philosophieren*, ed. S. Rödl and H. Tegtmeyer. Berlin: Walter de Gruyter, 231–248.
Vendler, Z. 1979. "Vicarious Experience." *Revue de Métaphysique et de Morale* 84 (2): 161–173.
Wegner, D. 2002. *The Illusion of Conscious Will*. Cambridge, MA: MIT Press.
Weiskrantz, L. 1986. *Blindsight: A Case Study and Its Implications*. Oxford: Oxford University Press.
Williams, B. 1973. "Imagination and the Self." In his *Problems of the Self*. Cambridge: Cambridge University Press, 26–45.
Williams, B. 1978. *Descartes: The Project of Pure Enquiry*. New York: Penguin Books.
Williams, B. 1981. "Persons, Character, and Morality." In his *Moral Luck*. Cambridge: Cambridge University Press, 1–19.
Wilson, T. D. 2002. *Strangers to Ourselves: Discovering the Adaptive Unconscious*. Cambridge, MA: Harvard University Press.
Wittgenstein, L. 1958. *The Blue and Brown Books*. New York: Harper & Row.
Wittgenstein, L. 1961. *Tractatus Logico-Philosophicus*. Trans. D. F. Pears and B. F. McGuinness. New York: Routledge.
Wittgenstein, L. 1973. *Philosophical Investigations*. Third edition. Trans. G. E. M. Anscombe. New York: Pearson.
Wright, C. 1998. "Self-Knowledge: The Wittgensteinian Legacy." In Wright, Smith, and Macdonald 1998, 13–45.
Wright, C., B. C. Smith, and C. Macdonald, eds. 1998. *Knowing Our Own Minds*. Oxford: Oxford University Press.
Xenophon. 2001. *Memorabilia*. Trans. A. L. Bonnette. Ithaca, NY: Cornell University Press.
Zahavi, D. 2005. *Subjectivity and Selfhood: Investigating the First-Person Perspective*. Cambridge, MA: MIT Press.

Index

For the benefit of digital users, indexed terms that span two pages (e.g., 52–53) may, on occasion, appear on only one of those pages.

Figures are indicated by *f* following the page number

alienation, 46, 47–50, 54–56, 57–59, 60–61, 62–63, 68, 77–78, 99–100, 244, 256–61, 271–72
Alshanetsky, Eli, 167n.2
Anscombe, G. E. M., 109n.12, 115n.19, 120n.24, 121, 135–38, 146n.2, 204n.9
anti-egoism. *See* self-consciousness: egoism vs. anti-egoism about
Aquinas, Thomas, 2, 175, 216–18, 216n.23
Ariely, Daniel, 12
Aristotle, 2, 214–17, 218n.25, 218n.27, 221, 250–51
armchair psychology. *See* psychology: armchair; skepticism: about armchair psychology
Armstrong, David M., 13n.14, 146n.2
attitudes, 32–33, 38n.9, 39, 211, 227n.1, 234–36, 239–41, 264–65, 266
 conscious vs. unconscious, 48–49, 94–98, 254, 261–63, 269–70, 271–72, 275–77
 subjective vs. objective, 85–88, 89–93, 94–97
Augustine of Hippo, 2, 101, 102–3, 142–43, 198, 248, 272–73

bad faith, 21, 77–78, 258–60, 271
Bar-On, Dorit, 1n.1, 3n.6, 14n.20, 35n.3, 39n.10, 47n.2, 59–62, 169n.4
belief, 32–33, 34–36, 37, 46–49, 50–51, 56–59, 65, 72–74, 77, 94–96, 128–30, 140–41, 176–77, 191, 192–95, 242–43
Berger, John, 265–66
Bermúdez, José Luis, 146n.2, 148n.5
Bilgrami, Akeel, 1n.1
blindsight, 49, 97–98
bodily awareness, 85n.3, 145–46
 nonpositional vs. positional, 148–49, 151–60
 Subject-Object Problem about, 123–24, 145–49, 160–61
bodily sensation, 145–46, 151–52, 153–54, 161n.15
body, 105, 107–9, 112–14, 143, 144–49, 151–61, 272
Boghossian, Paul, 172–73, 175, 176
Brewer, Bill, 146n.2, 147n.4

Burge, Tyler, 18n.25, 136n.38, 170n.6
Byrne, Alex, 1n.1, 3n.6, 30, 36n.5, 38n.8, 41n.14, 47n.2, 50–56, 57, 60–61, 62–63, 64–65, 68, 70, 77

Campbell, John, 110n.14
Cappelen, Herman, 138–41
Carroll, Lewis, 178–81
Carruthers, Peter, 1n.1, 14n.15, 200n.5, 229–33, 269–70
Cassam, Quassim, 1n.1, 3–4, 12, 14n.15, 18n.25, 39n.12, 147n.4, 148n.5, 170n.7, 229n.3, 250n.6, 252n.8, 269–70, 273n.21
Cogito ergo sum, 102–3, 105, 133, 142
Collingwood, R. G., 227–28, 246–47
concepts, 65, 186–87, 192, 221
 generality of, 110–11, 119–20, 174–75
 psychological, 17–19, 36, 70, 74, 75, 77, 103, 116–17n.21, 197, 206, 214–18, 225–26
 and reflection, 167–68, 177–78, 180, 182–84, 185–86, 201–6, 207–14, 220–22, 224–25, 265–67, 275–77
consciousness, 19–21, 64, 66, 74, 81, 125–26, 142–43, 151, 191–92, 258–59, 274–75
 nonpositional, 19–20, 64, 65–73, 74, 81–82, 92n.10, 97–100, 149–51
 positional, 66–67, 81, 92n.10, 149–51
 as subject, 83, 92–93, 95n.13, 96–98, 101, 104, 114–18, 123–25, 140

Delphic Maxim, 1, 23–24, 102, 248, 249, 268
Descartes, René, 2, 102–3, 105, 106–7, 130n.33, 142–43, 145–46, 197, 198, 244, 269
Dever, Josh, 138–41
desire, 6–7, 41, 47, 87–88, 89–92, 139–40, 192–93, 200, 242–43, 244, 271
Dilthey, Wilhelm, 246
Dretske, Fred, 38n.9
Dreyfus, Hubert, 157n.10, 248n.1

egocentric thought, 110–14, 120–23, 152–53, 156
 monadic vs. relational, 110, 118–21, 126–28

egoism. *See* self-consciousness: egoism vs. anti-egoism about
emotion, 32–33, 217, 264–65
Evans, Gareth, 19n.27, 37–43, 49, 50, 57, 59, 71n.4, 106n.9, 111n.15, 112, 113–14, 115n.19, 118n.22, 123, 124n.27, 131n.34, 136n.38, 140–41, 147n.4, 148–49, 156–57, 158, 202n.7, 208n.15
expression, 14–15, 58–60, 58n.15, 168–69, 180, 181, 185, 188–89, 255–58, 260–62, 265–66
expressivism, 59–62

facticity, 153n.8, 258–60
Fernandez, Jordi, 1n.1, 45n.1
Finkelstein, David, 1n.1, 39n.10, 39n.12, 47n.2, 59–62, 169n.4
first-person perspective. *See* perspective: first- vs. third-person
first-person pronoun. *See* "I"
Foot Philippa, 175–76
Freud, Sigmund, 248, 254, 276n.25

Gallois, André, 1n.1, 45n.1
Gertler, Brie, 1n.1, 3n.6, 30
Gladwell, Malcolm, 12

Hegel, G. W. F., 131n.34, 246
Heidegger, Martin, 274–75
Henrich, Dieter, 222n.29
Hieronymi, Pamela, 193n.22, 273n.20
human beings, 1, 1n.2, 4–5, 21, 132–34, 258–59, 273–77
  as rational animals, 9–12, 20n.29, 66–67n.2, 191–95
  as self-knowers by nature, 2–3, 15–17, 23–24, 165–66, 170–71, 191–95, 246–47, 248–51, 268, 275–77
Hume, David, 103–4, 105, 107, 126, 129–30, 211–12
Husserl, Edmund, 66, 198

"I," 27, 82–83, 102–4, 105–15, 118–30, 142–43, 274–75
  essentialism vs. inessentialism about, 138–41
  referentialism vs. anti-referentialism about, 134–38
  vs. "it," 124–25, 132–30
  vs. "you," 131–33
illumination. *See* transparency: and illumination
imagination, 41, 84–85, 88n.8, 196n.1, 217–18, 223–24

inference, 52, 53n.9, 62–63, 167–68, 171–75, 178–81, 183, 185–86, 187–88
inhabitant's perspective. *See* perspective: inhabitant vs. spectatorial
intention, 52, 54–55, 68–70, 76, 194–95, 200–6, 212–13

Kahneman, Daniel, 12
Kant, Immanuel, 15–16, 19, 103–4, 109–10, 142–43, 198, 217–18, 219–22, 222n.29, 272
"Know thyself". *See* Delphic Maxim
knowledge, 13, 65, 66, 67, 68, 94–95
  tacit, 64–65, 68, 183–84, 209–12
Kornblith, Hilary, 11, 18n.25, 196–97, 222–23, 228–29, 229n.3, 239n.12
Korsgaard, Christine, 5n.7, 6–7, 15–16, 18n.25, 165–66, 170–71, 173n.8, 189–91, 193, 263–64

language, 166–67, 193, 261–67
  semantic analysis of, 86–88
Lavin, Douglas, 175n.9, 225
Lawlor, Krista, 270–72
Lear, Jonathan, 257n.10, 261–62, 276n.25
Lehrer, Jonah, 12
Lichtenberg, G. W., 103–4, 105–7, 129n.31
Locke, John, 198n.3
Longuenesse, Béatrice, 124n.27, 147n.4

Mach, Ernst, 27, 82–83, 107–9, 108*f*
Macpherson, Fiona, 209n.17
Magidor, Ofra 138n.40
Malle, Bertram, 238n.11
Martin, Michael, 146n.3
McDowell, John, 7n.8, 16n.23, 124n.28, 136n.38, 146n.2, 148n.5, 170n.6
McGinn, Colin, 16n.23, 18n.25, 170n.6
Millikan, Ruth Garrett, 138n.40
mind, 2, 4–5, 9–10, 13, 14–15, 16, 101, 102–4, 126, 130n.33, 143, 145, 193
Mlodinow, Leonard, 12
mode-to-content shift, 212–14
modes of presentation, 74–76, 99n.16, 209–12, 263–64
Moore, G. E., 34–36, 103n.5, 151
Moore's Paradox, 34–36
Moran, Richard, 1n.1, 3n.5, 5n.7, 7n.9, 8n.10, 18n.25, 38n.8, 45–50, 55, 59, 60–61, 77, 93–96, 168–69, 170n.7, 243n.17, 257n.10, 259n.13, 261–63
Musholt, Kristina, 86n.4, 116n.20, 131n.34

Nagel, Thomas, 5n.7, 109n.13

Nichols, Shaun, 1n.1, 14n.16
Nisbett, Richard, 231, 232, 233–34, 235–36, 238–39, 240–41
neo-expressivism. *See* expressivism
nudge, 10, 12

O'Brien, Lucy, 1n.1, 45n.1, 47n.3
Oedipus, 27, 115, 117, 248–49
O'Shaughnessy, Brian, 146n.2, 176–77
other minds, 131–33, 161

pain, 27–28, 31–32, 33, 35–36, 59–60, 91–92, 145–46, 153–54
Peacocke, Christopher, 14n.19, 17n.24, 56–59, 60–61, 62–63, 64, 77, 95–96n.14, 113n.17, 116n.20, 170n.7
perception, 16, 40–41, 49–50, 70–72, 112–14, 145–46, 152, 155–56, 186–88, 206–9, 211–12, 214
Perry, John 86n.4, 109n.12, 115–18, 124n.28, 138–39, 141n.41
perspective
    first- vs. third-person, 5–12, 13, 14–15, 32, 33–34, 39–40, 84, 89–93, 104, 269
    inhabitant vs. spectatorial, 31–33, 38–39, 47–50, 53n.9, 55, 60–61, 96–97, 107–9, 116, 123, 168–69, 188–89, 243–47, 258–59
Plato, 1n.2, 2n.3, 248–27, 249n.4, 266–67
processualism, 233–41
proprioception, 99n.16, 145–46, 151–52, 153, 154–56, 158–59
psychoanalysis, 48, 254, 261, 275–77
psychology, 8, 12, 28, 242n.15
    armchair, 23, 196–200, 204–6, 211–12, 215, 217–25
    developmental, 18–19n.26, 160n.14
    rational, 142–43, 272
    social, 228, 231, 232, 237n.10, 252

questions, 17–19, 73–74, 128–29, 173–74, 182, 192–95, 211n.19

rational (vs. nonrational), 170–71, 192–93, 242–47. *See also* human beings: as rational animals
rational psychology. *See* psychology: rational
rationality, 2, 10, 17–19, 36, 165–66, 170–71, 173n.8, 175–78, 189–95, 242–47, 250–51
Recanati, François, 75n.6, 86n.4, 99n.16, 116n.20
reflection, 5, 19–21, 23–24, 66, 67–68, 70, 74, 76, 99n.16, 101–2, 125, 149, 150–51, 165–71, 178–84, 186–91, 200, 212–22, 224–25, 260–61, 263–64

concepts of, 212, 266–68
object-oriented, 184–86, 188, 190
pure vs. impure, 166, 257–58n.11
self-, 2, 184–86, 190–91, 248–49, 249n.5, 250–55, 261–68
transient vs. transformative 189, 260–61, 264–67
reflectivism, 22, 63, 64–68, 76, 77, 101–2, 104–5, 109–10, 125–31, 144, 229, 241, 251, 263, 267
Renz, Ursula, 250n.6
representation, 5–6, 7–8, 15–16, 41–42, 74–76, 142–43, 194–95, 220–22, 255–61, 264–65
    egocentric vs. allocentric, 110–14, 120–24
    implicit vs. explicit, 81, 98–100, 101–2, 110–14, 120–21, 175, 212–14, 263–64
    modes of. *See* modes of presentation
    as subject, 83–84, 85–88, 92–93, 138–41
Rödl, Sebastian, 1n.1, 3n.5, 13n.12, 16n.23, 131n.34, 200n.6
Ryle, Gilbert, 204–5

Sacks, Oliver, 154–56
Sartre, Jean-Paul, 1, 4–5, 19–21, 22, 41n.15, 44, 45, 64, 66–68, 74–76, 77–78, 81, 83, 91–92, 97, 124–25, 133–34, 139, 144, 147–54, 157–61, 187n.18, 191–92, 198, 218n.27, 224n.31, 251, 257–60, 273–77
Schwitzgebel, Eric, 4, 12, 199n.4, 223–25, 250n.7
Searle, John, 153n.6, 208n.13
self-awareness, 2, 4, 5, 13n.12, 15–16n.22, 20, 21, 62–63, 67–68, 77–78, 99–100, 101, 103, 104n.6, 116, 118, 124–25, 191–92, 257, 275
    vs. other-awareness, 132–34
self-blindness, 36–37
self-consciousness, 22–23, 101–43. *See also* "I"
    egoism vs. anti-egoism about, 102–4, 105–10, 114, 126–31, 132, 142–43
    Kantian conceptions of, 15–16, 18–19, 170–71, 189–91
    Sartrean conceptions of, 4–5, 19–21, 251, 273–77
    vs. consciousness-as-subject, 22–23, 83, 96–97, 104, 114–18, 123–25, 126, 139–41
self-knowledge, 27–28, 96–97
    contemporary work on, 2–4, 13–14, 27–28, 29–31, 45–63, 93–94
    correlation model of, 13–15

self-knowledge, (*cont.*)
  epistemic approaches to, 13–15, 30, 58–59, 61, 93–94
  failures of, 3–4, 10–11, 27–28, 77–78, 95–97, 99, 229–32, 243–46, 254, 255–57, 258–60, 270–72, 275–77
  immediate/Cartesian, 2–3, 27–28, 32, 48–50, 59–61, 148, 229, 231–32, 242, 249–50, 257, 269–70, 276–77
  metaphysical approaches to, 2–3, 4–5, 13n.12, 14–15, 20–21, 22, 28–29
  privileged, 3, 4–5, 8–9, 11, 12, 13–14, 27–28, 29, 32–33, 34–42, 93–94
  skepticism about (*see* skepticism: about self-knowledge)
  substantial/Socratic, 3–4, 12, 250, 269–72, 276–77
  trivial, 3–4, 12, 250
  value of, 3, 5, 189, 191, 247, 248–77
self-reference. *See* "I"
self-reflection. *See* reflection: self-
self-understanding. *See* understanding: self-; skepticism: about self-understanding
Setiya, Kieran, 52n.8, 69n.3
Shoemaker, Sydney, 3n.5, 3n.6, 5n.7, 14n.17, 16n.23, 18n.25, 35n.3, 36–37, 106n.9, 115n.19, 124n.28, 134–35, 170n.6, 198n.3, 273n.19
Silins, Nico, 57n.13
skepticism
  about armchair psychology, 196–97
  about the first-person perspective, 9–12
  about self-knowledge, 3–4, 13–14, 30–31
  about self-understanding, 228–32, 237–41, 244–45n.19, 245–46
Smit, Houston, 222n.29
Socrates, 1n.2, 23–24, 248, 249–50, 266–67, 268–70
solipsism, 132–34
standpoint. *See* perspective
Stanley, Jason, 86n.4
Stich, Stephen, 1n.1, 14n.16
Strawson, P. F., 109n.11, 109n.12, 124n.27, 131, 143, 208–9, 218n.26, 222n.29
subject (vs. object), 104, 105, 107–9, 110, 112, 123–25, 144–46, 160–61, 274–75

Sunstein, Cass, 12

Taking Condition, 173–78, 179–82, 185–86, 188, 190, 264–65
Taylor, Charles, 112–13
Thaler, Richard 12
thinking, 20n.29, 31–32, 61–62, 102–4, 105–7, 131, 135–36, 142–43, 145, 167n.1, 176, 197, 211n.19, 246, 267–68, 272
third-person perspective. *See* perspective: first- vs. third-person
Thompson, Michael, 136n.37
thought. *See* thinking
transcendence, 66, 91–92, 124–25, 149, 151, 161, 187n.18, 258–60
transparency
  approaches to, 46–62, 64–78, 214, 242–46
  and illumination, 260–61 (*see also* reflection: transformative)
  phenomenon of, 37, 39–43, 241–42
  problem of, 28–29, 37–39, 43–44, 45, 126–27, 213–14

understanding, 1, 15, 119, 159–60, 171–72, 173, 174, 177–78, 180, 182–84, 209–12, 219–22, 225–26
  applicative vs. conceptual, 98–99, 183–84, 186–87, 192
  self-, 2, 5, 77–78, 190, 200n.6, 227–28, 227n.1, 233–36, 241–44, 246–47, 251, 262–63, 264–67, 273–77

Vendler, Zeno, 84, 85, 86
Vignemont, Frédérique de, 146n.3

Whitman, Walt, 27
Williams, Bernard, 85, 129n.31, 248n.1
Wilson, Timothy, 8n.11, 12, 231, 232, 233–34, 235–36, 238–39, 240–41
Wittgenstein, Ludwig, 59–60, 103–4, 105–9, 120n.24, 135
world, 42, 105, 146, 152, 222, 271
Wright, Crispin, 1n.1, 3n.6, 14n.18, 29–30

Xenophon, 249

Zahavi, Daniel, 5n.7